The New Testament

Translated from the Greek Text
United Bible Societies
Third Edition

By

Clyde C. Wilton

Pastor Emeritus
Emmanuel Baptist Church
Bryan, Texas

Order this book online at www.trafford.com
or email orders@trafford.com

Most Trafford titles are also available at major online book retailers.

Printed in the United States of America.

ISBN: 978-1-4269-4856-5 (sc)
ISBN: 978-1-4269-4855-8 (hc)

Library of Congress Control Number: 2010917313

Trafford rev. 11/16/2010

 www.trafford.com

North America & international
toll-free: 1 888 232 4444 (USA & Canada)
phone: 250 383 6864   fax: 812 355 4082

Preface

I grew up on a farm between Jermyn and Jacksboro, which is between Wichita Falls and Fort Worth, Texas. My parents, Elmer and Eula Wilton, raised my brothers, L.V. and Anthony, and me. They were godly people and hard workers—usually on the job from sunup till sundown. They taught us that the Bible was a book of authority and full of wisdom.

When I graduated from Jermyn High School, I went off to college. It was a fun time for me. We had strict rules at home, but when I left for college I could make my own decisions. By the second year, church was no longer important to me and my Bible was idle. I had my first taste of beer and whiskey. I began playing poker with the boys, and I started taking ballroom dancing to be popular with the girls. I thought I was doing great, until one day I had an encounter with the Almighty. My world caved in. I became obsessed with thoughts of Eternity and the emptiness of the things of this world. Death and Judgment were knocking at my door, and I was mortified! My life-style no longer held an attraction for me. Everyone seemed to be concerned about education, but not about eternal life. I left the university and went back to the homeplace with Ma and Pa.

For more than a year, I lived and worked on the farm with my parents. I was enthralled in the study of the Bible, and it was my constant companion for many months. My ambitions were modified and my life-style was changed forever. I could see sin in its deadliest form. I could see the stupidity of drinking liquor and the sinfulness of playing poker or indulging in any form of gambling. Dancing and worldly living had no redemptive value to me. I was now able to see the saintly lives of my parents and could see the value in the need for godly rules to live by.

The Bible became important to me, and I began to proclaim it. Now I could find time to go to church. My time became too precious to squander, so I committed myself to a life of Christian service. I went back to college and met a wonderful woman, LaRue Haley, who later became my wife. Our four children, Aaron, Fawncyne, Kathy, and Stanley, as well as our in-laws, grandchildren, and great-grandchildren, have blessed us along the way. I have served as pastor of several churches and as an Air Force Chaplain for many years.

I grew up with the King James Version of the Bible. Years later, I discovered that there were other versions of the Bible. Then, still later, there were even many more translations. Some words were changed, and it seemed that the meanings often changed, as well. Some preachers and Bible students were very critical of the new translations. They were very dogmatic in their harsh evaluation of the translators. What did it all mean? Were the critics of the evaluation of the new translations a revelation of profound wisdom, or was it a case of sanctified ignorance? To make a sensible and scholarly evaluation of a translation, it would be important to know what the Greek New Testament and the Hebrew Old Testament said. That was my motivation for studying the Greek and Hebrew texts.

I had studied Greek when I was in college, and later I studied Greek and Hebrew at the seminary. For several years, though, I only used the English translations. So, my study began. Since that time, I have made it a daily task to study Greek and Hebrew.

In my translation, I have used 20 different versions of the Bible, many concordances, commentaries, the Septuagint, the Vulgate, several Greek texts, and other Bible helps. I have sought to be accurate in translating the thoughts from the Greek to the English. This incredible journey has taken me about 30 years to complete, and now I offer The Wilton Translation to you. My prayer is that it will be a blessing to many people.

*Special thanks go to
LaRue, my wife of almost 61 years,
for her constant encouragement,
and to
Maryanne Rivers,
for her unending technical support,
and to
my son, Aaron Wilton,
for his advice and help in editing this edition.*

Index of Books

Total Words 136,872

* This number includes all the epistles of Paul.

Introduction to Matthew

The first three Gospels, Matthew, Mark and Luke, are similar in their account of the gospel of Jesus. Therefore, they are called the Synoptic Gospels. Synoptic (syn "together with" and optic "seeing") means seeing things together or taking a common view. The Gospel of John has a different approach in the presentation of the good news of Jesus.

The early church fathers were unanimous in believing that Matthew, one of the 12 apostles, was the author of the Gospel of Matthew. His name means "gift of the Lord," and he was a tax collector until he left his job to follow Jesus. Matthew's other name was Levi.

The Gospel of Matthew was written primarily to Jews and from a Jewish point of view. It was probably written in Greek; however, some scholars think that it was written in Aramaic. The author was concerned about the fulfillment of the Old Testament Scriptures. However, he did not restrict the Gospel to the Jews. His purpose was to prove that Jesus was the promised Messiah and that he fulfilled the Old Testament Scriptures. He tells about the Magi coming to worship Jesus. The Great Commission (Matthew 28: 18-20) indicates that the Gospel is for everyone.

Of the 136,872 words in the New Testament, Matthew used 18,348 words. He used 1,678 different words. Mark used 1,344 different words with a total of 10,304. Luke used 2,044 different words with a total of 19,459 words. John used 1,021 different words with a total of 15,631 words. The Gospel writers used 63,741 words, which is a little less than half of the 136,872 words used in the New Testament.

Matthew 1:1-25

(1) The book of the genealogy of Jesus Christ, the son of David, the son of Abraham:
(2) Abraham was the father of Isaac,
Isaac was the father of Jacob,
Jacob was the father of Judah and his brothers,
(3) Judah was the father of Perez and Zerah by Tamar,
Perez was the father of Hezron,
Hezron was the father of Ram,
(4) Ram was the father of Amminadab,
Amminadab was the father of Nahshon,
Nahshon was the father of Salmon,
(5) Salmon was the father of Boaz by Rahab,
Boaz was the father of Obed by Ruth,
Obed was the father of Jesse,
(6) Jesse was the father of David the king.
David was the father of Solomon by the wife of Uriah,

(7) Solomon was the father of Rehoboam,
Rehoboam was the father of Abijah,
Abijah was the father of Asa,
(8) Asa was the father of Jehoshaphat,
Jehoshaphat was the father of Joram,
Joram was the father of Uzziah,
(9) Uzziah was the father of Jotham,
Jotham was the father of Ahaz,
Ahaz was the father of Hezekiah,
(10) Hezekiah was the father of Manasseh,
Manasseh was the father of Amos,
Amos was the father of Josiah,
(11) Josiah was the father of Jechoniah and his brothers, at the time of the Babylonian captivity.
(12) After the Babylonian captivity:
Jechoniah was the father of Shealtiel,
Shealtiel was the father of Zerubbabel,
(13) Zerubbabel was the father of Abiud,
Abiud was the father of Eliakim,
Eliakim was the father of Azor,
(14) Azor was the father of Zadok,
Zadok was the father of Achim,
Achim was the father of Eliud,
(15) Eliud was the father of Eleazar,
Eleazar was the father of Matthan,
Matthan was the father of Jacob,
(16) Jacob was the father of Joseph the husband of Mary, of whom was born Jesus, who is called Christ.

(17) So all the generations from Abraham to David were fourteen generations, and from David to the Babylonian captivity were fourteen generations, and from the Babylonian captivity to Christ were fourteen generations.

(18) Now this is the way the birth of Jesus came about. When his mother was betrothed to Joseph, before they came together, she became pregnant by the Holy Spirit. (19) Joseph, her husband, being a righteous man, did not want to publicly humiliate her, so he decided to divorce her secretly. (20) While he was thinking about these things, an angel of the Lord appeared to him in a dream and said, "Joseph, son of David, Do not fear to take Mary as your wife. It is by the Holy Spirit that she has conceived this child. (21) She will bear a son, and you shall call his name Jesus, for he will save his people from their sins!"

(22) This all happened to fulfill what the Lord had spoken through the prophet: (23) "Behold, the virgin will conceive and bear a son, and his name will be Emmanuel" — which means, "God with us."

(24) When Joseph woke up, he did what the angel of the Lord told him to do. He took his wife (25) but did not consummate the marriage until she gave birth to a son. He called his name Jesus.

Matthew 2:1-23

(1) When Jesus was born in Bethlehem of Judea in the days of Herod the king, behold, wise men from the East came to Jerusalem, (2) saying, "Where is the newborn king of the Jews? For we saw his star in the East, and have come to worship him."

(3) When Herod the king heard this, he was troubled, and all Jerusalem with him. (4) When he had called together all the chief priests and scribes of the people, he inquired from them where the Christ was to be born. (5) They said to him, "In Bethlehem of Judea, for so it has been written by the prophet:

(6) 'And you, Bethlehem in the land of Judah,
are by no means least among the rulers of Judah.
For from you shall come a ruler
who will shepherd my people Israel.' "

(7) Then Herod secretly called the wise men and accurately ascertained the exact time of the appearing of the star, (8) and sending them to Bethlehem, he said, "As you go, search diligently for the child. When you find him, report to me, so I can go and worship him." (9) So after their audience with the king, they went their way, and lo, the star they had seen in the East went before them until it came and stood over the place where the child was. (10) When they saw the star, they rejoiced with exceedingly great joy. (11) When they came into the house, they saw the child with his mother, and they fell down and worshipped him. Then, opening their treasures, they presented to him gifts of gold, frankincense, and myrrh. (12) And having been warned in a dream not return to Herod, they departed to their own country by a different way.

(13) When they had departed, behold, an angel of the Lord appeared to Joseph in a dream, saying, "Get up and take the child and his mother and flee to Egypt, and stay there until I tell you, for Herod is going to search for the child to destroy him." (14) So he got up and took the child and his mother by night and departed to Egypt, (15) and he was there until the death of Herod. This was to fulfill what the Lord had spoken through the prophet:

"Out of Egypt I called my son."

(16) Then Herod, when he saw that he had been outwitted by the wise men, was in a furious rage, and he sent and destroyed all the male children in Bethlehem and its vicinity who were two years old and under, according to the time which he had ascertained from the wise men. (17) Then was fulfilled what was spoken through Jeremiah the prophet, saying,

(18) "A voice was heard in Ramah,

weeping and loud mourning,
Rachel weeping for her children
and refusing to be comforted,
because they were no more."

(19) Herod died and, behold, the angel of the Lord appeared in a dream to Joseph in Egypt, saying, "Get up and take the child and his mother and go into the land of Israel, for those who sought the life of the child are dead."

(21) So he got up and took the child and his mother into the land of Israel. (22) When he heard that Archelaus reigned in place of his father Herod, he was afraid to go there, and being warned in a dream, he departed into the district of Galilee. (23) He went to a city called Nazareth and dwelt there, so that the words spoken through the prophets might be fulfilled:

"He shall be called a Nazarene."

Matthew 3:1-17

(1) Now in those days arrived John the Baptist in the desert of Judea preaching, (2) saying, "Repent, for the reign of heaven is near." (3) For this is he who was spoken of by the prophet Isaiah, saying,

"A voice of one crying in the desert:
'Prepare the way of the Lord,
Make straight his paths.' "

(4) John's clothing was made of camel's hair, and a leather belt was around his waist. His food was grasshoppers and wild honey. (5) Then went out to him Jerusalem and all Judea and all the whole region around the Jordan, (6) and people were baptized in the Jordan River, confessing their sins. (7) When John saw many of the Pharisees and Sadducees coming to the baptism, he said to them, "You brood of vipers, who warned you to flee from the coming wrath? (8) Produce fruit worthy of repentance; (9) and do not think to say among yourselves: 'We have Abraham as our father'; for I tell you that God is able to raise up children to Abraham out of these stones. (10) The ax is already placed at the root of the trees; therefore, every tree that does not produce good fruit is cut down and thrown into the fire. (11) I, indeed, baptize you in water for repentance; but the one coming after me is stronger than I, and I am not worthy to carry his shoes. He will baptize you in the Holy Spirit and fire. (12) His winnowing fork is in his hand, and he will thoroughly cleanse his threshing-floor, and he will gather his wheat into the barn, but the chaff he will burn with unquenchable fire."

(13) Then Jesus arrived from Galilee at the Jordan to be baptized by him. (14) But John tried to dissuade him, saying, "I need to be baptized by you, and you come to me?"

(15) But Jesus said to him, "Let it be done now; for it is proper for us to fulfill all righteousness." Then he consented.

(16) When Jesus was baptized, he went up immediately from the water; and behold, the heavens were opened, and he saw the Spirit of God coming down, like a dove, upon him; (17) and behold, a voice came from heaven, saying, "This is my beloved Son, in whom I am well pleased."

Matthew 4:1-25

(1) Then Jesus was led by the Spirit into the desert to be tempted by the devil. (2) After he had fasted forty days and forty nights, he was hungry. (3) The tempter came to him and said, "Since you are the Son of God, command that these stones become loaves of bread." (4) Jesus answered, "It is written:

'Man shall not live by bread alone,

but by every word that comes from the mouth of God.' "

(5) Then the devil took Jesus to the holy city and placed him on the pinnacle of the temple, (6) and he said to him, "Since you are the Son of God, cast yourself down, for it is written:

'He will put his angels in charge of you;

with their hands they will support you,

lest you strike your foot against a stone.' "

(7) Jesus said to him, "Again it is written:

'You shall not tempt the Lord your God.' "

(8) Again, the devil took him to an exceedingly high mountain and showed him all the kingdoms of the world and their splendor, (9) and he said to him, "All these things I will give you if you will fall down and worship me."

(10) Then Jesus said to him, "Go away, Satan! For it is written:

'You shall worship the Lord your God,

and him only shall you serve.' "

(11) Then the devil left him, and behold, angels came and ministered to him.

(12) When Jesus heard that John had been arrested, he withdrew to Galilee; (13) and leaving Nazareth he went to live in Capernaum beside the sea in the district of Zebulun and Naphtali, (14) to fulfill what was spoken through Isaiah the prophet:

(15) "Land of Zebulun and the land of Naphtali

along the sea beyond the Jordan,

Galilee of the Gentiles —

(16) the people living in darkness

have seen a great light,

and to the ones living in the shadow of death,

light has dawned."

(17) From that time Jesus began to proclaim this message: "Repent, for the reign of heaven is at hand."

(18) When Jesus walked by the Sea of Galilee, he saw two brothers, Simon, called Peter, and Andrew his brother, casting a net into the sea, for they were fishermen. (19) He said to them, "Come and follow me and I will make you fishers of men." (20) And immediately they left their nets and followed him.

(21) Jesus, going on from there, saw two other brothers, James and John. They were in a boat with their father Zebedee, mending their nets. He called them, (22) and immediately they left the boat and their father and followed him.

(23) Jesus went to all Galilee, teaching in their synagogues, proclaiming the gospel of the reign of heaven, and healing every disease and every illness among the people. (24) His fame reached into all Syria, and people brought to him all those who were sick and in pain, demon-possessed, lunatics, and paralytics, and he healed them. (25) The great crowds that followed him were from Galilee, the Ten Cities, Jerusalem, Judea and from beyond the Jordan.

Matthew 5:1-48

(1) When Jesus saw the crowds, he went up into the mountain; and he sat down, and his disciples came to him. (2) And opening his mouth he began to teach them, saying,

(3) "Blessed are the poor in spirit, for theirs is the reign of heaven.

(4) "Blessed are those who mourn, for they shall be comforted.

(5) "Blessed are the meek, for they shall inherit the earth.

(6) "Blessed are those hungering and thirsting for righteousness, for they shall be satisfied.

(7) "Blessed are the merciful, for they shall obtain mercy.

(8) "Blessed are the pure in heart, for they shall see God.

(9) "Blessed are the peacemakers, for they shall be called sons of God.

(10) "Blessed are those who are persecuted for the sake of righteousness, for theirs is the reign of heaven.

(11) "Blessed are you when you are reviled and persecuted and men shall say all kinds of evil against you falsely, on my account. (12) Rejoice and leap for joy, because your reward is great in heaven, for so they persecuted the prophets before you.

(13) "You are the salt of the earth; but if salt has become insipid, how shall its saltiness be restored? It is no longer good for anything, except to be thrown out and trodden underfoot by men.

(14) "You are the light of the world. A city set on a mountain cannot be hidden. (15) Neither do people light a lamp and put it under a peck measure, but on the lampstand, where it gives light to everyone in the house. (16) Even so, let your light shine before men, so that they may see your good

works and give praise to your Father in heaven.

(17) "Do not think that I came to destroy the law or the prophets. I did not come to destroy, but to fulfill. (18) I assure you that as long as heaven and earth endures, not a yodh or a small hook will disappear from the law until everything is accomplished. (19) Whoever then annuls one of the least of these commandments and so teaches others shall be ranked least in the realm of heaven; but whoever practices and teaches them shall be ranked great in the realm of heaven. (20) For I tell you, unless your righteousness surpasses the righteousness of the scribes and Pharisees, you will never enter into the realm of heaven.

(21) "You have heard that it was said to the people of long ago, 'You shall not kill, and whoever kills shall be liable to the court.' (22) But I say to you, whoever is angry with his brother is liable to the court; and whoever shall say to his brother, 'Raca,' shall be liable to the Sanhedrin, and whoever says, 'You Fool!' shall be liable to the fires of Gehenna.

(23) "Therefore, if you are offering your gift at the altar and there remember that your brother has something against you, (24) leave the gift before the altar, and go first and be reconciled to your brother, and then come and offer your gift. (25) Make friends quickly with your opponent while you are on the way to court, lest he deliver you to the judge, and the judge to the guard, and you be put in prison. (26) Truly I say to you, you will not get out until you have paid the last cent.

(27) "You have heard that it was said: 'You shall not commit adultery.' (28) But I say to you that everyone who looks upon a woman to lust for her has already committed adultery in his heart. (29) So if your right eye causes you to stumble, pluck it out and throw it away, for it is better that one of the members of your body perish than that your whole body be thrown into hell. (30) And if your right hand causes you to stumble, cut it off and throw it away, for it is better that one of the members of your body perish rather than your whole body go into hell.

(31) "And it was said: 'Whoever divorces his wife, let him give her a certificate of divorce.' (32) But I say to you that everyone divorcing his wife, except for fornication, causes her to commit adultery, and whoever marries the divorced woman commits adultery.

(33) "Again, you have heard that the people of long ago said: 'You shall not break an oath, but you shall fulfill your vows to the Lord.' (34) But I say to you, Do not swear at all; either by heaven, for it is the throne of God; (35) or by earth, for it is the footstool of his feet; or by Jerusalem, for it is the city of the great king; (36) or to swear by your head, because you cannot make one hair white or black. (37) But let your word be, 'Yes, Yes' and 'No, No'; for it is evil to say more.

(38) "You have heard that it was said: 'An eye for an eye, and a tooth for a tooth.' (39) But I say to you, do not resist an evil person. But if anyone slaps you on your right cheek, turn to him the other also. (40) And if anyone wants to sue you and take your shirt, let him take your coat also.

(41) And whoever will force you to go one mile, go with him two. (42) Give to him who asks of you, and do not turn away from him who wants to borrow from you.

(43) "You have heard that is was said: 'Love your neighbor, but hate your enemy.' (44) But I say to you: Love your enemies, and pray for those who persecute you, (45) so that you may become sons of your Father who is in heaven, because he makes the sun rise on the evil as well as the good, and he sends rain on the just and the unjust. (46) For if you only love those who love you, what reward do you have? Do not even the tax collectors do the same? (47) And if you only greet your brothers, what more are you doing than others? Do not even the Gentiles do the same? (48) Therefore, be perfect as your heavenly Father is perfect.

Matthew 6:1-34

(1) "Be careful not to parade your religion before men, to be seen of them; otherwise, you will have no reward from your Father who is in heaven.

(2) "So when you give alms, do not sound a trumpet before you, as the hypocrites do in the synagogue and in the streets. Truly I tell you, they have their reward in full payment. (3) When you give alms, do not let your left hand know what your right hand is doing, (4) so that your alms will be done in secret; and your Father who sees in secret will reward you.

(5) "And when you pray, do not be like the hypocrites, because they love to stand and pray in the synagogues and in the street corners, so people will see them. Truly I tell you, they have their reward in full payment. (6) But when you pray, enter into your private room and shut the door and pray to your Father who is unseen; and the Father who sees you in secret will reward you. (7) When you pray, do not use empty phrases as the Gentles do; for they think that they will be heard for their many words. (8) Therefore, do not be like them, for God, your Father, knows what you need before you ask him. (9) Therefore pray like this:

'Our Father who is in heaven,
hallowed be your name.
(10) Your kingdom come,
your will be done,
on earth as it is in heaven.
(11) Give us our daily bread.
(12) And forgive us our debts,
as we have also forgiven our debtors.
(13) And lead us not into temptation,
but rescue us from the evil one.'

(14) For if you forgive others who trespass against you, your heavenly Father will also forgive you; (15) but if you do not forgive others, neither will your

Father forgive your trespasses.

(16) "And when you fast, do not be gloomy like the hypocrites, for they disfigure their faces so it will look like they are fasting. Truly I tell you, they have their reward in full payment. (17) But when you fast, anoint your head and wash your face, (18) so you will not appear to be fasting; but your Father who is unseen will reward you.

(19) "Do not lay up for yourselves treasures upon earth, where moth and rust destroy, and where thieves break through and steal. (20) But lay up treasures in heaven, where neither moth nor rust can destroy, and where thieves do not break in and steal. (21) For where your treasure is, there will be your heart also.

(22) "The eye is the lamp of the body. If your eye is healthy, your whole body will be illuminated. (23) But if your eye is diseased, your whole body will be in darkness. If therefore the inner light is darkness, how great is that darkness!

(24) "No one can serve two masters. For he will hate the one and love the other or he will hold to the one and despise the other. You cannot serve God and mammon.

(25) "Therefore I tell you, do not be anxious for your life, what you shall eat or what you shall drink, or for your body, what you shall put on. Is not life more than food and the body more than clothing? (26) Look at the birds of heaven, they do not sow or reap or gather into barns, yet your heavenly Father feeds them. Are you not more important than they? (27) Which of you by being anxious can add one minute to his life? (28) And why be anxious concerning clothing? Observe how the lilies of the field grow. They do not toil or spin. (29) But I tell you that Solomon in all his glory was not clothed as one of these. (30) But if God so clothes the grass of the field, which is today and thrown into the oven tomorrow, will he not provide much more for you? O you of little faith! (31) Therefore do not be anxious saying, 'What shall we eat?' or 'What shall we drink?' or 'What shall we put on?' (32) For the Gentiles seek after all these things, and your heavenly Father knows that you need all these things. (33) But first seek his kingdom and his righteousness, and all these things shall be added to you. (34) Therefore do not be anxious for tomorrow. Let tomorrow take care of itself. Each day has enough trouble of its own.

Matthew 7:1-29

(1) "Judge not, lest you be judged. (2) For the way you judge, you will be judged, and the measure you give will be the measure you get. (3) And why do you see the splinter in your brother's eye, but you do not consider the log in your own eye? (4) Or how can you say to your brother, 'Let me take out the splinter in your eye' and there is a log in your own eye! (5) Hypocrite! First take the log out of your eye, and then you will see clearly

to take the splinter out of your brother's eye.

(6) "Do not give holy things to the dogs, and do not cast your pearls before pigs, lest they trample them by their feet and turn to tear you to pieces.

(7) "Ask and it will be given to you; seek and you will find; knock and the door will be opened to you. (8) For everyone asking receives; and one seeking finds; and to the one knocking, the door will be opened to him. (9) Or what man is there among you, if his son asks for bread, will give him a stone? (10) Or if he asks for a fish, will give him a snake? (11) If, therefore, you being evil, know how to give good gifts to your children, how much more will your Father in heaven give good gifts to those asking him? (12) Therefore treat others the way you would like to be treated; for this is the law and the prophets.

(13) "Enter through the narrow gate. For the gate is wide and the road is broad that leads to destruction, and many enter through it. (14) But the gate is small and the road is narrow that leads to life, and only a few find it.

(15) "Watch out for the false prophets, who come to you in sheep's clothing, but inwardly they are greedy wolves. (16) You will recognize them by their fruits. Can grapes be gathered from thorn bushes, or figs from thistles? (17) So, every good tree produces good fruit, but the corrupt tree produces bad fruit. (18) A good tree cannot produce bad fruit, neither can a corrupt tree produce good fruit. (19) Every tree that does not produce good fruit is cut down and cast into the fire. (20) Therefore, you will recognize them by their fruits.

(21) "Not everyone saying to me, 'Lord, Lord,' will enter into the reign of heaven, but only the ones doing the will of my Father in heaven. (22) Many will say in that day, 'Lord, Lord, did we not prophesy in your name, and did we not cast out demons, and did we not do many mighty works in your name?' (23) Then I will declare to them, 'I never knew you, depart from me, you evildoers!'

(24) "Therefore, everyone who hears these words of mine and does them will be like a wise man who built his house upon the rock; (25) and the rain fell, and the floods came, and the winds blew against that house; but it did not fall, for it had been built on the rock. (26) And everyone who hears these words of mine and does not do them will be like a foolish man who built his house upon the sand. (27) The rain fell, and the floods came, and the winds blew against that house, and it fell, and great was the fall of it!"

(28) When Jesus had finished speaking, the crowds were amazed at his teaching, (29) for he taught them with authority and not like their scribes.

Matthew 8:1-34

(1) When Jesus came down from the mountain, great crowds

followed him. (2) Behold, a leper came and bowed down before him, saying, "Lord, if you are willing, you can make me clean."

(3) Jesus stretched out his hand and touched him, saying, "I am willing, be clean." Immediately he was cured of his leprosy. (4) Jesus said to him, "See that you tell no one, but go and show yourself to the priest and offer the gift that Moses commanded for a proof of your cure."

(5) As he entered into Capernaum, a centurion came to him, seeking his help, (6) saying, "My boy is lying paralyzed at home and is in terrible pain."

(7) Jesus said to him, "I will go and heal him."

(8) But the centurion said, "Lord, I am not worthy for you to come under my roof, but only say the word, and my boy will be healed. (9) For I also am a man under authority, with soldiers under me, and I say to one, 'Go,' and he goes, and to another, 'Come,' and he comes, and to my slave, 'Do this,' and he does it."

(10) When Jesus heard this, he was astonished, and he said to those following him, "Truly, I tell you, I have not found such faith in Israel. (11) And I tell you that there will be many coming from the east and west, and they will recline with Abraham, Isaac and Jacob in the kingdom of heaven. (12) But the sons of the kingdom will be cast out into utter darkness, where there will be weeping and the gnashing of teeth."

(13) Then Jesus said to the centurion, "Go, as you have believed, it will be done to you." And the boy was healed in that hour.

(14) When Jesus entered Peter's house, he saw his mother-in-law in bed with fever. (15) Jesus touched her hand and the fever left her, and she arose and served them.

(16) That evening they brought to him many who were demon-possessed, and he cast out the spirits with a word, and he healed those who were sick. (17) This was to fulfill the prophecy of the prophet Isaiah, saying, "He took our weaknesses and bore our diseases."

(18) When Jesus saw the crowd around him, he commanded that they go to the other side. (19) A scribe came to him and said, "Teacher, I will follow you wherever you go."

(20) Jesus said to him, "Foxes have holes and the birds of the air have nests, but the Son of man does not have a place to lay his head."

(21) Another disciple said to him, "Lord, permit me first to go and bury my father."

(22) But Jesus said to him, "Follow me and let the dead bury their own dead."

(23) He got into a boat and his disciples followed him. (24) Suddenly, there was a great storm in the sea, so that the boat was covered by the waves; but Jesus was sleeping. (25) They came to Jesus and woke him and said, "Lord save us! We are perishing!"

(26) He replied, "You little-faiths! Why are you fearful?" Then he

arose and rebuked the winds and the sea, and it was completely calm.

(27) And the men were astonished, saying, "What manner of man is this, that even the winds and sea obey him?"

(28) When he came to the other side into the country of the Gadarenes, two demon-possessed men coming out of the tombs met him. They were exceedingly dangerous, so that no one was able to pass that way. (29) And they cried out, saying, "What do we have to do with you, Son of God? Did you come here to torture us before our time?"

(30) In the distance was a herd of many pigs feeding. (31) And the demons begged him, "If you cast us out, send us into the heard of pigs."

(32) Jesus said to them, "Go!" So those going out went into the pigs, and behold, they rushed over the cliff into the sea, and they perished in the water. (33) Those feeding the pigs fled, and going into the city, they reported all things that had happened to those who had been demon-possessed. (34) Then all the city came out to meet Jesus, and seeing him, they begged him to leave their neighborhood.

Matthew 9:1-38

(1) Jesus got into a boat and returned to his own city. (2) And immediately they brought to him a paralytic, on a pallet. When Jesus saw their faith, he said to the paralytic, "Son, be of good cheer, for your sins are forgiven!"

(3) At this, some of the scribes said among themselves, "This man is blaspheming!"

(4) Jesus, knowing their thoughts, said, "Why are you thinking evil in your hearts? (5) For which is easier to say, 'Your sins are forgiven,' or 'Rise up and walk?' (6) But in order that you may know that the Son of man has authority to forgive sins on the earth...." Then he said to the paralytic, "Rise, take up your pallet and go to your house." (7) And he got up and went to his house. (8) The crowds, seeing what happened, were awestricken, and they praised God, who had given such authority to men.

(9) When Jesus was going from there, he saw a man, whose name was Matthew, sitting at the customhouse, and he said to him, "Follow me." And he got up and followed him.

(10) Later, Jesus dined in the house of Matthew, and many of the tax collectors and sinners came and sat down at the table with Jesus and his disciples. (11) When the Pharisees saw this, they said to his disciples, "Why does your teacher eat with tax collectors and sinners?"

(12) Jesus heard this, and said, "Those who are healthy have no need to see a physician, but those who are ill. (13) But go and learn what this means, 'I desire mercy and not sacrifice.' For I did not come to call the righteous, but sinners."

(14) Then the disciples of John came to him, saying, "Why do we and

the Pharisees fast, but your disciples do not fast?"

(15) Jesus said to them, "Can the attendants of the bridegroom mourn as long as the bridegroom is with them? The days will come when the bridegroom is taken away from them; then they will fast. (16) No one sews a patch of unshrunk cloth on an old garment, for the patch pulls away from the garment and leaves a bigger hole. (17) Neither do men put new wine in old wineskins; otherwise, the wineskins burst, and the wine is spilled and the wineskins are destroyed. But they put new wine into new wineskins, and they are both preserved."

(18) While he was speaking to them, a ruler came and knelt before him, saying, "My daughter just died, but come and lay your hand on her, and she will live." Jesus got up and went with him, and so did his disciples.

(20) And behold, a woman, who had suffered from a flow of blood for twelve years, came behind him and touched the hem of his garment; (21) for she was saying to herself, "If only I touch his garment, I will be healed!"

(22) Jesus turned, and seeing her, said, "Be of good cheer, your faith has healed you." And instantly that woman was healed.

(23) When Jesus came into the ruler's house, he saw the flute-players and the distressed crowd, and he said, "Depart; for the girl is not dead, but is sleeping." And they ridiculed him. (25) But when the crowd was put out, he entered and took her by the hand, and the girl got up. (26) And this news went to all that land.

(27) As Jesus passed by, two blind men followed him, crying out and saying, "Have mercy on us, son of David!" (28) When Jesus came into the house, the blind men approached him, and Jesus said to them, "Do you believe I am able to do this?"

They said, "Yes, Lord."

(29) Then he touched their eyes, saying, "Let it be according to your faith."

(30) Their eyes were opened. And Jesus sternly admonished them to tell no one. (31) But they went out and spread the news to everyone in that land.

(32) As they were going out, a demon-possessed, dumb man was brought to him. (33) When the demon was cast out, the dumb man spoke. The crowds were amazed, saying, "Nothing like this has ever been seen in Israel."

(34) But the Pharisees said, "He casts out demons by the ruler of the demons."

(35) Jesus went about in all the cities and villages, teaching in their synagogues, proclaiming the good news of the kingdom and healing every disease and every illness. (36) Jesus, seeing the crowds, had compassion for them, because they were distressed and helpless, like sheep without a shepherd. (37) Then he said to his disciples, "The harvest is plentiful, but the workers are scarce; (38) beg the Lord of the harvest, therefore, to send forth

workmen into his harvest."

Matthew 10:1-42

(1) Jesus called his disciples to him and gave them authority over unclean spirits to cast them out and to heal every disease and every infirmity. (2) These are the names of the twelve apostles: first, Simon, called Peter, and Andrew his brother; James the son of Zebedee and John his brother; (3) Philip and Bartholomew; Thomas and Matthew the tax collector; James the son of Alphaeus and Thaddaeus; (4) Simon the Canaanite and Judas Iscariot, who betrayed him.

(5) These twelve Jesus sent forth after instructing them, saying, "Do not go to the Gentiles and do not enter any city of the Samaritans; (6) but rather go to the lost sheep of the house of Israel. (7) As you go, proclaim this message, 'The reign of heaven is at hand.' (8) Heal the sick, raise the dead, cleanse the lepers, cast out demons; freely you received, freely give. (9) Do not take gold, silver, or brass in your belts, (10) or a sack for your journey, or extra clothes, or sandals, or a staff; for a workman is worthy of his food.

(11) "When you enter into a city or village, seek someone who is worthy and stay with him until you leave. (12) And when you enter into the house, give it your greeting. (13) If the house is worthy, let your peace come upon it; but if it is not worthy, let your peace return to you. (14) And if they do not receive you or listen to your message, go outside that house or that city and shake the dust off your feet. (15) I tell you the truth, it will be more tolerable for the land of Sodom and Gomorrah in the Day of Judgment than for that city.

(16) "Remember, I am sending you forth as sheep in the midst of wolves; therefore, be as wise as snakes and as innocent as doves. (17) And beware of men; for they will deliver you to councils, and in their synagogues they will flog you; (18) and you will be dragged before governors and kings for my sake, for a testimony to them and to the Gentiles. (19) But when they deliver you up, do not be anxious of how you are to speak or what you are to say; for it will be given to you in that hour; (20) for it is not you who speaks, but the Spirit of your Father who is speaking in you.

(21) Brother will deliver up brother to death, and father his child, and children against parents to be put to death. (22) And you will be hated by all men on account of my name, but those enduring to the end will be saved. (23) When you are persecuted in one place, flee to another; for I tell you the truth, you will not have gone through all the cities of Israel before the Son of man comes.

(24) "A disciple is not above his teacher, nor a slave above his master. (25) It is enough for the disciple to be as his teacher, and the slave to be as his master. If they have called the master of the house Beelzebul, how much more will they call the members of his household? (26) Therefore, do

not fear them; for nothing is covered that will not be uncovered, and the hidden that will not be made known. (27) What I say to you in darkness, speak in the light, and what you hear whispered, proclaim on the housetops. (28) And do not fear those who kill the body but are not able to kill the soul; but rather fear the one who is able to destroy both soul and body in hell. (29) Are not two sparrows sold for a cent? And not one of them will fall to the ground without your Father's knowledge. (30) But as for you, all the hairs of your head are numbered. (31) Therefore, fear not; you are of more value than many sparrows.

(32) "So everyone who acknowledges me before men, I will acknowledge before my Father who is in heaven. (33) And whoever denies me before men, I will deny before my Father who is in heaven. (34) Do not think that I came to bring peace on the earth; I came not to bring peace, but a sword. (35) For I came to make hostile a man against his father and a daughter against her mother and a bride against her mother-in-law, (36) and the enemies of a man are those of his household. (37) Those who love father or mother more than me are not worthy of me; and those loving son or daughter more than me are not worthy of me; (38) and he who does not take up his cross and follow after me is not worthy of me. (39) He who finds his life will lose it, and he who loses his life for my sake will find it.

(40) "He who receives you receives me, and he who receives me receives the one who sent me. (41) He who receives a prophet in the name of a prophet will receive the reward of a prophet, and he who receives a righteous man in the name of a righteous man will receive the rewards of a righteous man. (42) And whoever gives to one of these little ones a cup of cold water because he is a disciple, truly, I say to you, he shall not lose his reward."

Matthew 11:1-30

(1) When Jesus had finished giving his disciples instructions, he left there and went to teach and preach in their cities.

(2) Now when John heard about the works of Christ, he sent a message by his disciples (3) and said to him, "Are you the one who is coming, or shall we look for another?"

(4) Jesus replied, "Go and report to John what you hear and see: the blind receive their sight, the lame walk, lepers are cleansed, the deaf hear, the dead are raised, and the poor are evangelized. (6) And blessed is he who is not offended in me."

(7) As they went away, Jesus began to speak to the crowds concerning John: "What did you go out into the wilderness to see? A reed being shaken by the wind? (8) But what did you go out to see? A man clothed in soft material? Behold, those in the houses of kings wear soft clothes. (9) But why did you go out? To see a prophet? Yes, I tell you, and

more than a prophet. (10) This is the one of whom it has been written,

'Behold, I send my messenger ahead of you,

who will prepare the way before you.'

(11) Truly, I say to you, there has not been a man born of woman who is greater than he. (12) And from the days of John the Baptist until now, the kingdom of heaven suffers violence, and men of violence take it by force. (13) For all the prophets and the law prophesied until John. (14) And if you are willing to accept it, he is the Elijah who was to come. (15) He who has ears, let him hear.

(16) "But to what shall I compare this generation? It is like children sitting in the market places and calling to others (17) saying,

'We piped to you, and you did not dance!

We mourned to you, and you did not wail!'

(18) For John came neither eating or drinking, and they say, 'He has a demon'; (19) the Son of man came eating and drinking, and they say, 'Behold, a man who is a glutton and a drunkard, a friend of tax collectors and sinners.' And wisdom is justified by her deeds."

(20) Then Jesus began to reproach the cities where his many powerful deeds had been done, because they had not repented. (21) "Woe to you, Chorazin! Woe to you, Bethasidia! For if Tyre and Sidon had witnessed the powerful deeds that have been done in your midst, they would have repented in sackcloth and ashes long ago. (22) However, I tell you, it shall be more tolerable for Tyre and Sidon than for you in the Day of Judgment. (23) And you, Capernaum, will you be exalted up to heaven? You shall be brought down to Hades; because if Sodom had witnessed the powerful deeds that have been done in your midst, it would have remained until today. (24) However, I tell you that it will be more tolerable in the Day of Judgment for the land of Sodom than for you."

(25) At that time Jesus declared, "I give thanks to you, Father, Lord of heaven and earth, because you have hidden these things from the wise and intelligent, and you have revealed them unto infants; (26) yes, Father, for thus it was well-pleasing in your sight. (27) All things have been delivered to me by my Father, and no one fully knows the Son except the Father; neither does anyone fully know the Father except the Son and to whom the Son wills to reveal.

(28) "Come to me, all who labor and are heavy-burdened, and I will give you rest. (29) Take my yoke upon you and learn from me, because I am meek and humble in heart, and you will find rest for your souls; (30) for my yoke is comfortable and my burden is light."

Matthew 12:1-50

(1) At that time Jesus went through the grainfields on the Sabbath; and his disciples were hungry, so they began to pluck the heads of grain and

to eat. (2) The Pharisees noticed this and said to him, "Look, your disciples are doing what is not lawful to do on the Sabbath."

(3) He said to them, "Have you not read what David did when he and those with him were hungry, (4) how he went into the house of God and they ate the consecrated bread which was not lawful for him or those with him to eat, but only the priests; (5) or have you not read in the law that on the Sabbath the priests in the temple profane the Sabbath but are guiltless? (6) And I say to you that one is here greater than the temple. (7) But if you had known what this means, 'I desire mercy and not sacrifice,' you would not have condemned the guiltless. (8) For the Son of Man is Lord of the Sabbath."

(9) He left there and went into their synagogue. (10) And behold, there was a man with a withered hand, and in order to find fault in Jesus they questioned him, saying, "Is it lawful to heal on the Sabbath?"

(11) He said to them, "What man among you, if he has one sheep and it falls into a ditch on a Sabbath, will he not take hold of it and lift it out? (12) How much more worth is a man than a sheep! So it is lawful to do good on the Sabbath."

(13) Then he said to the man, "Stretch out your hand!" And he stretched it out, and it was restored to health, like the other. (14) But the Pharisees went out and plotted against him to find a way to destroy him.

(15) Knowing this, Jesus withdrew from there. Many people followed him, and he healed them all, (16) and he sternly ordered them not to make him known. (17) This was to fulfill the words of the prophet Isaiah:

(18) "Behold, my servant whom I have chosen,
my beloved with whom my soul is well-pleased.
I will put my spirit upon him,
and he will proclaim justice to the Gentiles.
(19) He will not quarrel nor shout,
nor will his voice be heard in the streets.
(20) He will not break a bruised reed,
and a smoking wick he will not quench,
until he brings justice to victory.
(21) And in his name the Gentiles will hope."

(22) Then a blind and dumb, demon-possessed man was brought to him, and Jesus healed him, so that he could speak and see. (23) The crowds were all astonished and they said, "Is not he the Son of David?"

(24) But when the Pharisees heard it, they said, "This man casts out demons only by the power of Beelzebul, prince of demons."

(25) Jesus, knowing their thoughts, said to them, "Every kingdom divided against itself is brought to desolation, and every city or house divided against itself will not stand; (26) and if Satan casts out Satan, he is divided against himself; therefore, how can his kingdom stand? (27) And if I cast out demons by Beelzebul, by whom do your sons cast them out?

Therefore they will be your judges. (28) But if I cast out demons by the spirit of God, then the kingdom of God has come upon you. (29) Or how can anyone enter into a strong man's house and seize his goods, unless he first ties up the strong man? Then he can plunder his house. (30) He who is not with me is against me, and he who does not gather with me scatters. (31) Therefore I tell you, every sin and blasphemy shall be forgiven men, but blasphemy against the Spirit will not be forgiven. (32) And whoever speaks a word against the Son of Man, it shall be forgiven him, but whoever speaks against the Holy Spirit, it shall not be forgiven him, either in this age or the one to come.

(33) "Make the tree good and its fruit will be good, or make the tree bad and its fruit will be bad, for the tree is known by its fruit. (34) You brood of snakes! How can you, being evil, say anything good? For out of the abundance of the heart the mouth speaks. (35) The good man out of his good treasure brings forth good, and the evil man out of his evil treasure brings forth evil. (36) And I tell you, on judgment day men will be held accountable for every idle word they speak; (37) for by your words you will be justified, and by your words you will be condemned."

(38) Then some of the scribes and Pharisees asked him, "Teacher, we would like to see a sign from you."

(39) Jesus said to them, "An evil and adulterous generation seeks for a sign, but no sign will be given them except the sign of the prophet Jonah. (40) For as Jonah was three days and three nights in the belly of the huge fish, so will the Son of man be in the heart of the earth three days and three nights. (41) The men of Nineveh will rise up at the judgment and condemn this generation, because they repented at the preaching of Jonah, and now one greater than Jonah is here. (42) The Queen of the South will rise up at the judgment and condemn this generation, because she came from the ends of the earth to hear the wisdom of Solomon, and now a greater than Solomon is here.

(43) "When an unclean spirit comes out of a man, it goes through dry places seeking rest, but does not find it. (44) Then it says, 'I will return to the house I left.' So it returns and finds it unoccupied, swept clean and put in order. (45) Then it goes and takes with it seven other spirits more wicked than itself, and they go in and dwell there; and the last state of that man is worse than the first. So it will also be with this evil generation."

(46) While he was still speaking to the crowds, his mother and his brothers were outside seeking to speak to him. (47) And someone said to him, "Your mother and your brothers are outside seeking to speak to you."

(48) He said to him, "Who is my mother, and who are my brothers?"

(49) And stretching out his hand toward his disciples he said, "Behold, my mother and my brothers! (50) For whoever does the will of my Father in heaven is my brother and sister and mother."

Matthew 13:1-58

(1) On that day Jesus went out of the house and sat beside the sea, (2) and great crowds were assembled near him so that he got in a boat and sat there and the crowds stood on the beach. (3) And he told them many things in parables, saying: "A sower went out to sow. (4) And as he sowed, some seeds fell by the wayside, and the birds came and devoured them. (5) Other seeds fell on the rocky places, where the soil did not have much depth; and they came up immediately, because they did not have depth of soil; (6) but when the sun came up, they were scorched, and because they did not have root they dried up. (7) Other seeds fell on thorny ground, and the thorns came up and choked them. (8) Other seeds fell upon good ground and produced fruit—a hundred, sixty or others thirty times that which was sown. (9) Let him who has ears, listen."

(10) The disciples came to him and said, "Why do you speak to them in parables?"

(11) He replied, "Because it is given to you to know the mysteries of the kingdom of heaven, but to them it has not been given. (12) For to him who has it will be given to him, and he will have abundance; but to him who has not, even what he has will be taken from him. (13) Therefore I speak to them in parables, because seeing, they do not see, and hearing, they do not understand. (14) This is the fulfillment of the prophesy of Isaiah:

'Hearing you will not understand,

and seeing you will not perceive.

(15) For the hearts of these people have become insensitive,

and their ears are heavy and their eyes are closed;

lest they should see with their eyes and hear with their ears,

and understand with their hearts,

and turn about for me to heal them.'

(16) But you are blessed because your eyes see and your ears hear. (17) For I tell you, many prophets and righteous men desired to see what you see and did not see it, and to hear what you hear, but did not hear it.

(18) "Therefore listen to the meaning of the sower of the parable: (19) When anyone hears the word of the kingdom and does not understand it, the evil one comes and snatches away that which was sown in his heart; this is the word sown by the wayside. (20) And the word sown on the rocky places is he who hears and immediately receives it with joy; (21) yet he has no root in himself, so it is short-lived; for when tribulation and persecution comes on account of the word, he is immediately offended. (22) The word sown among the thorns is the one who hears the word, but the cares of the world and the deceitfulness of riches choke the word, and it becomes barren. (23) But the word sown on the good ground is the one who hears and understands it, who indeed bears fruit and produces a hundred, sixty or thirty times that which was sown."

(24) Jesus told them another parable, saying, "The kingdom of heaven is like a man sowing good seed in his field; (25) but while men were sleeping, his enemy came and sowed weeds among the wheat and went away. (26) But when the seeds sprouted and came up and bore fruit, the weeds also appeared.

(27) "So the slaves of the householder came and said to him, 'Sir, did you not sow good seed in your field? Where did the weeds come from?'

(28) "He said to them, 'An enemy did this.'

"So the slaves said to him, 'Then do you want us to go out and gather the weeds?'

(29) "But he said, 'No, because while gathering the weeds, you might root up the wheat. (30) Let both grow until the harvest; and at harvest time I will tell the reapers: Gather first the weeds and bind them in bundles to burn, but gather the wheat into my barn.' "

(31) He told them another parable, saying, "The kingdom of heaven is like a mustard seed, which a man took and sowed in his field; (32) it is the smallest of the seeds, but when it grows, it is the largest of the herbs and becomes a tree, and the birds of the sky come and dwell in its branches."

(33) He told them another parable, saying, "The kingdom of heaven is like yeast, which a woman took and hid in three measures of meal until the whole batch was leavened."

(34) Jesus spoke all these parables to the crowds; indeed he only spoke to them in parables. (35) This was to fulfill what was spoken by the prophet, saying,

"I will open my mouth in parables,
I will utter things hidden from the foundation of the world."

(36) Then he sent the crowds away and went into the house. And his disciples came to him, saying, "Explain to us the parable of the weeds in the field."

(37) Answering he said, "The Son of man is the one sowing the good seed. (38) And the field is the world; and the good seed are the sons of the kingdom; and the weeds are the sons of the evil one; (39) and the enemy who sowed them is the devil; and the harvest is the end of the age; and the reapers are the angels. (40) Therefore as the tares are gathered up and burned with fire, so it will be at the end of the age; (41) the Son of man will send forth his angels and they will gather out of his kingdom all stumbling blocks and the evil doers; (42) and he will cast them into the furnace of fire, where there will be wailing and gnashing of teeth. (43) Then the righteous will shine forth as the sun in the kingdom of their Father. Let him who has ears, listen.

(44) "The kingdom of heaven is like a treasure hidden in a field, which a man found and hid, and in his joy he goes and sells everything he has and purchases that field.

(45) "Again, the kingdom of heaven is like a merchant seeking beautiful pearls; (46) and finding one valuable pearl, he went and sold

everything that he had and bought it.

(47) "Again, the kingdom of heaven is like a net cast into the sea and gathering fish of every kind; (48) and when it was filled, men drew it to the shore, and they sat down and sorted the good into vessels, but the bad they cast out. (49) Thus it will be at the end of the age. The angels will go forth and separate the evil from the righteous (50) and will cast them into the furnace of fire; there will be wailing and gnashing of teeth.

(51) "Have you understood all these things?"

They said to him, "Yes."

(52) So he said to them, "Therefore every scribe trained for the kingdom of heaven is like a householder who brings forth out of his treasure things both new and old."

(53) When Jesus had finished these parables, he departed from there. (54) And going into his native town, he taught them in their synagogues, so that they were astonished and said: "Where did this man get this wisdom and miraculous powers? (55) Is not this man the carpenter's son? Is not Mary his mother? And are not James, Joseph, Simon and Judas his brothers? (56) And are not his sisters with us? How can this man do all these things?" (57) And they were offended in him.

But Jesus said to them, "A prophet is not without honor except in his native town and in his own house." (58) And he did not do many miracles there because of their lack of faith.

Matthew 14:1-36

(1) At that time Herod the tetrarch heard the fame of Jesus, (2) and he said to his servants, "This is John the Baptist; he has risen from the dead! That is why miraculous powers are at work in him."

(3) For Herod had seized John and bound him and put him in prison on account of Herodias, the wife of Philip his brother. (4) For John had said to him, "It is not lawful for you to have her." (5) Herod wanted to kill him, but he feared the people, because they considered him to be a prophet.

(6) On the birthday of Herod, the daughter of Herodias danced before them, and it pleased Herod so much (7) that he promised with an oath to give her whatever she asked. (8) So she was instructed by her mother to say, "Give me the head of John the Baptist here on a platter."

(9) The king was grieved, but because of the oath and the guests, he commanded it to be done, (10) so he sent and had John beheaded in prison; (11) and the head of John the Baptist was brought on a platter and given to the girl, and she took it to her mother. (12) His disciples came and took the body and buried it. Then they went and told Jesus.

(13) When Jesus heard this, he departed from there in a boat and went to a solitary place in the desert, and when the people heard about it, they followed him on foot from the towns. (14) When he got out of the boat

he saw a great crowd. He had compassion for them and healed their sick.

(15) When it was evening, the disciples came to him and said, "This is a desert place and the day is past; send the crowds away so they can go into the villages and buy food for themselves."

(16) Jesus said to them, "They do not need to depart. You give them something to eat."

(17) They said to him, "We only have five loaves here and two fish."

(18) Jesus said, "Bring them here to me." (19) And he ordered the crowds to sit down on the grass, and he took the five loaves and two fish, and looking up into heaven, he blessed them; then he broke and gave the bread to the disciples and they gave to the people. (20) They all ate and were satisfied, and they took up twelve baskets of broken pieces left over. (21) Those who ate were about five thousand men, not counting the women and children.

(22) Then Jesus immediately directed his disciples to embark into a boat and go to the other side before him, while he dismissed the crowds. (23) After dismissing the crowds, he went up the hill alone to pray. When evening came, he was there alone. (24) But the boat by this time was a long way from the shore, and it was being tossed by the waves, for the wind was against them. (25) Between three to six in the morning, Jesus came to them, walking upon the sea. (26) And the disciples, seeing him walking upon the sea, were terrified, and they said, "It is a ghost!" And they screamed with fright.

(27) Immediately Jesus said to them, "Be of good cheer, it is I; do not be afraid."

(28) Peter answered him, "Lord, if it is you, command that I come to you upon the water."

(29) Jesus said, "Come." And Peter came out of the boat walking upon the water and he came to Jesus.

(30) But seeing the strong wind, he was frightened, and beginning to sink, he cried out, "Lord, save me!"

(31) Immediately Jesus stretched out his hand and caught him and said to him, "Man of little faith, why do you doubt?" (32) They went up into the boat and the wind ceased. (33) And those in the boat worshipped him saying, "Truly, you are the Son of God."

(34) When they had crossed over, they came to the land of Gennesaret. (35) The men of that place recognized him, and they spread the word throughout that neighborhood; and the people brought to him all who were ill, (36) and they begged him to let them touch the fringe of his cloak, and as many as touched it were made whole.

Matthew 15:1-39

(1) Then some Pharisees and scribes from Jerusalem came to Jesus,

saying, (2) "Why do your disciples transgress the tradition of the elders? For they do not wash their hands before they eat."

(3) Jesus replied, "And why do you transgress the commandment of God for the sake of your tradition? (4) For God said, 'Honor your father and your mother, and whoever insults his father or mother, let him be put to death.' (5) But you say to your father or mother, 'whatever you should have received from me is dedicated to God,' (6) thus you claim that it is not necessary to honor your father; so you have annulled the Word of God to suit your tradition. (7) You hypocrites! Isaiah accurately prophesied about you, saying:

(8) 'This people honor me with their lips,
but their hearts are far from me.
(9) They vainly worship me;
their teachings are the doctrines of men.' "

(10) And he called the people to him and said, "Listen, and understand. (11) It is not what enters into the mouth that defiles the man, but the things coming out of the mouth, that defiles him."

(12) Then the disciples came to him and said, "Do you know that the Pharisees who heard you were offended?"

(13) Jesus replied, "Every plant that my heavenly Father did not plant will be uprooted. (14) Leave them alone; they are blind leaders of the blind; the blind cannot lead the blind, they both will fall into a pit."

(15) Peter said to him, "Explain the parable to us."

(16) So he said, "Are you also still without understanding? (17) Do you not understand that everything entering into the mouth goes into the stomach and is cast out into the latrine? (18) But the things that come out of the mouth come from the heart, and that is what defiles the man. (19) For out of the heart come forth evil thoughts, murders, adulteries, fornications, thefts, false witnessing, and blasphemies. (20) These are the things which defile the man; but to eat with unwashed hands does not defile the man."

(21) Then Jesus left that place and came to the region of Tyre and Sidon. (22) And a Canaanite woman came out from that vicinity and began crying out, "Lord! Son of David, have mercy on me. My daughter is tormented by a demon."

(23) But Jesus did not answer her a word. And the disciples came to him, saying, "Send her away, because she is crying out after us!"

(24) Jesus said, "I was sent only to the lost sheep of the house of Israel."

(25) And she came and fell down before him, saying, "Lord, Help me!"

(26) He said, "It is not good to take the children's bread and cast it to the dogs."

(27) And she said, "Yes, Lord, but even the dogs eat from the crumbs falling from their master's table."

(28) Then Jesus replied to her, "O woman, great is your faith; it will

be done to you as you wish." And her daughter was healed at once.

(29) Jesus left there and went along by the Sea of Galilee; and he went up into the mountain and sat down there. (30) And many people came to him, bringing the lame, crippled, blind, mute and many others, and they put them down at the feet of Jesus; and he healed them. (31) And the people were amazed when they saw the mute speaking, the crippled whole, the lame walking, and the blind seeing; and they praised the God of Israel.

(32) Jesus called his disciples to him and said, "I have compassion for the people, because they have been with me for three days and they have nothing to eat; and I do not want to send them away without food, lest they faint on the way home."

(33) And the disciples said to him, "Where in this desert place could we get enough food to feed such a great crowd of people?"

(34) And Jesus said to them, "How many loaves do you have?" They replied, "Seven, and a few small fish."

(35) And Jesus, having instructed the people to recline on the ground, (36) took the seven loaves and the fish, and having given thanks, he broke them and gave them to the disciples, and they gave them to the people. (37) They all ate and were satisfied, and they took up seven baskets full of what was left over of the broken pieces. (38) Those who ate were four thousand men, not counting the women and children.

(39) Then he sent the people away and got into the boat and went to the region of Magadan.

Matthew 16:1-28

(1) The Pharisees and Sadducees came to Jesus, and to test him, they asked him to show them a sign from heaven.

(2) He replied, "When it is evening you say, 'Fair weather, for the sky is red.' (3) And in the morning you say, 'Today, stormy weather, for the sky is dark.' You know how to discern the sky, but you do not know how to discern the signs of the times. (4) A wicked and adulterous generation seeks for a sign, but no sign will be given to it except the sign of Jonah." And he left them and departed.

(5) When the disciples crossed the lake, they had forgotten to bring any bread. (6) And Jesus said to them, "Watch out and pay attention to the leaven of the Pharisees and Sadducees."

(7) And they reasoned among themselves, saying, "We brought no bread."

(8) But Jesus, aware of this, said, "You of little faith. Why are you reasoning with yourselves because you have no bread? (9) Do you not know? Do you not remember the five loaves of the five thousand and how many baskets you took up? (10) Or the seven loaves and the four thousand and how many baskets you took up? (11) How is it that you do not

understand that I am not talking about bread? But beware of the leaven of the Pharisees and Sadducees."

(12) Then they understood that he was not talking about the leaven of the bread, but about the teaching of the Pharisees and Sadducees.

(13) When Jesus came into the region of Caesarea Philippi, he asked his disciples, "Who do men say the Son of man is?" (14) And they said, "Some say John the Baptist, some Elijah, and others Jeremiah or one of the prophets."

(15) He said to them, "But you, who do you say that I am?"

(16) And Simon Peter answering said, "You are the Christ, the Son of the Living God."

(17) And Jesus answering said, "Blessed are you, Simon, son of Jonah, for flesh and blood did not reveal this to you, but my Father in heaven. (18) And I also tell you that you are Peter, and I will build my church upon this rock, and the gates of Hades will not overcome it. (19) I will give you the keys of the kingdom of heaven, and whatever you bind upon earth will have been bound in heaven, and whatever you loose on earth will have been loosed in heaven." (20) Then he instructed his disciples not to tell anyone that he was the Christ.

(21) Then from that time Jesus began to show his disciples that he must go to Jerusalem and suffer many things from the elders and chief priests and scribes, and be killed and on the third day to be raised up.

(22) Peter took him aside and began to admonish him, saying, "God have mercy on you, Lord! This shall never happen to you."

(23) Jesus turned to Peter and said, "Get behind me, Satan! You are a stumbling block to me; for you are not thinking the things of God, but of man."

(24) Then Jesus said to his disciples, "If anyone wishes to come after me, let him deny himself and take up his cross and follow me. (25) For whoever wishes to save his life will lose it, and whoever loses his life for my sake will find it. (26) For what shall a man profit if he gains the whole world, and loses his soul? Or what shall a man give in exchange for his soul? (27) For the Son of man is coming with his angels in the glory of his Father, and he will reward each person according to his works. (28) Truly, I say to you there are some standing here who will not taste of death until they see the Son of man coming in his kingdom."

Matthew 17:1-27

(1) Six days later, Jesus took Peter, James, and John, his brother, and led them to a high mountain by themselves. (2) There he was transfigured before them. His face shone like the sun, and his garments became white as light. (3) And behold Moses and Elijah were talking to him.

(4) Peter spoke up and said, "Lord, it is good for us to be here; if you wish I will build here three tents, one for you, one for Moses, and one for Elijah."

(5) While he was still speaking, behold a bright cloud overshadowed them, and a voice from the cloud said, "This is my beloved Son, in whom I am well pleased. Listen to him!"

(6) When the disciples heard this, they fell on their faces, for they were terribly frightened.

(7) Jesus, coming to them and touching them, said, "Get up and do not fear." (8) They looked up and saw no one except Jesus.

(9) As they were going down the mountain, Jesus instructed, them, "Do not tell the vision to anyone until the Son of Man has been raised from the dead."

(10) The disciples asked him, "Why do the scribes say that Elijah must come first?"

(11) Jesus replied, "Indeed, Elijah comes and will restore all things. (12) But I tell you, Elijah has already come, and they did not recognize him, but treated him as they wished. So also the Son of Man is going to suffer at their hands." (13) Then the disciples understood that he spoke to them concerning John the Baptist.

(14) When they reached the crowd, a man came to him and fell on his knees, (15) saying, "Lord, have mercy on my son, for he has epilepsy and suffers greatly, for often he falls into the fire or into the water.

(16) "I brought him to your disciples, but they were not able to heal him." (17) Jesus replied, "O unbelieving and perverse generation. How long am I to be with you? How long am I to bear with you? Bring him here to me."

(18) Jesus rebuked the demon, and it came out of him, and he was immediately healed.

(19) Then the disciples came to Jesus privately and said, "Why were we not able to drive it out?"

(20) He said to them, "Because of your little faith; For truly I tell you, if you have faith as a grain of mustard seed, you can say to this mountain, 'Be removed from here to there,' and it will be removed; and nothing will be impossible to you."

(22) While they were going about in Galilee, Jesus said to them, "The Son of Man is about to be delivered into the hands of men, (23) and they will kill him, and on the third day he will be raised." The disciples were crushed with grief.

(24) When they came to Capernaum, a collector of taxes came to Peter and said, "Does your teacher pay the temple tax?"

"Yes," he said.

(25) When Peter came to the house, Jesus spoke to him first, "What do you think, Simon? From whom do the kings of the earth collect duty and

taxes, from their sons or from strangers?"

(26) Peter answered, "From strangers."

Jesus said, "Then the sons are exempt; (27) but lest we offend them, go to the sea and cast a net. Take the first fish you catch and open it's mouth and you will find a four-drachma coin. Take it and give to them for me and you."

Matthew 18:1-35

(1) At that time the disciples came to Jesus and said, "Who is the greatest in the kingdom of heaven?"

(2) And he called a little child and put him in the midst of them (3) and said, "Truly I say to you, unless you repent and become as this little child, you will never enter into the kingdom of heaven. (4) Whoever then humbles himself as this little child is the greatest in the kingdom of heaven; (5) and whoever welcomes one little child like this in my name, welcomes me. (6) But whoever causes one little one who believes in me to stumble, it would be better for him that a millstone should be tied around his neck and that he should be thrown into the sea.

(7) "Woe to the world for stumbling blocks; it is inevitable that there will be stumbling blocks, but woe to the man through whom they come. (8) If your hand or your foot causes you to stumble, cut it off and throw it away, for it is better to enter into life maimed or crippled than to have two hands and two feet and to be thrown into the fire of Gehenna. (9) And if your eye offends you, pluck it out and throw it away, for it is better to enter into life with one eye than to have two eyes and to be thrown into the fire of Gehenna.

(10) "See that you do not despise one of these little ones, for I tell you that their angels in heaven are always in the presence of my Father in heaven.

(12) "What do you think? If a man has a hundred sheep and one wanders away, will he not leave the ninety-nine on the hillside and look for the one who wandered away? (13) And if he finds it, truly I tell you that he rejoices over it more than over the ninety-nine that had not wandered off. (14) So it is not the will of your Father in heaven that one of these little ones should perish.

(15) "If your brother sins, go and show him his fault, while you are alone with him. If he listens to you, you have won your brother. (16) If he does not listen to you, take one or two more with you, so that by the mouth of two or three witnesses every fact will be confirmed. (17) And if he refuses to listen to them, tell it to the church, and if he refuses to listen to the church, let him be as a gentile and a tax collector.

(18) "Truly I tell you, whatever you bind on earth, will have been bound in heaven, and whatever you loose on earth will have been loosed in

heaven. (19) Again I tell you the truth that if two of you shall agree on earth about whatever they ask, it will be done for them by my Father in heaven. (20) For where two or three are assembled in my name, there I am in their midst."

(21) Then Peter came to Jesus and said, "How many times do I have to forgive my brother who sins against me? Seven times?"

(22) Jesus said, "I do not tell you until seven times, but until seventy times seven.

(23) "Therefore, the kingdom of heaven is like a king who decided to settle accounts with his slaves. (24) As he began, a debtor was brought to him who owed him ten thousand talents. (25) He could not pay, so his lord commanded that he, his wife and children, along with everything that he had, be sold and payment be made.

(26) "Therefore, the slave fell down before his master's feet, saying, 'Have patience with me, I will pay you everything.' (27) And the lord, filled with compassion, released him and forgave him the debt.

(28) "But that slave went out and found one of his fellow slaves who owed him a hundred denarii, and seized him by the throat, and said, 'Pay me what you owe me!' (29) Therefore the fellow slave fell down before him, saying, 'Have patience with me, I will pay you.' (30) But he refused and went and put him in prison until he could pay the debt. (31) When the other slaves knew what had happened, they were grieved exceedingly, and they went and told their lord what had happened.

(32) "Then the lord summoned him and said, 'Wicked slave! I forgave you all that debt, because you entreated me; (33) should you not have had mercy on your fellow slave as I had mercy on you?' (34) And the lord, being angry with him, delivered him to the tormentors until he could pay back his debt.

(35) "So also our Father in Heaven will do to you, unless you forgive your brother from you heart."

Matthew 19:1-30

(1) Now when Jesus had finished this discourse, he departed from Galilee and came to the borders of Judea beyond the Jordan. (2) Large crowds followed him.

(3) The Pharisees came to him to test him, saying, "Is it lawful for a man to divorce his wife for any reason?"

(4) Jesus answered, "Have you not read that the Creator in the beginning 'made them male and female,' (5) and he said, 'For this reason a man shall leave his father and his mother and cleave to his wife, and the two shall become one flesh.' (6) So they are no longer two but one flesh. Therefore what God has joined together, let no one divide."

(7) They said to him, "Why then did Moses command a man to give

a certificate of divorce and send her away?"

(8) He said to them, "Moses, because of the hardness of your hearts, allowed you to divorce your wives, but it was not so from the beginning. (9) And I say to you that whoever divorces his wife, except for the cause of fornication, and marries another commits adultery."

(10) They said to him, "If that is the case with a man and his wife, it is not expedient to get married."

(11) Jesus replied, "Not all men can receive this precept, only those who have the gift. (12) For there are eunuchs from birth, and some have been made eunuchs by men, and some have made themselves eunuchs for the sake of the kingdom. He who has power to receive it, let him receive it."

(13) Then they brought to Jesus children for him to lay his hands on them and to pray. But the disciples rebuked them.

(14) But Jesus said, "Let the children come to me, and do not hinder them, for of such is the kingdom of heaven." (15) And he put his hands on them and departed.

(16) And behold, one came to Jesus and said, "Teacher, what good thing can I do that I may have eternal life?"

(17) Jesus said, "Why do you question me concerning the good? There is one who is good. And if you wish to enter life, keep the commandments."

(18) He said, "Which?"

And Jesus said, " 'You shall not kill, you shall not commit adultery, you shall not steal, you shall not bear false witness, (19) you shall honor your father and your mother,' and, 'you shall love your neighbor as yourself.' "

(20) And the young man said to him, "All these things I have kept. What more do I lack?"

(21) Jesus said to him, "If you want to be perfect, go and sell what you have and give to the poor, and you will have treasure in heaven, and come follow me."

(22) When the young man heard this, he went away grieved, for he had great wealth.

(23) Then Jesus said to his disciples, "Truly I tell you that it is very hard for a rich man to enter the kingdom of heaven. (24) Again I tell you, it is easier for a camel to go through the eye of a needle than for a rich man to enter the kingdom of heaven."

(25) When the disciples heard this, they were exceedingly astonished, saying, "Who then can be saved?"

(26) Jesus looked at them and said, "With men this is impossible, but with God all things are possible."

(27) Then Peter said to Jesus, "Behold, we have left everything to follow you; what then shall we have?"

(28) Jesus said to them, "Truly I tell you that you who have followed me, in the regeneration when the Son of man sits on his glorious throne, will

also sit on the twelve thrones judging the twelve tribes of Israel. (29) And everyone who has left houses or brothers or sisters or fathers or mothers or children or farms for my sake will receive many times as much, and shall inherit eternal life. (30) But many who are first will be last, and many who are last will be first.

Matthew 20:1-34

(1) "The kingdom of heaven is like a landowner who went out early in the morning to hire workmen to work in his vineyard. (2) He agreed with the workmen to pay a denarius for the day's work, and he sent them into his vineyard.

(3) "And he went out about 0900 hours and saw others standing idle in the market place. (4) He said to them, 'You go also into the vineyard, and I will pay you what is right.' (5) And they went. Again he went out at 1200 hours and at 1500 hours, likewise. (6) About 1700 hours, he went out again and found others standing and he said to them, 'Why have you been standing here idle all day?'

(7) "They said to him, 'Because no one has hired us.'

"He said to them. 'You go into the vineyard also.'

(8) "When evening came, the owner of the vineyard said to the steward, 'Call the workmen and pay them their wages, beginning with the last and ending with the first.'

(9) "The ones who began at 1700 hours came and received a denarius. (10) And those who were hired first came and they thought they would receive more, but each of them also received a denarius. (11) When they received their pay, they began to grumble against the landowner, saying, (12) 'These last have worked only one hour, and you have made them equal to us who have borne the burden of the day and the scorching heat.'

(13) "The landowner said to one of them, 'Friend, I am not treating you unfairly. Did you not agree with me for a denarius? (14) Take what is yours and go; I choose to give the last as I give you. (15) Am I not free to do what I desire with my money? Or is your eye evil because I am good?' (16) So the last will be first, and the first will be last."

(17) Jesus, on his way to Jerusalem, took his disciples aside and said to them, (18) "Behold, we are going up to Jerusalem; and the Son of man will be delivered to the chief priests and scribes, and they will condemn him to death, (19) and they will deliver him to the Gentiles, to be mocked, flogged, and crucified; and on the third day he will be raised."

(20) Then came to him the mother of the sons of Zebedee with her two sons, kneeling and asking a favor of him.

(21) Jesus said to her, "What do you want?"

She said to him, "Promise me that my two sons will sit, one on the right and one on the left, with you in your kingdom."

(22) Jesus answering said, "You do not know what you ask. Can you drink the cup that I am about to drink?"

They said, "We can."

(23) Jesus said to them, "Indeed, you will drink my cup, but to sit at my right and at my left is not for me to give; but it is for those for whom it has been prepared by my father."

(24) When the ten heard about this, they were indignant with the two brothers. (25) Then, Jesus calling them, said, "We know that the rulers of the Gentiles lord it over them, and the high officials exercise authority over them. (26) It is not so among you, but whoever among you wishes to be great must be their servant, (27) and whoever among you wishes to be first must be their slave. (28) For the Son of man did not come to be served, but to serve, and to give his life a ransom for many."

(29) As they were going from Jericho, great crowds followed them. (30) Behold, two blind men were sitting by the roadside; hearing that Jesus was passing by, they cried out, "Lord, Son of David, have mercy on us!" (31) But the crowd rebuked them telling them to be quiet. But they cried out louder, "Lord, Son of David, have mercy on us!"

(32) Jesus stopped and called them to him and said, "What do you want me to do for you?"

(33) They said to him, "Lord, that our eyes be opened."

(34) Jesus, having compassion on them, touched their eyes, and immediately they could see, and they followed him.

Matthew 21:1-46

(1) When they came near to Jerusalem and came to Bethphage to the Mount of Olives, Jesus sent two of his disciples (2) saying, "Go into the village opposite you, and you will immediately find a donkey, having been tied with her colt; untie them and bring them to me. (3) If anyone questions you, you will say, 'The Lord needs them,' and he will immediately release them." (4) This happened to fulfill what was said through the prophet:

(5) "Tell the daughter of Zion, Behold, the king is coming to you, meek and riding on a donkey, on a colt, the beast of burden."

(6) The disciples went and did as Jesus had instructed them. (7) They brought the donkey and the colt and put on them their clothes, and Jesus mounted. (8) The very large crowd spread their clothes on the road, and others cut branches from the trees and spread them on the road. (9) And the crowds going before him and the ones following him shouted, "Hosanna to the son of David, Blessed is the one coming in the name of the Lord! Hosanna in the highest!"

(10) When Jesus entered into Jerusalem, the whole city was stirred, saying, "Who is this?"

(11) The crowds answered, "This is Jesus the prophet, who is from

Nazareth of Galilee."

(12) Jesus entered the temple, and he cast out all who were buying
and selling in the temple; he turned over the money changers' tables and the
benches of those selling doves, (13) and he said, "It is written, 'My house
shall be called the house of prayer.' But you are making it 'a cave of
robbers.' "

(14) The blind and the lame came to him in the temple, and he
healed them. (15) But when the chief priests and the scribes saw the
marvelous things which he did and the children shouting in the temple,
"Hosanna to the son of David," they were indignant.

(16) They said to him, "Do you not hear what they are saying?"
Jesus answered, "Yes, have you never read, 'Out of the mouth of infants and
nursing babes you have perfected praise?' "

(17) Then he left there and went to the city of Bethany and spent the
night there. (18) At dawn, as Jesus was going up to the city, he was hungry,
(19) and seeing a fig tree by the roadside, he went to it and found nothing on
it except leaves; and he said to it, "Never again shall you bear fruit!" And
immediately the fig tree dried up.

(20) When the disciples saw it, they were amazed, and they said,
"How is it that the fig tree withered so quickly?"

(21) Jesus said to them, "Truly, I say to you, if you have faith and do
not doubt, not only will you do what is done to the fig tree, but if you say to
this mountain, 'Be taken up and cast into the sea,' it will be done. (22) And
whatever you pray for in faith, you will receive."

(23) Jesus entered the temple, and while he was teaching, the chief
priests and elders of the people came to him and said, "By what authority do
you do these things, and who gave you this authority?"

(24) Jesus said to them, "I have a question to ask you, and if you tell
me the answer, I will tell you by what authority I do these things. (25) Was
the baptism of John from Heaven, or was it from men?" They reasoned
among themselves, "If we say, 'from heaven,' he will say to us, 'then why
did you not believe him?' (26) But if we say, 'from men,' we fear the people,
for all believe that John was a prophet."

(27) So they answered Jesus, "We do not know." And Jesus said to
them, "Neither do I tell you by what authority I do these things.

(28) "What do you think about this? A man had two sons, and he
said to the first, 'Son, go work in the vineyard today.' (29) But he answered,
'I will not,' but later he repented and went. (30) He went to the second and
said the same thing. And he said 'I will, sir.' But he did not go. (31) Which of
the two did the will of the father?" They answered, "The first." Jesus said to
them, "Truly, I say to you, the tax collectors and prostitutes go into the
kingdom of God before you. (32) For John came to you in the way of
righteousness, and you did not believe him, but the tax collectors and
prostitutes believed him; and when you saw it, you did not afterward repent

and believe him.

(33) "Listen to another parable. There was a landowner who planted a vineyard; and he put a hedge around it, and dug a wine press in it and built a tower. Then he rented it to farmers and went on a journey. (34) When the harvest time drew near, he sent his slaves to the farmers to collect his rent.

(35) "The farmers took his slaves and beat one, killed another, and stoned another. (36) A second time he sent other slaves to them, more than the first time, and they treated them the same way.

(37) "Finally, he sent his son to them, saying, 'They will respect my son.'

(38) "But when the farmers saw the son, they said to themselves, 'This is the heir. Come, let us kill him and take his inheritance.' (39) And they cast him outside the vineyard and killed him. (40) Therefore, when the owner of the vineyard comes, what will he do to those farmers?"

(41) They replied to him, "He will bring those bad men to a bad end and rent out his vineyard to other farmers, who will pay the rent at harvest time."

(42) Jesus said to them, "Have you not read in the Scriptures, 'The stone which the builders rejected has become the corner stone; this is the work of the Lord, and it is marvelous in our eyes'?

(43) "Therefore I tell you that the kingdom of God will be taken from you and given to a nation that will yield a harvest. (44) And the one who falls upon this stone will be broken in pieces, but he on whom it falls will be crushed." (45) When the chief priests and the Pharisees heard the parables, they knew that he was speaking about them. (46) They tried to arrest him, but they feared the people, because they considered him a prophet.

Matthew 22:1-46

(1) Jesus spoke to them again in parables: (2) "The kingdom of heaven is like a king who made a marriage feast for his son. (3) He sent his slaves to call the ones who had been invited to the marriage feast, but they did not want to come.

(4) "Again he sent other slaves saying, 'Tell those who have been invited that the banquet is ready! My oxen and grain-fed cattle have been butchered, and everything is ready. Come to the wedding feast!'

(5) "But they went away unconcerned, one to his own farm, another to his place of business; (6) and the rest seized the slaves, intimidated them and killed them. (7) The king was furious; and he sent his soldiers and destroyed those murderers and burned their city.

(8) "Then he said to his slaves, 'The marriage feast is ready, and those who were invited were not worthy. (9) Therefore, go to the crossroads and as many as you find, bring them to the marriage feast.' (10) And those

slaves went out into the streets and got together all they could find, evil as well as good. And the wedding hall was packed with guests.

(11) "When the king entered, he saw a man there who was not wearing wedding clothes, (12) and he said to him, 'Comrade, how did you get in here without wedding clothes?' The man was speechless.

(13) "Then the king said to his servants, 'Bind his feet and hands, and throw him into outer darkness, where there will be weeping and gnashing of teeth.' (14) For many are invited, but few are chosen."

(15) Then the Pharisees got together to plan how to trap Jesus in his speech. (16) So they sent to him their disciples along with the Herodians, saying, "Teacher, we know that you are truthful and teach the way of God in truth; and you are not influenced by others, because you do not court the favor of anyone. (17) Therefore tell us what you think, is it right to pay taxes to Caesar, or not?"

(18) Jesus, aware of their malicious plot, replied, "You hypocrites, why are you trying to trap me! (19) Show me the coin used for the tax." And they brought to him a denarius.

(20) Jesus said to them, "Whose image and whose inscription is this?"

(21) They said, "Caesar's."

Then he said to them, "Therefore, give Caesar what belongs to him, and give God what belongs to him."

(22) Hearing this, they were amazed, and leaving him, they went away.

(23) On that same day some Sadducees, who did not believe in a resurrection, came and questioned him, (24) saying, "Teacher, Moses said, 'If a man dies without children, his brother must marry his widow and have children for him.' (25) Now there were seven brothers among us. The first married, and died, and having no children, he left his widow to his brother. (26) Likewise the second died, and the third, even to the seventh. (27) Last of all, the woman died. (28) Therefore, in the resurrection, whose wife will she be? For they all had her."

(29) Jesus answered them, "You are led astray because you do not understand the Scriptures or the power of God. (30) For in the resurrection they do not marry nor are they given in marriage, for they are like the angels in heaven. (31) And concerning the resurrection of the dead, have you not read what God said to you? (32) 'I am the God of Abraham, the God of Isaac, and the God of Jacob'? He is not the God of the dead but of the living." (33) When the crowds heard this, they were astonished at his teaching.

(34) When the Pharisees heard that Jesus had silenced the Sadducees, they gathered themselves together. (35) And one of them, a lawyer, asked Jesus a question to test him, (36) "Teacher, what is the greatest commandment in the law?"

(37) Jesus said to him, "You shall love the Lord your God with all

your heart, with all your soul, and with all your mind. (38) This is the greatest commandment and is of first importance. (39) And the second is like it, 'You shall love your neighbor as yourself.' (40) On these two commandments, hang all the law and the prophets."

(41) While the Pharisees were assembled, Jesus questioned them, (42) saying, "What do you think about the Christ? Whose son is he?"

They said, "David."

(43) He asked them, "How is it then that David, inspired by the Spirit, calls him Lord, saying,

(44) 'The Lord said to my Lord, Sit at my right hand,

until I put your enemies under your feet.'

(45) If David calls him Lord, how is he his son?"

(46) No one was able to answer him a word, and from that day no one ever dared to question him again.

Matthew 23:1-39

(1) Then Jesus spoke to the crowds and to his disciples: (2) "The scribes and the Pharisees sit in the chair of Moses. (3) Therefore all that they tell you, do and observe, but do not do as they do, for they say one thing and do another. (4) They bind heavy burdens and put them on the shoulders of men, but they are not willing to lift one finger to help. (5) For everything they do is to be seen by men. For they broaden their phylacteries and enlarge their tassels; (6) and they love the chief place in the banquets and the chief seats in the synagogues; (7) and they love to be called 'rabbi' in the market place. (8) But you are not to be called, 'rabbi,' for you have one Rabbi and you are all brothers. (9) And call no man 'father' on earth, for you have one Father, and he is in heaven. (10) Nor are you to be called 'teacher,' for you have one Teacher, the Messiah. (11) The greatest among you will be your servant. (12) For whoever exalts himself will be humbled, and whoever humbles himself will be exalted.

(13) "Woe to you, scribes and Pharisees, hypocrites! You shut the door of the kingdom of heaven in men's faces; you do not enter yourselves, nor do you allow others to enter.

(15) "Woe to you, scribes and Pharisees, hypocrites! You travel over sea and land to make one proselyte, and then you make him a son of hell, twice as much as you are.

(16) "Woe to you, blind leaders! You say, 'It is nothing to swear by the temple, but whoever swears by the gold of the temple is bound by his oath.' (17) Blind Fools! Which is greater, the gold on the altar, or the temple that sanctifies the gold? (18) And you say, 'It is nothing to swear by the altar, but whoever swears by the gift of the alter is bound by his oath.' (19) You blind men! For which is greater, the gift or the alter that sanctifies the gift? (20) Therefore, the one who swears by the alter swears by all things on it.

(21) And the one who swears by the temple swears by him who dwells in it. (22) And the one who swears by heaven swears by the throne of God and the one who sits upon it.

(23) "Woe to you, scribes and Pharisees, hypocrites! You tithe the mint, the dill, and the cumin, but you have left out the more important things of the law, justice, mercy, and faith. These things you should have done, without neglecting the other things. (24) You blind leaders! You strain out the gnat, but you swallow the camel!

(25) "Woe to you, scribes and Pharisees, hypocrites! You clean the outside of the cup and the plate, but on the inside you are filled with robbery and self indulgence! (26) Blind Pharisees, hypocrites! You resemble whitewashed graves, which look outwardly beautiful, but within are full of bones of dead men and all kinds of uncleanness. (28) Thus outwardly you appear to men as righteous, but within you are full of hypocrisy and wickedness.

(29) "Woe to you, scribes and Pharisees, hypocrites! You build the tombs of the prophets, and you adorn the monuments of the righteous; (30) and you say, 'If we had lived in the days of our fathers we would not have taken part in shedding the blood of the prophets.' (31) So you yourselves witness that you are the sons of the ones who killed the prophets. (32) Perform then with your hand what your fathers began.

(33) "You snakes! You brood of vipers! How can you escape the judgment of hell? (34) Therefore, I am sending you prophets, wise men, and scribes. Some you will kill, even crucify, and some you will whip in your synagogues and persecute from city to city. (35) So upon you will come all the righteous blood that has been shed on the earth, from the blood of Abel the righteous to the blood of Zacharias, son of Barachias, whom you murdered between the sanctuary and the alter. (36) Truly, I tell you, all these things will come on this generation.

(37) "Jerusalem! Jerusalem! You who kill the prophets and stone those sent to you! How often I wished to gather your children together as a hen gathers her chickens under her wings, but you did not desire it! (38) So your house is left to you, desolate. (39) For I tell you, from now you will not see me until you say, 'Blessed is the one coming in the name of the Lord.' "

Matthew 24:1-51

(1) Jesus left the temple and was going away when his disciples came to him to show him the buildings of the temple. (2) Jesus said to them, "Look at all these buildings. Truly I tell you, there will not be one stone left upon another that will not be torn down."

(3) Jesus was sitting on the Mount of Olives when his disciples came to him privately and said, "Tell us when this will be, and what will be the sign of your coming and the completion of the age?"

(4) Jesus answered, "See that no one leads you astray, (5) for many will come in my name saying, 'I am the Christ,' and many will be led astray. (6) You will hear about wars and rumors of wars. Be not disturbed for this must happen, but the end is not yet. (7) For nation will rise against nation and kingdom against kingdom, and there will be famines and earthquakes in many places. (8) All these are the beginning of birth pangs. (9) Then they will arrest you and hand you over to be persecuted and kill you, and you will be hated by all the nations because of my name. (10) Then many will be offended, and they will betray one another, and they will hate one another. (11) Many false prophets will arise and lead many astray. (12) And because of the increase of lawlessness, the love of many will grow cold. (13) But those who endure will be saved. (14) And this gospel of the kingdom will be proclaimed to the entire world for a testimony to all the nations, and then the end will come.

(15) "So when you see the abomination of desolation, spoken through Daniel the prophet, standing in the holy place (let the reader understand), (16) let those in Judea flee to the mountains; (17) let the one on the housetop not come down to get his belongings out of his house; (18) let the one in the field not go back to get his clothes. (19) Woe to the pregnant women and nursing mothers in those days. (20) Pray that the flight will not be in winter or on a Sabbath; (21) for the affliction will be great, such has not happened from the beginning of the world until now and will not happen again. (22) Except those days were cut short, no one would survive, but because of the chosen, those days will be cut short. (23) Then if anyone says to you, 'Behold! Here is the Christ!' or 'There he is,' do not believe it. (24) For many false Christs and false prophets will rise up and will perform great signs and miracles, so as to deceive the elect, if possible. (25) Behold I have told you. (26) Therefore if they say to you 'Look, he is in the desert,' do not go forth, or if they say 'Look, he is in the private rooms,' do not believe it. (27) For as the lightening comes from the east and flashes to the west, so will be the coming of the Son of Man. (28) The eagles will gather where the carcass is.

(29) "Immediately after the misery of those days, 'the sun will be darkened, and the moon will not give it's light, and the stars will fall from the sky, and the powers of the heavens will be shaken.'

(30) "Then shall appear the sign of the Son of Man from heaven, and then all the tribes of the earth will mourn; and they will see the Son of Man coming on the clouds of heaven with power and great glory. (31) And he will send his angels with a loud trumpet call, and they will gather his elect from the four winds, from one end of the heavens to the other.

(32) "Learn a lesson from the parable of the fig tree. When the branch of the tree becomes tender and the leaves come out, you know that summer is near. (33) So likewise you, when you see these things, you will know that he is near, at the door. (34) Truly I tell you that this generation

will not pass away until all these things happen. (35) Heaven and earth will pass away, but my words will never pass away.

(36) "But concerning that day and hour no one knows, neither the angels of heaven nor the Son of Man. Only the Father knows. (37) For as the days before the flood came, they were eating and drinking, marrying and giving in marriage, until the day Noah entered the ark. (39) And they did not know until the flood came and took all of them, so will be the coming of the Son of Man. (40) There will be two men in the field, one will be taken and the other one left. (41) Two women will be grinding at the mill, one will be taken and the other one left. (42) Watch therefore, because you do not know what day your Lord is coming. (43) But know this, that if the owner of the house had known what time the thief was coming, he would have watched and prevented him from breaking into his house. (44) Therefore be ready, because the Son of Man will come at an unexpected hour.

(45) "Who then is the faithful and wise slave, whom his master put in charge of this household to give them their food at the proper time? (46) Blessed is the slave whom his master finds working when he arrives. (47) Truly I tell you, he will put him in charge of all his possessions. (48) But if the wicked slave says in his heart, 'My master delays his coming,' (49) and begins to strike his fellow slaves, and eats and drinks with the drunkards, (50) the master of that slave will come on a day that he does not expect and an hour that he is not aware of. (51) He will cut him to pieces and assign him a place with hypocrites, where there will be weeping and grinding of the teeth.

Matthew 25:1-46

(1) "Then the kingdom of heaven will be compared to ten virgins who took their lamps and went forth to meet the bridegroom. (2) Five of them were foolish and five were wise. (3) For although the foolish ones took their lamps, they did not take oil with them. (4) But the wise took vessels of oil along with the lamps. (5) While the bridegroom delayed, they all got drowsy and went to sleep.

(6) "At mid-night there was a shout, 'Behold, the bridegroom! Go forth to meet him!'

(7) "Then all the virgins arose and trimmed their lamps. (8) The foolish ones said to the wise, 'Give us some of your oil, because our lamps are going out.'

(9) "But the wise answered, 'We do not have enough to share with you; go rather to the store and buy for yourselves.'

(10) "While they were going away to buy the oil, the bridegroom came, and those who were ready went in with him to the wedding feast, and the door was shut.

(11) "Later the other virgins came saying, 'Lord, Lord, open the door

for us!'

(12) "But he answered, 'Truly, I do not know you.'

(13) "Therefore, be ready, for you do not know the day or the hour.

(14) "For it will be like a man going on a journey who called his slaves and entrusted to them his possessions. (15) He gave five talents to one, two to another, and one to another—to each according to his own ability—and then he went on his journey. (16) Immediately the one who received five talents went out and traded with them and made five more talents; (17) so also, the one who received two talents went out and traded with them and made two other talents. (18) But the one who received the one talent went away and dug a hole in the ground and hid his master's money.

(19) "After a long time the master of those slaves returned and settled accounts with them. (20) The one who had received the five talents came to him, saying, 'Lord, you gave me five talents; behold, I gained five other talents.'

(21) "Then his master said to him, 'Well done, good and faithful slave. You have been faithful over a few things; I will put you in charge of many things. Enter into the joy of your master.'

(22) "The one who had received the two talents came to him, saying, 'Lord, you gave me two talents; behold, I gained two other talents.'

(23) "His master said to him, 'Well done, good and faithful slave; you have been faithful over a few things; I will put you in charge of many things. Enter into the joy of your master.'

(24) "Then the one who had received the one talent said, 'I knew you to be a hard man, reaping where you did not sow, and gathering where you had not threshed. (25) So I was afraid, and I went and hid your talent in the ground. Behold, here is what is yours.'

(26) "His master said to him, 'Wicked and slothful slave! You knew that I reaped where I did not sow and gathered where I had not threshed. (27) You should have put my money in the bank, so that at my coming I could have received my money with interest. (28) Take therefore the talent from him and give it to the one who has ten talents. (29) For everyone who has will be given more, and he will have abundance; but the one who does not have, even what he has will be taken from him. (30) And cast the worthless slave into the outer darkness; there will be weeping and grinding of the teeth.'

(31) "When the Son of Man comes in his glory with all his angels with him, then he will sit on his throne of glory. (32) All the nations will be assembled before him, and he will separate them one from another, as the shepherd separates the sheep from the goats; (33) and he will set the sheep on his right, and the goats on his left.

(34) "Then the king will say to those on his right, 'Come, you blessed of my Father, inherit the kingdom which has been prepared from the foundation of the world. (35) For I was hungry and you fed me, I was thirsty

and you gave me something to drink, I was a stranger and you entertained me, (36) I was naked and you clothed me, I was sick and you visited me, I was in prison and you came to me.'

(37) "Then the righteous will answer him, 'When did we see you hungry and fed you, or thirsty and gave you something to drink? (38) And when did we see you a stranger and entertained you, or naked and clothed you? (39) And when did we see you sick or in prison and came to visit you?'

(40) "The king will reply to them, 'Truly, I tell you, whenever you did it to the least of these brothers of me, you did it to me.'

(41) "Then he will say to those on his left, 'Depart from me, you who are cursed, into the eternal fire prepared for the devil and his angels. (42) For I was hungry and you did not feed me, I was thirsty and you did not give me anything to drink, (43) I was a stranger and you did not entertain me, naked and you did not clothe me, sick and in prison and you did not visit me.'

(44) "Then they will also answer, 'Lord, when did we see you hungry or thirsty or a stranger or naked or sick or in prison, and we did not minister to you?'

(45) "Then he will reply, 'Truly I tell you, whenever you did not do it to the least of these, neither did you do it to me.'

(46) "And these will go away into eternal punishment, but the righteous into eternal life."

Matthew 26:1-75

(1) When Jesus had finished his teaching, he said to his disciples, (2) "You know that after two days will be the Passover, and the Son of Man will be delivered up to be crucified."

(3) Then the chief priests and the elders of the people came together in the court of the high priest (whose name was Caiaphas) (4) to plot together to seize Jesus by treachery and kill him. (5) But they said, "Not during the feast, lest there be a riot among the people."

(6) When Jesus was in Bethany in the house of Simon the leper, (7) a woman came to him with an alabaster jar of very expensive ointment, and she poured it on his head while he was reclining at the table. (8) When the disciples saw this, they were very angry; and they said, "Why this waste? (9) For this could have been sold for a large sum and given to the poor."

(10) Jesus, aware of this, said, "Why do you trouble the woman? For she has done a beautiful thing to me. (11) You always have the poor with you, but you will not always have me. (12) For she has poured this ointment over my body to prepare me for burial. (13) Truly I tell you, wherever in all the world this gospel is proclaimed, what this woman has done will be told as a memorial of her."

(14) Then Judas Iscariot, one of the twelve, went to the chief priests (15) and said, "What will you give me to deliver him to you?" And they

gave him thirty silver shekels. (16) From that time he sought an opportunity to betray him.

(17) On the first day of the Unleavened Bread, the disciples of Jesus came to him, saying, "Where do you want us to prepare for you to eat the Passover?"

(18) He answered, "Go into the city to a certain man and say to him, 'The Teacher says, My time is near; I want to celebrate the Passover with my disciples.' " (19) The disciples did as Jesus instructed them, and they prepared the Passover supper.

(20) When evening came, Jesus was reclining with the Twelve. (21) As they were eating, he said, "Truly, I say to you, one of you will betray me."

(22) They were exceedingly sorrowful and began each one to say to him, "Is it I, Lord?"

(23) Jesus answered, "The man who dips his hand in the dish with me will betray me. (24) Indeed the Son of Man goes as it has been written in Scripture concerning him, but woe to the man through whom the Son of Man is betrayed! It would have been better if that man had never been born."

(25) And Judas, the one betraying him, said, "Is it I, Rabbi?"

Jesus said, "You said it."

(26) While they were eating, Jesus took bread, and blessing it, he broke it and gave it to his disciples, and said, "Take and eat; this is my body."

(27) Then he took a cup, and when he had giving thanks he gave it to them, saying, "Drink from it, all of you, (28) for it is my blood of the covenant being shed for many for the forgiveness of sin. (29) And I tell you, I will not drink again from the fruit of the vine until that day when I will drink it new with you in the kingdom of my Father." (30) And after singing a hymn, they went out to the Mount of Olives.

(31) Then Jesus said to them, "All of you will be ashamed in me tonight. For it is written, 'I will strike the shepherd, and the sheep of the flock will be scattered,' (32) but after I am resurrected, I will go back to meet you in Galilee."

(33) But Peter said to him, "If all men are ashamed in you, I will never!"

(34) Jesus said to him, "Truly, I tell you, tonight before a rooster crows, you will deny me three times."

(35) Peter said to him, "Even if I must die with you, I will never deny you." And so said all the disciples.

(36) Then Jesus went with them to a place called Gethsemane and said to his disciples, "Sit down here while I go over there to pray." (37) And Jesus took with him Peter and the two sons of Zebedee, and he began to be grieved and to be distressed. (38) Then he said to them, "I am overwhelmed with distress in my soul, even unto death. Remain here and watch with me."

(39) Jesus went a little farther and fell on his face praying, "My

Father, if it is possible, let this cup pass from me; yet, not as I will, but as you will."

(40) Then he returned to the disciples and found them sleeping. He said to Peter, "So you were not able to watch with me for one hour? (41) Watch and pray, lest you enter into temptation; indeed the spirit it willing, but the flesh is weak."

(42) Again a second time he went away and prayed, "My Father, if this cup cannot pass away except I drink it, let your will be done."

(43) And again he found them sleeping, for their eyes were heavy. (44) So he left them again and went away and prayed a third time, saying the same words.

(45) Then he returned to the disciples and said to them, "Are you still sleeping and resting? Behold, the hour is at hand, and the Son of man is betrayed into the hands of sinners. (46) Get up, let us go, for the betrayer is here."

(47) While Jesus was still speaking, Judas, one of the Twelve, came with a large crowd with swords and clubs from the chief priests and elders of the people. (48) Now the betrayer had given them a signal, saying, "He is the one I will kiss; arrest him." (49) And he immediately approached Jesus and said, "Hail, Rabbi," and he affectionately kissed him.

(50) Jesus said to him, "Comrade, do what you are here for." Then they laid hands of Jesus and arrested him. (51) At that moment, one of those who were with Jesus stretched out his hand and drew his sword and cut off the ear of the slave of the high priest.

(52) Then Jesus said to him, "Put your sword back into its place; for those who take a sword will perish by a sword. (53) Or do you not know that I can ask my Father, and he will provide for me now with more that twelve legions of angels? (54) How then would the Scriptures be fulfilled that says it must happen this way?"

(55) At that time Jesus said to the crowds, "Are you coming out as against a robber with swords and clubs to arrest me? I sat daily teaching in the temple, and you did not arrest me. (56) But all this has happened that the Scriptures of the prophets might be fulfilled." Then all the disciples left him and fled.

(57) Those who had arrested Jesus led him away to Caiaphas, the high priest, where the scribes and elders were assembled. (58) And Peter followed him from a far distance up to the court of the high priest; and entering within, he sat to see the end.

(59) The chief priests and the whole Council sought false witnesses to testify against Jesus so they could put him to death. (60) And they did not find any, though many false witnesses came forward. But later two came and (61) said, "This man said, 'I can destroy the temple of God and rebuild it in three days.' "

(62) The high priest stood up and said to him, "Do you have nothing to say concerning the evidence of these men against you?"

(63) Jesus remained silent. And the high priest said to him, "I adjure you by the living God that you tell us if you are the Christ, the Son of God."

(64) Jesus said to him, "You have said it. But I tell you, hereafter you will see the Son of man sitting on the right hand of the power and coming on the clouds of the sky."

(65) Then the high priest tore his clothes, and said, "He has blasphemed. Why do we still need witnesses? Have you not heard his blasphemy? (66) What do you think?"

They said, "He deserves death."

(67) Then they spit in his face and violently abused him; and they slapped him, (68) saying, "Prophesy to us, Christ. Who struck you?"

(69) Now Peter was sitting outside in the court; and a maid came to him, and said, "You were also with Jesus the Galilean."

(70) But he denied before everyone, saying, "I do not know what you are talking about."

(71) And going out into the porch, someone else said to those there, "This man was with Jesus the Nazarene."

(72) And he denied with an oath, "I do not know the man."

(73) A little while later, those standing by came up and said to Peter, "Truly, you are one of them, for your accent gives you away."

(74) Then Peter began to curse and to swear, "I do not know the man!" And immediately a rooster crowed.

(75) Peter remembered the words of Jesus, saying, "Before a rooster crows you will deny me three times." And going outside, he wept bitterly.

Matthew 27:1-66

(1) Early in the morning, all the chief priests and the elders of the people gathered to find a way to put Jesus to death. (2) They bound Jesus, and led him away and delivered him to Pilate the governor.

(3) When Judas, the betrayer, saw that he was condemned, he was filled with remorse. He returned the thirty silver shekels to the chief priests and elders, (4) saying, "I sinned because I betrayed an innocent man!"

They said to him, "What is that to us? That is your problem!" (5) And Judas tossed the thirty silver shekels into the temple and left and went out and hanged himself.

(6) The chief priests took the thirty silver shekels and said, "It is not lawful to put them in the treasury, because it is the price of blood." (7) So after consultation they bought the Potter's Field for a burial for strangers. (8) It has ever since been called "The Field of Blood." (9) Then was fulfilled the words spoken through the prophet Jeremiah: "They took the thirty silver shekels, the price of the one whose price had been fixed by the sons of Israel,

(10) and they gave them for the Potter's Field, as the Lord directed me."

(11) Jesus stood before the governor, who interrogated him, saying, "Are you the king of the Jews?"

Jesus responded, "It is as you say."

(12) He was accused by the chief priests and elders, but he gave no answer. (13) Then Pilate said, "Do you not hear what things they are accusing you of?" (14) But he did not answer him a single word, so the governor was greatly amazed.

(15) At the festival season it was the governor's custom to release one of the prisoners chosen by the crowd. (16) At that time they had a notorious prisoner, whose name was Barabbas. (17) Therefore, when they were assembled, Pilate said to them, "Whom do you wish that I may release to you, Barabbas or Jesus, called Messiah?" (18) For he knew that they had delivered him because of envy.

(19) Now as he sat on the tribunal seat, his wife sent a message to him, saying, "Have nothing to do with that righteous man, for I have suffered many things in a dream because of him."

(20) But the chief priests and elders persuaded the crowds to ask for Barabbas and execute Jesus.

(21) So the governor said to them, "Which of the two do you want me to release to you?"

And they said, "Barabbas."

(22) Pilate said to them, "What then shall I do with Jesus, called Christ?"

They all said, "Crucify him!"

(23) But he said, "Why, what crime has he committed?"

But they shouted louder, saying, "Crucify him!"

(24) Pilate, seeing that nothing was accomplished, but that a riot was starting, took water and washed his hands in front of the crowd, saying, "I am innocent of this man's blood. You will see."

(25) All the people answered, "His blood be on us and on our children."

(26) Then he released to them Barabbas, but Jesus was whipped and delivered to be crucified.

(27) Then the governor's soldiers took Jesus into the praetorium, and they gathered the whole barracks around him. (28) They stripped him and put a purple robe around him; (29) and they plaited a crown of thorns and placed it on his head, and they put a reed in his right hand; and bowing the knee in front of him, they mocked him, saying, "Hail, king of the Jews"; (30) and spitting at him they took the reed and struck him on his head. (31) After they had mocked him, they stripped him of the robe and put his own clothes on him and led him away to crucify him.

(32) As they were going forth, they found a man of Cyrene, whose name was Simon, whom they forced to carry Jesus' cross. (33) And they

came to Golgotha, which means a place of a skull. (34) They gave him wine mixed with gall to drink, but when he tasted it, he refused to drink it. (35) When they crucified him, they divided his garments by casting lots; (36) and sitting down, they guarded him there. (37) They placed above his head the charge against him, which read, "THIS IS JESUS THE KING OF THE JEWS." (38) Then they crucified with him two robbers, one on the right and one on the left. (39) Those passing by cursed him, wagging their heads, (40) and saying, "The one who can destroy the temple and restore it in three days! If you are the Son of God, come down from the cross!"

(41) Likewise the chief priests, mocking with the scribes and elders, said, (42) "He saved others; he cannot save himself. He is the King of Israel. Let him come down from the cross now, and we will believe in him. (43) He trusted in God, let him rescue him now if he wants him. For he said, 'I am the Son of God.' " (44) In the same way the robbers also taunted him.

(45) From the sixth hour darkness covered all the earth until the ninth hour. (46) About the ninth hour Jesus cried out with a loud voice, saying, "Eli, Eli, lema sabachthani?" —that is "My God, my God, why have you forsaken me?"

(47) Some who were standing by and hearing him said, "He is calling Elijah!" (48) And immediately one of them ran and took a sponge. He filled it with vinegar, put it on a reed, and gave it to him to drink.

(49) But the rest said, "Wait, let us see if Elijah comes to save him."

(50) And Jesus again cried out with a loud voice and released his spirit. (51) At that time the veil of the temple was torn in two from top to bottom; and the earth was shaken and the rocks were split; (52) and the tombs were opened, and many bodies of saints who had fallen asleep were raised. (53) They came forth from the tombs after the resurrection of Jesus and entered into the holy city and appeared to many.

(54) When the centurion and ones guarding Jesus felt the earthquake and seeing what was happening, they were terribly frightened, and they said, "Truly, this man was the Son of God!"

(55) Now there were many women looking on from a distance. They had followed Jesus from Galilee, ministering to him. (56) Among them were Mary Magdalene, Mary, the mother of James and Joseph, and the mother of the sons of Zebedee.

(57) When evening came, a rich man named Joseph, from Arimathea, who himself was a disciple of Jesus, (58) came to Pilate and asked for the body of Jesus. And Pilate commanded it to be given to him. (59) Taking the body, Joseph wrapped it in a clean linen cloth (60) and placed it in his new tomb, which he had carved in the rock; and after rolling a large stone at the entrance of the tomb, he went away. (61) Mary Magdalene and the other Mary were sitting there facing the tomb.

(62) The next day, which was after the Day of Preparation, the chief priests and the Pharisees met and went to Pilate, (63) saying, "Sir, we

remember how that deceiver said while he was alive, 'After three days I will
rise again.' (64) Therefore give orders for the grave to be closely guarded for
three days, lest his disciples come and steal the body and say to the people
that he was raised from the dead; and the last deceit would be worse than the
first."

(65) Pilate said to them, "You have a guard, make it as secure as you
can." (66) So they went and secured the tomb by putting a seal on the stone
and setting a guard.

Matthew 28:1-20

(1) Late on the Sabbath, at the dawn of the first day of the week,
Mary Magdalene and the other Mary came to see the tomb.

(2) There had been a mighty earthquake. For an angel of the Lord
descended from heaven and rolled away the stone and sat upon it. (3) His
appearance was like lightening, and his clothes were as white as snow. (4)
The guards were so afraid of him that they became like dead men.

(5) The angel said to the women, "Do not fear, because I know that
you seek Jesus, who was crucified. (6) He is not here; for he was raised, as he
said. Come see the place where he lay. (7) And go quickly and tell his
disciples that he was raised from the dead, and behold, he is going before
you to Galilee. There you will see him. Lo, I have told you."

(8) So going away quickly from the tomb, with fear and great joy,
they ran to tell his disciples. (9) Suddenly Jesus met them, saying, "Hail."
And they approached him and grasped his feet and worshipped him.

(10) Jesus said to them, "Fear not. Go and tell my brothers to go to
Galilee, and there they will see me."

(11) As the women were on their way, some of the guards came into
the city and told the chief priests everything that had happened. (12) And
when they had assembled and worked out their strategy with the elders, they
bribed the soldiers with a sufficient amount of money, (13) and said to them,
"Tell the people that his disciples came by night and stole his body while we
were sleeping. (14) If this report gets to the governor, we will persuade him,
and we will free you from your anxiety." (15) So they took the money and
did as they were instructed. The rumor was spread about and is current in
Jewish circles to this day.

(16) So the eleven disciples went to Galilee, the mountain where
Jesus had directed them. (17) When they saw him, they worshipped him, but
some doubted. (18) Jesus came to them and talked to them, saying, "All
authority in heaven and in earth has been given to me. (19) Therefore as you
go make disciples of all nations, baptizing them in the name of the Father
and of the Son and of the Holy Spirit, (20) teaching them to observe all that I
have commanded you; and lo, I am with you always, even to the end of the
age."

Introduction to Mark

There is no internal evidence that Mark wrote the Gospel of Mark, but it was the unanimous testimony of the early church that it was written by John Mark. Papias (c. 140 A.D.) quotes an earlier source that said Mark was a close associate of Peter and that he accurately recorded the preaching of Peter. Mark carefully preserved this material, and it became the chief source of his gospel. Mark was the surname of the writer of the second gospel. It was Markos in Greek and Markus in Latin. His original, or Jewish, name was John.

Mark was the son of the Mary who owned the house in Jerusalem where the church met. It was there that the disciples were praying when Peter was put in jail. And it was there that Peter returned when the angels delivered him from the jail. It was probably there in the Upper Room that Jesus met with his disciples the night before the crucifixion. And from there they went to the Garden of Gethsemane. It is commonly believed that Mark was the young man who fled without his clothes when the temple police tried to sieze him (Mark 14:51,52). Mark had been associated with the church from the beginning. He went with Paul and Barnabas on their first missionary journey, but he deserted them at Parga in Pamphilia and returned to Jerusalem.

Peter referred to Mark as his son (1 Peter 5:13), and at the end of Paul's ministry he wanted Mark to be with him (2 Timothy 4:11). Perhaps Mark wrote his gospel from Rome (c. 65 A.D.). It is commonly believed that Mark's gospel was the first gospel written and that Matthew and Luke borrowed from it as they wrote their gospels. The Gospel of Mark is the shortest of the gospels with 10,304 words, and there are 1,344 different words. This gospel moves quickly from one episode in the life of Jesus to another. Millions have been blessed by reading this simple, yet vivid account of the ministry of Jesus.

Mark 1:1-45

(1) The beginning of the gospel of Jesus Christ, the Son of God.
(2) As it is written in Isaiah the prophet,
"Look, I send my messenger before you,
who will prepare your way —
(3) a voice of one shouting in the wilderness,
'Prepare the way of the Lord, make a straight road for him.' "
(4) John the Baptist appeared in the wilderness proclaiming a baptism of repentance for the forgiveness of sins. (5) All the country of Judea and all Jerusalem went out to him, and he baptized them in the Jordan River, confessing their sins. (6) John was dressed in camel's hair, and he had a leather belt around his waist, and he lived on grasshoppers and wild honey.

(7) And he proclaimed, "After me is coming one who is stronger than I, the straps of whose sandals I am not worthy to untie. (8) I baptized you in water, but he will baptize you in the Holy Spirit."

(9) In those days Jesus came from Nazareth of Galilee and was baptized in the Jordan by John. (10) And immediately he went up from the water, and he saw the heavens opening and the Spirit as a dove descending upon him like a dove. (11) And a voice came from heaven, "You are my beloved Son. In you I am well-pleased."

(12) Immediately the Spirit drove him into the wilderness, (13) and he was in the wilderness 40 days, tempted by Satan; and he was with the wild animals, and the angels ministered to him.

(14) After John had been put in prison, Jesus came into Galilee proclaiming the gospel of God (15) saying, "The time has come, and the kingdom of God is at hand. Repent and believe in the gospel."

(16) As Jesus was passing along the Sea of Galilee, he saw Simon and his brother Andrew casting a net into the sea, for they were fishermen. (17) Jesus said to them, "Come with me, and I will make you to become fishers of men." (18) They immediately left their nets and followed him. (19) He went a little farther and he saw James, the son of Zebedee, and John his brother, and they were in their boats mending their nets. (20) And immediately he called them, and they left their father Zebedee in the boat with the hired hands and went with him.

(21) They entered into Capernaum, and immediately on the Sabbath Jesus went into their synagogue and began to teach. (22) Immediately the people were amazed at his teaching, for he taught as one with authority and not as the scribes. (23) And immediately there was a man in their synagogue with an unclean spirit, and he cried out, (24) "What do you want with us, Jesus of Nazareth? Have you come to destroy us? I know who you are, the Holy One of God."

(25) Jesus rebuked him, "Be quiet and come out of him." (26) The unclean spirit threw the man into convulsions and crying out in a loud voice came out of him.

(27) All were amazed, so that they were questioning among themselves, saying, "What is this? A new teaching with authority! He commands the unclean spirits, and they obey him." (28) And at once his fame went out everywhere to all the surrounding region of Galilee.

(29) Immediately they went out of the synagogue, and they went into the house of Simon and Andrew; and James and John were with them. (30) Simon's mother-in-law was in bed with a fever, and immediately they tell him about her. (31) Jesus went to her and, holding by the hand, he lifted her up; and the fever left her, and she served them.

(32) When evening came, at the setting of the sun, the people brought all the sick and the demon-possessed. (33) The whole city was assembled at the door. (34) And Jesus healed many who were sick with various diseases, and he cast out many demons. He did not permit the

demons to speak because they knew him.

(35) Very early in the morning, while it was still dark, Jesus arose and went out and into a desolate place, and there he prayed. (36) Simon and those with him looked for him, (37) and when they found him, they said to him, "Everyone is looking for you."

(38) Jesus said to them, "Let us go to other villages and there I will preach, for that is why I came." (39) And he went throughout all Galilee preaching in their synagogues and casting out demons.

(40) A leper came to him begging and kneeling before him and said, "If you are willing, you can make me clean!"

(41) Jesus had compassion, and he stretched out his hand and touched him and said, "I am willing. Be clean." (42) And immediately the leprosy left him, and he was cleansed.

(43) Jesus immediately sent him away with an earnest appeal: (44) "Say nothing to anyone; but go and show yourself to the priest and make an offering for your cleansing according to what Moses commanded, for a testimony to the people." (45) But he went out proclaiming and spreading the news concerning what had happened, so that Jesus was no longer able to openly enter into a city; but he was out in desolate places, and the people came to him from all directions.

Mark 2:1-28

(1) After some days, Jesus came back to Capernaum, and the people heard that he had come home; (2) so many came together that there was no more room for them, even at the door, and he spoke the word to them. (3) The people brought to him a paralyzed man who was carried by four men. (4) Since they were not able to bring him to Jesus because of the crowd, they tore off the roof of the house where he was, and they lowered the paralytic who was lying on the mattress. (5) And Jesus, seeing their faith, said to the paralytic, "Son, your sins are forgiven."

(6) There were some scribes sitting there and reasoning in their hearts, (7) "Why does this man speak this way? He blasphemes! Who can forgive sins but God alone?"

(8) Jesus immediately, knowing in his spirit what they were thinking, said to them, "Why are you reasoning in your hearts about these things? (9) Which is easier, to say to the paralytic, 'Your sins are forgiven,' or to say, 'Arise, take up your bed and walk.' (10) But that you may know that the Son of Man has authority to forgive sins" — he says to the paralytic, (11) "I say to you, arise, take up your bed and go to your house."

(12) He arose immediately and, taking up his bed, he went out in the sight of everyone. They were all amazed and they glorified God, saying, "We have never seen anything like this!"

(13) Jesus went out again by the seashore, and all the crowds came to

him, and he taught them. (14) As he passed by, he saw Levi the son of Alphaeus sitting at the tax office, and he said to him, "Follow me." And he arose and followed him.

(15) Jesus dined in the house of Levi, and many tax collectors and sinners reclined at the table with him and his disciples, for there were many who followed him. (16) The scribes and Pharisees, seeing that he was eating with tax collectors and sinners, said to his disciples, "Why does he eat with tax collectors and sinners?"

(17) Jesus, hearing them, said to them, "Those who are healthy do not need to see a physician, but those who are sick; I came not to call the righteous, but sinners."

(18) The disciples of John and the Pharisees were fasting, and people came to Jesus and said, "Why do the disciples of John and the disciples of the Pharisees fast, but your disciples do not fast?"

(19) Jesus said to them, "Can the wedding guests fast while the bridegroom is with them? As long as the bridegroom is with them, they cannot fast. (20) But the days will come when the bridegroom will be taken away from them, and then in that day they will fast.

(21) "No one sews an unshrunk patch on an old garment; otherwise, the patch pulls away from it, the new from the old, and a worse tear is made. (22) And no one puts new wine into old wineskins; otherwise, the wine will burst the wineskins, and the wine is lost, and so are the skins; but new wine is put into fresh wineskins."

(23) One Sabbath Jesus passed through the grainfields, and his disciples began to pluck the heads of grain. (24) The Pharisees said to him, "Look! Why do that which is unlawful to do on the Sabbath?"

(25) He said to them, "Have you not read what David and those who were with him did when they were hungry? (26) And how he entered the house of God in the days of Abiathar the high priest and ate the consecrated bread, which it is not lawful to eat, except the priests; and he also gave to those who were with him?"

(27) Jesus said to them, "The Sabbath was made for man, not man for the Sabbath. (28) So the Son of Man is Lord of the Sabbath."

Mark 3:1-35

(1) Jesus again entered into the synagogue, and there was a man who had a withered hand. (2) And they carefully watched him to see if he would heal him on the Sabbath, so that they might accuse him. (3) And Jesus said to the man with the withered hand, "Stand up in the midst of everyone."

(4) Then Jesus said to them, "Is it lawful on the Sabbath to do good or evil, to save life or to kill?" But they were silent.

(5) Looking around at them with anger and utterly distressed at the hardness of their hearts, he said to the man, "Stretch out your hand." And he

stretched out his hand, and it was completely restored. (6) The Pharisees immediately went out and began to plot with the Herodians against Jesus to destroy him.

(7) Jesus and his disciples went away to the sea, and a large crowd from Galilee followed him from Judea. (8) When they had heard what he had done, they came to him, from Jerusalem, Idumea, beyond the Jordan and the region of Tyre and Sidon. (9) And he told his disciples to prepare a boat for him so the crowd would not crush him. (10) For many were healed, so that as many as were diseased pressed upon him, that they might touch him. (11) The unclean spirits, when they saw him, fell down before him and cried out, "You are the Son of God." (12) And he sternly charged them not to make him known.

(13) Then Jesus went up into the mountain and summoned the men he wanted, and they came to him. (14) He appointed twelve—calling them apostles—to be with him and to be sent out to preach (15) and have authority to cast out demons. (16) These are the twelve that he appointed: Simon (he named Peter), (17) James the son of Zebedee and John the brother of James (he named them Boanerges, Sons of Thunder), (18) Andrew, Philip, Bartholomew, Matthew, Thomas, James the son of Alphaes, Thaddaeus, Simon the Cananaean, (19) and Judas Iscariot, who betrayed him.

(20) Jesus entered a house, and the crowds came together again, so that they were unable to eat bread. (21) When his family heard about this, they went to seize him, for they were saying, "He is out of his mind."

(22) And the scribes from Jerusalem came down and said, "He has Beelzebul; and by the ruler of the demons he casts out demons."

(23) Jesus called them and spoke to them in parables, "How can Satan cast out Satan? (24) If a kingdom is divided against itself, that kingdom cannot stand. (25) If a house is divided against itself, that house cannot stand. (26) And if Satan rises up against himself and is divided, he cannot stand, but his end has come. (27) But no one can enter a strong man's house and plunder his property, unless he first binds the strong man, then he can plunder his house. (28) Truly, I say to you, all the sins and blasphemies that the sons of men shall utter will be forgiven. (29) But whoever blasphemes against the Holy Spirit will never be forgiven, but will be guilty of an eternal sin" — (30) because they had said, "He has an unclean spirit."

(31) Jesus' mother and brothers came, and standing outside, they sent someone to call him. (32) A crowd was standing around him, and they told him, "Behold, your mother, brothers and sisters are outside seeking you."

(33) Jesus responded by saying, "Who are my mother and brothers?"

(34) And looking around at those sitting in a circle, he said, "Behold, my mother and brothers! (35) Whoever does the will of God is my brother and sister and mother."

Mark 4:1-41

(1) Again Jesus began to teach by the seashore. A very large crowd had assembled, so that he embarked in a boat in the sea and he sat in it, and the people on the land were gathered around him. (2) He taught them many things in parables, and in his teaching he said to them, (3) "Listen! A farmer went out to sow. (4) As he sowed, some of the seed fell along the path, and the birds came and devoured them. (5) Other seed fell on rocky ground where the soil was shallow, and immediately it sprang up, because it had no depth of soil. (6) When the sun rose it was scorched, and because it had no root, it withered. (7) Other seed fell among thorns, and the thorns came up and choked it, and it did not produce fruit. (8) Other seed fell into the good soil and brought forth grain, coming up, growing, and yielding thirty, or sixty, or even a hundred times as much as was sown."

(9) Then he said, "He who has ears to hear, let him hear."

(10) When Jesus was away from the crowd, those around him and the twelve inquired about the parables. (11) He said to them, "To you the mystery of the kingdom has been revealed, but for those outside, everything is in parables, (12) so that,

'seeing they may not perceive,
and hearing they may not understand;
otherwise they might repent and be forgiven.' "

(13) Then Jesus said to them, "If you do not understand this parable, how will you be able to understand any of them? (14) The farmer sows the word. (15) These are the ones along the path, where the word was sown, and when they hear it, immediately Satan comes and takes the word that had been sown in their hearts. (16) Others are like seed sown on the rocky ground. When they hear the word, they immediately receive it with joy, (17) but they do not have root in themselves so their joy is short-lived. When affliction or persecution comes on account of the word, immediately they fall away. (18) Others, like seed sown among thorns, hear the word, (19) but the cares of the age and the false glamour of wealth, and the cravings for many other things come in and choke the word, and it is barren. (20) But others, like seed sown on good soil, hear the word and welcome it and yield thirty, or sixty, or a hundred times as much as was sown."

(21) Jesus said to them, "Is a lamp brought in to be placed under the bushel or under the couch? Is it not rather to be put on the lampstand? (22) For there is nothing hidden that is not to be manifested; nor is there anything covered that is not to be revealed. (23) If anyone has ears to hear, let him hear."

(24) Jesus continued, "Be careful what you hear. With the measure you use, it will be measured to you. (25) For he who has, it will be given to him; and he who has not, even that which he has will be taken from him."

(26) He said, "The kingdom of God is like a man casting seed on the

soil, (27) and whether he is sleeping at night or rising in the day, the seed sprouts and grows, and he knows nothing about it. (28) The earth bears fruit on its own accord, first the blade, then the head, then the fully developed wheat in the head. (29) But when the fruit is ripe, he immediately sends forth the sickle, because the harvest is ready."

(30) Then Jesus said, "How can we compare the kingdom of God, or by what parable can we use to illustrate it? (31) It is like a grain of mustard seed, which, when it is sown on the soil is smaller than all the seeds of the earth; (32) yet when it is sown, it comes up and becomes greater than all the herbs, and makes great branches so that the birds of the air can dwell under its shade." (33) Jesus used many such parables to speak the word to them as they were able to receive it. (34) He did not speak to them without a parable, but privately he explained everything to his disciples.

(35) Jesus said to them on that day when evening had come, "Let us go over to the other side." (36) They left the crowd, and they took him away in the boat in which he was sitting, and other boats were also with him. (37) Then a violent storm arose, and the waves struck the boat, so that is was almost filled with water. (38) Jesus was in the stern asleep on the cushion. They woke him and said to him, "Teacher, are you not concerned that we are perishing?"

(39) He got up and rebuked the wind and said to the sea, "Hush! Be calm!" The wind ceased and there was a great calm.

(40) He said to them, "Why are you afraid? Do you not have faith?"

(41) They were awestruck and said to one another, "Who then is this man, that both the wind and the sea obey him?"

Mark 5:1-43

(1) They landed on the other side of the sea in the country of the Gerasenes. (2) And when Jesus got out of the boat, immediately a man with an unclean spirit came out of the tombs and met him. (3) He had been dwelling among the tombs, and no one was able to bind him with a chain. (4) For he had often been shackled and chained, but the chains had been torn apart and the shackles broken, and no one was able to subdue him. (5) He was always, by day and by night, among the tombs in the mountains screaming and cutting himself with stones.

(6) The man, far away, saw Jesus and ran and fell down before him; (7) and shouting with a loud voice, he said, "What do we have in common, Jesus, Son of the Most High God? I implore you, in the name of God, do not torment me!" (8) For Jesus had been saying to him, "You unclean spirit, come out of the man!"

(9) Jesus asked him, "What is your name?"

He said to him, "My name is Legion, for we are many." (10) And he earnestly begged Jesus not to send them out of that neighborhood.

(11) There was a great herd of swine nearby grazing by the hillside, (12) and he begged him saying, "Send us to the swine, that we may enter them." (13) And he let them do so. The unclean spirits came out and entered into the swine, and the herd, about two thousand in number, rushed down over the cliff into the lake and were drowned. (14) Then the swineherds fled and reported it in the city and in the fields, and the people came to see what had happened. (15) They came to Jesus and they saw the demon-possessed man, who had had the legion, sitting and dressed and in his right mind, and they were afraid; (16) and those who saw told what had happened to the demon-possessed man and what had happened to the swine. (17) And they began to beg Jesus to leave their neighborhood.

(18) As Jesus was getting into the boat, the demon-possessed man begged Jesus to let him go with him; (19) but Jesus did not permit him to go, but he said to him, "Go to your house and to your people and tell them what the Lord has done for you, and how he has had mercy on you." (20) And he departed and began proclaiming in the Decapolis all the things that Jesus had done for him, and they all were amazed.

(21) When Jesus had crossed over again in the boat to the other side, a great crowd gathered around him; he was beside the lake. (22) Then came Jarius, one of the rulers of a synagogue, and when he saw Jesus he fell at his feet, (23) and he earnestly begged him, saying, "My little daughter is at the point of death. Come, and lay your hands on her that she may be healed and live!" (24) So Jesus went with him.

A great crowd followed him, even pressing upon him. (25) And there was a woman who had suffered from hemorrhages for twelve years; (26) and she had suffered many things under the care of many physicians and she had spent all she had, and she had profited nothing but got worse. (27) She, hearing about what Jesus had done, came in the crowd behind Jesus and touched his clothes. (28) For she said, "If I touch even his clothes, I will be healed." (29) And immediately the flow of blood was stopped, and she knew that her body had been healed.

(30) At once Jesus, knowing that power had gone out from him, turned around and said, "Who touched my clothes?"

(31) The disciples said to him, "You see the crowd pressing against you. Why do you ask, 'Who touched me?' "

(32) Jesus looked around to see who had done it. (33) Then the woman, realizing what had happened to her, came in fear and trembling and fell down before him and told him the whole truth.

(34) Jesus said to her, "Daughter, your faith has healed you. Go in peace, and be free from this disease."

(35) While he was still speaking, some came from the house of the ruler of the synagogue, saying, "Your daughter is dead. Why trouble the teacher any longer?" (36) But Jesus, ignoring the message, said to the ruler of the synagogue, "Do not fear, only believe." (37) Jesus did not permit anyone to go with him except Peter and James and John, the brother of James.

(38) They came to the house of the ruler of the synagogue, and there he saw confusion, and people weeping and wailing loudly. (39) He entered and said to them, "Why all this confusion and weeping? The child is not dead but asleep." (40) Then they began to ridicule him.

Then Jesus put everyone out and took the father and the mother of the child and those with him, and they went in where the child was. (41) He took the child by the hand and said to her, "Talitha, koum," which means, "Little girl, I say to you, arise." (42) Immediately the little girl got up and began to walk about (she was twelve years old). At that they were utterly amazed. (43) Jesus sternly ordered them to let no one know about this, and he told them to give her something to eat.

Mark 6:1-56

(1) Jesus left there and went to his hometown, and his disciples followed him. (2) It was the Sabbath, and he began teaching in the synagogue, and many who heard him were amazed, saying, "Where did this man get these things; what is this wisdom given to him and how does he work these miracles through his hands? (3) Is not this man the carpenter, the son of Mary, the brother of James, Jose, Judas and Simon? And are not his sisters here with us?" And they were offended with him. (4) Jesus said to them, "A prophet is not without honor except in his own home town and among his relatives and his family." (5) And he could not do mighty works there, except laying on of hands and healing a few sick people; (6) he marveled because of their unbelief.

Jesus went around the villages teaching; (7) and he called the twelve to him and began to send them forth, two by two, and he gave them authority over the unclean spirits; (8) and these were his instructions: "Take nothing for your journey, except only a staff—no bread, no wallet, no money in your belts. (9) Wear sandals but do not put on two shirts. (10) Whenever you enter a house, remain there until you leave that place. (11) Whenever you are not welcomed or heard, as you leave, shake off the dust under your feet as a testimony against them."

(12) So they went out and proclaimed that people should repent; (13) and they cast out many demons, and they anointed with oil many sick people and healed them.

(14) King Herod heard about this, for the fame of Jesus spread, and people were saying, "John the Baptist has been raised from the dead; therefore mighty power works in him."

(15) Others were saying, "He is Elijah."

And others were saying, "He is a prophet like one of the prophets."

(16) When Herod heard, he said, "John the Baptist, whom I beheaded, has been raised from the dead."

(17) For Herod himself had sent out and arrested John and put him

in prison because of Herodias, the wife of Philip, his brother, whom he married. (18) John had said to Herod, "It is not lawful for you to have your brother's wife." (19) Herodias had a grudge against him and wanted to kill him, but could not. (20) For Herod feared John and protected him, knowing that he was a righteous and holy man. When Herod heard John, he was very perplexed, yet he heard him gladly.

(21) Herodias had her chance one day when Herod had a birthday party and gave a banquet for his chief officials, his military commanders, and the leading men of Galilee. (22) The daughter of Herodias came in and danced. She pleased Herod and those reclining with him. The king said to the girl with an oath, "Ask of me whatever you want; and I will give it to you." (23) And he swore to her, "Whatever you ask I will give it to you, up to half of my kingdom."

(24) She went out and asked her mother, "What shall I ask for?"

She said, "The head of John the Baptist."

(25) She immediately rushed in with her request to the king, saying, "I want you to give me at once the head of John the Baptist on a platter."

(26) The king was deeply grieved, but because of the oaths and the guests, he did not want to reject her. (27) Immediately the king sent an executioner with orders to bring his head. He went in the prison and beheaded John (28) and put the head on a platter and gave it to the girl, and she gave it to her mother. (29) When the disciples heard what had happened, they came and took his body and put it in a tomb.

(30) The apostles returned to Jesus and reported to him what they had done and what they had taught. (31) And Jesus said to them, "Come to a private place in the desert and rest a little while." For there were so many people coming and going that they had no opportunity to eat. (32) So they went by boat to a private place in the desert. (33) Many saw them leave and recognized them, and people ran on foot from all the cities to the place and arrived there ahead of them. (34) When Jesus landed, he saw a large crowd, and he had compassion on them, because they were like sheep without a shepherd; and he began to teach them many things.

(35) When it was late in the day, the disciples approached him and said, "This is a desert place and it is getting late. (36) Dismiss them, so they can go to the farms and villages to buy for themselves something to eat."

(37) He replied, "You give them something to eat."

And they said to him, "Shall we go and spend 200 denarii for bread and give it to them?"

(38) Jesus said to them, "How many loaves do you have? Go and see."

They found out and they said, "Five, and two fish."

(39) And he instructed them all to recline on the green grass. (40) They reclined in groups by hundreds and by fifties. (41) Jesus, taking the five loaves and the two fish, looked up to heaven and gave thanks, and broke the loaves; and he gave them to the disciples to give to the people, and the two

fish he divided among them all. (42) And they all ate and were satisfied. (43) They took up twelve full baskets of the broken pieces and also of the fish. (44) Those who ate the loaves were five thousand men.

(45) Immediately Jesus insisted that his disciples embark in the boat and go before him to the other side, to Bethsaida, while he dismissed the crowd. (46) And after he had bid them farewell, he went away to the hill to pray. (47) When evening came, the boat was in the middle of the lake, and he was on the land. (48) It was about the fourth watch of the night that Jesus, seeing them straining at the oars, for the wind was against them, came toward them walking on the lake; he intended to walk by them, (49) but when they saw him walking on the lake, they thought that he was a ghost, and they cried out. (50) For they saw him and were frightened. But he immediately spoke to them and said, "Be of good cheer, It is I. Do not be afraid." (51) He got into the boat with them, and the wind ceased, and they were greatly amazed, (52) for they did not understand the meaning of the loaves; their hearts had been hardened.

(53) When they crossed over, they came to the land of Gennesaret and anchored there. (54) When they came out of the boat, the people immediately recognized Jesus. (55) The people hurried about that whole neighborhood, and they began to carry the sick on pallets to where he was reported to be. (56) Whenever he entered the villages, the cities or the country, they put the sick in the streets, and they begged him to let them touch the tassel of his robe; and as many as touched him were healed.

Mark 7:1-37

(1) Some of the Pharisees with some scribes who had come from Jerusalem came to Jesus, (2) and they noticed that some of his disciples were eating bread with unclean hands—that is, unwashed hands. (3) (For the Pharisees and all the Jews do not eat unless they ceremonially wash their hands, holding to the traditions of the elders, (4) and when they come from the market places they do not eat unless they purify themselves, and they hold to many other traditions, as washing of cups, pots and vessels of bronze.)

(5) So the Pharisees and scribes questioned Jesus, "Why do your disciples not live according to the traditions of the elders, but eat with unclean hands?"

(6) Jesus said to them, "Well did Isaiah prophesy concerning you hypocrites, as it is written:
    'This people honor me with their lips,
    but their hearts are far from me;
    (7) They worship me in vain,
    teaching the doctrines of the precepts of men.'
(8) Leaving the commandment of God, you hold to the tradition of men."

(9) Jesus continued, "Well you set aside the commandment of God so that you may keep your tradition. (10) For Moses said, 'Honor your father and mother,' and, 'He who curses his father or mother, let him die.' (11) But you say that if a man says to his father or mother: 'Whatever support you might receive from me is Korban' (that is, a gift to God), (12) then you are exempt from doing anything for your father or mother, (13) annulling the word of God by the tradition you received; you do many other similar things."

(14) Jesus called the crowd to him and said to them, "Listen to me, all of you, and understand. (15) Nothing from the outside can enter a man to defile him; but the things coming out of the man defiles him."

(17) When Jesus left the crowd and entered into a house, his disciples questioned him concerning the parable. (18) And he said, "Are you also without understanding? Do you not know that everything outside entering a man cannot defile him, (19) because it cannot enter into the heart, but into his stomach, and passes out into the drain?" (Thus he made all foods clean.)

(20) Jesus continued, "That which comes out of the man defiles him. (21) For from within, out of the heart of man, comes forth evil thoughts, fornication, thefts, murders, (22) adulteries, greediness, iniquities, deceit, lewdness, envy, blasphemy, arrogance and folly. (23) All of these evil things comes from within and defile a man."

(24) Then Jesus arose and went away into the district of Tyre. He entered into a house and wished to be unrecognized; however, he could not escape notice. (25) But immediately a woman who had a daughter with an unclean spirit, hearing about him, came and fell at his feet. (26) The woman was a Greek, a Syrophenician by race, and she begged him to cast the demon out of her daughter. (27) Jesus said to her, "First let the children be fed; for it is not good to take the bread of the children and throw it to the dogs."

(28) And she replied, "Yes, Lord; and yet the dogs under the table eat from the crumbs of the children."

(29) Jesus said to her, "For your reply go, the demon has gone out of your daughter." (30) She went away to her house, and she found the child lying on the bed, and the demon had departed.

(31) Again Jesus went out of the district of Tyre and went through Sidon to the lake of Galilee in the midst of the district of Decapolis. (32) They brought to him a deaf man who spoke with difficulty, and they begged him to lay his hand on him. (33) Jesus took the man away from the crowd privately and put his fingers into his ears; and spitting he touched his tongue, (34) and looking up to heaven he groaned, and said to him, "Ephphatha!" (which means, "Be opened!") (35) His ears were opened and his tongue was loosed, and he spoke correctly. (36) Jesus forbade them to tell anyone, but the more he charged them, the more zealously they proclaimed it. (37) The people were most exceedingly astounded, saying, "He has done all things well; he makes the deaf to hear and the dumb to speak!"

Mark 8:1-38

(1) In those days again when there was a huge crowd and there was nothing to eat, Jesus called to him his disciples and said to them, (2) "I have compassion for these people, for they have been with me for three days and they have nothing to eat. (3) If I send them to their homes fasting, they may faint in the way, for some of them are a long way from home."

(4) His disciples replied, "Where can anyone get enough food for these people in this desolate place."

(5) Jesus replied, "How many loaves do you have?"

They said, "Seven."

(6) He directed the crowd to recline on the ground. And taking the seven loaves, he gave thanks and broke them and gave them to the disciples to serve, and they served the people. (7) They also had a few fish; and he blessed them and he told the disciples to serve them to the crowd. (8) They ate and were satisfied, and they took up seven baskets full of pieces that were left over. (9) There were about four thousand men. Then he dismissed them. (10) Immediately he got in a boat with his disciples and went to the region of Dalmanutha.

(11) The Pharisees came and began to argue with him. To test him, they asked him for a sign from heaven. (12) Sighing deeply in his spirit, he said, "Why does this generation seek a sign? Truly I tell you no sign will be given to this generation." (13) He left them, and again he got in a boat and went to the other side.

(14) They forgot to take bread; they had only one loaf with them in the boat. (15) Jesus warned them, "Be careful! Watch out for the leaven of the Pharisees and the leaven of Herod."

(16) They reasoned among themselves about the fact that they had no bread. (17) Jesus, knowing their thoughts, said, "Why are you talking about not having bread? Do you not yet perceive or comprehend? Have your hearts been hardened? (18) Having eyes do you not see, and having ears do you not hear? And do you not remember? (19) When I broke the five loaves and gave to the five thousand, how many baskets full of fragments did you pick up?"

They said to him, "Twelve."

(20) "When the seven loaves were given to the four thousand, how many baskets full of fragments did you pick up?"

They said to him, "Seven."

(21) He said to them, "And do you not yet understand?"

(22) They came to Bethsaida. Some people brought a blind man and begged Jesus to touch him. (23) Jesus took hold of the hand of the blind man and led him outside the village. He spit on his eyes and putting his hands on him asked him, "Do you see anything?"

(24) Looking up he said, "I see men, but they look like trees

walking."

(25) Then again Jesus puts the hands on his eyes, and he looked steadily and his eyesight was restored so that he saw everything clearly. (26) He sent him to his house, saying, "Do not enter into the village."

(27) Then Jesus and his disciples went to the villages of Caesarea Philippi. On the way he asked his disciples, "Who do men say that I am?"

(28) They answered, "John the Baptist, and others Elijah, but others one of the prophets."

(29) And he asked them, "But you, who do you say I am?"

Peter answering said to him, "You are the Christ."

(30) He warned them not to tell anyone about him.

(31) Then he began to teach them that the Son of Man must suffer many things and be rejected by the elders, the chief priests, the scribes, be put to death, and after three days rise again. (32) He spoke about this plainly. And Peter took him aside and began to rebuke him.

(33) But Jesus, turning around and seeing his disciples, rebuked Peter, saying, "Get behind me, Satan, because you are not thinking the things of God, but the things of men."

(34) Then he called the crowd with the disciples to him, and he said to them, "If anyone wishes to come after me, let him deny himself and take up his cross and follow me. (35) For whoever wishes to save his life will lose it, but whoever will lose his life for my sake and the gospel will save it. (36) For what does it profit a man to gain the whole world and forfeit his soul? (37) For what can a man give in exchange for his soul? (38) For whoever is ashamed of me and my words in this adulterous and sinful generation, the Son of Man will be ashamed of him when he comes in the glory of the Father with the holy angels."

Mark 9:1-50

(1)Jesus said to them, "Truly, I say to you, some who are standing here will not taste of death until they have seen the kingdom of God come with power."

(2) Six days later Jesus took Peter, James and John and led them up into a high mountain where they were alone. And Jesus was transfigured before them, (3) and his garments became exceedingly white, so much that no person on earth could make them as white. (4) Elijah appeared to them, accompanied by Moses, and they were talking with Jesus.

(5) Peter said to Jesus, "It is good for us to be here; let us put up three tents, one for you, one for Moses and one for Elijah." (6) (He really did not know what to say, because they were stricken with awe.)

(7) Then there came a cloud overshadowing them, and a voice came out of the cloud, "This is my beloved son, hear him!" (8) Suddenly, looking around, they no longer saw anyone except Jesus only with themselves.

(9) As they were coming down from the mountain, Jesus ordered them not to tell anyone about what they had seen until the Son of man had risen from the dead. (10) So they kept the matter to themselves, and they discussed what he meant by "risen from the dead."

(11) Then they asked him, "Why do the scribes say that Elijah must come first?"

(12) Jesus replied, "Elijah does come first to restore all things. How is it written that the Son of man will suffer many things and be rejected? (13) But I tell you that Elijah has come, and they did to him whatever they wished, as it was written concerning him."

(14) When they came to the disciples, they saw a large crowd gathered around them and scribes were arguing with them. (15) When the crowd saw Jesus, they were greatly amazed, and they all immediately ran up to him and greeted him.

(16) Jesus asked them, "Why are you arguing with them?"

(17) One of the crowd spoke to him, "Teacher, I brought my son to you, for he has a spirit that makes him speechless; (18) whenever it seizes him, it convulses him, and he foams at his mouth and grinds his teeth, and he becomes completely exhausted. I asked your disciples to cast it out, but they were not able to do so."

(19) Jesus said to them, "O unbelieving generation, how long shall I be with you! How long shall I put up with you! Bring him to me."

(20) So they brought him to him. When the spirit saw Him, it immediately convulsed him, and falling and rolling on the ground, he foamed at the mouth.

(21) Jesus asked the boy's father, "How long has he had this problem?"

He said, "From childhood; (22) and oftentimes it has thrown him into fire and into water to destroy him; but if you can, have compassion on us and help us!"

(23) Jesus responded, "You say, 'if you can!' All things are possible to him who believes."

(24) The father of the child immediately cried out, "I believe; help my unbelief!"

(25) Jesus, seeing the crowd rapidly gathering, rebuked the unclean spirit, "You dumb and deaf spirit, I command you, come out of him and never enter him again."

(26) The spirit cried out and violently caused convulsing and then left him; the boy looked like a dead person, and many were saying, "He is Dead!" (27) But Jesus took hold of his hand and lifted him, and he stood up.

(28) When Jesus went into the house, the disciples asked him privately, "Why were we not able to cast it out?"

(29) Jesus replied, "This kind can only be cast out by prayer."

(30) Then they left that place and went through Galilee, and he did not want others to know where he was; (31) for he was teaching his

disciples. He told them, "The Son of man will be betrayed by the hands of men. They will kill him, and after three days he will rise again." (32) They did not understand what he meant, and they feared to question him.

(33) They came to Capernaum. When they were in the house, Jesus questioned them, "What were you arguing about on the journey?" (34) They were silent, because they had been arguing with one another about who was the greatest.

(35) Jesus, sitting down, called the Twelve and said to them, "If anyone wants to be first, he must be last and servant of all."

(36) Then he took a child and placed him in their midst, and taking the child in his arms said to them, (37) "Whoever receives one of these children receives me; and whoever receives me, does not receive me, but the one having sent me."

(38) John said to him, "Teacher, we saw someone casting out demons in your name. He was not following us so we sought to stop him."

(39) But Jesus said, "Do not stop him; for no one can do a mighty work in my name and then quickly speak evil of me. (40) For who is not against us is for us. (41) For whoever gives you a cup of water in my name, because you belong to Christ, truly I tell you, he will not lose his reward. (42) And whoever offends one of these little ones who believe in me, it would be better for him that a heavy millstone were tied around his neck and thrown into the sea. (43) If your hand causes you to sin, cut it off; for it would be better to enter into life crippled than to have two hands and to go to hell, where the fire is unquenchable. (45) If your foot causes you to sin, cut it off. It is better to enter into life lame than to have two feet and be cast into hell. (47) If your eye causes you to sin, pluck it out. It is better to enter into the kingdom of God one-eyed than with two eyes and be cast into hell, (48) where the worm does not die and the fire is not quenched. (49) For everyone will be salted with fire.

(50) "Salt is good; but if salt becomes saltless, how will it be restored? Have salt in yourselves, and be at peace with one another."

Mark 10:1-52

(1) Jesus left that place and went into the region of Judea and beyond the Jordan, and the crowds came to him again, and as usual he taught them. (2) Some Pharisees approached him and tested him by asking, "Is it lawful for a man to divorce his wife?"

(3) Jesus answered them, (4) "What did Moses command you?"

They said, "Moses permitted a man to write a certificate of divorce and send her away."

(5) Jesus said to them, "It was because of the hardness of your hearts that Moses wrote you this law. (6) But from the beginning of creation God made them male and female; (7) and for this reason a man shall leave his

father and mother, (8) and the two shall become one flesh. So they are no longer two, but one flesh. (9) What, therefore, God has joined together, let no man separate."

(10) When they were in the house again, the disciples questioned him about this. (11) Jesus said to them, "Whoever divorces his wife and marries another, commits adultery against her, (12) and if she divorces her husband and marries another, she commits adultery."

(13) People were bringing little children to Jesus so he could touch them, but the disciples rebuked them. (14) When Jesus saw this, he was indignant; and he said to them, "Permit the children to come to me, and do not hinder them, for of such is the kingdom of God. (15) Truly I say to you, whoever does not receive the kingdom of God like a child will never enter into it." (16) And he put his arms around them, and laying his hands upon them, he blessed them.

(17) As Jesus went forth on his way, a man came running to him. He kneeled before him and asked him, "Good Teacher, what must I do to inherit eternal life?"

(18) Jesus said to him, "Why do you call me good? No one is good except God alone. (19) You know the commandments: Do not murder, do not commit adultery, do not steal, do not bear false witness, do not cheat, honor your father and your mother."

(20) He said to him, "Teacher, all these things I have kept since my childhood."

(21) Jesus, looking upon him, loved him and said to him, "One thing you lack, go and sell everything you have and give to the poor, and you will have treasures in heaven, and come follow me." (22) At these words his countenance fell, and he went away grieved, for he had great wealth.

(23) Jesus, looking around, said to his disciples, "How hard it is for the wealthy to enter the kingdom of God."

(24) The disciples were amazed at his words. But Jesus said to them again, "Children, how hard it is for the wealthy to enter the kingdom of God! (25) It is easier for a camel to go through the eye of a needle than for a rich man to enter the kingdom of God."

(26) They were exceeding astonished saying to themselves, "Then who can be saved?"

(27) Jesus, looking at them, said, "With men it is impossible but not with God, for all things are possible with God."

(28) Peter said to him, "Behold, we have left everything and have followed you."

(29) Jesus replied, "Truly I say to you, no one has left house or brothers or sisters or mother or father or children or land for my sake and the sake of the gospel (30) who will not receive a hundredfold now in this present age, houses, brothers, sisters, mothers, children and lands with persecutions; and in the coming age, eternal life. (31) Many who are first will be last, and many last will be first."

(32) They were on the road to Jerusalem, with Jesus going ahead of them, and the disciples were amazed, and those following were afraid. And taking the Twelve aside again he began to tell them what was going to happen to him. (33) "We are going to Jerusalem, and the Son of Man will be betrayed by the chief priests and the scribes; and they will condemn him to death, and they will deliver him to the Gentiles, (34) and they will mock him, and spit upon him, and whip him, and kill him; but after three days he will rise again."

(35) James and John, the sons of Zebedee, approached Jesus and said to him, "Teacher, we would like for you to do for us whatever we ask."

(36) He said to them, "What do you want me to do for you?"

(37) They said to him, "Grant us to sit, one at your right and one at your left, in your glory."

(38) Jesus said to them, "You do not know what you ask. Can you drink from the cup which I drink, or to be baptized with the baptism which I am baptized?"

(39) They said to him, "We can."

Jesus said to them, "The cup which I drink you will drink and the baptism which I am baptized you will be baptized, (40) but to sit at my right or at my left is not for me to give. But it is for those to whom it has been reserved."

(41) When the ten heard this, they became indignant with James and John. (42) Jesus called them to him and said, "You know that those who are recognized as rulers of the Gentiles lord it over them, and their high officials exercise authority over them. (43) It is not so among you. But whoever wishes to become great among you will become your servant, (44) and whoever wishes to become first among you will become slave of all. (45) For even the Son of Man did not come to be served but to serve and give his life a ransom for many."

(46) Then they came to Jericho. As Jesus and his disciples and a large crowd were going out of Jericho, Bartimaeus, the son of Timaeus, a blind beggar, was sitting by the roadside. (47) When he heard that it was Jesus of Nazareth, he began to cry out and say, "Jesus, Son of David, have mercy on me!"

(48) Many rebuked him and told him to be quiet, but he shouted out louder, "Son of David, have mercy on me!"

(49) Jesus stopped and said, "Call him."

They called the blind man and said to him, "Be of good courage, get up, he is calling you." (50) He threw away his garment and leaped up and came to Jesus.

(51) Jesus said to him, "What do you want me to do?"

The blind man said to him, "Rabboni, that I may see again!"

(52) Jesus said to him, "Go, your faith has healed you." Immediately he received his sight, and he followed him on the road.

Mark 11:1-33

(1) When they approached Jerusalem and came to Bethphage and Bethany at the Mount of Olives, Jesus sent two of his disciples (2) and said to them, "Go into the village opposite you, and just as you enter you will find a colt that has never been ridden; untie it and bring it here. (3) If anyone says to you, 'What are you doing?' say, 'The Lord has need of it and we will promptly bring it back.' "

(4) They went and found a colt tied at a door at a street corner, and they untied it. (5) Some of the men standing by said to them, "Why are you untying the colt?" (6) They answered as Jesus had told them; and they let them go. (7) They brought the colt to Jesus, and they saddled it with their clothes, and Jesus sat on it. (8) And many spread their clothes on the road, and others spread leafy branches, which they had cut from the fields. (9) And those going before and those following cried out,

"Hosanna!

Blessed is he who comes in the name of the Lord!

(10) Blessed is the coming reign of our father David!

Hosanna in the highest!"

(11) Jesus entered into Jerusalem and went into the temple. He inspected everything there, but as it was already late, he went with the twelve to Bethany.

(12) On the next day when he left Bethany he was hungry. (13) In the distance he saw a fig tree with leaves, and he came to it thinking that he might find something on it; however, he found nothing but leaves, since it was not the season for figs. (14) Jesus responded by saying, "Never again will anyone eat fruit from you." His disciples were listening to him.

(15) When they came to Jerusalem, Jesus went into the temple and began casting out the ones selling and buying in the temple. He turned over the tables of the moneychangers and the seats of the ones selling doves, (16) and he did not permit anyone to carry a vessel through the temple; (17) and he taught them saying, "Is it not written,

'My house has been called a house of prayer for all the nations?'

But you have made it a den of robbers."

(18) The chief priests and scribes heard him, and they sought how they might destroy him, for they feared him, because all the people were amazed at his teaching.

(19) When evening came, they went out of the city.

(20) Early in the morning they passed by the fig tree and saw that it had withered from the roots.

(21) Peter remembered and said to Jesus, "Rabbi, look! The fig tree that you cursed has withered."

(22) Jesus responded, "Have faith in God. (23) Truly I tell you, whoever says to this mountain, 'Be taken and cast into the sea' and not

doubting in his heart but believes what he says will happen, it will be done for him. (24) Therefore I tell you, whatever you ask in prayer, believe that you receive it, and you will. (25) When you stand praying, forgive, if you have anything against anyone, so that your Father in heaven may forgive your trespasses."

(27) They came again to Jerusalem. As he was walking in the temple, the chief priests, the scribes and the elders came to him, (28) and they said to him, "By what authority are you doing these things, or who gave you this authority to do these things?"

(29) Jesus said to them, "I will ask you one question. Answer me, and I will tell you by what authority I do these things. (30) Was the baptism of John from heaven or from men? Answer me."

(31) They reasoned among themselves and said, "If we say, 'From heaven,' he will say, 'Why then did you not believe him?' (32) But if we say, 'From men'...." (They feared the people, for all regarded John as a true prophet.) (33) So they answered Jesus, "We do not know."

Jesus said to them, "Neither will I tell you by what authority I do these things."

Mark 12:1-44

(1) Then Jesus began to teach them in parables: "A man planted a vineyard, and he put a hedge around it, dug a winepress and built a tower. Then he rented it to farmers and went on a journey. (2) At the proper time he sent a slave to the farmers, so that he might collect his share of the fruit of the vineyard. (3) The farmers seized him, beat him, and sent him away empty. (4) Again he sent to them another slave; and that one they wounded the head and insulted him. (5) Then he sent another one, and that one they killed, and he sent many others; some were beaten and others were killed. (6) He still had one left to send, a beloved son. Finally he sent him to them saying, 'They will respect my son.' (7) But those farmers said to themselves, 'This one is the heir, come let us kill him, and the inheritance will be ours.' (8) So they took him and killed him, and threw him outside the vineyard.

(9) "What then will the owner of the vineyard do? He will come and destroy the farmers, and give the vineyard to others. (10) Have you not read this scripture:
'The stone which the builders rejected
has become the corner stone;
(11) this is the work of the Lord,
and it is marvelous in our eyes?' "
(12) Then they tried to arrest him for they knew that the parable was for them, but they feared the people, so they left him and they went away.

(13) Then they sent to him some of the Pharisees and Herodians that they might trap him in his speech. (14) They came to him and said, "Teacher,

we know that you are honest; and you are not partial to anyone, and you do not seek human approval, but you teach the true way of God. Is it lawful to give tribute to Caesar or not? Should we give or should we not give?"

(15) Jesus, perceiving their hypocrisy, said to them, "Why are you trying to trap me? Bring me a coin so I can see it."

(16) They brought it, and Jesus said to them, "Whose image and inscription is this?"

They said to him, "Caesar's."

(17) Jesus said to them, "Give to Caesar what belongs to Caesar and to God what belongs to God." They were amazed at him.

(18) Then Sadducees, who say that there is no resurrection, came to him with this question, (19) "Teacher, Moses wrote for us that if a man's brother should die leaving a wife without a child, he should take the wife of his brother and raise up children for his brother. (20) There were seven brothers. The first took a wife and died with no children. (21) And the second took her, and he died with no children, and the third likewise. (22) In fact all the seven had her, but they left no children. Last of all the woman died also. (23) In the resurrection whose wife will she be? For the seven had her as wife."

(24) Jesus said to them, "Are you led astray because you do not know the scriptures nor the power of God? (25) For when the dead rise, they neither marry nor be given in marriage, but are as the angels in heaven. (26) But concerning the resurrection of the dead, have you not read in the book of Moses what God said to him at the burning bush, 'I am the God of Abraham, and the God of Isaac and the God of Jacob'? (27) He is not the God of the dead but of the living. You are greatly mistaken."

(28) One of the scribes, who had been listening to their discussions and seeing that Jesus skillfully answered them, came to Jesus with a question, "Which is the first of all the commandments?"

(29) Jesus answered, "The first is: 'Hear, O Israel, The Lord our God is one Lord. (30) And you shall love the Lord your God with all your heart, with all your soul, with all your mind, and with all your strength.' (31) The second is this: 'You shall love your neighbor as yourself.' There are no greater commandments than these."

(32) The scribe said to him, "Well said, Teacher, you are right in saying that he is one and there is none besides him. (33) And to love him with all the heart and with all the understanding and with all the strength, and to love one's neighbor as himself is more than all the burnt offerings and sacrifices." (34) Jesus, seeing how wisely he responded, said to him, "You are not far from the kingdom of God." No one dared to question him anymore.

(35) While Jesus was teaching in the temple, he asked, "How can the scribes say that Christ is the son of David? (36) David himself, inspired by the Holy Spirit, said,

'The Lord said to my Lord:
Sit at my right hand,
until I put your enemies under your feet.'
(37) David himself calls him Lord. So how is he his son?" The large crowd heard him gladly.

(38) In his teaching he said, "Beware of the scribes, who like to walk about in robes and are greeted in the market places (39) and have the chief seats in the synagogues and chief places in the banquets. (40) They devour the houses of the widows and in pretence make long prayers. They will receive the greater condemnation."

(41) Jesus sat down in front of the collection box, and he observed the crowd putting copper coins in the collection box. Many rich men put in large sums. (42) One poor widow came and put in two copper coins, worth a fraction of a cent. (43) He called his disciples to him and said to them, "I tell you the truth, this poor widow has put in more that all the others who were putting into the collection box. (44) For they all put in from their abundance, but this woman has put in all she had, her whole living."

Mark 13:1-37

(1) As Jesus went out of the temple, one of his disciples said to him, "Look Teacher, what huge stones! What wonderful buildings!"

(2) Jesus said to him, "Do you see all these great buildings? There will not be left one stone upon another; all will be thrown down."

(3) When Jesus was sitting on the Mount of Olives, Peter, James, John and Andrew questioned him privately, (4) "Tell us, when will these things be? And what will be the sign that they are all about to be fulfilled?"

(5) Jesus began, "Beware lest someone leads you astray. (6) Many will come in my name, saying, 'I am he,' and they will deceive many. (7) When you hear of wars and rumors of wars, do not be disturbed; it must happen; but the end is not yet. (8) Nation will rise against nation and kingdom against kingdom. There will be earthquakes in various places and there will be famines. These are the beginnings of birth pains.

(9) "Look out for yourselves. They will deliver you to the courts and in the synagogue you will be whipped, and you will stand before rulers and kings for my sake, to testify to them. (10) And the gospel must first be proclaimed to all nations. (11) When you are arrested and brought to trial, be not anxious beforehand of what to say, but speak that which is given to you in that hour; it is not you who will be speaking but the Holy Spirit.

(12) "Brother will deliver brother to death, and a father a child, and children will rise up against parents and have them put to death. (13) You will be hated by all men because you bear my name, but the ones enduring to the end will be saved.

(14) "When you see the abomination of desolation standing where it

ought not be—let the reader understand—then let the ones in Judea flee to the mountains; (15) let not the ones on the roof of the house come down or enter the house to take anything out; (16) and those in the fields let them not return to take out their clothes. (17) How dreadful it will be for expectant mothers and those who have nursing babies in those days. (18) Pray that it will not be in winter, (19) for in those days there will be such afflictions that have never been from the beginning, when God created the world, until now and shall never be again. (20) Unless the Lord shortens the days, no flesh would be saved, but because of the elect, his chosen ones, he will shorten the days. (21) At that time if anyone says to you, 'Look, here is the Christ!' or 'Look, there he is,' do not believe it. (22) For there will rise up many false Christs and false prophets and they will perform signs and wonders to lead astray, if possible, the elect.

(23) "But you beware. I have told you everything before it happens.

(24) "But in those days after that affliction, the sun will be darkened, and the moon will not give her light, (25) and the stars will fall out of heaven, and the heavenly powers will be shaken. (26) Then you will see the Son of man coming in the clouds with great power and glory. (27) Then he will send the angels and they will assemble the elect from the four winds, from the extremity of the earth to the extremity of heaven.

(28) "Now learn the parable of the fig tree: When the branches become tender and put forth leaves, you know that summer is near. (29) So also you, when you see these things happening, you know that he is near, even at the door. (30) I tell you the truth, this generation will not pass away until these things happen. (31) The sky and the earth will pass away but my words will never pass away.

(32) "Concerning that day or the hour no one knows, not the angels in heaven neither the Son, only the Father. (33) Watch, be awake. For you do not know when the time will come. (34) It is like a man going on a journey and giving his authority to his slaves, to each his work, and he commands the doorkeeper to keep watch.

(35) "Watch therefore because you do not know when the Lord of the house will return, either in the evening, or at midnight, or when the rooster crows, or at dawn; (36) lest, coming suddenly, he will come finding you asleep. (37) What I say to you, I say to everyone, 'Watch!' "

Mark 14:1-72

(1) It was two days before the Passover and the Feast of the Unleavened Bread. The chief priests and scribes sought how to seize Jesus by deceit and murder him. (2) For they said, "Not at the feast lest there be a riot of the people."

(3) When Jesus was in Bethany in the house of Simon the leper he was reclining at the table, and a woman came in with an alabaster jar of

perfume made from very expensive nard. She broke the jar and began to pour it over the head of Jesus. (4) There were some who became angry, and they said to themselves, "Why this waste of the perfume! (5) This could have been sold for three hundred denarii and the money given to the poor." And they angrily rebuked her.

(6) But Jesus said, "Leave her alone. Why do you criticize her? She has done a beautiful thing for me. (7) For you always have the poor with you, and whenever you wish you can do good to them, but you will not always have me. (8) She did what she could; she has anointed my body beforehand for the burial. (9) I tell you the truth, wherever the gospel is proclaimed in the entire world, also what this woman did will be spoken for a memorial of her."

(10) Then Judas Iscariot, one of the Twelve, went to the chief priest to betray Jesus to them. (11) When they heard him they were delighted, and they promised to give him money. So he sought for an opportunity to betray him.

(12) On the first day of the Feast of Unleavened Bread, when the Passover lamb was sacrificed, the disciples asked him, "Where do you want us to go to prepare for you to eat the Passover?"

(13) So Jesus sent two of his disciples with these instructions, "Go into the city and you will meet a man carrying a pitcher of water; follow him, (14) and wherever he enters, tell the master of the house that the Teacher asks, 'Where is my guest room where I may eat the Passover with my disciples?' (15) Then he will show you a large upstairs room, furnished and ready. And there prepare the meal."

(16) The disciples left and they went to the city and found everything as they had been told, and they prepared the Passover supper.

(17) When evening came, Jesus went with the Twelve. (18) As they reclined and ate, Jesus said, "I tell you the truth, one of you—one who is eating with me—will betray me."

(19) They were grieved and they said to him, one by one, "It is not I, is it?"

(20) He said to them, "It is one of the Twelve—one who is dipping with me in the bowl. (21) The Son of Man is going as it is written concerning him, but woe to that man through whom the Son of Man is betrayed. It would have been better for him if he had not been born."

(22) As they were eating, Jesus took bread, blessed and broke it and gave it to them, saying, "Take, this is my body."

(23) Then taking a cup he gave thanks and gave it to them, and they all drank of it. (24) And he said to them, "This is my blood of the covenant, being shed for many. (25) I tell you the truth, no more will I drink of the fruit of the vine until that day when I drink it new in the kingdom of God." (26) Then they sang a hymn and went out to the Mount of Olives.

(27) Jesus said to them, "All of you will be ashamed of me and fall away, because it is written:

'I will strike the shepherd,
and the sheep will be scattered.'
(28) "But after I have risen I will go before you into Galilee."
(29) Peter said to him, "If everyone is ashamed, I will not be!"
(30) Jesus said to him, "I tell you the truth, this day, even tonight, before the rooster crows twice, you will deny me three times."
(31) But he more emphatically declared, "If I must die with you, I will never deny you!" Likewise they all agreed.
(32) They came to a place called Gethsemane and Jesus said to his disciples, "Sit here while I pray." (33) He took Peter, James and John with him, and he began to be deeply distressed and troubled. (34) He said to them, "My soul is deeply grieved, even unto death; remain here and watch."
(35) He went forward a little and fell to the ground, and he prayed that if possible that hour might pass from him. (36) He said, "Abba (Father), all things are possible with you; remove this cup from me; but not what I will, but what You will!"
(37) When he returned he found them sleeping, and he said to Peter, "Simon, are you asleep? Could you not keep watch for one hour? (38) Watch and pray lest you fall into temptation. The spirit is willing, but the flesh is weak."
(39) Again he went away and he prayed saying the same words. (40) Again he returned to find them sleeping, for their eyes were heavy. They did not know how to answer him.
(41) He came the third time and said to them, "Are you still sleeping and resting? It is enough. The hour has come. Look, the Son of Man is betrayed into the hands of sinners. (42) Rise! Let us go. My betrayer is at hand!"
(43) While he was still speaking Judas, one of the Twelve, arrived. With him was a crowd with swords and clubs from the chief priests and the scribes and the elders.
(44) The betrayer had given them a sign, saying, "The one I kiss is he; seize him and take him away under guard." (45) Judas came immediately to him and said, "Rabbi!" And he fervently kissed him. (46) They laid their hands on him and arrested him. (47) But one who was standing by drew his sword and cut off the ear of the servant of the high priest.
(48) Jesus said to them, "Have you come with swords and clubs to arrest me as though I am a robber? (49) I was with you in the temple teaching daily, and you never laid hands on me, but this is the fulfillment of the Scriptures." (50) Then they all left him and fled.
(51) A young man, clothed with a nightgown over his naked body, was following him and they caught him, (52) but he, leaving the nightgown, fled naked.
(53) They led Jesus away to the high priest, and all the chief priests, the elders and the scribes came together. (54) Peter followed from afar until

he was in the courtyard of the high priest. He found a seat with the temple guard and he began to warm himself by the bright fire.

(55) The chief priests and all the Sanhedrin were looking for evidence against Jesus so as to put him to death, but they found none. (56) Many had testified falsely against him, but their testimonies did not agree.

(57) Some stood up and falsely testified against him, saying, (58) "We heard him saying, 'I will overthrow this handmade temple and after three days I will build another not made with hands.' " (59) Yet in this their testimonies did not agree.

(60) Then the high priest stood up in the midst and asked Jesus, "Have you no answer to the charges that these men bring against you?" (61) But Jesus was silent and gave no answer.

Again the high priest asked him, "Are you the Christ, the Son of the Blessed?"

(62) Jesus said, "I am, and you will see the Son of Man sitting at the right hand of Power and coming on the clouds of heaven."

(63) The high priest tore his clothes and said, "What more evidence do we need? (64) You heard the blasphemy. What do you think?" And they all condemned him to be worthy of death.

(65) Then some began to spit at him; they blindfolded him and struck him in the face and mocked him saying, "Prophesy!" And the guards took him and beat him.

(66) Peter was below in the courtyard and one of the maidservants of the high priest came, (67) and seeing Peter warming himself, looked at him and said, "And you were with Jesus the Nazarene!"

(68) But he denied, saying, "I do not know or understand what you are talking about." Then he went outside into the porch.

(69) Again the maidservant saw him and she began talking to those standing by, "This man is one of them."

(70) Peter again denied, and after awhile the ones standing by said to Peter, "Certainly you are one of them, for you are a Galilean."

(71) He began to curse and to swear, "I do not know this man of whom you are talking about." (72) Immediately, for the second time, a rooster crowed. Peter remembered what Jesus had said to him, "Before the rooster crows twice you will have denied me three times." And thinking about it he began weeping.

Mark 15:1-47

(1) Very early in the morning, the chief priests, with the elders and scribes and all the Sanhedrin, made their decision. They bound Jesus and led him away and they took him to Pilate. (2) And Pilate questioned him, "Are you the king of the Jews?"

Jesus replied, "You said it."

(3) The chief priests accused him of many things. (4) Pilate again questioned him, "Do you have no answer in your defense? See how many charges they are bringing against you?" (5) But Jesus made no answer, so Pilate was amazed.

(6) Now at the feast it was the custom to release one prisoner at the people's request. (7) There was one prisoner named Barnabas who was in custody with the rebels who had committed murder in the uprising. (8) When the crowd came to Pilate to ask for the usual favor, (9) he answered them saying, "Do you want me to release to you the king of the Jews?" (10) For he knew that the chief priests had delivered him because of their envy. (11) But the chief priests stirred up the crowd to ask for Barabbas instead.

(12) Pilate again asked them, "What then shall I do with the man you call the king of the Jews?"

(13) Again they cried out, "Crucify him!"

(14) But Pilate said to them, "Why? What crime has he done?" But they shouted out louder, "Crucify him!"

(15) So Pilate, resolving to please the mob, delivered Jesus to be whipped and crucified.

(16) Then the soldiers led him away inside the palace (the Governor's headquarters) and called together the whole battalion. (17) They put a purple robe around him and plaiting a thorny crown they put it upon him. (18) Then they began to salute him, "Hail, king of the Jews!" (19) They struck him on the head with a club and spit at him, and kneeling before him, they worshipped him. (20) After they had mocked him, they took off the purple robe and put his clothes on him. Then they led him out to crucify him.

(21) A man called Simon, a Cyrenian, the father of Alexander and Rufus, was passing by coming in from the country, and they forced him to carry his cross. (22) They brought Jesus to the place called Golgotha, which means "Place of a Skull." (23) They gave him wine spiced with myrrh, but he did not take it. (24) Then they crucified him, and they divided his clothes by casting lots to see what each might get.

(25) It was about 9:00 o'clock when they crucified him. (26) The superscription giving the charge against him read: "THE KING OF THE JEWS." (27) They crucified two robbers with him, one on the right and one on the left of him. (29) Those passing by cursed him and wagging their heads at him they said, "Aha! You who would destroy the temple and build it back in three days! (30) Come down from the cross and save yourself."

(31) Likewise the chief priests and the scribes joined in the mocking and saying to one another, "He saved others, but he cannot save himself. (32) Let the Christ, the king of Israel, come down from the cross that we may see and believe." The ones who were crucified with him also taunted him.

(33) At midday darkness came over all the land until 3:00 o'clock. (34) At that time Jesus cried out in a loud voice, "Eloi, Eloi, lama sabachthani?" which means, "My God, my God, why have you forsaken

me?"

(35) Some of those standing by heard and said, "Look, he is calling Elijah."

(36) One man came running with a sponge soaked in vinegar on the end of a stick and gave it to him to drink, saying, "Let him alone. Let us see if Elijah comes to take him down."

(37) Then Jesus uttered a loud cry and expired. (38) The veil of the temple was split in two from top to bottom. (39) The centurion, standing in front of him, and seeing how he died, said, "Certainly this man was the son of God!"

(40) There were also women present who were looking from a distance. Among them were Mary Magdalene, Mary the mother of James the younger and of Joses, and Salome, (41) who served and followed him when he was in Galilee, and also many others came with him to Jerusalem.

(42) When the evening came, since it was the day of preparation, that is, the day before the Sabbath, (43) Joseph from Arimathea, an honorable councilor, who was himself expecting the kingdom of God, took courage and went to Pilate and asked for the body of Jesus. (44) Pilate, surprised to hear that he had already died, called the centurion to ask him if he had already died. (45) When he received the report from the centurion, he released the body to Joseph. (46) He had brought a piece of new linen and, taking the body down, he wrapped it with the linen and put him in a tomb that had been hewn out of rock and then rolled a stone against the door of the tomb. (47) Mary Magdalene and Mary the mother of Joses saw where he was laid.

Mark 16:1-20

(1) When the Sabbath was past, Mary Magdalene, Mary the mother of James, and Salome brought spices to anoint him. (2) It was very early, as the sun was rising, on the first day of the week when they came to the tomb. (3) They said to themselves, "Who will roll away the stone from the entrance of the tomb?"

(4) They looked up and saw that the exceedingly large stone had been rolled away. (5) They entered into the tomb and they saw a young man clothed in a white robe sitting on the right. They were utterly astounded.

(6) He said to them, "Do not be so astounded. You seek Jesus the Nazarene who was crucified. He has risen! He is not here. Look, the place where they laid him. (7) But go and tell his disciples and Peter that he will go before you into Galilee, and there you will see him, just as he told you."

(8) The women went out and fled from the tomb, for trembling and bewilderment had come over them, and they told no one because they were afraid.

(9) Jesus, rising early on the first day of the week, appeared first to Mary Magdalene, from whom he had cast out seven demons. (10) She went

to his followers who were grieving and weeping to tell them the good news; (11) and the ones who heard that he was alive and that she had seen him, did not believe it.

(12) Later Jesus was manifested in a different form to two of them who were going into the country, (13) and they reported it to the rest, but neither did they believe.

(14) And later Jesus appeared to the eleven as they reclined; and he scolded them because of their disbelief and the hardness of their hearts, because they did not believe those who had seen him and told them that he had risen. (15) He said to them, "As you go into all the world proclaim the gospel to all creatures. (16) Those who believe and are baptized will be saved, but those disbelieving will be condemned. (17) Signs will follow those who believe: In my name they will cast out demons; they will speak with new tongues; (18) they will take up serpents; and if they drink deadly poison it will not hurt them; and they will place their hands on the sick and they will recover."

(19) So then after the Lord Jesus had spoken to them, he was taken up into heaven and sat at the right hand of God. (20) Then those going forth proclaimed everywhere, while the Lord worked with them and confirmed the word through the accompanying signs.

The Shorter Ending of Mark

The women reported promptly to Peter and his friends the things that they had been told. Later Jesus sent his disciples to the west with the sacred and immortal proclamation of eternal salvation. Amen.

Introduction to Luke

The Gospel of Luke is directed to Theophilus (one who loves God). He may have been responsible for seeing that the writings were copied and distributed. The evidence is commanding that Luke is the author of the two books, "The Gospel of Luke" and "The Acts of the Apostles," even though his name is not mentioned in either of the books. We learn some things about his personal life from the writings of Paul. He is "the beloved physician" (Col. 4:14); he was one of Paul's fellow workers (Philemon 1:24); and when Paul was awaiting execution only Luke was with him (2 Tim. 4: 11).

Luke was a Gentile, well-educated in Greek culture, a physician by profession, and a master in grammatical construction. He spent many years in research and prayerful study in preparation for his contribution to the New Testament. He wrote more of the New Testament than any other person. We are indebted to Luke, for without him we would not have heard about The Good Samaritan or the Prodigal Son. And we would not have known about the message of the angels to the shepherds announcing the birth of Jesus.

Luke had an outstanding command of the Greek language with a vocabulary that was extensive and rich. The Gospel of Luke is the longest of the gospels with 19,459 words with 2,044 different words. In both of his books he uses 3,078 words, which is more than half of the 5,436 different words used in the New Testament.

Luke 1:1-80

(1) Since many have written a narrative concerning the things which have happened, (2) as reported by eye-witnesses and custodians of the word, (3) it seemed good to me also, after fully investigating their sources, for me to write an orderly account for you, most excellent Theophilus, (4) so that you may know the certainty concerning the things which you have been informed.

(5) There was, in the days of Herod, king of Judea, a priest of the course of Abijah whose name was Zechariah, and his wife, Elizabeth, was of the daughters of Aaron. (6) They were righteous before God and blameless, observing all the commandments and ordinances of the Lord. (7) They had no children. Elizabeth was barren, and they were elderly.

(8) When it was time for Zechariah to serve as priest, (9) according to the custom of the priesthood, he was chosen by lot to enter the temple and burn incense, (10) and all the people were outside praying at the hour of incense. (11) There appeared to him an angel to the right of the altar of incense. (12) And seeing the angel, Zechariah was troubled, and fear fell

upon him.

(13) But the angel said to him, "Fear not, Zechariah, because your petition has been heard, and your wife Elizabeth will bear you a son, and you shall call his name John. (14) And you will have joy and gladness, and many will rejoice at his birth, (15) for he will be great before the Lord; and he will not drink wine nor strong drink, and he will be filled with the Holy Spirit, even from birth. (16) He will turn many of the sons of Israel to the Lord their God. (17) And he will go before him in the spirit and power of Elijah, to turn the hearts of fathers and children, and the disobedient to the wisdom of the just, to make ready a people prepared for the Lord."

(18) Zechariah said to the angel, "How shall I know this? For I am old and my wife is advanced in years?"

(19) The angel answered, "I am Gabriel, who stands in the presence of God, and I was sent to tell you this good news, (20) and behold, you will be silent and unable to speak until the day these things happen, because you did not believe my words which will be fulfilled in due time."

(21) The people were waiting for Zechariah and wondering at his delay in the temple. (22) When he went out he could not speak to them, and they knew that he had seen a vision in the temple. He made signs to them and remained speechless. (23) When his days of service were completed, he returned home.

(24) Afterward his wife Elizabeth conceived, and she hid herself for five months, saying, (25) "The Lord has looked upon me and has taken away my reproach among men."

(26) In the sixth month God sent Gabriel to Nazareth, a city of Galilee, (27) to a virgin betrothed to a man whose name was Joseph of the house of David, and the virgin's name was Mary. (28) He came to her and said, "Rejoice, favored one, the Lord is with you."

(29) Mary was deeply troubled at his words and wondered what this greeting meant. (30) And the angel said to her, "Fear not, Mary, for you have found favor with God. (31) Behold, you will conceive and bear a son, and you shall call his name Jesus. (32) He will be great, and he will be called the Son of the Most High; and the Lord God will give to him the throne of his father David; (33) and he will reign over the house of Jacob forever, and of his kingdom there will be no end."

(34) Mary said to the angel, "How will this be, since I have no husband."

(35) The angel answered her, "The Holy Spirit will come upon you, and the power of the Most High will overshadow you; therefore the holy child will be called the Son of God; (36) and behold, Elizabeth, your relative, has conceived and will bear a son in her old age, and she, who was called barren, is now in her sixth month. (37) For with God nothing is impossible."

(38) Mary said, "Behold I am the servant of the Lord; may it be to me as you say." Then the angel left her.

(39) Immediately Mary hurried to the hill country to a city of Judea,

(40) and she entered into the house of Zechariah and greeted Elizabeth. (41) When Elizabeth heard the greeting of Mary, the baby leaped in her womb, and Elizabeth was filled with the Holy Spirit, (42) and she cried out with a loud voice, "Blessed are you among women, and blessed is the fruit of your womb. (43) Who am I that the mother of my Lord should come to me? (44) For behold when the sound of your greeting came to me, the baby in my womb leaped for joy. (45) Blessed is she who believed that the Lord would fulfill the things spoken to her."

(46) Then Mary said,
"My soul magnifies the Lord
(47) and my spirit rejoices in God my Savior,
(48) for he has been mindful
of the low estate of his slave.
For behold, henceforth all generations will call me blessed,
(49) for the Mighty One has done great things for me;
holy is his name.
(50) His mercy is from age to age
to those who fear him.
(51) He did mighty things with his arm;
he has confused the inmost thoughts of the proud.
(52) He has dethroned monarchs,
and has exalted the humble.
(53) He has filled the hungry with good things,
and he has sent away the rich empty.
(54) He has helped his servant Israel,
in remembrance of his mercy,
(55) as he spoke to our fathers,
to Abraham and his descendants for ever."

(56) Mary remained with her about three months and then returned home.

(57) The time came for Elizabeth to be delivered; and she gave birth to a son. (58) The neighbors and relatives heard how the Lord had magnified his mercy to her, and they rejoiced with her. (59) On the eighth day they circumcised the child and intended to name him Zechariah after his father, (60) but the mother said, "No, but he shall be called John."

(61) They said to her, "None of your kindred is called by this name."

(62) They made signs to the father inquiring what he wanted him to be named, (63) and asking for a tablet he wrote, "John is his name." And they all marveled. (64) Immediately his mouth was opened, and with his tongue he began praising God.

(65) And fear came on all their neighbors. Those dwelling in the hill country of Judea were talking about all these things. (66) Those who heard were saying, "What then will this child be?" For the hand of the Lord was with him.

(67) Zechariah, his father, was filled with the Holy Spirit and

prophesied, saying,

(68) "Blessed be the God of Israel,
because he has visited and redeemed his people.
(69) He has raised a horn of salvation for us,
in the house of his servant David,
(70) as he spoke through his holy prophets.
(71) Salvation from our enemies,
from the hand of those hating us,
(72) to show mercy to our fathers,
and to remember his holy covenant,
(73) the oath he swore to our father Abraham,
to grant us (74) deliverance from the hand of our enemies,
that we may serve him without fear
(75) in holiness and righteousness
before him all of our days.
(76) And you, O child, will be called a prophet of the Most High;
for you will go before the Lord to prepare his ways,
(77) to give knowledge of salvation to his people
in the forgiveness of their sins,
(78) because of the tender mercy of our God,
and so the day will dawn upon us from on high
(79) to give light to those sitting in the shadow of darkness,
to guide our feet into the way of peace."

(80) The child grew and became strong in spirit, and he was in the desert until he made his public appearance in Israel.

Luke 2:1-52

(1) In those days a decree went out from Caesar Augustus that all the world should be enrolled. (2) This first enrollment was when Quirinius was governor of Syria. (3) Each man went to his native city to be enrolled. (4) Joseph went from Nazareth, a city of Galilee, to Bethlehem, Judea, the city of David, because he was of the house and lineage of David, (5) to be enrolled with Mary, who was pregnant. (6) The time came for her to be delivered, (7) and she gave birth to her firstborn son and wrapped him in cloths and laid him in a manger, because there was no place for them in the inn.

(8) There were shepherds in the same neighborhood living in the fields and keeping watch over their flock by night. (9) An angel of the Lord came upon them, and the glory of the Lord shone around them, and they were fearfully frightened. (10) Then the angel said, "Fear not, for behold, I bring good news to you—tidings of great joy, which will be for all the people, (11) because today a Savior has been born to you in the city of David who is Christ the Lord. (12) This is a sign to you: you will find a baby

wrapped in cloths and lying in a manger." (13) And suddenly there was with the angel a great heavenly army praising God and saying,

(14) "Glory to God in the highest,
and on earth peace among men of his good pleasure!"

(15) When the angel left them and returned to heaven, the shepherds said to one another, "Let us now go to Bethlehem and to see what the Lord has made known to us."

(16) So they went in haste and found Mary and Joseph and the baby lying in the manger, (17) and seeing, they made known the word spoken to them concerning this child. (18) All who heard marveled concerning the things spoken to them by the shepherds, (19) but Mary kept all these things and treasured them in her heart. (20) The shepherds returned, glorifying and praising God for all the things they had heard and seen, as it had been told them.

(21) On the eighth day they circumcised him and named him Jesus, according to the name given by the angel even before he was conceived.

(22) When the time of their purification had been completed according to the law of Moses, they went up to Jerusalem to present themselves to the Lord, (23) as it is written in the law of the Lord, "Every firstborn male shall be called holy to the Lord," (24) and to offer a sacrifice according to the teaching of the law of the Lord, "a pair of turtle-doves or two young pigeons."

(25) Behold there was a man in Jerusalem whose name was Simeon. He was a just and devout man and he was expecting the consolation of Israel; and the Holy Spirit was upon him, (26) and it had been told him by the Holy Spirit that he would not see death until he had seen the Lord's Christ. (27) The Spirit led him into the temple, and when the parents brought the child Jesus to sanctify him according to the custom of the law, (28) Simeon took Jesus up in his arms and praised God and said,

(29) "Now, Master, let your slave depart in peace,
according to your word.
(30) For my eyes have seen your salvation,
(31) which you have prepared in the presence of all the people,
(32) a revealing light to the Gentiles,
and a glory for your people Israel."

(33) The father and the mother were astonished at the things said about him, (34) and Simeon blessed them, and he said to Mary his mother, "Behold, this child is destined for the fall and the rising of many in Israel and for a sign to be spoken against— (35) and a sword shall pierce your heart—so that the secret thoughts of many hearts will be revealed."

(36) There was also Hanna, a prophetess, the daughter of Phanuel, of the tribe of Asher. She was elderly and had lived with her husband seven years after their marriage, (37) and she was now a widow of eighty-four, who never left the temple but worshipped the Lord with fasting and praying

night and day. (38) At that very hour she came and gave thanks to God and spoke about the child to all who were looking forward to the redemption of Jerusalem.

(39) When they had done everything required by the law of the Lord, they returned to Galilee, to their own city, Nazareth. (40) And the child grew strong and was filled with wisdom, and the grace of God was upon him.

(41) Every year his parents went to Jerusalem to the feast of the Passover. (42) When Jesus was twelve years old they went to the feast as usual, (43) and when the feast was over, and as they were returning, the boy Jesus stayed in Jerusalem. (44) And thinking that Jesus was in the caravan, they traveled a day and searching for him among their relatives and acquaintances, (45) and not finding him, they returned to Jerusalem seeking him. (46) After three days they found him in the temple sitting in the midst of the teachers, listening to them and asking them questions. (47) All who heard him were amazed at his intelligence and his answers. (48) When they saw him, they were astonished, and his mother said to him, "Son, why did you do this to us? Behold, your father and I have been greatly distressed looking for you."

(49) Jesus said to them, "Why did you seek me? Did you not know that I must be in the affairs of my Father?"

(50) They did not understand him. (51) He went down with them to Nazareth, and was obedient to them. And his mother treasured up all these things in her heart. (52) And Jesus increased in wisdom and in stature and in favor with God and men.

Luke 3:1-38

(1) In the fifteenth year of the reign of Tiberius Caesar, Pontius Pilate being governor of Judea, Herod the tetrarch of Galilee, and his brother Philip the tetrarch of the region of Iturea and Trachonitis, and Lysanias the tetrarch of Abilene, (2) in the time of the high priesthood of Anna and Caiaphas, the word of God came to John the son of Zechariah in the wilderness. (3) John went into all the neighborhood of the Jordan proclaiming a baptism of repentance for the forgiveness of sins. (4) As it is written in the book of Isaiah the prophet,

"A voice crying in the wilderness,
'Prepare the way of the Lord,
make his ways straight.
(5) All ravines shall be filled
and all mountains and hills shall be leveled.
The crooked shall be made straight
and the rough ways smooth.
(6) And all flesh shall see the salvation of God.' "

(7) John said to the crowds coming to him to be baptized, "Offspring of vipers, who warned you to flee from the coming wrath? (8) Produce fruits worthy of repentance; and do not say to yourselves, 'We have Abraham as our father'; for I tell you that God can raise up from these stones children to Abraham. (9) And even now the ax is resting at the root of the tree; therefore, every tree not producing good fruit will be cut down and thrown into the fire."

(10) The crowds asked him, "What then shall we do?"

(11) John said to them, "Let the one who has two coats give to him who has none, and the one having food, let him do likewise."

(12) Tax collectors, coming to be baptized, asked him, "Teacher, what shall we do?"

(13) He said to them, "Collect no more than what is required of you."

(14) And soldiers asked him, "And we, what shall we do?"

John told them, "Do not intimidate or accuse falsely, and be satisfied with your wages."

(15) While the people were in suspense, they were all reasoning in their hearts concerning John, "Perhaps he is the Christ."

(16) John said to them, "I indeed baptize you with water, but there is coming one mightier than I, of whom I am not worthy to loosen the leather straps of his sandals. He will baptize you with the Holy Spirit and fire. His winnowing shovel is in his hand to thoroughly cleanse the threshing floor and to gather the wheat into his barn, but the chaff he will burn up with unquenchable fire." (18) So with many and varied exhortations John evangelized the people, (19) but Herod the tetrarch, being rebuked by him concerning Herodias, the wife of his brother, and all the other evil things he did, (20) and adding to all his evil, he locked up John in prison.

(21) Now when all the people had been baptized and Jesus had been baptized, and when Jesus was praying, heaven was opened (22) and the Holy Spirit came down upon him in a bodily form like a dove. And a voice came from heaven, "You are my beloved Son, I am well pleased with you!"

(23) Jesus was about thirty years old when he began his work, being the son (as was supposed) of Joseph, the son of Eli, (24) the son of Matthat, the son of Levi, the son of Melchi, the son of Jannai, the son of Joseph, (25) the son of Mattathias, the son of Amos, the son of Naum, the son of Esli, the son of Naggai, (26) the son of Maath, the son of Mattathias, the son of Semein, the son of Josech, the son of Joda, (27) the son of Joanan, the son of Rhesa, the son of Zerubbabel, the son of Salathiel, the son of Neri, (28) the son of Melchi, the son of Addi, the son of Kosam, the son of Elmadam, the son of Er, (29) the son of Jesus, the son of Eliezer, the son of Jorim, the son of Matthat, the son of Levi, (30) the son of Symeon, the son of Judah, the son of Joseph, the son of Jonam, the son of Eliakim, (31)the son of Melea, the son of Menna, the son of Mattatha, the son of Nathan, the son of David, (32) the son

son of Jesse, the son of Obed, the son of Boaz, the son of Sala, the son of Naasson, (33) the son of Aminadab, the son of Admin, the son of Arni, the son of Hesron, the son of Phares, the son of Judah, (34) the son of Jacob, the son of Issac, the son of Abraham, the son of Thara, the son of Nachor, (35) the son of Seruch, the son of Rhagau, the son of Phalek, the son of Eber, the son of Sala, (36) the son of Cainam, the son of Arphaxad, the son of Shem, the son of Noah, the son of Lamech, (37) the son of Methuselah, the son of Enoch, the son of Jeret, the son of Maleleel, the son of Cainam, (38) the son of Enos, the son of Seth, the son of Adam, the son of God.

Luke 4:1-44

(1) Jesus, full of the Holy Spirit, returned from the Jordan and was being led by the Spirit in the desert and was being tempted forty days by the devil. (2) In those days he ate nothing, and when they were ended he was hungry.

(3) The devil said to him, "Since your are the Son of God, tell this stone to become a loaf."

(4) Jesus answered him, "It is written that man shall not live by bread alone."

(5) The devil led Jesus up and showed him all the kingdoms of the inhabited earth in a moment of time (6) and said to him, "I will give to you all this authority and this glory of the world, because it has been given to me, and I give it to whom I will; (7) therefore, prostrate yourself before me in worship, and it will all be yours."

(8) Jesus answered, "It is written: 'You shall worship the Lord your God, and him only shall you serve!' "

(9) Then the devil led Jesus to Jerusalem and set him on the apex of the temple and said to him, "Since you are the Son of God, throw yourself down; (10) for it is written, 'He will command his angels to carefully protect you, (11) and their hands will carry you, lest you stumble on a stone.' "

(12) Jesus replied, "It also says, 'You shall not test the Lord your God.' "

(13) When the devil had finished all temptations, he left him for awhile.

(14) Jesus returned to Galilee in the power of the Spirit, and a report went forth throughout the entire neighborhood concerning him. (15) He taught in all their synagogues, being praised by everyone.

(16) Jesus came to Nazareth, where he had been brought up, and he entered into the synagogue on the Sabbath day according to his custom, and he stood up to read. (17) A roll of the prophet Isaiah was handed to him and, having unrolled the scroll, he found the place where it was written:

(18) "The Spirit of the Lord is upon me,
because he anointed me to evangelize the poor.

He has sent me to proclaim liberty to the captives,
and to give sight to the blind,
to release the oppressed,
(19) to proclaim the acceptable year of the Lord."

(20) Then Jesus, rolling up the scroll, returned it to the attendant and sat down. The eyes of all in the synagogue were gazing at him. (21) He began speaking to them, "Today, while you are listening, this scripture has been fulfilled."

(22) Everyone spoke favorably of him, and they were amazed at the gracious words that came out of his mouth. They said, "Is not this man the son of Joseph?"

(23) Jesus said to them, "No doubt you will quote this parable to me: 'Physician heal yourself!' and you will say, 'Do the things in your home town that we have heard you did in Capernaum.' "

(24) He continued, "Truly I tell you that no prophet is acceptable in his native place. (25) I tell you of a truth that there were many widows in the days of Elijah in Israel, when it did not rain for three years and six months and there was a great famine over all the land; (26) and Elijah was sent to no one except to Sarepta, a widow woman of Sidon. (27) Also, there were many lepers in the days of Elisha the prophet, but not one of them was cleansed except Naaman the Syrian."

(28) Everyone in the synagogue, hearing these words, was filled with rage, (29) and they rose up and cast him outside the city and led him to a brow of the hill on which their city was built so they could throw him over the cliff; (30) but he, passing through the midst of them, went away.

(31) Jesus went down to Capernaum, a city of Galilee, and he began teaching them on the Sabbath day. (32) The people were astounded at his teaching, because he taught with authority. (33) There was a man in the synagogue with a spirit of an unclean demon, and he shouted with a loud voice, (34) "Ha! What do you want with us, Jesus of Nazareth? Have you come to destroy us? I know who you are: the Holy one of God."

(35) Jesus rebuked him, saying, "Hush! Come out of him!" Then the demon, throwing him down in the midst of them but not injuring him, came out of him.

(36) They were all awestruck, and they said to one another, "What does this mean? He commands with authority and power and unclean spirits come out." (37) So the report of him went forth to every place of the neighborhood.

(38) Jesus, leaving the synagogue, entered into the house of Simon, and his mother-in-law was suffering with a high fever, and they consulted him about her. (39) Jesus, standing over her, rebuked the fever, and it left her. She immediately got up and served them.

(40) As the sun was setting, all who had sick people with various diseases brought them to him and he, putting his hands on each of them, healed them. (41) Demons also came out of many, shouting, "You are the

Son of God." Jesus, rebuking them, would not allow them to speak, because they knew that he was the Christ.

(42) At dawn Jesus went into the desert place; but the crowds searched for him and when they found him, they tried to keep him from leaving them. (43) But he said to them, "I must preach the kingdom of God to the other cities also, because that is why I was sent." (44) And he continued to preach in the synagogues of Judea.

Luke 5:1-39

(1) Jesus stood by the Lake of Gennesaret as the people crowded upon him to hear the word of God, (2) and he saw two boats by the lake. The fishermen had gone out of them and were washing their nets. (3) Jesus entered into one of them, which belonged to Simon, and he asked him to shove off a little from the shore. And sitting, he taught the people from the boat.

(4) After his teaching, Jesus said to Simon, "Launch out into the deep, and let down your nets for a catch."

(5) Simon answered, "Master, we have toiled all through the night, and we have caught nothing! But, upon your word, I will let down the nets."

(6) And, doing this, they caught such an enormous number of fish that their nets were being torn. (7) So he motioned to his partners in the other boat that they should come to help them. And they came and filled both boats so that they were sinking.

(8) Simon Peter, seeing this, fell at the knees of Jesus, saying, "Depart from me, Lord, for I am a sinful man." (9) For astonishment had seized him and all those with him at the catch of the fish which they had taken, (10) as was the case of James and John, sons of Zebedee, who were partners with Simon.

Jesus said to Simon, "Fear not; from now on you will be taking men that they may live." (11) They, bringing their boats to the land and leaving everything, followed Jesus. (12) When Jesus entered into one of the cities, behold a man full of leprosy, seeing him, fell on his face and begged him, saying, "Lord, if you will, you can make me clean."

(13) Stretching out his hand, he touched him, saying, "I am willing, be clean!" Immediately the leprosy left him.

(14) Jesus ordered him, "Tell no one, but go and show yourself to the priest, and make an offering for your cleansing as commanded by Moses, as an evidence of your cure." (15) But rather the word about him continued to spread, and many crowds came together to hear and to be healed from their infirmities, (16) but he was withdrawing into the wilderness and praying.

(17) One day when he was teaching, there were Pharisees and teachers of the law sitting by who had come from every village of Galilee and Judea and from Jerusalem, and the power of the Lord was in him to heal.

(18) Behold, men were carrying a man on a pallet who was paralyzed, and they sought to bring him in to lay him before Jesus. (19) But, not finding a way to carry him in because of the crowd, they went up on the roof and let him down through the tiles, with the pallet in front of Jesus.

(20) And Jesus, seeing their faith, said, "Man, Your sins have been forgiven."

(21) The scribes and Pharisees began to reason and saying to one another, "Who is this man who speaks blasphemies? Who can forgive sins, except God alone?"

(22) Jesus, knowing their thoughts, said to them, "Why are you reasoning in your hearts? (23) Which is easier, to say, 'Your sins have been forgiven,' or to say, 'Rise and walk'? (24) But that you may know that the Son of Man has authority on earth to forgive sins...." — He said to the one who was paralyzed, "I say to you, arise, and, taking your pallet, go to your house."

(25) And immediately rising up before them and taking the pallet which he had been lying on, he went away to his house praising God.

(26) All were seized with astonishment and they praised God; and they were filled with fear, saying, "We have seen incredible things today!"

(27) After these things, Jesus went out and saw a tax collector, named Levi, sitting in his tax office, and he said to him, "Follow me." (28) And leaving everything, he arose and followed Jesus.

(29) Levi made a great feast for Jesus in his house, and there was a great crowd of tax collectors and others who were reclining with them. (30) The Pharisees and their scribes complained to his disciples, saying, "Why do you eat and drink with tax collectors and sinners?"

(31) And Jesus answering, said to them, "Those who are healthy have no need of a physician, but those who are ill. (32) I have not come to call the righteous, but sinners to repentance."

(33) They said to him, "The disciples of John fast frequently and offer prayers, and so do the disciples of the Pharisees, but your disciples eat and drink."

(34) Jesus said to them, "Can you make the attendants of the groom fast while the groom is with them? (35) But the days will come when the groom is taken away; then they will fast in those days."

(36) He also told them a parable: "No one tearing a patch from a new garment puts it on an old garment; otherwise, he will only tear the new garment, and the new patch will not match the old. (37) And no one puts new wine into old wineskins; otherwise, the new wine will burst the wineskins, and it will be spilled and the wineskins will perish. (38) But new wine must be put into new wineskins. (39) And no one wants new wine after drinking the old; for he says, 'The old is better.' "

Luke 6:1-49

(1) One Sabbath Jesus and his disciples went through grainfields, and his disciples, picking heads of grain and rubbing them with their hands, ate them. (2) Some of the Pharisees said, "Why are you doing what is not lawful to do on the Sabbath?"

(3) Jesus answered them, "Have you not read what David did when he and those with him were hungry — (4) how he entered into the house of God and taking the consecrated bread, which was only lawful for the priests to eat, he ate and gave to those with him?"

(5) Then he said to them, "The Son of Man is Lord of the Sabbath."

(6) On another Sabbath Jesus entered into a synagogue to teach, and a man was there whose right hand was withered. (7) The Pharisees carefully watched Jesus to see if he would heal on the Sabbath, so that they might find fault with him. (8) Jesus knew their thoughts, and he said to the man with the withered hand, "Arise and stand before us." And, rising up, he stood.

(9) Then Jesus said to them, "I ask you, is it lawful to do good or to do evil on the Sabbath, to save or to destroy life?"

(10) Jesus, looking around to all of them, said to the man, "Stretch out your hand." He did, and his hand was restored to him. (11) But they were filled with madness, and they discussed what they might do to Jesus.

(12) In those days Jesus went up into the mountain to pray, and he spent the whole night praying to God. (13) When it was day, he called his disciples to him, to choose from them twelve whom he named apostles: (14) Simon, whom he named Peter, Andrew, his brother, James, John, Philip, Bartholomew, (15) Matthew, Thomas, James, the son of Alphaeus, Simon, the one called Zealot, (16) Judas, the son of James, and Judas Iscariot, who betrayed him.

(17) He came down with them and stood on a level place. There was a great crowd of his disciples and a great multitude of people from all Judea and Jerusalem and the seacoast of Tyre and Sidon, (18) who came to hear Jesus and to be healed from all their diseases; and the ones being tormented by unclean spirits were healed. (19) All the crowd sought to touch him, because power went out from him, and he healed them all.

(20) Jesus, lifting up his eyes, said to his disciples:

"Blessed are you who are poor, for the reign of God is yours.

(21) Blessed are you, who are hungering now,

for you will be satisfied.

Blessed are you, who are weeping now, for you will laugh.

(22) Blessed are you when men hate you and when they ostracize you and insult you and slander your name as evil on the account of the Son of Man.

(23) "Rejoice in that day and skip for joy, for, behold, your reward is great in heaven; for in the same way their fathers did to the prophets.

(24) "But woe to you rich, for you have in full your consolation.

(25) Woe to you who are full now, for you will be hungry.

Woe to you who are laughing now, for you will mourn and weep.

(26) Woe to you when all men speak well of you,

for that is the way their fathers treated the false prophets.

(27) "But I say to you who hear: Love your enemies, do good to those who hate you, (28) bless the ones cursing you, and pray for those harassing you. (29) To the one striking you on the cheek, turn to him the other also; and from the one taking your coat, do not prevent him from taking your shirt. (30) Give to the ones asking you, and from those who take your things, do not demand that they bring them back. (31) Treat others as you would like for them to treat you.

(32) "If you only love those who love you, what credit is that to you? Even the sinners love those who love them. (33) And if you do good only to those who do good to you, what credit is that to you? Even sinners do that. (34) And if you lend only to those whom you expect repayment, what grace is that! Even sinners lend to sinners, expecting to be repaid in full. (35) But love your enemies and do good and lend, despairing of no one; and your reward will be great, and you will be sons of the Most High, for he is kind to the ungrateful and wicked. (36) Be merciful, even as your father is merciful.

(37) "Do not judge, and you will not be judged; do not condemn, and you will not be condemned. Forgive, and you will be forgiven. (38) Give, and it will be given to you. Good measure, pressed down, shaken and running over, will be put into your lap; for the measure you give will be the measure you get."

(39) Then Jesus told them a parable: "Can a blind man lead a blind man? Will they not both fall into a ditch? (40) A disciple is not above his teacher; but everyone having been perfected will be as his teacher.

(41) "Why do you see the chaff in your brother's eye, but do not discern the log in your own eye? (42) How can you say to your brother, 'Brother, let me take the chaff out of your eye,' you, who does not see the log in your own eye? Hypocrite, first take the log out of your eye, then you can see clearly to take the chaff out of your brother's eye.

(43) "A good tree does not bear bad fruit, nor does a bad tree bear good fruit. (44) For each tree is known by its own fruit; for men do not gather figs from thorn bushes nor do they pick a grape from a bramble bush. (45) The good man out of the good treasure of his heart brings forth that which is good, and the evil man out of an evil heart brings forth that which is evil. For out of the abundance of the heart his mouth speaks.

(46) "Why do you call me, 'Lord, Lord,' and do not the things which I say? (47) Everyone coming to me and hearing my words and doing them is compared (48) to a man building a house who dug deep and put his foundation upon the rock; and a flood came and a river dashed against that house, but it could not shake it, because it was well-built. (49) But the one hearing and not doing is like a man who built a house upon the sand without

a foundation, which the river dashed against, and immediately it collapsed, and the ruin of that house was great."

Luke 7:1-50

(1) When Jesus finished his teaching to the people, he entered Capernaum. (2) A certain centurion had a slave, who was dear to him and was about to die. (3) And hearing about Jesus, he sent to him elders of the Jews, asking him to come and heal his slave. (4) When they came to Jesus, they pleaded with him earnestly, saying, "This man is worthy of your help; (5) for he loves our nation, and he built for us a synagogue." (6) Jesus went with them.

When he was not far from the house, the centurion sent friends to him, saying to him, "Lord, do not trouble yourself, for I am not worthy for you to enter under my roof, (7) and I did not consider myself worthy to come to you; but say the word, and let my servant be healed. (8) I also am a man set under authority, having soldiers under my command; and I say to one, 'Go,' and he goes, and I say to another, 'Come,' and he comes, and I say to my slave, 'Do this,' and he does it."

(9) Jesus, hearing these words, marveled at him, and turning, he said to the crowd following him, "I tell you, I have not found such faith in Israel!" (10) The messengers returned to find the slave in perfect health.

(11) On the next day, Jesus went to a city called Nain, and his disciples and a large crowd went with him. (12) As he drew near the gate of the city, behold, a man had died, and he was being carried out. He was the only son of a widow, and many people of the city were with her. (13) The Lord, seeing her, had compassion on her, and he said to her, "Do not weep."

(14) Jesus went to the coffin and touched it, and the pallbearers stopped, and he said, "Young man, I say to you, get up." (15) And the dead man sat up and began talking, and he delivered him to his mother.

(16) They were awestricken, and they glorified God, saying, "A great prophet has risen among us!" and, "God has visited his people!" (17) The report of these things spread throughout all Judea and the surrounding neighborhood.

(18) The disciples of John told him about these things, and John, calling two of his disciples, (19) sent them to the Lord to ask him, "Are you the Coming One, or do we wait for another?"

(20) The men came to Jesus and said, "John the Baptist sent us to ask you if you are the Coming One, or do we wait for another?"

(21) In that hour Jesus was healing many from their diseases, plagues, and evil spirits, and he gave sight to many of the blind. (22) Jesus, answering, said to them, "Go and report to John what you saw and heard: the blind receive their sight, the lame walk, the lepers are cleansed, the dumb hear, the dead are raised, and the poor are evangelized. (23) Blessed is he

who is not offended in me."

(24) When the messengers of John went away, Jesus began to speak to the crowds about John: "What did you go out into the wasteland to gaze upon? Was it a reed being shaken by the wind? (25) But what did you go out to see? A man elegantly dressed? Behold, the ones who are gorgeously dressed and live in luxury are in royal palaces. (26) But what did you go out to see? A prophet? Yes, I tell you, and more than a prophet! (27) This is he of whom it is written:

'Behold, I send my messenger before you

to prepare your way before you.'

(28) I tell you, No one born of a woman is greater than John; but the least in the kingdom is greater than he."

(29) All the people, even the tax collectors, hearing this, acknowledged the justice of God, being baptized with the baptism of John; (30) but the Pharisees and the lawyers rejected the counsel of God for themselves, not being baptized by his baptism.

(31) "To what then can I compare the men of this generation and what are they like? (32) They are like children playing in the market place and calling to one another:

'We piped to you, but you did not dance,

we mourned, but you did not weep.'

(33) For John the Baptist came neither eating bread nor drinking wine, and you say, 'He has a demon.' (34) The Son of Man came eating and drinking, and you say, 'Behold, a glutton and a drunkard, a friend of tax collectors and sinners!' (35) But wisdom is vindicated by all her children."

(36) One of the Pharisees invited Jesus to dine with him, and he entered into his house and reclined to eat. (37) And, behold, a sinful woman who was in the city and knowing that Jesus was dining with the Pharisee, brought an alabaster flask of perfume; (38) and standing behind him at his feet weeping, she began to wet his feet with her tears and wipe them off with the hairs of her head, and she fervently kissed his feet and anointed them with the perfume. (39) When the Pharisee who had invited Jesus saw what happened, he said to himself, "If this man were a prophet, he would know that this woman is a sinner."

(40) Jesus answered him, saying, "Simon, I have something to say to you."

And he said, "Teacher, speak."

(41) "A certain creditor had two debtors; one owed five hundred coins and the other fifty. (42) They had nothing to pay, so he canceled their debts. Which of them, then, will love him more?"

(43) Simon answering, said, "I suppose the one to whom he canceled the larger debt."

Jesus said to him, "Rightly you have judged."

(44) And turning to the woman, Jesus said to Simon, "Do you see this woman? I came into your house. You gave me no water for my feet, but

this woman wet my feet with her tears and wiped them with her hair. (45) You did not give me a kiss, but this woman, since I entered, has not ceased fervently kissing my feet. (46) You did not anoint my head with oil, but this woman, with perfume, has anointed my feet. (47) Therefore, I tell you, her many sins are forgiven, because she loved much; the one to whom little is forgiven has little love."

(48) Jesus said to her, "Your sins have been forgiven."

(49) Those who were reclining with Jesus began to say to themselves, "Who is this that can even forgive sins?"

(50) Jesus said to the woman, "Your faith has saved you; go in peace."

Luke 8:1-56

(1) After this, Jesus journeyed throughout every town and village proclaiming the good news of the kingdom of God. The Twelve were with him, (2) and certain women who were healed from evil spirits and infirmities: Mary called Magdalene (from whom seven demons had been expelled), (3) and Joanna, wife of Chuza the steward of Herod, and Susanna, and many others who were contributing to support them from their own possessions.

(4) When a great crowd of people from every city came to him, he taught them by a parable: (5) "A sower went out to sow his seed, and as he sowed, some fell on the path where it was walked on, and the birds of the air devoured it. (6) Other seed fell upon the rock, and it grew up but withered because it had no moisture. (7) Others fell in the midst of thorns, and the thorns, growing up with it, choked it. (8) Others fell upon the good ground, and it matured and produced a crop, a hundred fold."

After this, he called out, "He who has ears to hear, let him hear!" (9) The disciples asked Jesus to explain the meaning of the parable. (10) So he said, "To you it has been given to know the mysteries of the reign of God, but to the rest in parables, that

'Seeing they may not perceive,
and hearing they may not understand.'

(11) "Now this is the parable: The seed is the word of God. (12) The ones on the path are the ones hearing, but then the devil comes and takes away the word from their hearts, so they may not believe and be saved. (13) The ones on the rock are those who hear the word and receive it with joy, but they have no root. For awhile they believe, but in the time of trial they fall away. (14) The ones in the midst of thorns are the ones hearing, but as they go, worries, riches and pleasures of life choke them, so that they do not bear fruit to maturity. (15) The ones in the good ground are those hearing the word and retain it in a just and good heart and bear fruit through perseverance.

(16) "No one lights a candle and hides it with a vessel or puts it under the bed, but he puts it on a lampstand, so that those coming in may see the light. (17) For nothing is hidden that will not be exposed or a secret that will not become known. (18) Listen carefully, therefore, how you hear; for whoever has, more will be given to him, and whoever has not, even what he seems to have will be taken from him."

(19) His mother and his brothers came to him, but they could not reach him because of the crowd. (20) And they reported to him, "Your mother and your brothers are standing outside, and they want to see you."

(21) But he, answering, said to them, "My mother and my brothers are these who are hearing and doing the word of God."

(22) One day Jesus and his disciples got into a boat, and he said to them, "Let us go to the other side of the lake." So they set sail. (23) And sailing, he fell asleep, and a violent storm came down on the lake, and they were being swamped and in danger.

(24) They went to Jesus and woke him, saying, "Master, Master, we are perishing!" But he, being awakened, rebuked the wind and the raging of the waves; and they ceased, and there was a calm.

(25) Jesus said to them, "Where is your faith?"

Being filled with fear and amazement they were saying to one another, "Who then is this, who commands the winds and the waters, and they obey him?"

(26) Then they sailed down to the country of the Gerasenes, which is opposite Galilee. (27) As Jesus went on land, a certain man out of the city met him. He had demons and for a long time had not worn clothes, and he did not stay in the house but lived among the tombs. (28) And seeing Jesus, he cried out with a loud voice and fell prostrate before him, saying, "What do you want with me, Jesus, son of the Most High God? I beg you, do not torment me!" (29) For Jesus had commanded the unclean spirit to come out of the man. For many times it had seized him, and he had been guarded and kept bound with chains and fetters, but breaking the chains, he was driven by the demon into the wastelands.

(30) Jesus asked him, "What is your name?"

And he said, "Legion," for many demons had entered into him. (31) And they besought him not to command them to go into the abyss.

(32) There was a large herd of swine nearby feeding on the hillside; and they begged him to let them go into those swine, and he allowed them to do so. (33) And the demons, coming out of the man, entered into the swine, and the herd rushed down the precipice into the lake and was drowned. (34) When the herdsmen saw what had happened, they fled and reported it in the city and in the country. (35) The people went out to see what had happened, and they came to Jesus and found the man from whom the demons had been cast out, clothed and in his right mind, and sitting at the feet of Jesus; and they were afraid. (36) The people were told by witnesses how the demon-possessed man had been healed. (37) Then all the people of the

neighborhood of the Gerasenes asked Jesus to leave them, for they were seized with fear. So he got in a boat and returned.

(38) The man who had been demon-possessed begged to go with him. But he sent him away, saying, (39) "Return to your house and tell what God has done for you." (39) So the man went away proclaiming throughout the entire city what Jesus had done for him.

(40) When Jesus returned, the crowds welcomed him, for they were expecting him. (41) Behold! a man, whose name was Jarius, a ruler of the synagogue, came and falling at the feet of Jesus, besought him to come to his house, (42) because his only begotten daughter, who was about twelve years old, was dying.

As he went, the people pressed upon him. (43) And there was a woman who had had a flow of blood for twelve years and had spent all her living, but no one was able to heal her. (44) She came up behind him and touched the fringe of his garment, and she was healed immediately.

(45) Jesus said, "Who touched me?"

When all denied it, Peter said, "Master, the crowds are around you and pressing upon you."

(46) But Jesus said, "I know someone touched me, for I know that power went out from me."

(47) When the woman realized that she had been detected, she came trembling, and falling down before Jesus, declared before all the people why she had touched him and how she had been immediately healed. (48) Jesus said to her, "Daughter, your faith has saved you; go in peace."

(49) While he was still speaking, someone came from the ruler of the synagogue saying, "Your daughter is dead. Do not bother the teacher any longer."

(50) Jesus, hearing this, said, "Fear not, only believe, and she will be healed."

(51) And coming to the house, he would not permit anyone to enter with him except Peter, John and James, and the child's father and mother. (52) Meanwhile, all were crying and beating themselves for her. And Jesus said, "Do not cry; for she is not dead but sleeping."

(53) They, knowing that she died, mocked him. (54) But Jesus took her by the hand and called, saying, "Child, arise." (55) And the spirit returned to her, and she got up immediately, and he told them to give her something to eat. (56) Her parents were amazed. He directed them to tell no one what had happened.

Luke 9:1-62

(1) Then Jesus, calling the twelve together, gave them authority over all the demons and power to heal the sick. (2) He sent them to proclaim the reign of God and to deliver the weak from their afflictions; (3) and he said to

them, "Take nothing for your journey—no staff, no bag, no bread, no money, and no extra clothes. (4) Whatever house you enter, remain there, and go out from there. (5) Whenever they do not receive you, shake the dust off your feet as you are going out of that city as a testimony against them." (6) And they, departing, went through the villages preaching the gospel and healing the sick everywhere.

(7) When Herod, the ruler, heard about all the things that were happening, he was perplexed, because it was said by some that John the Baptist had been raised from the dead, (8) and by some that Elijah had appeared, and by others that one of the ancient prophets had risen. (9) Herod said, "John I beheaded; but who is this of whom I hear such things?" And he sought to see him.

(10) The apostles, having returned, told Jesus what they had done. Then Jesus, taking with him the apostles, departed privately to a city called Bethsaida. (11) And the crowds, knowing, followed him, and he welcomed them and spoke to them about the reign of God, and he cured those who had need of healing. (12) As the day began to decline, the Twelve came to him and said, "Send the crowd away so that they may go into the surrounding villages and farms to find lodging and food, for we are here in this desert place."

(13) Jesus said to them, "You give them something to eat."

But they said, "We have only five loaves and two fish—unless we go and buy food for these people." (14) (For there were about five thousand men.)

He said to his disciples, "Have them to recline in groups of about fifty each." (15) And they made them recline. (16) Then Jesus, taking the five loaves and two fish and looking up to heaven, blessed them and broke and gave to the disciples to set before the people. (17) And they all ate and were satisfied; and the leftovers were gathered up and put in twelve baskets.

(18) One day when Jesus was praying in private his disciples were with him, and he questioned them, "Who do the crowds say that I am?"

(19) They answering said, "John the Baptist, but others Elijah, and others that a certain prophet has risen."

(20) And he said to them, "But who do you say that I am?"

And Peter answered, "The Christ of God!"

(21) Jesus commanded them not to tell this to anyone, (22) saying, "The Son of Man must suffer many things and be rejected by the elders and high priests and scribes and to be killed and on the third day to be raised up."

(23) And he said to everyone, "If anyone wishes to come after me, let him deny himself and take up his cross daily, and follow me. (24) For whoever wishes to save his life will lose it, but whoever loses his life for my sake will save it. (25) For what does it profit a man if he gains the whole world and loses his own soul or destroys himself? (26) For whoever is ashamed of me and of my words, the Son of Man will be ashamed of him

when he comes in his glory and the glory of the Father and of the holy angels. (27) Truly, I say to you, some are standing here who will not taste of death until they see the reign of God."

(28) About eight days later, Jesus took Peter, James and John to the mountain to pray. (29) As he prayed, the appearance of his face was changed, and his garments became dazzlingly white. (30) And behold, two men talked with him, who were Moses and Elijah, (31) who appeared in glory and spoke of his departure, which he was about to accomplish in Jerusalem. (32) Peter and the ones with him had fallen asleep, but when they became fully awake, they saw the glory of Jesus and the two men standing with him. (33) As the men were leaving, Peter said to Jesus, "Master, it is good for us to be here; let us make three tents, one for you, one for Moses, and one for Elijah" — not knowing what he was saying.

(34) While he was saying these things, a cloud appeared and overshadowed them; and they were frightened as they entered into the cloud. (35) Then came a voice from the cloud, saying, "This is my Son who has been chosen, listen to him!" (36) When the voice spoke, they found Jesus alone. They were silent and told no one in those days of the things that they had seen.

(37) On the following day, coming down from the mountain, a large crowd met Jesus. (38) And behold, a man cried out from the crowd, saying, "Teacher, I beg you to look upon my son, because he is my only child. (39) Behold, a spirit seizes him, and he suddenly cries out, and it throws him into a convulsion and makes him foam at the mouth, and before it leaves him, he is bruised badly. (40) I begged your disciples to cast it out, but they could not."

(41) Jesus answered, "O faithless and perverted generation, how long shall I put up with you? Bring your son here." (42) As he was being brought to him, the demon threw him to the ground in a convulsion, but Jesus rebuked the unclean spirit, and he cured the boy and returned him to his father. (43) All the people were astounded at the majesty of God.

While they were all marveling at all the things Jesus did, he said to his disciples, (44) "Listen carefully to what I tell you: the Son of Man will soon be betrayed into the hands of sinners." (45) But they did not understand his words; it was veiled from them so they did not perceive it, and they feared to ask him to explain.

(46) They began to argue among themselves as to which of them was the greatest. (47) Jesus, knowing the thoughts of their hearts, took a child and stood him by his side. (48) And he said to them, "Whoever receives this child in my name receives me, and whoever receives me receives the one who sent me, for it is the least one among you who is great."

(49) John said to him, "Master, we saw someone casting out demons in your name, and we tried to stop him, because he does not follow us."

(50) But Jesus said to him, "Do not stop him, for he who is not against you is for you."

(51) When the time came for Jesus to be received up, he set his face to go to Jerusalem, (52) and he sent messengers before him. They entered a village of Samaritans to prepare for him, (53) but they would not receive him because he was going to Jerusalem. (54) When his disciples, James and John, saw this, they said, "Lord, do you want us to call down fire from heaven to destroy them?" (55) Jesus turned and rebuked them. (56) Then they went to another village.

(57) As they were going on their way, a man said to Jesus, "I will follow you wherever you go."

(58) Jesus said to him, "Foxes have holes and birds of the air have nests, but the Son of Man has no place to lay his head."

(59) Jesus said to another, "Follow me."

But he replied, "Let me first go and bury my father."

(60) Jesus said to him, "Let the dead bury their own dead, but you go and proclaim the reign of God."

(61) Another said, "I will follow, Lord, but first let me say farewell to those in my house."

(62) But Jesus said to him, "No one, putting a hand on a plow and looking back, is fit for the reign of God!"

Luke 10:1-42

(1) After this the Lord appointed seventy-two others and sent them to go before him to every city that he had planned to visit. (2) And Jesus said to them, "The harvest indeed is great, but the workers are few; therefore, ask the Lord of the harvest to send forth workers to gather his crops. (3) Go, behold, I send you as lambs in the midst of wolves! (4) Carry no pouch, or knapsack; wear no shoes and greet no one on the way. (5) When you enter a house, first say, 'Peace to this house!' (6) And if a son of peace is there, your peace will rest upon him. (7) Stay in that same house eating and drinking what they provide, for the workman is worthy of his wages. Do not go from house to house.

(8) "When you enter a city and if they receive you, eat what they set before you. (9) Heal the sick and say to them, 'The reign of God is at hand.' (10) But when you enter a city that does not welcome you, go out into the streets and say, (11) 'Even the dust of your city that clings to our feet we wipe off against you; nevertheless know this, that the reign of God has come near you.' (12) I tell you that on that day it will be more tolerable for Sodom than for that city.

(13) "Woe to you, Chorizan! Woe to you, Bethsaida! If these miracles had happened in Tyre and Sodom, they would have repented long ago in sackcloth and sitting in ashes. (14) Nevertheless, it will be more tolerable in the judgment than for you. (15) And you, Capernaum,

'Will you be lifted up to heaven?

You will be brought down to Hades!'

(16) "He who hears you hears me; and he who rejects you rejects me; and he who rejects me rejects the one who sent me."

(17) The seventy-two returned with great joy saying, "Lord, even the demons obey us in your name."

(18) And Jesus said to them, "I saw Satan fall from heaven like lightening. (19) Behold, I have given you the authority to walk on serpents and scorpions, and over all the power of the enemy, and nothing shall hurt you. (20) Nevertheless do not rejoice in the fact that the spirits obey you; but rejoice that your names are written in heaven."

(21) In that same hour Jesus rejoiced in the Holy Spirit and said, "I praise you, Father, Lord of heaven and earth, because what you have hidden from the wise and clever you have revealed to the simple. Yes, Father, for such was your good pleasure.

(22) "All things have been delivered to me by my father, and no one knows who the son is except the father, and no one knows who the father is except the son and to whom the son wishes to reveal him."

(23) Then he turned to his disciples and said to them privately, "Blessed are the eyes that see what you see! (24) For I tell you that many prophets and kings desired to see what you see yet never saw it, and to hear what you hear yet never heard it."

(25) Behold, a certain lawyer stood up to test Jesus, saying, "Teacher, what must I do to inherit eternal life?"

(26) Jesus said to him, "What is written in the law? How do you understand it?"

(27) And he answered, "You shall love the Lord your God with all your heart, and with all your soul, and with all your strength, and with all your mind; and your neighbor as yourself."

(28) Jesus said to him, "You have answered correctly. Do this and you will live."

(29) But he, wishing to justify himself, said to Jesus, "And who is my neighbor?"

(30) And Jesus answered, "A certain man was going down from Jerusalem to Jericho, and he fell in with robbers, who stripped him and beating him went away leaving him half-dead. (31) A certain priest happened to be going down that road, and he saw him, but he went by on the other side. (32) And likewise, a Levite came to the place where he was, and seeing him, he passed by on the other side. (33) But a certain Samaritan traveler came by, and when he saw him, he had compassion upon him; (34) and he went to him and bound up his wounds, pouring on oil and wine, and putting him on his own animal, he brought him to an inn and cared for him. (35) On the next day he gave two coins to the innkeeper and said, 'Take care of him, and whatever more you spend, I will repay you when I return.'

(36) "Which of these three do you think became neighbor to the one

falling among the robbers?"

(37) He said, "The one showing mercy to him."

Jesus said to him, "Go and you do likewise."

(38) As they went along, Jesus entered into a certain village, and a certain woman, whose name was Martha, welcomed him into her house. (39) And she had a sister whose name was Mary, who sat at the feet of the Lord listening to his teaching. (40) But Martha was very busy with much serving. So she went to Jesus and said, "Lord, are you not concerned about my sister leaving me alone to serve? Tell her therefore to help me!"

(41) The Lord said to her, "Martha, Martha, you are anxious and troubled about many things, (42) but one thing is needful. Mary has chosen the better part, which shall not be taken from her."

Luke 11:1-54

(1) When Jesus ceased praying in a certain place, one of his disciples said to him, "Lord, teach us to pray, as John taught his disciples."

(2) Then Jesus said to them, "When you pray, say:
'Father, let your name be sacred,
let your reign come.
(3) Give us our daily bread.
(4) Forgive us our sins,
for we forgive those who are indebted to us;
and do not lead us into temptation.' "

(5) Then Jesus said to them, "Who of you will go to a friend at midnight and say to him, 'Friend, lend me three loaves, (6) since a friend of mine has come to me from a journey to visit me, and I have nothing to set before him.'

(7) "That one from inside may say, 'Do not bother me; the door is already locked and the children are with me in bed and I cannot get up to give to you.' (8) I tell you, though he will not get up and give to him because he is his friend, yet because of his importunate solicitation he will get up and give to him whatever he needs.

(9) "So I say to you, ask and it will be given to you; seek and you will find; knock and it will be opened to you. (10) For everyone asking receives, and whoever seeks finds, and the door will be opened to him who knocks.

(11) "What father among you, whose son asks for a fish, will give him a snake? (12) Or if he asks for an egg, will he give him a scorpion? (13) Therefore if you, being evil, know how to give good gifts to your children, how much more will your Father in heaven give the Holy Spirit to those who ask him!"

(14) Jesus cast out a mute demon, and when the demon was cast out, the dumb man spoke, and the crowds were astonished. (15) But some of

them said, "He casts out demons by Beelzebul, the chief of demons." (16) Others, tempting him, demanded a sign from heaven by him.

(17) Jesus, knowing their thoughts, said to them, "Every kingdom divided against itself is made desolate, and a divided house falls. (18) And if Satan is divided against himself, how can his kingdom stand? For you say that I cast out demons by Beelzebul. (19) If I cast out demons by the power of Beelzebul, by whom do your sons cast them out? Therefore, they will be your judges. (20) But it I cast out demons by the finger of God, then the reign of God has come to you.

(21) "When a strong man, fully armed, guards his courtyard, his property is secure. (22) But when a stronger one comes and conquers him, he takes his armor on which he had trusted and divides his plunder.

(23) "He who is not with me is against me, and he who does not gather with me scatters.

(24) "When the unclean spirit goes out of a man, it goes through dry places seeking rest, but, finding none, it says, 'I will return to the house I left.' (25) And when it returns, it finds it clean and furnished. (26) Then it goes and takes with it seven other spirits more evil than itself, and they enter and dwell there. The last state of that man is worse than the first."

(27) While Jesus was saying these things, a certain woman from the crowd raised her voice and said, "Blessed the womb that bore you, and the breasts that nursed you."

(28) But he said, "Yea rather, blessed the ones hearing the word of God and obeying it."

(29) As the multitudes came together, Jesus began to speak, "This is an evil generation. It seeks a sign, but no sign will be given except the sign of Jonah. (30) For as Jonah became a sign to the Ninevites, so also will the Son of Man to this generation. (31) The queen of the south will rise up in judgment with the men of this generation and condemn them. For she came from the extremities of the earth to hear the wisdom of Solomon, and behold, a greater than Solomon is here! (32) The men of Nineveh will stand up in judgment with this generation and condemn it, for they repented at the preaching of Jonah, and behold, a greater than Jonah is here!

(33) "No one lights a lamp and places it in a secret place or under a basket, but on a lampstand, so that those entering may see the light. (34) Your eye is the lamp of your body; when your eye is good, your whole body is full of light, but when it is evil, your body is full of darkness. (35) Be careful, therefore, lest the light in you is darkness. (36) If then your whole body is full of light, no part having any darkness, it will be fully illuminated, as when a shining light enlightens you."

(37) As Jesus spoke, a Pharisee asked him to dine with him, so he went in and reclined. (38) The Pharisee, seeing that he did not first wash himself before dinner, was astonished.

(39) Then the Lord said to him, "You Pharisees clean the outside of the cup and the platter, but on the inside you are full of rapacity and evil.

(40) Foolish men! Did not he who made the outside make the inside also? (41) Nevertheless, give alms of the things from within, and behold, all things are clean to you.

(42) "Woe to you Pharisees! For you tithe mint and rue and every herb, but you disregard justice and the love of God. The latter you ought to do without disregarding the former.

(43) "Woe to you Pharisees! For you love the chief seats in the synagogue and greetings in the market places.

(44) "Woe to you! For you are as unseen tombs over which men walk without knowing it."

(45) In response a certain lawyer said to Jesus, "Teacher, by saying these things, you are insulting us also."

(46) Jesus replied, "Woe to you lawyers also! For you burden men with difficult burdens to carry, but you do not touch the burdens with one of your fingers.

(47) "Woe to you! For you build tombs for the prophets, but your fathers killed them. (48) So you witness that you approve of the works of your fathers, because they killed them, and you build their tombs. (49) Therefore, the wisdom of God said, 'I will send to them prophets and apostles and some of them they will kill and others they will persecute,' (50) that the blood of the prophets which they shed from the foundation of the world might be required of this generation, (51) from the blood of Abel to the blood of Zechariah, who was killed between the altar and the sanctuary. Yes, I tell you, it will be required of this generation.

(52) "Woe to you lawyers! You took the key of knowledge. You yourselves did not enter, and you restrained those who were entering."

(53) When Jesus went away, the scribes and the Pharisees were terribly angry and they provoked him to speak of many things, (54) lying in ambush to catch him in his speech.

Luke 12:1-59

(1) Meanwhile, thousands of people were assembled, so that they tread upon one another. Jesus first spoke to his disciples: "Be on your guard against the leaven of the Pharisees, which is hypocrisy. (2) For there is nothing that has been completely covered and hidden that will not be made known. (3) Therefore the things spoken in darkness will be heard in the light, and what you whispered in the private rooms will be proclaimed on the housetops.

(4) "And I say to you, my friends, do not fear those who can kill the body but can do nothing more. (5) But I warn you to fear the one who, after death, has the authority to cast into hell. Yes, I tell you, fear that one! (6) Are not five sparrows sold for two coins? And not one is forgotten by God. (7) But even all the hairs of your head have been numbered. Fear not, for you

are more important than sparrows.

(8) "I tell you, all who confess me before men, the Son of Man will confess before the angels of God, (9) but those denying me before men will be denied before the angels. (10) Everyone who speaks a word against the Son of Man, it will be forgiven him, but the one blaspheming against the Holy Spirit will not be forgiven. (11) When they bring you before synagogues and rulers and authorities, do not be anxious about what you will say, (12) for the Holy Spirit will teach you in that hour what you should say."

(13) Someone from the crowd said to Jesus, "Teacher, tell my brother to divide the inheritance with me."

(14) He said to him, "Man, who appointed me to be a judge or a divider over you?"

(15) And Jesus said, "Watch for and guard against all covetousness, for the abundant life is not determined by one's possessions."

(16) Then Jesus told them a parable. "The land of a rich man produced abundantly. (17) And he thought within himself, 'What shall I do, because I have no place to store my grain?'

(18) "Then he said, 'This I will do: I will tear down my old barns and build larger ones, and I will store all my grain and my goods there. (19) And I will say to my soul, "Soul, you have laid up many goods for many years, relax, eat, drink, and be merry." '

(20) "But God said to him, 'Foolish man! This night your life is demanded from you, and who will get your possessions?'

(21) "So it is to those who lay up treasures for themselves but are not rich toward God."

(22) Jesus said to his disciples, "Therefore I say to you, do not be anxious about your life, what you will eat, or about your body, what you will wear. (23) For life is more than food, and the body is more than clothing. (24) Consider the ravens: they do not sow neither do they reap and they have neither storehouse nor barn, yet God feeds them. How much more value are you than birds! (25) Who of you, by being anxious, can add length to your life? (26) Therefore if you have no control over the least, why be anxious about the other things?

(27) "Consider how the lilies grow. They do not labor or spin, but I tell you, Solomon in all his glory was not clothed in such splendor. (28) And if God so clothes the grass in a field today and tomorrow it is thrown into an oven, how much more will he clothe you? (29) And you, do not seek what you will eat and what you will drink, and do not be in suspense. (30) For all the nations seek after these things, and your Father knows that you need them; (31) but seek his reign, and these things will be given to you. (32) Fear not, little flock, for it is the good pleasure of your Father to give you the kingdom. (33) Sell your possessions and give alms. Make for yourselves eternal purses, a treasure in heaven that will last forever, where a thief cannot come nor a moth cannot corrupt. (34) For where your treasure is,

there also will be your heart.

(35) "Let your loins be girded and your lamps burning, (36) and be like men waiting for their master to return from the wedding festivities, so that when he comes and knocks they may immediately open the door for him. (37) Blessed are those slaves who are watching when the master comes. Truly, I say to you, he will gird himself and have them to recline, and serve them. (38) And blessed are those slaves if he comes in the second or third watch and finds them watching. (39) But remember this, if the householder had known what time the thief was coming, he would have not allowed him to break in his house. (40) So you be prepared, for the Son of Man will come at an hour that you do not expect."

(41) Then Peter said, "Is this parable for us or for everyone?"

(42) And the Lord said, "Who then is the faithful and wise steward, whom his master will set over his household attendants to give them food at the appropriate time? (43) Blessed is that slave who is found faithful when his lord returns. (44) Truly, I tell you, he will set him over all his possessions. (45) But if that slave says in his heart, 'My lord has delayed his return,' and he beats his menservants and maidservants, and he eats and drinks and gets drunk, (46) and the lord of that slave returns in a day that he did not expect and in an hour that he did not know, he will cut him asunder and will assign him a place with the untrustworthy. (47) That slave, knowing the will of his lord but not preparing or doing it, will be severely beaten. (48) But the one not knowing, yet deserving punishment, will be beaten with few blows. So to everyone who has been given much, much will be demanded of him. More will be asked of the one to whom more has been entrusted.

(49) "I came to cast fire upon the earth, and I wish that it had already started. (50) I have a baptism to be baptized with, and I am constrained until it is accomplished. (51) Do you think that I came to establish peace on earth? No, I tell you, but rather division. (52) From this time there will be five in one house, three against two and two against three. (53) The father will be divided against son and son against father, mother against the daughter and daughter against the mother, mother-in-law against her daughter-in-law and daughter-in-law against the mother."

(54) Jesus said to the crowds, "When you see a cloud rising in the west, immediately you say, 'A storm is coming,' and so it is. (55) And when a south wind is blowing you say, 'There will be heat,' and so it is. (56) Hypocrites, you know how to forecast the weather, but how is it that you cannot analyze the present time?

(57) "Why do you not judge for yourselves what is just? (58) As you are going with your accuser to appear before a ruler, do your best to be reconciled with him on the way, lest he drags you to the judge, and the judge deliver you to the jailer, and the jailer cast you into prison. (59) I tell you, you will not be released until you have made the last payment."

Luke 13:1-35

(1) At that time there were some present who told Jesus about the Galileans whose blood Pilate mixed with their sacrifices. (2) Jesus responded by saying, "Do you think that those Galileans were the greatest sinners in Galilee because they suffered these things? (3) I tell you, unless you repent, you will all likewise perish. (4) Or, do you think that those eighteen who were killed by the falling tower of Siloam were guiltier than all the others who lived in Jerusalem? (5) I tell you, no! But unless you repent, you will all likewise perish."

(6) Then Jesus told this parable, "A certain man had planted a fig tree in his vineyard, and he came to gather fruit, but he found none. (7) So he said to the vinedresser, 'Behold, for three years I have been seeking fruit from this fig tree but I have found none. Cut it down. Why should I leave it here to take up space?' (8) But he replied, 'Lord, leave it for another year, and I will dig and put manure around it. (9) Then if it does not produce, cut it down.' "

(10) Jesus was teaching in one of the synagogues on a Sabbath. (11) Behold, there was a woman who had been crippled by a weak spirit for eighteen years, and she was bent double and unable to stand erect. (12) Jesus, seeing the woman and calling her to come to him, said, "Woman, you have been loosed from your weakness." (13) Then he put his hands on her, and she immediately stood erect, and she praised God.

(14) The synagogue ruler, being angry with Jesus because he healed on the Sabbath day, said to the crowd, "There are six days for us to work. Those seeking to be healed should come on those days and not on the Sabbath day."

(15) The Lord answered him, "Hypocrites! Do you not on the Sabbath untie your ox or the donkey from the manger and lead it to water? (16) This woman, being a daughter of Abraham, was bound by Satan for eighteen years. Was it not fitting to loose her from this bondage on the Sabbath day?" (17) When Jesus said these things, the opposition was put to shame, and the entire crowd rejoiced because of all the glorious things which were done by him.

(18) Jesus said, "What is the kingdom of God like, and to what shall I compare it? (19) It is like a mustard seed, which a man took and planted in his garden, and it grew and became a tree, and the birds of the air lodged in its branches."

(20) Again he said, "To what shall I compare the kingdom of God? (21) It is like leaven which a woman took and mixed in three measures of oil until it was all leavened."

(22) Jesus went throughout the cities and villages as he went on his way to Jerusalem. (23) Someone said to him, "Lord, are only a few saved?"

Jesus said to them, (24) "Struggle to enter through the narrow door, because I tell you, many will seek to enter but will not be able. (25) When the householder gets up and closes the door, you on the outside will begin to knock on the door saying, 'Lord, open to us,' and he will answer, 'I do not know you.' (26) Then you will begin to say, 'We ate and drank with you, and you taught in our streets.' (27) And he will say, 'I do not know you. Depart from me all you workers of unrighteousness.' (28) There will be weeping and gnashing of the teeth when you see Abraham and Isaac and Jacob and all the prophets in the kingdom of God, but you yourselves thrown outside. (29) And they will come from the east and west and from the north and south and will recline in the kingdom of God. (30) Behold, some of the last will be first and some of the first will be last."

(31) In that hour some of the Pharisees approached Jesus and said to him, "Depart and leave here, because Herod wants to kill you."

(32) Jesus said, "Go tell that fox, 'I cast out demons and heal sicknesses today and tomorrow, and on the third day I complete my work.' (33) Nevertheless, it is necessary for me to journey today and tomorrow and on the following day, for it is impossible for a prophet to perish outside Jerusalem!

(34) "Jerusalem, Jerusalem, who kills the prophets and stones the ones sent to you! Oftentimes I have yearned to gather her children as a bird gathers her brood under her wings, and you would not let me. (35) Behold! Your house is forsaken. And I tell you that you will not see me until you say, 'Blessed is the one coming in the name of the Lord.' "

Luke 14:1-35

(1) Jesus went to dine in the house of one of the leaders of the Pharisees on a Sabbath, and they carefully watched him. (2) Behold, there in front of him was a man with dropsy. (3) Jesus asked the lawyers and Pharisees, "Is it lawful or not to heal on the Sabbath?" (4) They were silent. So Jesus took hold of the man and healed him and sent him on his way.

(5) Jesus said to them, "If your son or an ox had fallen into a pit, would you not pull him out on a Sabbath day?" (6) This they were not able to answer.

(7) Jesus, observing that the ones invited were choosing the chief seats, told them a parable: (8) "When you are invited to a wedding feast, do not recline at the chief seats, for a more honorable man than you may have been invited. (9) When he arrives, the host will say to you, 'Give this man your place.' Then, with shame, you will take the last place. (10) But when you are invited, go and recline at the last place, so that when the host comes to you, he will say, 'Friend, go up higher.' Then you will be honored before all those reclining with you. (11) For everyone exalting himself will be humbled, and the one humbling himself will be exalted."

(12) Jesus also said to the host, "When you prepare a dinner or a

banquet, do not call your friends, or your brothers, or your relatives, or your rich neighbors, lest they invite you in return, and it becomes a recompense. (13) But when you have a party, invite the poor, the maimed, the lame, and the blind, (14) and you will be blessed, because they will not recompense you. For you will be recompensed in the resurrection of the just."

(15) One of those at the table heard this and said, "Blessed is he who eats bread in the kingdom of God."

(16) Jesus said to him, "A certain man prepared a great banquet and invited many, (17) and he sent his slave at the hour of the supper to tell those who had been invited, 'Come, for all things are prepared.'

(18) "And they all began with one mind to make excuses. The first said, 'I bought a farm and I need to go see it. Have me excused.'

(19) "Another said, 'I bought five yoke of oxen and I am going to test them. Have me excused.'

(20) "Another said, 'I married a wife; therefore, I cannot come.'

(21) "The slave returned and reported these things to his master. Then the master of the house was angry. He said to his slave, 'Go out quickly into the streets and alleys of the city and bring in here the poor, the maimed, the blind and the lame.'

(22) "The slave said, 'Master, it has been done, yet there is room for more.'

(23) "The master said to the slave, 'Go out into the roads and hedges and compel them to come in, so that my house may be filled. (24) For I tell you that not one of those who were invited shall taste of my banquet.' "

(25) Great crowds accompanied him; and Jesus turned to them and said, (26) "If anyone comes to me and does not hate his father, mother, wife, children, brothers, sisters, and even his own life, he cannot be my disciple. (27) Whoever does not bear his cross and follow me cannot be my disciple.

(28) "For if any of you wanted to build a tower would you not first consider carefully the cost to see if you could complete it? (29) If you lay the foundation but are not able to finish, all those observing you will begin to mock, (30) saying, 'This man began to build but was not able to finish.'

(31) "Or what king, going to fight another king in war, will not first seriously evaluate to see if he is able with ten thousand to meet his enemy with twenty thousand coming against him? (32) Otherwise, he will send a delegation while he is far away and seek peace. (33) So, therefore, whoever of you does not say farewell to all his possessions cannot be my disciple.

(34) "Salt is good, but if it becomes insipid, what can restore it? (35) It is not good for the soil nor for the manure pit. It is thrown out. He who has ears to hear, let him hear."

Luke 15:1-32

(1) The tax collectors and sinners were all coming to Jesus to hear

him. (2) And the Pharisees and scribes were grumbling among themselves, saying, "This man receives sinners and eats with them."

(3) Then Jesus told them this parable: (4) "What man among you, if he has a hundred sheep and loses one of them, will he not leave the ninety-nine in the wilderness and go seeking the lost sheep until he finds it? (5) And when he finds it, he puts it upon his shoulders rejoicing. (6) When he goes home he calls together his friends and neighbors and says to them, 'Rejoice with me, because I found my lost sheep.' (7) I tell you, there will likewise be more joy in heaven over one repentant sinner than over ninety-nine righteous people who have no need of repentance.

(8) "Or what woman, if she has ten silver coins and loses one of them, will she not light a lamp and sweep the house and seek diligently until she finds it? (9) And when she finds it, she calls together her friends and neighbors and says to them, 'Rejoice with me, because I found my silver coin that was lost.' (10) Likewise, I tell you, there is joy before the angels of God over one repentant sinner."

(11) Jesus said, "A certain man had two sons. (12) The younger one said to his father, 'Father, give me my share of the estate.' So he divided the property between them.

(13) "A few days later the younger son gathered all his belongings and departed to a far country, and there he squandered his wealth by prodigal living. (14) When he had spent everything, there came a severe famine throughout that country, and he became desperate. (15) So he went and attached himself to a citizen of that country, who sent him into his field to feed swine. (16) He wanted to eat the pods that the swine ate, but no one gave to him.

(17) "Then, coming to himself, he said, 'How many are my father's hired hands with an abundance of food, and I am here starving! (18) I will arise and go to my father and I will say to him, "Father, I have sinned against heaven and before you, and (19) I am no longer worthy to be called your son. Make me as one of your hired hands." '

(20) "So he arose and went to his father. While he was still far away, his father saw him and was moved with compassion. Running to him, he fell upon his neck and fervently kissed him.

(21) "The son said to him, 'Father, I have sinned against heaven and before you, I am no longer worthy to be called your son.'

(22) "The father said to his hired hands, 'Quickly! Bring out the best robe and put it around him, and put a signet ring on his hand and sandals on his feet. (23) Bring and kill the fatted calf. Let us eat and celebrate! (24) For this my son was dead and he is alive again, he was lost and he has been found.' And they began to celebrate.

(25) "The older brother was in the field, and as he came near the house, he heard music and dancing, (26) and he called one of the lads to him and asked him what was happening. (27) He said to him, 'Your brother has

come, and your father killed the fatted calf because he is back and in good health.'

(28) "The older brother was angry and refused to enter, so the father came out to plead with him, (29) but he responded by saying to his father, 'Lo, these many years I have served you and I have never disobeyed your orders, and you have never given me a goat to celebrate with my friends. (30) But when this son of yours, who has squandered your property living with prostitutes, comes home, you killed for him the fatted calf!'

(31) "The father said to him, 'Son, you are always with me, and everything I have is yours. (32) But we had to celebrate and rejoice because this brother of yours was dead, but now he lives. He was lost but he was found.' "

Luke 16:1-31

(1) Jesus also said to the disciples, "There was a certain rich man who had a steward who was accused of wasting his possessions. (2) So he summoned him and said, 'What is this that I hear about you? Hand in the records of your stewardship, for you can no longer be my steward.'

(3) "The steward said to himself, 'What can I do, because my master is taking away my employment. I am not strong enough to dig and I am ashamed to beg. (4) I know what I will do so that, when I lose my employment, people will receive me into their houses.'

(5) "So he called in each of his master's debtors and said to the first, 'How much do you owe my Master?'

(6) "He said, 'Eight hundred measures of oil.'

"He said to him, 'Take your bill and sit down quickly and write four hundred.'

(7) "Then to another he said, 'How much do you owe?'

"And he said, 'A hundred measures of wheat.'

"He said to him, 'Take the bill and write eighty.'

(8) "The master praised the unrighteous steward because he acted astutely. For the worldly are wiser in their generation than the children of light. (9) I tell you, make friends for yourselves by means of unrighteous mammon, so that when it fails, they may receive you into the eternal home.

(10) "Whoever is faithful in little things is faithful also in big things; whoever is unjust in little things also is unjust in big things. (11) If therefore you cannot be trusted with elusive wealth, who will entrust you with the true riches? (12) And if you have not been faithful in that which belongs to another, who will give you that which is yours forever?

(13) "No servant can serve two masters; for either he will hate the one and love the other, or he will hold fast to the one and despise the other. You cannot serve God and Wealth."

(14) The Pharisees, who were lovers of money, heard all these things

and mocked Jesus.

(15) He said to them, "You are justifying yourselves before men, but God knows your hearts. For what is exalted among men is an abomination in the sight of God. (16) The Law and the Prophets were until John; since then the kingdom of God is preached, and everyone is rushing into it. (17) But it is easier for heaven and earth to pass away than for one stroke of a letter of the law to become void.

(18) "Everyone divorcing his wife and marrying another commits adultery, and the one marrying the divorcee commits adultery.

(19) "There was a certain rich man who dressed in a purple robe and fine linen, and every day he feasted in great splendor. (20) At his gate was placed a certain man named Lazarus, covered with sores, (21) who was desiring to eat the food falling from the rich man's table. Even the dogs came and licked his sores.

(22) "When the poor man died he was carried away by the angels to the arms of Abraham. The rich man also died and was buried. (23) And in Hell, he was in torment, and he lifted up his eyes and saw Abraham far away and Lazarus in his arms. (24) So he called to him, 'Father Abraham, have mercy on me and send Lazarus that he may dip his finger in water and cool my tongue, because I am suffering in this flame.'

(25) "But Abraham said, 'Son, remember that you received good things in your life, and likewise Lazarus the bad things. Now he is comforted here and you are suffering. (26) And besides all this, between you and us there is a great chasm firmly fixed, so that anyone wishing to pass from here to you cannot. Neither can anyone cross from there to us.'

(27) "Then he said, 'I beg you, Father, send him to the house of my father, (28) so that he may witness to them, for I have five brothers, lest they also come to this place of torment."

(29) "Abraham replied, 'They have Moses and the prophets. Let them hear them.'

(30) "But he said, 'No, Father Abraham. If someone from the dead should go to them, they would repent.'

(31) "But he said to him, 'If they do not hear Moses and the prophets, neither would they be persuaded if someone should rise from the dead.' "

Luke 17:1-37

(1) Jesus said to his disciples, "It is inevitable that temptations to sin will come, but woe to him through whom they come. (2) It would be better for him to be thrown into the sea with a millstone hung around his neck rather than cause one of these little ones to sin.

(3) "Listen carefully. If your brother sins, rebuke him, and if he repents, forgive him. (4) And if seven times in the day he sins against you,

and seven times turns to you saying, 'I repent,' forgive him."

(5) The apostles said to the Lord, "increase our faith."

(6) The Lord said, "If you had faith the size of a mustard seed, you could have said to this black mulberry tree, 'Be uprooted and be planted in the sea,' and it would have obeyed you.

(7) "If one of you had a slave plowing or herding sheep and came in from the field would you say to him, 'Come quickly and recline'? (8) But rather would you not say, 'Prepare my meal and gird yourself and serve me while I eat and drink, and then you may eat and drink'? (9) Would he thank the slave for doing what he was told to do? (10) So you also, when you do what is commanded of you, say, 'We are unworthy slaves; we have only done our duty.' "

(11) Jesus, on the way to Jerusalem, passed along the borders of Samaria and Galilee. (12) As he entered a village, ten lepers met him. They stood at a distance (13) and they shouted, "Jesus, Master, have mercy on us!"

(14) And seeing them he said, "Go show yourselves to the priests." As they went they were healed. (15) One of them, seeing that he was healed, returned with a loud voice praising God, (16) and he fell upon his face at the feet of Jesus, giving thanks to him. And he was a Samaritan.

(17) Jesus asked, "Were not ten healed? Where are the nine? (18) Was there no one to return and give praise to God except this foreigner?"

(19) And he said, "Stand up and go. Your faith has saved you."

(20) When the Pharisees questioned Jesus as to when the reign of God was coming, he replied, "The reign of God does not come with visible signs (21) nor will they say, 'Behold, here! or there!' For behold, the reign of God is within you."

(22) Jesus said to his disciples, "The days will come when you will desire to see one of the days of the Son of Man and you will not see it. (23) And they will say to you, 'Behold there!' or 'Behold here!' Do not go after them, nor follow them. (24) For as the lightening flashes and lights up the sky from one side to the other, so will be the Son of Man in his day. (25) But first he must suffer many things and be rejected by this generation.

(26) "As it was in the days of Noah, so it will be in the days of the Son of Man. (27) They were eating, drinking, marrying, and giving in marriage until the day Noah entered the ark, and the flood came and destroyed them all. (28) Likewise as it was in the days of Lot. They were eating, drinking, buying, selling, planting and building. (29) But the day Lot left Sodom, it rained fire and brimstone from heaven and destroyed them all.

(30) "It will be like that on the day when the Son of Man is revealed. (31) On that day if one is on the housetop and his goods are in the house, he should not go down to get them, and likewise if one is in the field, he should not turn back for his goods. (32) Remember Lot's wife! (33) Whoever seeks to save his life will lose it, and whoever loses his life will save it. (34) I tell you, in that night there will be two men on one couch; one will be taken and

the other one left. (35) Two women will be grinding grain together; one will be taken and the other one left."

(37) They said to him, "Where, Lord?"

And he said to them, "Where the body is, there the vultures will be gathered together."

Luke 18:1-43

(1) Jesus told them a parable to teach them that they ought to always pray and never to despair. (2) He said, "There was a judge in a certain city who neither feared God nor respected man. (3) There was a widow in that city who kept coming to him saying, 'Protect me against my adversary!'

(4) "He refused for awhile, but afterwards he said to himself, 'Though I do not fear God nor respect man, (5) but because this widow is troubling me, I will give her justice before she exhausts me by her continual coming.' "

(6) The Lord said, "Hear what the unrighteous judge says. (7) Will not God vindicate his chosen ones who cry to him day and night? How long will he delay? (8) I tell you, he will give them swift justice. But when the Son of Man comes, will he find faith on the earth?"

(9) Jesus told this parable to some who trusted in themselves that they were righteous and despised everyone else: (10) "Two men went up into the temple to pray, one a Pharisee and the other a tax collector. (11) The Pharisee stood and prayed to himself, 'O God, I thank you that I am not as the rest of the men—swindlers, evildoers, adulterers—or even as this tax collector. (12) I fast twice a week. I tithe all my income.' (13) But the tax collector, standing far off, would not lift his eyes to heaven, but beating his breast, said, 'O God, be merciful to me, the sinner!'

(14) "I tell you, this man went down to his house justified rather than the other. For everyone who exalts himself will be humbled, and everyone humbling himself will be exalted."

(15) Some people brought infants to Jesus so that he might touch them, but the disciples, seeing this, rebuked them. (16) But Jesus said, "Let the little children come to me, for of such is the reign of God. (17) Truly I tell you, whoever does not receive the reign of God like a child cannot enter into it."

(18) Then a certain ruler questioned Jesus, "Good Teacher, What must I do to inherit eternal life?"

(19) Jesus said to him, "Why do you call me good? Only God alone is good. (20) You know the commandments: 'Do not commit adultery, do not murder, do not steal, do not bear false witness, honor your father and your mother.' "

(21) He said, "I have kept all these commandments from childhood."

(22) Jesus, hearing this, said to him, "Yet one thing you lack: sell

everything you have and distribute it to the poor and you will have treasure in heaven, and come follow me."

(23) When he heard this he became greatly grieved, because he was a very wealthy man.

(24) Jesus, looking at him, said, "It is very difficult for the wealthy to enter the reign of God. (25) It is easier for a camel to go through the eye of a needle than for a rich man to enter the reign of God."

(26) Those who heard him said, "Then who can be saved?"

(27) Jesus said, "The things that are impossible with men are possible with God."

(28) Peter said to him, "Behold, we have left all to follow you."

(29) Jesus said to him, "I solemnly assure you that no one has left house, wife, brothers, parents or children for the sake of the reign of God (30) who has not received multiplied blessings in this life and life everlasting in the coming age."

(31) Jesus privately spoke to the Twelve, "Behold, we are going up to Jerusalem, and all things written by the prophets concerning the Son of man will be accomplished. (32) He will be delivered to the Gentiles; and he will be mocked and insulted and spit upon, (33) and after they have scourged him they will kill him, and on the third day he will rise again."

(34) They did not understand. His words were obscure to them, and they did not know what he was talking about.

(35) As Jesus drew near Jericho, a blind beggar sat by the side of the road begging. (36) When he heard the crowd passing by, he asked what was happening. (37) They told him, "Jesus the Nazarene is passing by."

(38) He cried out, "Jesus, Son of David, have mercy on me."

(39) Those who led the way sternly ordered him to be quiet; but he shouted louder, "Son of David, have mercy on me!"

(40) Jesus stood and commanded that he be brought to him. When he came near him, he asked him, "What do you want me to do?"

(41) He replied, "Lord, let me see again."

(42) Jesus said to him, "See again; your faith has healed you." Immediately he received his sight and followed Jesus, praising God. (43) When the people saw it, they all praised God.

Luke 19:1-48

(1) Jesus entered and was passing through Jericho. (2) Behold, there was a rich man named Zacchaeus who was chief of the tax collectors. (3) He sought to see who Jesus was, but he was short and could not see over the crowd. (4) So he ran ahead and climbed up into a fig-mulberry tree to see Jesus, because he was coming that way.

(5) When Jesus came to that place, he looked up and said to him, "Zacchaeus, Come down quickly, for I must go to your house today." (6) He

came down immediately and received him joyfully.

(7) When the people saw this they all began to complain saying, "He has gone in to be the guest of a sinful man!"

(8) Zacchaeus, standing, said to the Lord, "Behold, Lord, half of my possessions I give to the poor, and if I have defrauded anyone, I will restore fourfold."

(9) Jesus said to him, "Today salvation has come to this house, because he also is a son of Abraham. (10) For the Son of man came to seek and to save that which was lost."

(11) As the people were listening to Jesus, he told them a parable as they were coming near to Jerusalem, and because they were thinking that the reign of God was about to manifest itself. (12) He said, "A man of noble birth went into a far country to receive for himself a kingdom and then return. (13) He called ten slaves, gave to them ten minas, and said to them, 'Trade with these until I return.'

(14) "But his citizens hated him, and they sent a delegation after him, saying, 'We do not want this man to reign over us.'

(15) "After he was made king, he returned and called the slaves to whom he had given the money, so that he might know what each had gained by trading.

(16) "The first one came to him and said, 'Lord, your mina has gained ten more.'

(17) "He said to him, 'Well done, good slave! Because you have been faithful in the least, you will have authority over ten cities.'

(18) "The second came to him and said, 'Lord, your mina, I have gained five more.'

(19) "He said to him, 'You will be over five cities.'

(20) "Then another one came saying, 'Lord, behold your mina, I have kept it wrapped up in a handkerchief. (21) I was afraid of you because you are a harsh man. You take up what you did not lay down and you reap what you did not sow.'

(22) "He said to him, 'Wicked slave, I will judge you by your own words. You knew that I was a harsh man, taking up what I did not lay down and reaping what I did not sow.

(23) " 'Why did you not deposit the money in the bank so that I could have collected it with interest?'

(24) "To those standing by he said, 'Take from him the mina and give to him who has ten minas.'

(25) "And they said to him, 'Lord, he has ten minas!'

(26) "I tell you that to everyone who has, more will be given, and to the one who has not, that which he has will be taken away. (27) But bring here those enemies of mine who did not want me to reign over them and slay them before me."

(28) After saying these things, Jesus went on ahead, going up to

Jerusalem. (29) When he came near Bethphage and Bethany, at the Mount of Olives, he sent two of his disciples, saying to them: (30) "Go to the village before you, and entering you will find a colt tied, on which no man ever sat. Untie it and bring it here. (31) If anyone asks you, 'Why are you untying it?' say to him, 'The Lord needs it.' "

(32) They went and found it to be as he had said. (33) As they were untying the colt, the owner said to them, "Why are you untying the colt?"

(34) They said, "The Lord needs it."

(35) Then they led it to Jesus, and throwing their garments on the colt, they put Jesus on it. (36) As Jesus was riding along, the people carpeted the road before him with their garments.

(37) As he was approaching the descent of the Mount of Olives, the entire crowd of the disciples began joyfully to praise God with a loud voice for all the miracles they had seen, (38) saying,

"Blessed is the king who comes
in the name of the Lord!
Peace in heaven
and glory in the highest!"

(39) Some of the Pharisees from the crowd said to him, "Teacher, rebuke your disciples."

(40) Jesus answered, "I tell you, if they were silent, the stones would cry out!"

(41) Jesus, coming in sight of the city, wept over it, (42) saying, "If only you knew, even today, the conditions of peace! — but now they are hidden from your eyes. (43) The days are coming when your enemies will encircle you with a rampart and hem you in on all sides. (44) They will throw you and your children to the ground, and they will not leave you one stone upon another, because you did not recognize the time of your visitation."

(45) Jesus entered the temple and began to cast out the traders (46) saying to them, "It is written, 'My house shall be a house of prayer,' but you have made it a den of robbers."

(47) Jesus was teaching daily in the temple, but the chief priests, scribes and the national leaders were seeking to destroy him; (48) but they did not know how to do it, because all the people hung upon his words.

Luke 20:1-47

(1) One day Jesus was teaching the people and preaching the gospel in the temple when the chief priests and scribes with the elders came upon him (2) and said to him, "Tell us by what authority do you do these things, or who gave you this authority?"

(3) Jesus said to them, "I also will ask you a question, and you tell me. (4) Was the baptism of John from heaven or from men?"

(5) They reasoned with themselves saying, "If we say, 'From heaven,' he will say, 'Why did you not believe him?' (6) If we say, 'From men,' all the people will stone us, for they are convinced that John was a prophet."

(7) So they answered, "We do not know."

(8) Jesus said to them, "Neither will I tell you by what authority I do these things."

(9) Then Jesus began to tell the people this parable: "A certain man planted a vineyard and leased it to some farmers and went away for a long time. (10) At harvest time the owner sent a slave to the farmers to receive his share of the crop, but the farmers beat him and sent him away empty. (11) He sent another slave, and that one also they beat and insulted and sent him away empty. (12) And he sent a third, but this one they wounded and threw him out.

(13) "Then the owner of the vineyard said, 'What shall I do? I will send my beloved son. Perhaps they will show respect for him.'

(14) "When the farmers saw him they reasoned among themselves, 'This is the heir. Let us kill him so that the inheritance will be ours.' So they threw him out of the vineyard and killed him.

(15) "What then will the owner of the vineyard do to them? (16) He will come and destroy these farmers and give the vineyard to others."

When they heard this, they said, "May it never be so!"

(17) Jesus looked at them and said, "What is the meaning of this scripture:

'The stone which the builders rejected
has become the keystone of the structure?'
(18) Everyone who falls upon that stone will be broken to pieces, but he on whom it falls will be pulverized."

(19) At this time the scribes and the chief priests tried to lay their hands on Jesus, but they feared the people. They realized that he had aimed the parable at them.

(20) So, observing carefully, they sent spies to him in the guise of honest men to trap him by crafty words so they could deliver him to the power and authority of the governor. (21) They questioned him, "Teacher, we know that you speak and teach what is right, and you do not show partiality but teach the way of God in truth. (22) Is it lawful or not for us to pay taxes to Caesar?"

(23) Jesus, perceiving their hypocrisy said to them, (24) "Show me a coin. Whose image and title are on it?"

(25) They replied, "Caesar's."

He said to them, "Then give to Caesar what belongs to him and give to God what belongs to him."

(26) They were unable to trap him publicly in his speech, and they were so astonished at his answer that they made no reply.

(27) Some of the Sadducees (those who do not believe that there will

be a resurrection) came to Jesus with a question: (28) "Teacher, Moses wrote for us that if a married man dies childless, his brother should take his widow and have children for his brother. (29) Now there were seven brothers. The first took a wife and died childless. (30) The second (31) and the third took her, and all the seven took her and they died without children. (32) Finally, the woman also died. (33) So then, in the resurrection whose wife will she be? For she was the wife of all of them."

(34) Jesus said to them, "The children of this age marry and are given in marriage, (35) but those counted worthy to a place in the age to come and to the resurrection from the dead will neither marry nor be given in marriage. (36) And being like angels they are no longer liable to death, and being children of the resurrection they are children of God. (37) As to the resurrection of the dead, Moses pointed that out at the bush when he called the Lord 'the God of Abraham and the God of Isaac and the God of Jacob.' (38) God is not a God of the dead, but of the living, for to him all are alive."

(39) Some of the scribes said, "Well said, teacher." (40) After that no one dared to question him.

(41) Then Jesus said to them, "How can they say that Christ is the Son of David? (42) For David says of himself in the Book of Psalms:

'The Lord said to my Lord: Sit at my right hand

(43) until I make your enemies your footstool.'

(44) "Now if David called him 'Lord' how can he be his son?"

(45) As all the people were listening, he said to his disciples, (46) "Beware of the scribes! They like to parade in robes, and they love salutations in the market places and the best seats in the synagogue and the places of honor at banquets, (47) but they rob the homes of the widows while in pretense they recite long prayers. They will receive greater condemnation."

Luke 21:1-38

(1) Jesus, looking up, saw the rich putting their gifts into the treasury, (2) and also a poor widow putting in her two small coins. (3) He said, "Truly I say to you, this poor widow has put in more than all the others. (4) They gave out of their surplus, but this woman, out of her poverty, put in all she had to live on."

(5) When some were talking about the temple, adorned with its beautiful stones and dedicated gifts, Jesus said, (6) "As for these things that you see, the days are coming when there shall not be left one stone upon another that will not be torn down."

(7) They asked him, "Teacher, when will this be, and what will be the sign that it is about to happen?"

(8) He said, "Watch carefully so that you will not be led astray, for many will come in my name, saying, 'I am he!' and 'The time is at hand!' Do

not follow them. (9) When you hear of wars and insurrections do not be terrified. These things must first take place, but the end is not immediately."

(10) Then he said to them, "Nation will rise against nation and kingdom against kingdom. (11) There will be great earthquakes, and in many places there will be pestilences and famines, and there will be horrible events, and great signs from heaven.

(12) "But before this happens they will lay their hands upon you and persecute you, delivering you to the synagogues and prisons, and you will be brought before kings and governors for the sake of my name. (13) This will be an opportunity for your testimony. (14) Do not prepare a speech for your defense (15) for I will give you eloquence and wisdom that none of your adversaries will be able to withstand or contradict. (16) You will even be betrayed by parents, brothers, relatives, and friends, and some of you will be put to death. (17) You will be hated by all for the sake of my name, (18) yet not a hair of your head will perish. (19) By your steadfast endurance you will posses your souls.

(20) "When you see Jerusalem encircled by armies, you will know that her devastation is near. (21) Those in Judea must flee to the mountains, and those in the city must escape, and those in the country must not return to it, (22) because these are days of vengeance in fulfillment of that which has been written. (23) Woe to the pregnant women and those who have nursing babies in those days. For there will be terrible misery in the land and great wrath upon this people. (24) They will fall by the edge of the sword and will be taken as prisoners to all nations, and Jerusalem will be trampled by the Gentiles, until the times of the Gentiles are fulfilled.

(25) "There will be signs in the sun, moon and stars. On the earth, nations will be in anguish, bewildered at the roaring and the tossing of the sea. (26) Men will faint from fear in anticipation of the things coming upon the earth. For the powers of the heavens will be shaken. (27) Then they will see the Son of man coming in a cloud with power and great glory. (28) When these things begin to take place, stand erect and lift up your heads, for your deliverance is near."

(29) Then he told them a parable: "Look at the fig tree and all the trees. (30) When they are budding, you see for yourselves that summer is near. (31) So also, when you see these things taking place, you know that the reign of God is near. (32) Truly, I tell you that this generation will not pass away until all this takes place. (33) Heaven and earth will pass away, but my words will never pass away.

(34) "Keep a watch on yourselves lest you become depressed with indulgence, drunkenness, and worldly cares, and suddenly that day comes upon you. (35) For like a trap it will come upon all who dwell upon the face of the whole earth. (36) Stay awake at all times, and pray constantly that you may be able to escape these coming events, and to stand before the Son of man."

(37) Jesus taught daily in the temple, but he went out to spend the

nights at the Mount of Olives. (38) All the people came early in the morning to the temple to hear him.

Luke 22:1-71

(1) The time of the feast of the unleavened bread, called the Passover, was near. (2) The chief priests and the scribes sought a way to destroy Jesus, for they feared the people.

(3) Satan entered into Judas, called Iscariot, who was a member of the Twelve. (4) He went and discussed with the chief priests and officers how he might betray Jesus, (5) and they were delighted to give him money. (6) He fully consented, and looked for an opportunity to betray him in the absence of the crowd.

(7) Then came the day of the unleavened bread on which it was necessary to kill the Passover lamb. (8) So Jesus said to Peter and John, "Go and prepare the Passover for us, that we may eat the Passover."

(9) They said to him, "Where do you want us to prepare it?"

(10) He said to them, "As you enter into the city, a man carrying a pitcher will meet you. Follow him into the house he enters. (11) Then say to the owner, 'The Teacher asks: Where is the guest room where I may eat the Passover with my disciples?' (12) That man will show you a large furnished room upstairs. Prepare that room."

(13) They went and found it as he had told them and they prepared the Passover.

(14) At the appointed hour, Jesus reclined with the apostles. (15) He said to them, "I have eagerly desired to eat this Passover with you before I suffer. (16) For I assure you that I will eat it no more until it is fulfilled in the kingdom of God."

(17) Jesus, taking a cup and giving thanks, said, "Take this and divide it among yourselves. (18) For I assure you I shall drink no more from the fruit of the vine until the kingdom of God comes."

(19) Jesus, taking a loaf and giving thanks, broke it and gave it to them, saying, "This is my body given to you. Do this for my memorial."

(20) Likewise, he took the cup after supper, saying, "This is the new covenant in my blood, which is poured out for you. (21) The hand of the one betraying me is with me on the table. (22) The Son of man goes according to what has been determined, but woe to that man through whom he has been betrayed." (23) They began to argue among themselves concerning who was about to do this.

(24) There was a contention among them about which of them was considered to be the greatest. (25) So Jesus said to them, "The kings of the nations lord it over their subjects, and those in authority are called benefactors. (26) But this is not for you, because the greater is like the younger, and the one governing is as the one serving. (27) For who is greater,

the one reclining or the one serving? Is it not the one reclining? But I am among you as one serving. (28) You are the ones who have stood by me in my trials; (29) so as my Father has appointed a kingdom for me, I also appoint one for you, (30) so that you may drink and eat at my table in my kingdom, and you will sit on thrones judging the twelve tribes of Israel.

(31) "Simon, Simon, Satan has demanded to have you to sift as wheat, (32) but I have made supplication for you that your faith will not fail; and when you have returned to me, strengthen your brothers."

(33) He replied, "Lord, I am prepared to go with you to prison and to death."

(34) Jesus replied, "I tell you, Peter, a rooster will not crow today until you have denied three times that you know me."

(35) Then Jesus said to them, "When I sent you out with no moneybag, knapsack or sandals, were you in need of anything?"

They replied, "Not a thing."

(36) He said to them, "But now let him who has a moneybag, take it, likewise a knapsack, and let the one who has no sword sell his garment and buy one. (37) For I tell you that which has been written will be fulfilled in me,

'He was classed with criminals,'
for the things concerning me are fulfilled."

(38) And they said, "Look, Lord, here are two swords."

Jesus said, "That is enough."

(39) Then he went forth as usual to the Mount of Olives, and his disciples followed him. (40) When he came to the place, he said to them, "Pray that you do not enter into temptation."

(41) He withdrew about a stone's throw, and knelt and prayed, (42) "Father, if you are willing, take this cup from me; nevertheless, not my will but let your will be done." (43) An angel from heaven appeared to strengthen him. (44) In agony he prayed more earnestly, and his sweat, like drops of blood, was falling to the earth.

(45) Then he arose from prayer, and he found his disciples asleep, exhausted with grief. (46) He asked them, "Why are you sleeping. Get up and pray so that you may not enter into temptation."

(47) While he was speaking a crowd came, led by one of the twelve, called Judas. He approached Jesus to kiss him. (48) Jesus said to him, "Judas, do you betray the Son of man with a kiss?"

(49) Those around Jesus, seeing what was happening, said, "Lord, shall we smite with a sword?" (50) One of them struck the slave of the high priest and cut off his right ear.

(51) Jesus said, "Not this way!"

(52) Jesus said to the chief priests, officers of the temple and elders coming upon him, "Why do you come against me as a robber with swords and clubs? (53) While I was teaching daily in the temple you did not stretch out your hand against me, but this is your hour and the power of darkness."

(54) Then they arrested Jesus and brought him into the house of the high priest. Peter followed far away. (55) They built a fire in the center of the court and Peter sat down among them. (56) A maidservant who was sitting near the light and gazing at him said, "This man was with him."

(57) Peter denied, saying, "Woman, I do not know him."

(58) A little later another person saw him and said, "You are one of them."

But Peter said, "Man, I am not!"

(59) About an hour later another man emphatically asserted, saying, "Truly this man was with him, for he is a Galilean."

(60) But Peter said, "Man, I don't know what you are talking about!" While he was speaking a rooster crowed.

(61) The Lord turned and looked at Peter, and Peter remembered that the Lord had told him, "Before the rooster crows today, you will deny me three times." (62) Then Peter went outside and wept bitterly.

(63) The men in charge mocked and beat Jesus. (64) Blindfolding him, they questioned him, "Prophesy! Who tagged you?" (65) They spoke many other insulting things against him.

(66) At the dawn of day the assembly of the elders of the people came together, including the chief priests and scribes, and they led him to the council. (67) They said to Jesus, "If you are the Christ, tell us."

(68) He replied, "If I tell you, you will not believe, and if I question you, you will not answer. (69) But from now on the Son of man will be sitting at the right hand of the power of God."

(70) And they all said, "Therefore, are you the Son of God?"

He replied to them, "I am as you say."

(71) They said, "Do we need any more evidence? We ourselves have heard it from his own lips."

Luke 23:1-56

(1) The entire assembly brought Jesus to Pilate. (2) They began to accuse him, saying, "We found this man misleading our nation, forbidding us to give tribute to Caesar and saying that he himself is Christ a king."

(3) Pilate questioned him, "Are you the king of the Jews?" Jesus replied, "Yes, I am."

(4) Pilate said to the chief priests and to the people, "I do not find this man guilty of any crime."

(5) They kept insisting, "He stirs up the people teaching all over Judea. He began in Galilee and has come here."

(6) When Pilate heard this he asked if the man was a Galilean. (7) And when he learned that he was under Herod's jurisdiction, he sent him to Herod, who was also in Jerusalem.

(8) When Herod saw Jesus, he rejoiced greatly, for he had wanted to

see him for a long time, because he had heard about him, and he hoped to see him perform a miracle. (9) He questioned him with many words, but Jesus did not answer him. (10) The chief priests and scribes were standing there vigorously accusing him. (11) Herod despised Jesus, and with his bodyguards, mocked him. They put gorgeous clothing upon him and sent him back to Pilate. (12) Herod and Pilate became friends that day — previously they had been enemies.

(13) Pilate called together the chief priests and the rulers and the people (14) and said to them, "You brought to me this man as one who was inciting the people to rebellion. I have examined him in your presence and I have found no basis for your allegations. (15) And neither did Herod, because he sent him back to us. It is obvious that this man has done nothing deserving death. (16) Therefore, after chastising him, I will release him."

(18) The whole crowd cried out, "Take this man and release to us Barabbas." (19) (This man had been thrown into prison for causing an insurrection in the city and for murder.) (20) Pilate, wishing to release Jesus, appealed to them again. (21) But they kept shouting, "Crucify, crucify him."

(22) A third time he said to them, "What evil has this man done? I have found nothing in him deserving the death penalty. Therefore, I will chastise him and release him."

(23) But they kept insisting with loud voices and demanding that he be crucified, and their voices prevailed. (24) So Pilate gave in to their demands. (25) He released the one who had caused insurrection and murder and had been thrown into prison, the one they had asked for, and he delivered Jesus to their will.

(26) As they led Jesus away, they laid hold on a certain Cyrenian named Simon who was coming from the country. They placed the cross on him to carry it behind Jesus. (27) A great crowd of people followed him, and the women were beating their breasts and grieving for him. (28) Jesus turned to them and said, "Daughters of Jerusalem, do not weep over me, but weep for yourselves and your children, (29) for the days are coming when the cry will be 'Happy are the sterile, and those who never bore children or nursed them!' (30) Then they will begin to say to the mountains, 'Fall on us,' and to the hills, 'cover us.' (31) For if they do these things when the tree is green, what will happen when it is dry?"

(32) Two criminals were also led away with Jesus to be crucified. (33) When they came to the place called Kranion, they crucified him with the criminals, one on the right and one of the left. (34) Jesus said, "Father, forgive them, for they do not know what they are doing." They divided his garments by casting lots.

(35) The people stood by watching, but the rulers were mocking him, saying, "He saved others; let him save himself if he is the Christ of God, the chosen one!"

(36) The soldiers also made fun of him as they offered him vinegar.

(37) They said, "If you are the King of The Jews, save yourself."

(38) There was an inscription over his head: "This is the King of the Jews."

(39) One of the dying criminals taunted him, saying, "Are you not the Christ? Save yourself and us!"

(40) But the other one, rebuking him, said, "Do you not fear God because you are condemned to die like him? (41) We deserve our punishment, for we are receiving the due rewards of our deeds, but this man has done nothing wrong."

(42) Then he said, "Jesus, remember me when you come into your kingdom."

(43) Jesus replied, "I assure you, today you will be with me in paradise."

(44) It was now about twelve o'clock and darkness came over all the land until three o'clock, (45) for the sun stopped shining; and the curtain in the sanctuary was split in two.

(46) Jesus called out in a loud voice, "Father, into your hands I commit my spirit." Then he expired.

(47) The centurion, seeing what had happened, glorified God, saying, "Certainly this man was righteous!"

(48) When all the people who had come together to see the show saw what had happened, they went home beating their breasts. (49) All the friends of Jesus and the women who came with him from Galilee were standing at a distance watching everything.

(50) There was a good and upright man named Joseph, who was a member of the Sanhedrin, (51) who had not agreed with the actions of the council. He was from Arimathea, a city of the Jews, and he was looking expectantly for the reign of God. (52) This man came to Pilate and asked for the body of Jesus. (53) He took it down and wrapped it in linen and placed it in a tomb hewn out of a rock where no one had ever been buried. (54) It was the day of Preparation and the Sabbath was about to begin.

(55) The women who had come with Jesus from Galilee saw the tomb and how his body was buried. (56) They went home to prepare spices and perfumes. On the Sabbath they rested in obedience to the law.

Luke 24:1-53

(1) On the first day of the week, at the break of dawn, the women came to the tomb bringing spices they had prepared. (2) They found the stone rolled away from the tomb, (3) but when they went in, they did not find the body of Jesus. (4) They were confused about this, and suddenly two men stood by them in flashing robes, (5) and being terrified they bowed their faces to the ground. The men said to them, "Why do you seek the living among the dead? (6) He is not here, but he has been raised up. Remember

how he told you when you were in Galilee (7) that the Son of man must be delivered into the hands of sinful men, and be crucified, and rise again on the third day." (8) They remembered his words.

(9) On their return from the tomb, they reported to all the Eleven and to all the rest what had happened. (10) The women were Mary Magdalene, Joanna, Mary the mother of James, and the other women, who told these things to the apostles. (11) Their words sounded to them like nonsense, and they refused to believe them. (12) But Peter got up and ran to the tomb; and stooping down, he saw the strips of linen lying by them, and he went away wondering what had happened.

(13) On that day two of the disciples were going to Emmaus, a village about seven miles from Jerusalem. (14) They were talking to one another about the things that had happened. (15) In the course of their discussion, Jesus himself came and walked with them, (16) but their eyes were blinded as to his identity.

(17) He said to them, "What are you talking about as you are walking?"

They stood still with sad faces, (18) and one of them, Cleopas, by name, said to him, "Are you the only stranger in Jerusalem who does not know what has recently happened there?"

(19) He said to them, "What things?"

They said to him, "The things concerning Jesus of Nazareth, who was a prophet mighty in action and words before God and all the people. (20) Our chief priests and rulers delivered him up to be sentenced to death, and they crucified him. (21) We were hoping that he was the one to redeem Israel. Besides all this, today is the third day since this happened. (22) Moreover, some of our women brought us some astonishing news. They were at the tomb at the break of dawn, (23) and they did not find his body. Instead, they came back saying that they had seen angels who said that he was alive. (24) Some of the ones who were with us went to the tomb and found it just as the women had said, but they did not see him."

(25) Jesus said to them, "O foolish men, and slow of heart to believe all the things spoken by the prophets! (26) Was it not necessary for Christ to suffer and enter into his glory?" (27) Then beginning with Moses and the prophets, he interpreted for them all the Scriptures concerning himself.

(28) They drew near the village of their destination, but Jesus appeared to continue on. (29) They prevailed upon him, saying, "Remain with us, because the sun is setting, and it will soon be night." So he went in with them.

(30) As they were reclining, Jesus took a loaf, and blessed and broke it, and gave it to them. (31) Then they opened their eyes and recognized him, and he disappeared. (32) They said to one another, "Did not our hearts burn within us as he opened up the scriptures while we were walking on the way?"

(33) They immediately got up and returned to Jerusalem; and they

found the Eleven gathered together and others with them, (34) who said, "Truly, the Lord has risen and has appeared to Simon!" (35) Then they told them what had happened on the road and how they recognized him as he broke the bread.

(36) As they were talking, Jesus appeared in their midst and said to them, "Peace to you."

(37) They became exceedingly terrified, because they thought they saw a ghost. (38) Jesus said to them, "Why are you troubled with disturbing thoughts? (39) See my hands and my feet that it is I, myself. Touch me and see. A ghost does not have flesh and bones." (41) They were disbelieving, yet they were filled with reverence and joy, and Jesus said to them, "Do you have anything here to eat?" (42) They gave him a piece of broiled fish, (43) and he took and ate it in their presence.

(44) Then he said to them, "When I was with you I told you that all things written concerning me in the Law of Moses, the prophets and the Psalms must be fulfilled." (45) Then he opened up their minds so that they could understand the Scriptures.

(46) He said to them, "Thus it has been written that the Christ must suffer and rise from the dead on the third day, (47) and that repentance and forgiveness of sins should be proclaimed in his name to all the nations, beginning at Jerusalem. (48) You are witnesses of these things. (49) I will send the promise of my Father upon you, but stay in the city until you are clothed with divine power."

(50) Jesus led them to Bethany and lifted up his hands and blessed them. (51) As he was blessing them he departed from them. (52) They returned to Jerusalem with great joy, (53) and they were continually in the temple praising God.

Introduction to John

John the apostle ("the disciple whom Jesus loved" John 13:13) wrote the gospel of John; however, his name is not mentioned. John was a Jew so he knew the hostility between the Jews and the Samaritans. He was acquainted with the Jewish customs and their concern about the law and the traditions of the elders, especially about the laws of the Sabbath.

The gospel was probably written toward the end of the first century (c. 85 A.D.). This was the view of the early church fathers. John tells us that his purpose in writing the gospel is that those who read will believe and be saved (John 20:31). John is more concerned about the spiritual and less about the formal and ritual. John tells us about the new birth (John 3:3) but has nothing to say about baptism; he tells us about foot washing (John 13:5) but nothing about the Lord's Supper.

John was a fisherman before be became a disciple of Jesus. So we do not expect him to have the vocabulary of a doctor, like Luke, or a lawyer, like Paul, or a government employee, like Matthew. But no one was more profound with the truth about eternal things than John.

The words of John were smaller than the words of Luke or of Matthew. John had about 8 words on each line; Matthew had about 7 and 1/2 words and Luke had about 7. In the Gospel of John there were 15,631 words with 1,021 different words (a new word every 15.3 words); in the Gospel of Matthew there were 18,348 words used with 1,683 different words (a new word every 10.9 words); In the Gospel of Luke there were 19,459 words with 2,044 different words (a new word every 9.5 words).

John 1:1-51

(1) The Word was in the beginning, and the Word was with God, and the Word was divine. (2) This one was originally with God. (3) Through him all things came to be, and apart from him not one thing came to be which was made. (4) In him was life, and the life was the light of mankind. (5) And the light shines in the darkness, and the darkness did not master it.

(6) There was a man named John sent from God. (7) This man came to be a witness, that he might witness concerning the light that all men might believe through him. (8) He was not that light, but that he might witness concerning the light. (9) The true light, which enlightens every man, was coming into the world. (10) He was in the world, and the world came to be through him, yet the world did not know him. (11) He came to his own, but his own did not accept him. (12) But as many as received him, He gave them the power to become children of God—to the ones believing in his name, (13) who were born not of the will of the flesh nor of the will of man but of God.

(14) And the Word became flesh and dwelt among us, and we beheld the glory of him, as the glory of the only begotten from the Father, full of grace and truth.

(15) John witnessed concerning him and cried out saying: "This man was He whom I said, 'The one coming after me, has come before me, because He was before me.' " (16) Because from the fullness from him we all received, even grace upon grace. (17) For the law was given through Moses; grace and truth came through Jesus Christ. (18) No one has ever seen God; the only begotten of God, being in the bosom of the Father, that one revealed him.

(19) And this is the witness of John, when the Jews sent to him from Jerusalem priests and Levites that they might ask him, "Who are you?" (20) He confessed and did not deny, but plainly declared, "I am not the Christ."

(21) And they asked him, "What then? Are you Elijah?"

And he said, "I am not."

"Are you the prophet?"

And he answered, "No."

(22) Therefore they said to him, "Who are you? Give us an answer that we may give to the ones having sent us. What do you say concerning yourself?"

(23) He said: "I am a voice crying in the wilderness, make straight the way of the Lord, as the Prophet Isaiah said."

(24) Now the ones having been sent were of the Pharisees. (25) And they questioned him and said to him, "Why then do you baptize since you are not the Christ, not Elijah, nor the prophet?"

(26) And John answered them saying, "I baptize in water. Among you stands one whom you do not know, (27) the one coming after me, of whom I am not worthy to loosen the strap of his sandal." (28) These things happened in Bethany where John was baptizing.

(29) The next day John saw Jesus coming toward him, and he said, "Behold, the Lamb of God, who is taking the sin of the world. (30) This is he as to whom I said, 'After me comes a man who is before me, because he was before me.' (31) And I did not know him, but that he might be manifest to Israel I came baptizing in water."

(32) And John witnessed saying, "I saw the spirit coming down as a dove from heaven, and he remained upon him. (33) And I did not know him, but the one sending me to baptize in water said to me, 'In whomever you see the spirit coming down and remaining upon, this is the one baptizing in the Holy Spirit.' (34) And I have seen, and have witnessed that this is the Son of God."

(35) Again the next day John stood with two of his disciples. (36) And looking at Jesus walking he said, "Behold, the Lamb of God!"

(37) The two disciples heard him speaking and they followed Jesus. (38) And Jesus, turning, beholding them following him, said to them, "What do you seek?"

And they said to him, "Rabbi (which means Teacher), where do you stay?"

(39) He said to them, "Come and you will see." Therefore they went and saw where he was staying, and they remained with him that day. It was about the tenth hour. (40) One of the two hearing John and following him was Andrew, the brother of Simon Peter. (41) This one first found his own brother and said to him, "We have found the Messiah" (which means Christ).

(42) He led him to Jesus. Jesus, looking at him, said, "You are Simon the son of John. You shall be called Cephas" (which means Rock).

(43) The next day Jesus wished to go forth into Galilee, and he found Philip. And Jesus said to him, "Follow me."

(44) Now Philip was from Bethsaida, the city of Andrew and Peter. Philip found Nathaniel and said to him, (45) "We have found him of whom Moses in the law and the prophets wrote, Jesus son of Joseph, from Nazareth."

(46) And Nathaniel said to him, "Can anything good come out of Nazareth?" Philip said to him, "Come and see."

(47) Jesus saw Nathaniel coming to him, and said, concerning him, "Behold, truly an Israelite in whom is no guile!"

(48) Nathaniel said to him, "Whence do you know me?" Jesus answered and said to him, "Before Philip called you, being under the fig tree, I saw you."

(49) Nathaniel answered him, "Rabbi, you are the Son of God, you are the king of Israel."

(50) Jesus answered and said to him, "Because I told you that I saw you under the fig tree, do you believe? You shall see greater things than these."

(51) And he said to him, "Truly, truly I say to you, you shall see the heaven, having been opened, and the angels of God ascending and descending upon the Son of Man."

John 2:1-25

(1) And on the third day there was a wedding in Cana of Galilee, and the mother of Jesus was there. (2) Jesus and his disciples were also invited to the wedding. (3) And being in need of wine, the mother of Jesus said to him, "They have no wine."

(4) And Jesus said to her, "What is that to me and to you, woman? My hour has not yet come."

(5) His mother said to the servants, "Do whatever he tells you."

(6) Now six stone water jars were sitting there according to the purifying of the Jews, each containing two or three measures. (7) Jesus said to them, "Fill the water jars with water." And they filled them up to the top.

(8) And he said to them, "Draw now and carry to the master of the

feast." And they did. (9) Now when the master of the feast tasted the water having become wine he did not know where it came from (but the servants having drawn the water knew). The master of the feast called the bridegroom (10) and said to him, "All men first set forth the good wine, and when they are inebriated, the inferior. You have kept the good wine until now." (11) This, the beginning of the signs of Jesus, he did in Cana of Galilee. And he manifested his glory and his disciples believed in him.

(12) After this, he and his mother and brothers and his disciples went down to Capernaum, and there they remained for a few days.

(13) And the Passover of the Jews was at hand, and Jesus went up to Jerusalem. (14) And he found in the temple those who were selling the oxen and sheep and pigeons, and the coin dealers sitting. (15) And having made a whip of ropes, he cast out the coins of the money changers and he overturned the tables. (16) And to the ones selling the pigeons he said, "Take these things hence. Do not make my Father's house a house of merchandise."

(17) His disciples remembered that it was written, "The zeal for your house will consume me."

(18) Then answered the Jews and said to him, "What sign do you show us, because you do these things?"

(19) Answered Jesus, "Destroy this temple and in three days I will raise it."

(20) Then the Jews said, "This temple was built in forty-six years and you will raise it in three days?"

(21) But he spoke about the temple of his body. (22) Therefore when he was raised from the dead, his disciples remembered that he had said this, and they believed the Scripture and the word that Jesus had spoken.

(23) Now when he was in Jerusalem at the Passover Feast, many believed in his name, beholding the signs that he was doing. (24) But Jesus did not commit himself to them because he knew all men, (25) and because he had no need that anyone should witness concerning man; for he knew what was in man.

John 3:1-36

(1) There was a man of the Pharisees, named Nicodemus, a ruler of the Jews. (2) This man came to Jesus by night and said to him, "Rabbi, we know that you are a teacher come from God; for no one can do these signs which you do, unless God is with Him."

(3) Jesus answered and said to him, "Truly, truly, I say to you, except one is born from above, he cannot see the kingdom of God."

(4) Nicodemus said to him, "How can a man, being old, be born? Can he enter a second time into his mother's womb to be born?"

(5) Jesus answered, "Truly, truly, I say to you, unless one is born of water and spirit, he cannot enter the kingdom of God. (6) That which is born

of the flesh is flesh, and that which is born of the spirit is spirit. (7) Do not marvel because I told you, 'You must be born from above.' (8) The wind blows where it wishes, and you hear the sound of it but you do not know where it comes from and where it goes. So is everyone having been born of the spirit."

(9) Nicodemus answered and said, "How is this possible?"

(10) Jesus answered and said to him, "Are you the teacher of Israel and do not know these things? (11) Truly, truly, I say to you, we speak of what we know, and we witness of what we have seen, but our witness you do not receive. (12) Since I told you the earthly things and you do not believe, how will you believe if I tell you the heavenly things? (13) And no one has gone up into heaven except the one coming down from heaven, the Son of Man, (14) and as Moses lifted up the serpent in the desert, so must the Son of Man be lifted up, (15) that everyone believing in him may have eternal life.

(16) "For God so loved the world that he gave his only begotten Son, that everyone believing in him may not perish but may have eternal life. (17) For God did not send the Son into the world to condemn the world, but that the world might be saved through him. (18) The one believing in him is not condemned, but the one not believing has already been condemned, because he has not believed in the name of the only begotten Son of God. (19) This is the condemnation, that the light has come into the world and men loved darkness rather than the light, for their deeds were evil. (20) For everyone doing evil hates the light, and does not come to the light, lest his deeds should be exposed, (21) but the one doing the truth comes to the light, that his works may be manifested that the works have been performed in God."

(22) After these things Jesus and his disciples came into the Judean land, and there remained with them and baptized. (23) And John was also baptizing at Aenon near Salim, because much water was there, and people came and were baptized. (24) For John had not yet been cast into prison. (25) Then there was a discussion of the disciples of John with a Jew about purifying. (26) And they came to John and said to him, "Rabbi, he who was with you beyond the Jordan, to whom you bore witness, behold this man baptizes and all men are coming to him!"

(27) John answered and said, "A man cannot receive anything unless it has been given to him from heaven. (28) You bear me witness that I said, 'I am not the Christ, but that I have been sent before that one.' (29) The one having the bride is the bridegroom; but the friend of the bridegroom, standing and hearing him, rejoices greatly at the bridegroom's voice. Therefore this joy of mine has been fulfilled. (30) That one must increase, but I must decrease.

(31) "The one coming from above is over all; the one being on the earth is of the earth and speaks of the earth. The one coming from heaven is over all. (32) What He has seen and heard, this he witnesses to, and the witness of him no man receives. (33) The one receiving his witness has

certified that God is true. (34) For he whom God sent speaks the words of God, for he does not give the spirit by measure. (35) The Father loves the Son, and has given all things into his hands. (36) The one believing in the Son has eternal life; but the one disobeying the Son will not see life, but the wrath of God abides upon him."

John 4:1-54

(1) When Jesus knew that the Pharisees had heard that he was making and baptizing more disciples than John (2) (though Jesus himself did not baptize, but his disciples), (3) he left Judea and went into Galilee. (4) He had to pass through Samaria. (5) He came therefore to a city called Sychar, near the field that Jacob gave to his son Joseph. (6) Jacob's well was there. Therefore Jesus, having become fatigued from the journey, sat on the well. It was about the sixth hour.

(7) A woman of Samaria came to draw water. Jesus said to her, "Give me a drink." (8) For his disciples had gone into the city to buy food.

(9) The Samaritan woman said to him, "How can you being a Jew, ask a drink from me, being a Samaritan woman?" (For Jews do not associate with Samaritans.)

(10) Jesus answered and said to her, "If you knew the gift of God, and who it is saying to you, 'Give me a drink,' you would have asked and he would have given you living water."

(11) She said to him, "Sir, you do not have a bucket and the well is deep; from what source do you have the living water? (12) Are you greater than our father Jacob, who gave us the well and drank from it himself, and his sons and his cattle?"

(13) Jesus answered and said to her, "Everyone drinking of this water will thirst again, (14) but whoever drinks of the water which I will give him will never thirst, but the water I will give him will become in him a fountain springing to eternal life."

(15) The woman said to him, "Sir, give me this water that I may not thirst, nor come here to draw."

(16) He said to her, "Go, call your husband, and come here."

(17) The woman answered and said to him, "I have no husband." Jesus said to her, "Well you say, 'I have no husband'; (18) for you had five husbands, and he whom you now have is not your husband; thus you said truly."

(19) The woman said to him, "Sir, I perceive that you are a prophet. (20) Our fathers worshipped in this mountain; and you say it is in Jerusalem where it is necessary to worship."

(21) Jesus said to her, "Believe me, woman, the hour is coming when neither in this mountain nor in Jerusalem will you worship the Father. (22) You worship what you do not know; we worship what we know, because

salvation is from the Jews. (23) But the hour is coming, and now is, when the true worshippers will worship the Father in spirit and truth; for such the father seeks to worship him. (24) God is spirit, and those who worship him must worship in spirit and truth."

(25) The woman said to him, "I know that the Messiah is coming (being interpreted Christ); when that one comes, he will show us all things."

(26) Jesus said to her, "I, the one speaking to you, am he."

(27) At this time his disciples came and marveled that he was speaking with a woman; however no one said, "What do you seek or why do you speak with her?"

(28) So the woman left her water jar and went into the city, and she said to the men, (29) "Come, see a man who told me all that I ever did; is not this the Christ?"

(30) They went forth from the city and came to him.

(31) In the meantime, his disciples urged him saying, "Rabbi, eat."

(32) But he said to them, "I have food to eat which you do not know about."

(33) Therefore the disciples said to one another, "Has anyone brought him food?"

(34) Jesus said to them, "My food is to do the will of the one having sent me and to finish his work. (35) Do you not say that the harvest comes in four months? Behold, I tell you, lift up your eyes and behold the fields because they are white to harvest. (36) Already the one reaping receives wages and gathers fruit to eternal life, so that the one sowing and the one reaping may rejoice together. (37) For in this the word is true 'One is sowing and another is reaping.' (38) I sent you to reap what you have not worked for; others have worked, and you have entered into their labor."

(39) And out of that city many of the Samaritans believed in him because of the word of the woman, witnessing, "He told me all that I ever did." (40) So when the Samaritans came to him, they asked him to remain with them; and he remained there two days. (41) And many more believed because of his word.

(42) They said to the woman, "We no longer believe because of your witness, for we have heard for ourselves, and we know that this man is truly the Savior of the world."

(43) Now after two days he went forth from there to Galilee. (44) For Jesus himself witnessed that a prophet has no honor in his own native country. (45) So when he came to Galilee, the Galileans received him, having seen all things that he had done in Jerusalem at the feast; for they also had gone to the feast.

(46) Then he came again to Cana of Galilee, where he had made the water wine. And there was a certain royal official whose son was sick in Capernaum. (47) And this man, hearing that Jesus had come from Judea to Galilee, went to him and requested that he come down and cure his son, for he was about to die.

(48) Therefore Jesus said to him, "Except you see signs and wonders you will not believe."

(49) The royal official said to him, "Sir, come down before my child dies!"

(50) Jesus said to him, "Go, your son lives."

The man believed the word, which Jesus said to him, and he went. (51) As he was going down his slaves met him saying that the boy lives. (52) Therefore he inquired of the hour when he began to get better. Then they said to him, "Yesterday at the seventh hour the fever left him."

(53) Therefore, the father knew that was the hour in which Jesus had said to him, "Your son lives"; and he believed and his whole household.

(54) This was the second sign Jesus did having come out of Judea into Galilee.

John 5:1-47

(1) After these things there was a feast of the Jews, and Jesus went up to Jerusalem. (2) Now there is in Jerusalem at the sheepgate a swimming pool, in Hebrew called Bethzatha, having five porches. (3) In these lay a multitude of invalids, blind, lame and withered. (5) And a certain man was there who had been ill for thirty-eight years. (6) Jesus, seeing this man lying and knowing that he had been there a long time, said to him, "Do you wish to become whole?"

(7) And the sick man answered, "Sir, I have no man to put me into the swimming pool when the water is troubled; but while I am coming another steps down before me."

(8) Jesus said to him, "Rise, take your pallet and walk."

(9) And immediately the man became whole, and he took his pallet and walked. Now that day was the Sabbath.

(10) Therefore the Jews said to the one having been healed, "It is the Sabbath, and it is not lawful for you to carry your pallet."

(11) But he answered them, "The one making me whole said to me, 'Take your pallet and walk.' "

(12) They asked him, "Who is the man who said to you, 'Take and walk?' "

(13) But the man who had been healed did not know who it was, for Jesus withdrew as there was a crowd in the place. (14) After these things Jesus found him in the temple and he said to him, "Behold, you are whole! Sin no longer lest something worse happens to you."

(15) The man went away and told the Jews that it was Jesus who had made him whole. (16) Therefore the Jews persecuted Jesus because he did these things on a Sabbath.

(17) But Jesus answered them, "My Father still works, and I work." (18) Therefore, because of this the Jews sought all the more to kill him, because he not only broke the Sabbath but also said that God was his Father,

making himself equal to God.

(19) Therefore Jesus answered and said to them, "Truly, truly, I say to you, the Son can do nothing of himself, except what he sees the Father doing; for whatever that one does, the Son also does likewise. (20) For the Father loves the Son and shows him all things which he does, and greater than these works he will show him, that you may marvel. (21) For as the Father raises the dead and gives them life, so also the Son gives life to whom he wills. (22) For the Father judges no one, but he has given judgment to the Son, (23) that all men may honor the Son as they honor the Father. The one not honoring the Son does not honor the Father who sent him. (24) Truly, truly, I say to you, the one hearing my word and believing the one having sent me has eternal life, and he comes not into judgment but has passed out of death into life. (25) Truly, truly, I say to you, an hour is coming and now is, when the dead will hear the voice of the Son of God and the ones hearing will live. (26) For as the Father has life in himself, so also the Son he gave to have life in himself. (27) And he gave him authority to execute judgment because he is the Son of Man.

(28) "Do not marvel at this, because an hour is coming when all the ones in the tombs will hear his voice— (29) the ones having done good will come forth to a resurrection of life, and the ones having done evil to a resurrection of judgment. (30) I can do nothing myself; I judge as I hear, and my judgment is just, because I do not seek my will but the will of the one having sent me.

(31) "If I witness concerning myself, my witness is not valid; (32) there is another one witnessing concerning me, and I know that the witness which he witnesses concerning me is true.

(33) "You have sent to John and he has witnessed the truth, (34) but the witness I receive is not from man; I say these things that you may be saved. (35) That man was a burning and shining lamp, and you were willing to rejoice for an hour in his light. (36) But the witness I have is greater than John; for the works, which the Father has given me to finish, these very works I do, witness that the Father has sent me. (37) And the Father having sent me has witnessed concerning me. His voice you have never heard nor his form you have never seen, (38) and his word is not abiding in you, because the one he sent you do not believe. (39) You search the Scriptures because you think that in them you have eternal life; and the Scriptures are witnessing concerning me; (40) yet you do not wish to come to me that you may have life.

(41) "I do not receive glory from men. (42) But I know that you do not have the love of God in yourselves . (43) I have come in the name of my Father and you do not receive me; if another comes in his own name, that one you will receive. (44) How can you believe, receiving glory from one another, and the glory from the only God you do not seek? (45) Do not think that I will accuse you to my father. There is one accusing you: Moses, in whom you have hoped. (46) For if you believed Moses, you would have

believed me; for that one wrote concerning me. (47) But if you do not believe his writings, how will you believe my words?"

John 6:1-71

(1) After this Jesus went across the Sea of Galilee (Tiberius). (2) And a large crowd followed him, because they saw the signs which he did on the ailing ones. (3) And Jesus went up to the mountain and there sat with his disciples. (4) Now the Passover, the feast of the Jews, was at hand.

(5) Then Jesus, lifting up his eyes beholding the large crowd coming toward him, said to Philip, "Whence can we buy bread that these people may eat?" (6) This he said to test him; for he knew what he was about to do.

(7) Philip answered him, "Two hundred denarii would not buy enough bread for each to receive a little."

(8) Andrew, one of his disciples, the brother of Simon Peter, said to him, (9) "There is a lad here who has five barley loaves and two fish; but what are they among so many?"

(10) Jesus said, "Make the people recline." Now there was much grass in the place. Therefore the men reclined, in number about five thousand. (11) Then Jesus took the loaves and having given thanks distributed to the ones lying down; so also the fish, as much as they desired.

(12) Now when they were filled he told his disciples, "Gather up the leftover fragments that nothing may be lost." (13) So they gathered the fragments of the five barley loaves, which were left over by the ones having eaten, and filled twelve baskets.

(14) Therefore the people seeing the sign which he did said, "This is truly the prophet, the one coming into the world." (15) Jesus therefore, knowing that they were about to come and seize him that they might make him king, departed to the mountain by himself.

(16) When evening came, his disciples went down to the sea, (17) and embarking in a boat came across the sea to Capernaum. And it was now dark, and Jesus had not yet come to them, (18) and the sea was agitated as a great wind blew. (19) Then, having rowed about three or four miles, they saw Jesus walking upon the water and coming near the boat. And they were frightened. (20) But he said to them, "It is I, fear not." (21) They wished therefore to take him into the boat, and immediately they were at the land to which they were going.

(22) On the next day the crowd, standing on the other side of the sea, saw that there was only one boat there, and that Jesus had not entered into the boat with his disciples, but that his disciples had gone away alone. (23) Other boats came from Tiberius near the place where they ate the bread after the Lord had given thanks.

(24) Therefore when the crowd saw that Jesus was not there or his disciples, they embarked in the boats and came to Capernaum seeking Jesus.

(25) And finding him across the sea, they said to him, "Rabbi, when did you come here?"

(26) Jesus answered them and said, "Truly, truly, I say to you, you seek me not because you saw signs but because you ate of the loaves and were satisfied. (27) Work not for the perishing food, but for the food remaining to eternal life, which the Son of Man will give you. For this one God the Father sealed."

(28) Therefore they said to him, "What may we do that we may work the works of God?"

(29) Jesus answered and said to them, "This is the work of God, that you believe in him whom he has sent."

(30) They said to him, "What signs then will you give that we may see and believe you? What work will you do? (31) Our fathers ate manna in the desert, as it is written, 'He gave them bread from heaven to eat.' "

(32) Therefore Jesus said to them, "Truly, truly, I say to you, it is not Moses who has given you the bread from heaven. (33) For the bread of God is the one coming down from heaven and gives life to the world."

(34) Then they said to him, "Lord, give us this bread always."

(35) Jesus said to them, "I am the bread of life. The one coming to me shall not be hungry, and the one believing in me shall never thirst. (36) But I told you and you have seen me yet you do not believe. (37) All that the Father gives me will come to me, and the one coming to me I will not cast outside. (38) Because I have come down from heaven, not that I might do my will, but the will of the one having sent me. (39) And this is the will of the one having sent me, that all of which he has given me, that none shall be lost, but all shall be raised up in the last day. (40) For this is the will of my Father, that everyone beholding the Son and believing in him shall have life eternal, and I will raise him up in the last day."

(41) Therefore the Jews grumbled at him because he said, "I am the bread having come down from heaven."

(42) And they said, "Is not this Jesus, the son of Joseph, whose father and mother we know? How does he now say, 'I have come down from heaven?' "

(43) Jesus answered and said to them, "Do not grumble with one another. (44) No one can come to me unless the Father, the one having sent me, should draw him, and I will raise him up in the last day. (45) It is written in the prophets: 'And they shall be all taught of God.' Everyone hearing and learning from God comes to me. (46) Not that anyone has seen the Father, except the one being with God, this one has seen the father. (47) Truly, truly, I say to you, the one believing has eternal life. (48) I am the bread of life. (49) Our fathers ate the manna in the desert and died. (50) This is the bread coming down from heaven that a man may eat of it and not die. (51) I am the living bread coming down from heaven; if anyone eats of this bread, he will live forever. And the bread which I shall give for the life of the world is my flesh."

(52) Then the Jews quarreled with one another, saying, "How can this one give us his flesh to eat?"

(53) Therefore Jesus said to them, "Truly, truly, I say to you, unless you eat the flesh of the Son of Man and drink his blood, you have no life in yourselves. (54) The one eating my flesh and drinking my blood has eternal life and I will raise him up in the last day. (55) For my flesh is real food, and my blood is real drink. (56) The one eating my flesh and drinking my blood abides in me, and I in him. (57) As the living Father sent me, and I live because of the Father, also that one who feeds on me will live because of me. (58) This is the bread, having come down out of heaven, not as the fathers ate and died. The one eating this bread will live forever." (59) These things he said, teaching in a synagogue in Capernaum.

(60) Therefore, many of his disciples, hearing, said, "This is a hard word; who can understand it?"

(61) But Jesus, knowing in himself that his disciples grumbled about this, said to them, (62) "Then what if you see the Son of Man ascending where he was at first? The spirit is the thing quickening; the flesh is of no profit. (63) The words, which I have spoken to you, are spirit and life. (64) But there are some of you who do not believe." For from the beginning Jesus knew who did not believe and who was the one betraying him.

(65) And he said, "This is why I told you that no one can come to me unless it has been given to him by my Father."

(66) After this many of his disciples went back and no longer walked with him.

(67) Therefore Jesus said to the twelve, "Do you also wish to go away?"

(68) Simon Peter answered him, "Lord, to whom shall we go? You have the words of eternal life; (69) and we have believed and have known that you are the Holy One of God."

(70) Jesus answered them, "Did I not chose you, the twelve? And one of you is a devil." (71) Now he spoke of Judas the son of Simon Iscariot. For this one, being one of the twelve, was about to betray him.

John 7:1-53

(1) After this Jesus walked in Galilee, because he did not wish to walk in Judea for the Jews were seeking to kill him. (2) Now the Jewish Feast of Tabernacles was at hand.

(3) Therefore his brothers said to him, "Depart hence and go to Judea, that also your disciples may see the works you do. (4) For no one works in secret if he seeks to be known openly. If you do these things, manifest yourself to the world." (5) For his brothers did not believe in him.

(6) Therefore Jesus said to them, "My time has not yet come, but your time is always here. (7) The world cannot hate you, but it hates me

because I witness about it that its works are evil. (8) You go up to the feast; I am not going up to the feast, because my time has not yet been fulfilled." (9) So saying these things to them, he remained in Galilee.

(10) But when his brothers went up to the feast, then he also went up, not publicly, but in secret.

(11) Therefore the Jews sought him at the feast and said, "Where is that man?"

(12) And there was much murmuring about him in the crowds. Some said, "He is a good man."

Others said, "No, but he deceives the people." (13) However, no one spoke openly concerning him because of fear of the Jews.

(14) But in the middle of the feast Jesus went up to the temple and taught. (15) Then the Jews marveled, saying, "How is it that this man has learning, not having been taught?"

(16) Jesus answered them and said, "My teaching is not mine, but of the one having sent me; (17) if anyone wishes to do his will, he will know concerning the teaching, whether it is from God or if I speak from myself. (18) The one speaking from himself seeks his own glory; but the one seeking the glory of the one having sent him is true, and in him is no wickedness. (19) Did not Moses give you the law? But none of you keeps the law. Why do you seek to kill me?"

(20) The people answered and said, "You have a demon. Who seeks to kill you?"

(21) Jesus answered and said to them, "One work I did and you all marvel. (22) Because Moses gave you circumcision (not that it is from Moses but from the fathers), on a Sabbath you circumcise a man. (23) If a man receives circumcision on a Sabbath, so that the Law of Moses may not be broken, are you angry with me because I made a man healthy on a Sabbath? (24) Do not judge according to appearance, but judge with righteous judgment."

(25) Therefore some of the Jerusalemites said, "Is not this the man whom they are seeking to kill? (26) And behold, he speaks openly, and they say nothing to him! Perhaps the rulers truly know that this man is the Christ. (27) But we know where this man comes from, but when the Christ comes no one will know where he comes from."

(28) Therefore Jesus cried out in the temple, teaching and saying, "You know me, and you know where I come from; but from myself I have not come, but the one having sent me is true, whom you do not know. (29) I know him, because I am from him, and that one sent me."

(30) Therefore they sought to arrest him, but no one laid hands on him because his hour had not yet come.

(31) Now many of the people believed in him, and they said, "When the Christ comes, will he do more signs than this man has done?"

(32) The Pharisees heard the people murmuring these things

concerning him, and the chief priests and Pharisees sent officers that they might arrest him.

(33) Then Jesus said, "I shall be with you a little longer, then I will go to the one having sent me. (34) You will seek me but you will not find me, and where I am you cannot come."

(35) Therefore the Jews said to themselves, "Where is this man about to go that we shall not find him? Does he plan to go to the ones scattered among the Greeks and teach the Greeks? (36) What is this word which he said, 'You will seek me and you will not find me,' and, 'Where I am you cannot come'?"

(37) Now in the last day of the great feast Jesus stood and cried out, saying, "If anyone thirsts, let him come to me and drink. (38) The one believing in me, as the Scripture said, 'From his inner self shall flow rivers of living water.' " (39) Now this he said concerning the Spirit whom the ones believing were about to receive; for the Spirit had not yet been given, because Jesus had not yet been glorified.

(40) Some of the people therefore hearing these words said, "This man is truly the Prophet."

(41) Others said, "This man is the Christ."

But others said, "Shall Christ come from Galilee?"

(42) "Has not the Scripture said that the Christ will come from the seed of David and from Bethlehem the village where David was?" (43) So there was a division among the people because of him. (44) And some wanted to arrest him, but no one laid hands on him.

(45) Then the officers went to the chief priests and Pharisees, who said to them, "Why did you not bring him?"

(46) The officers answered, "Never has a man spoken as he speaks!"

(47) Therefore the Pharisees answered them, "Are you also led astray? (48) Have any of the rulers or the Pharisees believed in him? (49) But these people, not knowing the law, are cursed."

(50) Nicodemus, the one having just come to him before, being one of them, said to them, (51) "Does our law judge a man unless it first hears him and knows what he does?"

(52) They answered and said to him, "Are you also from Galilee? Search and you will see that a prophet never comes from Galilee."

(53) And they went each to his own house.

John 8:1-59

(1) But Jesus went to the Mount of Olives. (2) And early in the morning he again came to the temple, and all the people came to him, and sitting he taught them. (3) The scribes and Pharisees brought a woman having been caught in adultery, and standing her in the midst, (4) they said to him, "Teacher, this woman has been caught in the act of adultery. (5) Now

in the law Moses commanded us to stone such; therefore, what do you say?"

(6) But this they said tempting him, that they might have something to accuse him. But Jesus stooping down wrote with the finger in the earth. (7) And as they remained questioning him, he stood erect and said to them, "Let the sinless one of you cast the first stone." (8) And again stooping down he wrote in the earth. (9) And they, hearing, went away one by one, beginning with the older ones, and he was left alone, with the woman.

(10) And standing erect, Jesus said to her, "Woman, where are they? Has no one condemned you?"

(11) And she said, "No one, Lord."

And Jesus said to her, "Neither do I condemn you. Go, and sin no more."

(12) Jesus spoke to them again, saying, "I am the Light of the World; the one following me will not walk in darkness, but will have the Light of life."

(13) Therefore the Pharisees said to him, "You witness concerning yourself; your witness is not true."

(14) Jesus answered and said to them, "Even if I witness concerning myself, my witness is true, because I know where I came from and where I go. But you do not know where I came from or where I go.

(15) "You judge according to the flesh, I judge no one. (16) But even if I judge, my judgment is true, because I am not alone, but I am with the one having sent me, the Father. (17) And even in your law it has been written that the witness of two men is true; (18) I am the one witnessing concerning myself, and the Father, the one having sent me, witnesses concerning me."

(19) Then they said to him, "Where is your father?"

Jesus answered, "You know neither me or my Father; if you knew me you would have also known my Father." (20) These words he spoke in the treasury, teaching in the temple; and no one arrested him, because his hour had not yet come.

(21) Again he said to them, "I go and you will seek me, and you will die in your sin. Where I go you cannot come."

(22) Therefore the Jews said, "Will he kill himself, because he says, 'Where I go you cannot come'?"

(23) "You are of the things below, I am of the things above; you are of this world, I am not of this world. (24) Therefore I said to you that you will die in your sins; if you do not believe that I am he, you will die in your sins."

(25) Then they said to him, "Who are you?"

Jesus said to them, "Why should I speak to you at all? (26) I have many things to say and to judge concerning you. But the one having sent me is trustworthy, and what I heard from him I tell the world."

(27) They did not know that he spoke to them of the Father. (28) Jesus said, "When you lift up the Son of Man, then you will know that I am

he, and from myself I do nothing, but say exactly what my father taught me. (29) And the one having sent me is with me; he did not leave me alone, because I always do the things that are pleasing to him."

(30) Speaking these words, many believed in him. (31) Then Jesus said to the Jews who had believed in him, "If you continue in my words, you are truly my disciples, (32) and you will know the truth and the truth will make you free."

(33) They answered him, "We are the descendants of Abraham, and we have never been enslaved to anyone. How can you say that 'You will become free'?"

(34) Jesus answered them, "Truly, truly, I say to you, everyone continuing in sin is a slave to sin. (35) The son remains in the family forever, but the slave does not. (36) So if the Son sets you free, you will really be free. (37) I know that you are descendants of Abraham; yet you seek to kill me, because you have no room for my message. (38) I speak of what I have seen with the Father, and you do what you have heard from your father."

(39) They answered him, "Abraham is our father."

Jesus said to them, "If you were Abraham's children, you would do the works of Abraham. (40) But, as it is, you seek to kill me, a man who has told you the truth straight from God. Abraham did not do such things. (41) You do the works of your father."

Then they said to him, "We were not born of fornication. We have one father, God."

(42) Jesus said to them, "If God were your father, you would have loved me, for I came forth from God and now I am here, for I have not come of my own accord, but that one sent me. (43) Why do you not understand my language? It is because you are unable to understand what I say. (44) You are of your father the devil, and you wish to do the desires of your father. That one was a murderer from the beginning, and stands not in the truth, because truth is not in him. When he lies, he speaks out of his own nature, because he is a liar and the father of lies. (45) But because I tell you the truth, why do you not believe me? (46) Can anyone of you prove me guilty of sin? If I am telling you the truth, why do you not believe me? (47) The one being of God hears the words of God. The reason you do not hear is because you are not of God."

(48) The Jews answered him, "Are we not right in saying that you are a Samaritan and have a demon?"

(49) Jesus answered, "I do not have a demon, but I honor my father, and you dishonor me. (50) But I do not seek my glory; but there is one seeking it, and he is judging. (51) Truly, truly, I say to you, if anyone keeps my word he will never see death."

(52) Then the Jews said to him, "Now we know that you have a demon. Abraham died, and the prophets, and you say, 'If anyone keeps my word, he will never taste death.' (53) Are you greater than Abraham, who died? And the prophets died; who do you claim to be?"

(54) Jesus answered, "If I glorify myself, my glory is nothing; my Father is glorifying me, of whom you say, 'He is our God.' (55) But you have not known him, but I know him, and if I say that I do not know him, I shall be a liar like you, but I know him and keep his word.

(56) "Your father Abraham rejoiced that he should see my day, and he saw it, and he rejoiced!"

(57) The Jews then said to him, "You are not yet fifty years old, and you have seen Abraham?"

(58) Jesus said to them, "Truly, truly, I tell you, before Abraham was, I am." (59) Then they picked up stones to throw at him; but Jesus, unobserved, went out of the temple.

John 9:1-41

(1) And passing along, he saw a man blind from birth. (2) His disciples asked him, saying, "Rabbi, who sinned, this man or his parents, that he was born blind?" (3) Jesus answered, "Neither this man nor his parents sinned; but that the works of God might be manifest in him, (4) it is necessary for us to work the works of the one having sent me while it is day; the night comes when no one can work. (5) While I am in the world, I am the Light of the World."

(6) Having said these things, he spit on the ground and made clay from the spittle, and put the clay on the eyes of him, (7) and said to him, "Go, wash in the swimming pool of Siloam" (which means having been sent). Therefore he went and washed, and he returned seeing.

(8) Therefore the neighbors and the ones seeing him previously as a beggar said, "Is this not the man who sits and begs?"

(9) Some said, "This is he."

Others said, "No, but he is like him."

That one said, "I am he."

(10) Therefore they said to him, "Then how were your eyes opened?"

(11) That one answered, "The man called Jesus made clay and anointed my eyes and said to me, 'Go to Siloam and wash,' so, going and washing, I saw."

(12) They said to him, "Where is that one?"

He said, "I do not know."

(13) They brought the one who had been blind to the Pharisees. (14) Now it was a Sabbath day when Jesus made the clay and opened his eyes. (15) The Pharisees also asked him how he received his sight. And he said to them, "He put clay on my eyes, and I washed and I see."

(16) Then some of the Pharisees said, "This man is not from God because he does not keep the Sabbath."

But others said, "How can a sinful man do such things?" So there was a division among them.

(17) So, again they said to the blind man, "What do you say about him, because he opened your eyes."

And he said, "He is a prophet."

(18) The Jews did not believe that he had been blind and had received his sight until they called the parents of the one having received his sight; (19) and they asked them saying, "Is this your son whom you say that was born blind? How then does he now see?"

(20) Then his parents answered, and said, "We know that this is our son and that he was born blind; (21) but how he sees we do not know nor do we know who opened his eyes. Ask him, he is of age, and he will speak for himself." (22) The parents said these things because they feared the Jews; for the Jews had already agreed that if anyone should acknowledge him to be Christ he would be put out of the synagogue. (23) Therefore his parents said, "He is of age, ask him."

(24) So a second time they called the man who had been blind and said to him, "Give glory to God; we know that this man is a sinner."

(25) Then that one answered, "I do not know if he is a sinner; one thing I know, I was blind, now I see."

(26) They said to him, "What did he do to you? How did he open your eyes?"

(27) He answered them, "I have already told you, and you would not listen. Why do you wish to hear again? Do you wish to become his disciples?"

(28) And they reviled him and said, "You are a disciple of that man! We are disciples of Moses. (29) We know that God has spoken by Moses, but we do not know where this man comes from."

(30) The man answered and said to them, "In this is a marvelous thing! And you do not know where he comes from—yet he opened my eyes! (31) We know that God does not hear sinners, but he listens to anyone who is god-fearing and does his will. (32) From the ages it has never been heard that anyone opened the eyes of a man born blind. (33) If this man were not from God he could do nothing."

(34) They answered and said to him, "You were born in complete sin, and you teach us!" And they cast him out.

(35) Jesus heard that they had cast him out, and finding him, he said, "Do you believe in the Son of Man?"

(36) That one answered and said, "And who is he, Lord, that I may believe in him?"

(37) And Jesus said to him, "You have seen him, and that one speaking with you is he."

(38) And he said, "I believe, Lord," and he worshipped him.

(39) And Jesus said, "For judgment, I came into this world, that the ones not seeing may see and the ones seeing may become blind."

(40) Some of the Pharisees, being with him, heard this, and said to him, "Are we also blind?"

(41) Jesus said to them, "If you were blind you would have no guilt, but now, because you say, 'We see,' your sin remains.

John 10:1-42

(1) "Truly, truly, I say to you, the one not entering through the gate of the sheepfold, but climbs up by another way, is a thief and robber. (2) But the one entering through the gate is the shepherd of the sheep. (3) To this one the porter opens, and the sheep hear his voice, and he calls his own sheep by name and leads them out. (4) When he puts forth all his own, he goes before them, and sheep follow him because they know his voice. (5) But they will never follow a stranger, but they will flee from him, because they do not know the voice of strangers."

(6) Jesus told them this allegory, but they did not understand what he said to them. (7) Therefore Jesus said again, "Truly, truly, I say to you, I am the gate of the Sheep. (8) All who came before me are thieves and robbers, but the sheep did not listen to them. (9) I am the gate. If anyone enters through me, he will be saved, and he will go in and he will go out, and he will find pasture. (10) The thief comes only to steal and kill and destroy. I came that they may have life, and have it abundantly.

(11) "I am the Good Shepherd. The Good Shepherd lays down his life for the sheep. (12) The hireling, not being a shepherd who owns the sheep, sees the wolf coming and leaves the sheep, and the wolf seizes the flock and scatters it. (13) He is not concerned about the sheep because he is a hireling. (14) I am the Good Shepherd, and I know my sheep and my sheep know me. (15) As the Father knows me, even so I know the Father, and I lay down my life for the sheep. (16) And I have other sheep that are not of this fold. I must bring them also, and they will hear my voice. So there will be one flock, one shepherd. (17) Therefore the Father loves me because I lay down my life that I may take it again. (18) No one takes it from me, but I lay it down of my own accord. I have authority to lay it down, and I have authority to take it up again. I received this injunction from my father."

(19) Again there was a division because of these words. (20) Many of them said, "He has a demon and he raves. Why listen to him?"

(21) Others said, "These are not the words of one who has a demon. Can a demon open the eyes of the blind?"

(22) Then there was the Feast of Dedication in Jerusalem. It was winter, (23) and Jesus walked in the temple in the portico of Solomon. (24) Therefore the Jews surrounded him and said to him, "How long will you hold us in suspense? If you are the Christ, tell us plainly."

(25) Jesus answered them, "I told you, but you do not believe. The works which I do in the name of my Father, they bear witness concerning

me, (26) but you do not believe because you are not of my sheep. (27) My sheep listen to my voice, and I know them, and they follow me, (28) and I give them eternal life, and they will never perish. No one can seize them from my hand. (29) My Father, who has given them to me, is greater than all, and no one can snatch them out of my Father's hand. (30) The Father and I are one."

(31) Again the Jews picked up stones that they might stone him. (32) Jesus said to them, "I have shown you many good works from the Father; for which of these works do you stone me?"

(33) The Jews answered him, "Concerning a good work we do not stone you, but for blasphemy, and because you, being a man, make yourself God."

(34) Jesus answered them, "Is it not written in your law, 'I said you are gods?' (35) If he called them 'gods,' to whom the word of God came, and Scripture cannot be broken, (36) do you say of him whom the Father sanctified and sent into the world, 'You are blaspheming,' because I said, 'I am the Son of God'? (37) If I do not the works of my Father, do not believe me; (38) but if I do, even though you do not believe me, believe the works, that you may know and continue to know that the Father is in me, and I am in the Father." (39) Again they sought to arrest him, but he went forth out of their hands.

(40) And he went away again across the Jordan to the place where John at first had been baptizing, and he remained there. (41) And many came to him and said, "John did no miracles, but everything that John said about this man was true." (42) And many believed in him there.

John 11:1-57

(1) Now there was a certain ailing man, Lazarus, from Bethany, the village of Mary and Martha. (2) This Mary was the one anointing the Lord with ointment and wiping of his feet with her hair. (3) Therefore the sisters sent to him, saying, "Lord, behold, he whom you love is ill."

(4) And hearing, Jesus said, "This sickness is not to death, but for the glory of God —that the Son of God may be glorified through it."

(5) Now Jesus loved Martha and her sister and Lazarus. (6) So when he heard that he was ill, he then remained where he was for two days. (7) Then after this, he said to his disciples, "Let us go into Judea again."

(8) The disciples said to him, "Rabbi, the Jews are seeking to stone you, and you go again there?"

(9) Jesus answered, "Are there not twelve hours in the day? If anyone walks in the day, he does not stumble, for the light of this world he sees. (10) But if anyone walks in the night, he stumbles, because the light is not in him." (11) After saying these things, he said to them, "Lazarus our friend has fallen asleep, but I am going that I may waken him."

(12) Therefore the disciples said to him, "Lord, if he has fallen asleep, he will be healed."

(13) But Jesus spoke concerning his death, but those men thought that he was talking concerning the sleep of slumber.

(14) So then Jesus told them plainly, "Lazarus died, (15) and I rejoice because of you, that I was not there so that you may believe. But let us go to him."

(16) Then Thomas, called Twin, said to his fellow disciples, "Let us also go that we may die with him."

(17) Therefore Jesus, on his arrival, found that he had already been in the tomb four days. (18) Now Bethany was near Jerusalem—less than two miles away. (19) And many of the Jews had come to Martha and Mary to comfort them concerning their brother. (20) Therefore when Martha heard that Jesus was coming she met him, but Mary sat in the house.

(21) Then Martha said to Jesus, "Lord, if you had been here, my brother would not have died. (22) But even now I know that whatever things you ask of God, God will give to you."

(23) Jesus said to her, "Your brother will rise again."

(24) Martha said to him, "I know that he will rise again in the last day."

(25) Jesus said to her, "I am the resurrection and the life. The one believing in me, even if he should die, he will live. (26) And everyone living and believing in me shall never die. Do you believe this?"

(27) She said to him, "Yes, Lord, I believe that you are the Christ, the Son of God, the one coming into the World."

(28) And saying this, she went away and called her sister Mary, secretly saying, "The Teacher is here and he calls for you." (29) And when that one heard, she arose quickly and came to him.

(30) Now Jesus had not yet come into the village, but was still in the place where Martha had met him. (31) Therefore the Jews—the ones being with her in the house comforting her—seeing that Mary got up quickly, and went out, followed her, thinking that she was going to the tomb to mourn there. (32) Therefore Mary, when she came to where Jesus was, seeing him, fell at his feet, and said to him, "Lord, if you had been here my brother would not have died."

(33) Therefore when Jesus saw her weeping and the Jews coming with her weeping, he was agitated in spirit and grieved. (34) And he said, "Where have you laid him?"

They said to him, "Lord, come and see."

(35) Jesus shed tears.

(36) Then the Jews said, "Lo! How he loved him."

(37) But some of them said, "Could not this man who opened the eyes of the blind have kept this man from dying?"

(38) Jesus then being agitated in himself, came to the tomb. It was a cave and a stone was lying upon it. (39) Jesus said, "Take away the stone."

Martha, the sister of the one having died, said to him, "Lord, now he stinks, for it is the fourth day."

(40) Jesus said to her, "Have I not told you that if you believe you will see the glory of God?"

(41) Then they took away the stone, and Jesus lifted up his eyes and said, "Father, I thank you that you have heard me. (42) I know that you always hear me, but I said this for the benefit of the people standing around, that they may believe that you did send me."

(43) And saying these things, he cried out with a great voice, "Lazarus, come out!" (44) The dead man, his feet and hands bound with bandages and his face bound around with cloth, came out.

Jesus said to them, "Unbind him and let him go."

(45) Then many of the Jews, the ones coming to Mary and seeing what Jesus did, believed in him. (46) But some of them went away to the Pharisees and told them the things that Jesus did.

(47) Therefore the chief priests and the Pharisees assembled the Sanhedrin and said, "What are we doing? This man does many miracles. (48) If we let him continue in this way, all men will believe in him, and the Romans will come and take away both our place and the nation."

(49) But a certain one of them, Caiphas, who was high priest that year, said to them, "You know nothing, (50) nor do you realize that it is expedient that one man should die for the people rather than the whole nation perish."

(51) But he did not say this from his own accord, but being high priest that year he prophesied that Jesus was about to die for the nation, (52) and not for the nation only, but that the children of God, having been scattered, he might gather into one. (53) So from that day they plotted to kill him.

(54) Therefore Jesus no longer walked openly among the Jews, but went away from there into the country near the desert, to a city called Ephraim. And he remained there with his disciples.

(55) Now it was near the Passover of the Jews, and many went up to Jerusalem from the country before the Passover, that they might purify themselves. (56) Therefore they sought Jesus, and standing in the temple they said to one another, "What do you think? Will he come to the feast?" (57) Already both the chief priests and Pharisees had given orders that if anyone knew where he was, he should report it so they could arrest him.

John 12:1-50

(1) Then Jesus came to Bethany six days before Passover, where Lazarus was, whom Jesus had raised from the dead. (2) Therefore they made a supper for him there, and Martha served, but Lazarus was one of the ones reclining at the table with him. (3) Then Mary, taking a pound of nard, an

expensive ointment, anointed the feet of Jesus and wiped his feet with her hair. And the house was filled with the odor of the ointment.

(4) And Judas Iscariot, one of his disciples (the one who was about to betray him), said, (5) "Why was this ointment not sold for three hundred denarii and given to the poor?" (6) But he said this, not because he was concerned about the poor, but because he was a thief, having the moneybag, and he pilfered from it.

(7) Therefore Jesus said, "Leave her alone, that she may keep it for the day of my burial. (8) For you will always have the poor with you, but you will not always have me."

(9) The great crowd of the Jews knew that Jesus was there, and they came, not only because of Jesus but also to see Lazarus, whom he had raised from the dead. (10) But the chief priests took counsel that they might also kill Lazarus, (11) because many of the Jews were going to Jesus and believing in him.

(12) The next day the great crowd coming to the feast, hearing that Jesus was coming to Jerusalem, (13) took branches of the palm trees and went out to meet him, and they cried out, "Hosanna, blessed is the one coming in the name of the Lord, even the King of Israel!"

(14) And Jesus, having found a young donkey, sat on it, as it is written, (15) "Fear not, daughter of Zion, behold, your king is coming, sitting on a donkey's colt." (16) At first his disciples did not understand this, but when Jesus was glorified, then they remembered that these things they did to him were the things written about him.

(17) Meanwhile the crowd that had been with him when he called Lazarus out of the tomb, raising him from the dead, had continued to bear witness. (18) Because the crowd had heard that he had done this sign, they went to meet him. (19) Therefore the Pharisees said to themselves, "Behold, we are gaining nothing! See, the world has gone after him."

(20) Now there were some Greeks among those going up to worship at the feast. (21) Therefore these approached Philip, who was from Behsaida of Galilee, and asked him saying, "Sir, we wish to see Jesus."

(22) Philip went and told Andrew; Andrew and Philip went and told Jesus. (23) And Jesus answered them saying, "The hour has come for the Son of Man to be glorified. (24) Truly, truly, I say to you, unless the grain of wheat, falling into the earth, dies, it remains alone, but if it dies it bears much fruit. (25) The one loving his life loses it, and the one having no concern for it in this world will keep it for eternal life. (26) If anyone serves me, let him follow me, and where I am, there will also be my servant. If anyone serves me, my Father will honor him.

(27) "Now my soul is troubled, and what shall I say, 'Father, save me from this hour'? But for this purpose I came to this hour. (28) Father, glorify your name."

Then a voice came out of heaven, "I have glorified it, and I will glorify it again."

(29) The crowd, standing and hearing it, said that it had thundered. Others said, "An angel has spoken to him."

(30) Jesus said, "This voice did not come for me, but for you. (31) Now is the judgment of this world; now the ruler of this world shall be cast out. (32) And I, if I am lifted up from earth, will draw all men to myself." (33) He said this to signify what kind of death he was about to die.

(34) Then the crowd answered him, "We have heard from the law that Christ continues forever. How can you say that the Son of Man must be lifted up? Who is this Son of Man?"

(35) Then Jesus said to them, "The light is among you for a short time. Walk while you have the light, lest the darkness overtakes you. The one walking in the darkness does not know where he is going. (36) While you have the light, believe in the light, that you may become sons of the light."

After Jesus finished speaking, he went away and was unobserved by them. (37) Though he had done so many signs before them, yet they did not believe in him, (38) that the word spoken by Isaiah the prophet might be fulfilled,

"Lord, who believed our report?
And to whom has the arm of the Lord been revealed?"

(39) Therefore they could not believe, because Isaiah again said,

(40) "He has blinded their eyes and hardened their hearts,
lest they might see with eyes and understand with the hearts,
and turn for me to heal them."

(41) Isaiah said this because he saw his glory and spoke about him.

(42) But nevertheless many even among the rulers believed in him, but because of the Pharisees they did not confess it, lest they should be put out of the synagogue. (43) For they loved the glory of men more than the glory of God.

(44) Then Jesus cried out and said, "The one believing in me does not believe in me, but in the one having sent me, (45) and the one seeing me sees the one having sent me. (46) I—a light—have come into the world that everyone believing in me may not continue in darkness. (47) And if anyone hears my words and does not keep them, I do not judge him, for I did not come to judge the world, but to save the world. (48) The one rejecting me and not receiving my words has a judge. That word which I spoke will condemn him in the last day. (49) Because I did not speak from my own accord, but the Father having sent me has commanded me what to say and how to speak. (50) And I know that his commandment is eternal life. Therefore whatever things I speak are what the Father has told me to speak."

John 13:1-38

(1) Now before the feast of Passover Jesus knew that his hour had

come to depart out of this world to the Father. Having loved his own in the world, he showed them the full extent of his love. (2) And during supper (the devil had already suggested to Judas that he should betray him), (3) Jesus, knowing that the Father had given all things into his hands, and that he had come from God and was going to God, (4) rose from the supper and laid aside his garments; and taking a towel he girded himself.

(5) Then he poured water into a basin and began to wash the feet of the disciples and to dry them with the towel with which he was girded.

(6) Then he came to Simon Peter who said to him, "Lord, do you wash my feet?"

(7) Jesus answered and said to him, "What I am doing you do not know yet, but later your will understand."

(8) Peter said to him, "You shall never wash my feet!"

Jesus answered him, "Unless I wash you, you have no part with me."

(9) Simon Peter said to him, "Lord, not only my feet but also the hands and the head!"

(10) Jesus said to him, "The one having bathed has no need to wash, except the feet, for his whole body is clean. And you are clean, but not all." (11) For he knew the one betraying him. Therefore he said, "You are not all clean."

(12) When he had washed their feet, he took his garments and reclined again. Then he said to them, "Do you know what I have done to you? (13) You call me, 'The Teacher' and 'Lord,' and rightly so, for I am. (14) Therefore, since I, 'The Teacher' and 'The Lord' washed your feet, you also ought to wash one another's feet. (15) For I have given you an example that as I have done to you, also you should do. (16) Truly, truly, I say to you, a slave is not greater than his lord, nor is the one sent greater than the one sending him. (17) Since you know these things, blessed are you if you do them.

(18) "I am not speaking concerning all of you. I know whom I have chosen, but that the Scripture may be fulfilled, 'The one eating my bread lifted up his heel against me.'

(19) "I tell you now before it happens, that when it happens you may believe that I am he. (20) Truly, truly, I say to you, the one receiving whomever I send receives me; and the one receiving me receives the one having sent me."

(21) Jesus, saying these things, was troubled in spirit, and he testified and said, "Truly, truly, I say to you, one of you will betray me."

(22) The disciples looked at one another, being uncertain of whom he spoke. (23) One of the disciples, whom Jesus loved, was reclining in the bosom of Jesus. (24) Therefore Simon Peter nodded to this one and said to him, "Ask who it is concerning whom he speaks."

(25) So that one falling back on the breast of Jesus, said to him, "Lord who is it?"

(26) Jesus answered, "It is that one to whom I shall give the piece of bread when I have dipped it." Then, dipping the piece of bread, he gave it to Judas, the son of Simon Iscariot. (27) After Judas took the bread, Satan entered into him.

(28) Then Jesus said to him, "What you are about to do, do quickly." But none of the ones reclining understood what he said. (29) For some thought, since Judas had the moneybag, that Jesus was telling him to buy what was need for the feast or to give something to the poor. (30) So, having taken the piece of bread, that one went out immediately; and it was night.

(31) Then when he went out, Jesus said, "Now is glorified the Son of Man, and God is glorified in him. (32) Since God is glorified in him, God will also glorify him in himself, and immediately he will glorify him. (33) Children, I will be with you only a little longer. You will seek me; and as I said to the Jews, I say to you that where I go you cannot come.

(34) "A new commandment I give you, that you love one another. As I have loved you, also you should love one another. (35) All men will know that you are my disciples, if you have love for one another."

(36) Simon Peter said to him, "Lord, where are you going?"

Jesus answered him, "Where I go, you cannot follow me now, but you will follow later."

(37) Peter said to him, "Lord, why can't I follow you now? I will lay down my life for you."

(38) Jesus answered, "Your life you will lay down for me? Truly, truly, I say to you, before a rooster crows you will disown me three times.

John 14:1-30

(1) "Do not let your heart be troubled. Believe in God; believe also in me. (2) In my Father's house are many rooms; otherwise, would I have told you that I go to prepare a place for you? (3) And if I go and prepare a place for you, I will come again and receive you to myself, that where I am you may be also. (4) And you know the way where I go."

(5) Thomas said to him, "Lord, we do not know the way."

(6) Jesus said to him, "I am the way and the truth and the life. No one comes to the Father except through me. (7) If you had known me, you would have known my Father also. From now you know him and have seen him."

(8) Philip said to Jesus, "Lord, show us the Father, and we will be satisfied."

(9) Jesus said to him, "Philip, I have been with you such a long time, and yet you do not know me? The one having seen me has seen the Father. How can you say, 'Show us the Father'? (10) Do you not believe that I am in the Father and the Father in me? The words, which I say to you, are not from

myself; but the Father living in me does his works. (11) Believe me that I am in the Father and the Father in me, or believe because of the works themselves. (12) Truly, truly, I say to you, the one believing in me the works which I do, that one will do also, and greater than these he will do, because I am going to the Father. (13) And whatever you ask in my name, this I will do, that the Father may be glorified in the Son. (14) If you ask anything in my name, I will do it.

(15) If you love me, you will keep my commandments. (16) And I will ask the Father, and he will give you another Counselor, that he may be with you forever— (17) the Sprit of truth, which the world cannot receive, because it neither sees him nor knows him. You know him because he dwells with you and will be in you. (18) I will not leave you as orphans; I am coming to you. (19) A little while and the world will no longer see me, but you will see me; because I live, you will live also. (20) In that day you will know that I am in my Father, and you in me, and I in you. (21) The one having my commandments and keeping them, that one is the one loving me. The one loving me will be loved by my Father, and I will love him and manifest myself to him."

(22) Judas (not Iscariot) said to him, "Lord, why are you about to manifest yourself to us and not to the world?"

(23) Jesus answered and said to him, "If anyone loves me, he will keep my word, and my Father will love him, and we will come to him and dwell with him. (24) The one not loving me does not keep my words; and the word which you hear is not mine but the Father who sent me.

(25) "These things I have spoken to you while remaining with you. (26) But the Counselor, the Holy Spirit, whom the father will send in my name, that one will teach you all things and will remind you of all things that I told you. (27) Peace I leave with you, my peace I give you. I do not give as the world gives. Do not let your heart be troubled nor let it be fearful. (28) You heard me say, 'I am going away and I will come to you.' If you loved me, you would have rejoiced that I am going to the Father, for the Father is greater than I. (29) Now I have told you before it happens, so that when it happens you will believe. (30) I will not speak with you much longer, for the ruler of the world is coming; and he has nothing in common with me, but the world must know that I love the Father, and as the Father has commanded me do, I do. Rise, let us leave.

John 15:1-27

(1) "I am the true vine and my Father is the vine-dresser. (2) Every branch in me not bearing fruit he cuts off, and every branch bearing fruit he prunes that it may bear more fruit. (3) Now you are clean because of the word which I have spoken to you. (4) Continue in me, and I will continue in you. As the branch cannot bear fruit from itself unless it remains on the vine,

so you cannot bear fruit unless you abide in me.

(5) "I am the vine, you are the branches. The one continuing in me and I in him bears much fruit, because apart from me you can do nothing. (6) If anyone does not abide in me, he is cast out as the branch is dried and cast into the fire and burned. (7) If you abide in me and my words in you, ask whatever you wish and it shall be done to you. (8) By this my Father is glorified: that you bear much fruit and show yourselves to be my disciples.

(9) "As the Father loved me, I have also loved you. Continue in my love. (10) If you keep my commandments, you will abide in love. (11) These things I have spoken to you that my joy may be in you and your joy may be complete. (12) My commandment is that you love one another as I have loved you. (13) No one has a greater love than this: that a man lay down his life for his friends. (14) You are my friends if you do what I command you. (15) I no longer call you slaves, because a slave does not know what his lord does. But I have called you friends, because I have made known to you all the things that I learned from my Father. (16) You did not choose me, but I chose you, and I appointed you to go and bear fruit that should remain; so that whatever you ask the Father in my name, he may give it to you. (17) I command you to love one another.

(18) "If the world hates you, you know that it hated me first. (19) If you were of the world it would love you, but you are not of the world. I chose you out of the world, therefore the world hates you. (20) Remember the word that I said to you: 'A slave is not greater than his lord.' If they persecuted me, they will also persecute you; if they kept my word, they will also keep yours. (21) But all these things they will do to you on account of my name, because they do not know the one having sent me. (22) They did not have sin until I came and spoke to them, but now they do not have an excuse for their sin. (23) The one hating me also hates my Father. (24) If I had not done the works among them which no other man did, they would not have sin. They have seen and hated both me and my Father. (25) But this is to fulfill the word written in their law: 'They hated me freely!' [a]

(26) "When the Counselor comes, whom I will send to you from the Father, that one will witness about me. (27) And you also must witness, because you have been with me from the beginning.

John 16:1-33

(1) "I have spoken these things to you that you will not be offended. (2) They will expel you from the synagogues. Indeed, the hour comes when whoever kills you will think he is offering a sacrifice to God. (3) And they will do these things because they have not known the Father or me. (4) But I

---

[a] without cause

have spoken these things to you so that when the hour comes you will remember that I told you. These things I did not tell you at first because I was with you.

(5) "But now I am going to the one having sent me; yet none of you asks me 'Where are you going?' (6) But because I have spoken these things, grief has filled your hearts. (7) But I tell you the truth, it is to your advantage that I go away, for if I do not go away, the Counselor will not come to you; but if I go, I will send him to you. (8) When that one comes, he will convict the world of sin, righteousness and judgment; (9) concerning sin, because they do not believe in me; (10) concerning righteousness, because I am going to the Father and you will see me no longer; (11) concerning judgment, because the ruler of this world has been judged.

(12) "I have yet many more things to tell you, but you cannot bear them now. (13) But when that one, the Spirit of Truth, comes, he will guide you into all the truth. For he will not speak from himself, but what things he hears he will speak, and he will declare to you what is coming. (14) He will glorify me because he will receive from me and declare it to you. (15) All that belongs to the Father is mine; therefore I said that he receives from me and will declare to you.

(16) "A little while, and you shall not see me, and again, a little while, and you will see me."

(17) Therefore some of the disciples said to one another, "What does he mean by this, 'A little while, and you will not see me, and again, a little while, and you will see me,' and 'because I am going to the Father'?" (18) Then they kept saying, "What does he mean by this, 'A little while?' We do not understand what he says."

(19) Jesus knew what they wanted to ask him, so he said to them, "Are you asking one another what I mean by saying, 'A little while, and you shall not see me, and again, a little while, and you will see me'? (20) Truly, truly, I say to you, that you will weep and mourn, but the world will rejoice. You will be grieved, but your grief will become joy. (21) When a woman is in travail she has pain because her time has come, but when she delivers the child, she no longer remembers the anguish because of the joy that a child was born into the world. (22) Therefore you now have grief, but I will see you again and your hearts will rejoice, and no one will take away your joy. (23) And in that day you will no longer question me. Truly, truly, I say to you, whatever you ask the Father in my name, he will give you. (24) Therefore you have not asked for anything in my name. Ask, and you will receive, that your joy may be complete.

(25) "I have spoken to you in figures of speech; but the hour is coming when I will no longer speak to you in allegories, but I will talk to you plainly concerning the Father. (26) In that day you will ask in my name, and I do not say to you that I will ask the Father on your behalf. (27) For the Father himself loves you because you have loved me and have believed that I came from God. (28) I came from the Father and have come into the world;

again, I am leaving the world and going to the Father."

(29) His disciples said, "Behold, now you are speaking clearly, and you are no longer speaking in allegories. (30) Now we can see that you know all things and you have no need for anyone to question you. By this we believe that you came from God."

(31) Jesus answered them, "Now do you believe? (32) Behold, the hour is coming—indeed it has arrived—when each of you will be scattered to his own place, and I will be left alone. Yet I am not alone, because the Father is with me.

(33) "These things I have told you that in me you may have peace. In the world you will have distress, but be confident, I have overcome the world."

John 17:1-26

(1) When Jesus had spoken these words, he lifted up his eyes to heaven and said, "Father, the hour has come. Glorify your son that the Son may glorify you. (2) Inasmuch as you gave him authority over all flesh, he may give eternal life to all whom you have given to him. (3) And this is eternal life: that they may know you the only true God, and Jesus Christ whom you have sent. (4) I have glorified you on earth by finishing the task you gave me to do. (5) And now, Father, glorify me in your presence with the glory which I had with you before the world came into existence.

(6) "I have made your name known to the men whom you gave to me out of the world. They were yours and you gave them to me, and they have kept your word. (7) Now they know that everything you have given to me is from you. (8) For the words which you gave to me I have given to them and they accept them. They were convinced that I came from you, and they believed that you sent me. (9) I implore you concerning them but not concerning the world, but for those whom you have given to me, for they are yours. (10) All I have is yours, and all you have is mine, and I have been glorified in them. (11) And I am no longer in the world, but they are in the world, and I come to you. Holy Father, keep those whom you have given to me in your name, so they may be one as we are one. (12) When I was with those whom you have given to me, I kept them in your name, and I guarded them and not one of them is lost except the son of perdition, that the Scripture might be fulfilled.

(13) "And now I come to you; about these things I speak while in the world that they may have my joy fulfilled in them. (14) I have given your word to them and the world has hated them, because they are not of the world as I am not of the world. (15) I do not ask you to take them out of the world, but that you should keep them from the evil one. (16) They are not of the world, as I am not of the world. (17) Sanctify them by the truth; your word is truth. (18) As you sent me into the world, I also send them into the

world. (19) I sanctify myself for them that they may be truly sanctified.

(20) "It is not for them only that I make this request, but also concerning the ones believing in me through their word, (21) that all may be one, as you, Father, in me, and I in you, that they also may be in us so that the world may believe that you sent me. (22) And the glory which you have given to me, I have given to them, that they may be as we are one: (23) I in them and you in me, that they may be in complete unity, that the world may know that you sent me and you have loved them as you have loved me. (24) Father, I want those whom you have given to me to be with me where I am, so that they may behold my glory which you gave to me because you loved me before the creation of the world. (25) Righteous Father, the world has not known you, and these men know that you have sent me. (26) And I made known to them your name, and I will continue to make it known so that the love which you loved me may be in them, and I in them."

John 18:1-40

(1) Jesus, having said these things, went forth with his disciples across the brook of Kidron, where there was a garden, into which he and his disciples entered.

(2) Now Judas, the one betraying him, knew the place, because Jesus had often met there with his disciples. (3) Judas, taking the temple guard and some attendants from the chief priests and from the Pharisees, came there with torches, lanterns and weapons.

(4) Therefore Jesus, knowing all things coming upon him, went forth and said to them, "Whom do you seek?"

5) They answered him, "Jesus, the Nazarene."

Jesus said, "I am he." Now Judas, the one betraying him also stood with them.

(6) When Jesus said, "I am he," they all drew back and fell on the ground.

(7) Therefore Jesus questioned them again, "Whom do you seek?"

And they said, "Jesus, the Nazarene."

(8) Jesus answered, "I told you that I am he; if therefore you seek me, let these men go." (9) This was to fulfill the word that he had spoken, "I have not lost one of those whom you gave me."

(10) Then Simon Peter, having a sword, drew it and struck the slave of the high priest, and cut off his right ear. (The name of the slave was Malchus.)

(11) Therefore Jesus said to Peter, "Put the sword into the sheath! Shall I not drink the cup which the Father has given me?"

(12) Then the temple guard with its commander and the Jewish officials took Jesus and bound him.

(13) They first brought him to Annas, for he was the father-in-law of

Caiphas, who was high priest that year. (14) Now Caiphas was the one who had advised the Jews that it was expedient that one man die for the people.

(15) Simon Peter and another disciple followed Jesus. That disciple was known to the high priest, (16) but Peter stood outside the door. Therefore, the other disciple, who was known to the high priest, went out and spoke to the doorkeeper and brought Peter in.

(17) Then the maidservant that kept the door said to Peter, "Are you also one of this man's disciples?"

He said, "I am not."

(18) The slaves and the attendants, having made a fire, were warming themselves because it was cold, and Peter was also standing with them and warming himself.

(19) Then the high priest questioned Jesus about his disciples and his teachings.

(20) Jesus answered him, "I have spoken openly to the world. I have always taught in synagogues and in the temple, where all the Jew come together. I spoke nothing in secret. (21) Why do you question me? Question the ones having heard me. Behold, these know what I said."

(22) And hearing these things, one of the attendants standing by slapped Jesus, saying, "Is this the way to answer the high priest?"

(23) Jesus answered, "If I have spoken evil, witness concerning the evil, but if correctly, why do you hit me?" (24) Then Annas sent Jesus, having been bound, to Caiphas the high priest.

(25) Now Simon Peter was standing and warming himself. Therefore they said to him, "Are you not also one of his disciples?"

That one denied it and said, "I am not."

(26) One of the slaves of the high priest, being a relative of the man whom Peter cut off the ear said, "Did I not see you in the garden with him?" (27) Again Peter denied it. And immediately a rooster crowed.

(28) Then they led Jesus from Caiphas to the praetorium. And it was early. The Jews did not enter the praetorium lest they would be defiled and unable to eat the Passover. (29) So Pilate went outside and said to them, "What accusation do you bring against this man?"

(30) They answered and said to him, "If this man were not a criminal we would not have delivered him to you."

(31) Therefore Pilate said to them, "You take him and according to your law judge him."

The Jews said to him, "It is not lawful for us to kill anyone." (32) This was to fulfill the word of Jesus signifying the circumstances of his imminent death. (33) Therefore Pilate entered again into the praetorium and called Jesus and said to him, "Are you the King of the Jews?"

(34) Jesus answered, "Do you say this of your own accord, or have others told you about me?"

(35) Pilate answered, "Am I a Jew? Your people and the chief priests delivered you to me. What have you done?"

(36) Jesus answered, "My kingdom is not of this world. If my kingdom were of this world, my attendants would have fought and I would not have been delivered to the Jews; but my kingdom is not hence."

(37) Then Pilate said to him, "Are you really a king?" Jesus answered, "You say that I am a king. For this I have been born and for this I have come into the world, that I might witness to the truth; everyone being of the truth hears my voice."

(38) Pilate said to him, "What is truth?" And having said this he went out again to the Jews and said to them, "I find no crime in him." (39) But you have a custom that I should release one prisoner at the time of Passover. Do you want me to release 'The king of the Jews'?"

(40) They cried out saying, "Not this man, but Barabbas." Now Barabbas was a robber.

John 19:1-42

(1) Then Pilate took Jesus and whipped him. (2) And the soldiers, having plaited a wreath of thorns, put it on his head, and they clothed him in a purple robe. (3) They came to him and said, "Hail, king of the Jews!" and they slapped him.

(4) And Pilate went out again and said to them, "Behold! I bring him out to you that you may know that I find no crime in him." (5) So Jesus came outside, wearing the thorny wreath and the purple robe. And Pilate said to them, "Behold! The man!"

(6) When the chief priests and the attendants saw him, they shouted, "Crucify! Crucify!"

Pilate said to them, "You take him and crucify him, for I do not find crime in him."

(7) The Jews answered him, "We have a law, and according to that law he ought to die, because he made himself the Son of God."

(8) When Pilate heard this, he was more frightened than before, (9) and he entered into the praetorium again and asked Jesus, "Where do you come from?" But Jesus gave no answer to him.

(10) Then Pilate said to him, "Will you not speak to me? Do you not know that I have authority to release you and I have authority to crucify you?"

(11) Jesus answered, "You would have no authority over me if it had not been given to you from above; therefore the one having delivered me to you has a greater guilt."

(12) From then on, Pilate sought to release him, but the Jews kept shouting, saying, "If you release this man, you are not a friend of Caesar. Everyone who makes himself a king opposes Caesar."

(13) Therefore Pilate, hearing these words, brought Jesus outside, and he sat on a tribunal in a place called the Stone Pavement (but in Hebrew,

Gabbatha).

(14) Now it was the preparation of the Passover, about the sixth hour, and he said to the Jews, "Behold! Your king."

(15) Then they shouted, "Away with him! Away with him! Crucify him!"

Pilate asked them, "Shall I crucify your king?"

The chief priests answered, "We have no king except Caesar."

(16) Then Pilate delivered him to them that he might be crucified.

Therefore they took Jesus. (17) And he, bearing his Cross, went forth to a place called the Place of the Skull (which in Hebrew is Golgotha), (18) where they crucified him, and with him two others — one on either side and Jesus in the middle.

(19) Pilate wrote a title and put it up on the cross, and it read: "JESUS THE NAZARENE, THE KING OF THE JEWS." (20) So therefore, many of the Jews read this title, because the place where Jesus was crucified was near the city, and it was written in Hebrew, Latin and Greek. (21) Then the chief priests of the Jews said to Pilate, "Do not write, 'The King of the Jews,' but that He said, 'I am King of the Jews.' "

(22) Pilate answered, "What I have written, I have written."

(23) When the soldiers crucified Jesus, they took his clothes and divided them into four parts, a part for each soldier. But the tunic was seamless, from the top throughout.

(24) They said therefore to one another, "Let us not tear it, but let us cast lots for it."

This happened that the Scripture might be fulfilled which said,

"They divided my garments among themselves

and over my clothes they cast a lot."

So the soldiers did these things.

(25) Now the mother of Jesus stood by the cross, and the sister of the mother of him, Mary the wife of Clopas, and Mary Magdalene. (26) Then Jesus, seeing his mother and the disciple whom he loved standing by, said to his mother, "Woman, behold your son." (27) Then he said to the disciple, "Behold your mother." From that hour the disciple took her into his own care.

(28) After this, Jesus knowing that all things were now completed, and that the Scripture would be fulfilled, said, "I thirst." (29) A vessel full of vinegar was there, so they filled a sponge with vinegar and wrapped around a hyssop plant and put it to his mouth. (30) Therefore when Jesus received the vinegar, he said, "It is finished," and bowing his head he gave up his spirit.

(31) Therefore the Jews, since it was the day of Preparation and that the bodies might not remain on the cross on the Sabbath, for that day was a great Sabbath, asked Pilate to have their legs broken that they might be taken down. (32) So the soldiers came and broke the legs of the first man and then of the other man who had been crucified with him. (33) But when they came

to Jesus and saw that he was already dead, they did not break his legs; (34) but one of the soldiers with his lance pierced his side, and there came out immediately blood and water. (35) And the one having seen it has given testimony, and the witness is true, and that one knows he tells the truth that you may also believe. (36) For these things happened that the Scripture might be fulfilled: "A bone of him shall not be broken," (37) and as another Scripture says: "They shall look upon him whom they pierced."

(38) Later, Joseph from Arimathea, being a secret disciple of Jesus because of his fear of the Jews, asked Pilate for the body of Jesus, and Pilate granted him permission. Therefore he came and took his body. (39) And Nicodemus, the one having come to him at first by night, came bearing a mixture of myrrh and aloes, about a hundred pounds. (40) Then they took the body of Jesus and bound it in sheets with spices, as is the burial custom of the Jews. (41) Now there was a garden in the place where he was crucified, and in the garden was a new tomb in which no one had ever been laid. (42) Therefore because it was the Jewish Preparation Day and that the tomb was near, they put Jesus there.

John 20:1-31

(1) Now on the first day of the week, early, before daylight, Mary Magdalene came to the tomb and saw that the stone had been moved from the tomb. (2) Therefore she ran to Simon Peter and to the other disciple whom Jesus loved, and said to them, "They took the Lord out of the tomb and we do not know where they put him."

(3) Then Peter and the other disciple went forth and came to the tomb. (4) The two ran together, but the other disciple outran Peter and came first to the tomb, (5) and he saw the sheets lying there but he did not enter. (6) Then came Simon Peter, following him, and he entered the tomb. And he saw the sheets lying there (7) and the napkin, which was on his head. The napkin was not lying with the sheets but, having been wrapped up, was in another place. (8) Then the other disciple, the one coming first to the tomb, entered, and he saw and believed. (9) For yet they did not understand the Scripture that he must arise again from the dead. (10) Then the disciples again went away to themselves.

(11) But Mary stood outside the tomb crying. As she was crying, she stooped into the tomb (12) and saw two angels in white, sitting where the body of Jesus had lain, one at the head and one at the feet.

(13) They asked her, "Woman, why do you cry?"

She said to them, "They took my Lord and I do not know where they put him." (14) Saying this, she turned around and saw Jesus standing, but she did not know that it was Jesus.

(15) Jesus said to her, "Woman, why do you cry? Whom do you seek?" Thinking that he was the gardener, she said to him, "Sir, if you did

carry him away, tell me where you put him, and I will take him."

(16) Jesus said to her, "Mary."

Mary, turning, said to him in Hebrew, "Rabboni" (which means Teacher).

(17) Jesus said to her, "Do not cling to me, for I have not yet ascended to the Father, but go to my brothers and tell them, 'I ascend to my Father and your Father, to my God and your God.' "

(18) Mary Magdalene went to the disciples announcing to them, "I have seen the Lord," and she told them what he had said to her.

(19) Then on the early evening of that first day of the week, the doors having been shut because they feared the Jews, Jesus came and stood in their midst and said, "Peace to you."

(20) And saying this, he showed them his hands and his side. Therefore the disciples seeing the Lord rejoiced.

(21) Then Jesus said to them again, "Peace to you. As the Father has sent me, I also send you."

(22) And saying this, he breathed on them and said to them, "Receive the Holy Spirit. (23) Of whomever sins you forgive, they have been forgiven; of whomever sins you retain, they have been retained."

(24) But Thomas (called Twin), one of the twelve, was not with them when Jesus came. (25) Therefore the other disciples said to him, "We have seen the Lord," but he said, "Unless I see the mark of the nails in his hands and put my finger into the place of the nail and put my finger into his side, I will not believe."

(26) A week later his disciples were in the house again, and Thomas was with them. Jesus came through the closed door and stood in their midst and said, "Peace to you."

(27) Then he said to Thomas, "Bring your finger here and see my hands, and bring your hand and put it into my side; be not faithless but faithful."

(28) Thomas answered him, "My Lord and my God!"

(29) Jesus said to him, "Have you believed because you have seen me? Blessed are the ones not seeing and yet have believed."

(30) Jesus did many other things before the disciples, which are not written in this book. (31) But these have been written that you may believe that Jesus is the Christ, the Son of God, and that believing you may have life in his name.

John 21:1-25

(1) After this Jesus manifested himself again to his disciples by the Sea of Tiberius. This is how it happened. (2) Simon Peter, Thomas (called Twin), Nathaniel from Cana of Galilee, the sons of Zebedee, and two other of his disciples were together.

(3) Simon Peter said to them, "I am going to fish."

They said to him, "We are also coming with you." They went forth and embarked in the boat, but they caught nothing that night. (4) But when early morning came, Jesus stood on the shore; however, the disciples did not know that it was Jesus.

(5) Jesus said to them, "Children, do you have any fish?"

"No," they answered him.

(6) So he said to them, "Cast your net on the right side of the boat, and you will find some." Therefore they cast, and they were no longer able to drag the net because of the multitude of fish.

(7) That disciple whom Jesus loved said to Peter, "It is the Lord!" Therefore Simon Peter, hearing that it was the Lord, girded himself with the upper garment, because he was clad only with an inner garment, and threw himself into the sea. (8) But the other disciples came in the little boat dragging the net of fish, for they were not far from the land, about one hundred yards away. (9) When they came to land, they saw a fish lying on a coal fire and bread.

(10) Jesus said to them, "Now bring some of the fish you caught."

(11) Simon Peter went up and dragged the net full of fish to the land. The net was not torn, even though there were so many — one hundred fifty-three large fish!

(12) Jesus said to them, "Come, eat breakfast." None of the disciples, knowing that it was the Lord, dared ask him, "Who are you?"

(13) Jesus came and took the bread and gave to them, and the fish likewise. (14) Now this was the third time Jesus, after he was raised from the dead, was manifested to the disciples.

(15) When they had finished breakfast, Jesus said to Simon Peter, "Simon, son of John, do you love me more than these?"

He said to him, "Yes, Lord, you know that I love you."

He said to him, "Feed my lambs."

(16) A second time he said to him, "Simon, son of John, do you love me?"

He said to him, "Yes, Lord you know that I love you."

He said to him, "Feed my lambs."

(17) A third time he said to him, "Simon, son of John, do you love me?"

Peter was grieved because he said to him the third time, "Do you love me?" And he said to him, "Lord, you know all things, you know that I love you."

Jesus said to him, "Feed my little sheep. (18) Truly, truly, I say to you, when you were younger you clothed yourself and walked where you desired; but when you are old you will stretch out your hands, and another will dress you and take you where you do not want to go."

(19) He said this to indicate the kind of death in which he would

glorify God. Then he said to him, "Follow me."

(20) Peter, turning, saw the disciple whom Jesus loved following, who also leaned on his breast at the supper and said, "Who is the one betraying you?" (21) Therefore, Peter seeing him, said to Jesus, "Lord, what about this man?"

(22) Jesus said to him, "If I wish for him to remain until I come, what is that to you? You follow me." (23) Therefore the rumor spread among the brethren that this disciple would not die, but Jesus did not say to him that he would not die, but, "If I wish for him to remain until I come, what is that to you?"

(24) This is the disciple witnessing concerning these things and who has written this book. And we know that his witness is true.

(25) There are many other things that Jesus did. If all of them were written, I suppose the world itself could not contain the books.

Introduction to Acts

Luke, the physician, was the author of Acts, which is the companion book of his gospel. The Gospel tells what Jesus "began to do and to teach" (1:1), and Acts continues the ministry of Jesus through his church. Geographically, the story begins in Jerusalem and extends to Rome, the political center of the empire. Historically, it covers the first 30 years of the church. It shows how the early church coped with pagan and Jewish thought. Luke's detailed account gives us a vivid description of the evangelism of the early church. The design of the book revolves around key persons: Peter and Paul, the role of the Holy Spirit in the growth of the church, the significant problems between the Jews and the Gentiles, and the internal problems of the membership of the church itself.

The "we" passages begin in Acts 16:10. Up to that time the author was a historian. When Paul was at Mysia, he wanted to enter Bithynia, but "the spirit of Jesus" would not let him do so. So instead of going north, he went west and came to Troas and spent the night there. That night he had a vision of a man of Macedonia, saying, "Come over to Macedonia and help us!" Was that man Luke? The narrative changes from third person to first person: "We put out to sea...and traveled to Philippi." Evidently, Luke stayed at Philippi. Paul and other workers with him went on to other places and had an extended ministry at Corinth. Later, they returned to Philippi on their way to Jerusalem, and at Philippi Luke again joins them: "We sailed from Philippi...and joined the others at Troas" (20:5).

Luke was with Paul when they arrived in Jerusalem (21:17). Paul was arrested in Jerusalem and put on trial in Caesarea. He was there for two years and later he appealed his case to Caesar in Rome. When Paul was put on the ship to go to Italy, Luke was there by his side. Was Luke gathering material for his book during these two years? Luke was with Paul when they arrived in Rome (28:15). At the end of the book Paul had been in his rented house for two years, and he was boldly preaching about the kingdom of God. This may have been the time Luke was writing his book. Paul was released, but later he was put in the dungeon and executed. When Paul wrote his last letter and awaiting execution, he wrote: "Only Luke is with me."

Paul used 32,394 words with 2,634 different words for his 13 letters. Luke used 37,897 words with 3,079 different words for his two books. So Luke wrote more of the New Testament than anyone else. They have blessed the peoples of the world for 2,000 years and will continue to do so until the end of time.

Acts 1:1-26

(1) In the first book, O Theophilus, I wrote about all the things concerning the work and teachings of Jesus, from the beginning (2) until the

day he was taken up, after giving instructions to the apostles whom he chose through the Holy Spirit, (3) to whom also he presented himself alive after he was crucified by being seen for 40 days by many infallible proofs by them and speaking of the things concerning the kingdom of God. (4) Eating with them, he commanded them: "Do not depart from Jerusalem, but wait for the promise of the Father which you have heard about. (5) John indeed baptized in water, but you will soon be baptized in the Holy Spirit."

(6) When they came together, they asked him "Lord, are you at this time restoring the kingdom to Israel?"

(7) He said to them, "It is not for you to know times and seasons which the Father placed in his authority; (8) but you will receive power, the Holy Spirit coming upon you, and you will be my witnesses in Jerusalem, and in all Judea, and Smaria, and to the extremity of the earth."

(9) After saying these things, the disciples watched him as a cloud took him up out of their sight.

(10) As they were gazing, as he departed to heaven, behold, two men stood by them in white clothes! (11) They said, "Men, Galileans, why do you stand here looking to heaven? This same Jesus who was taken up from you into heaven will return in the same way that you beheld him going into heaven." (12) Then they returned from the Mount of Olives to Jerusalem, a little more than a half-mile away. (13) When they arrived, they went into the upper room where they were staying. Those present were Peter, John, James, Andrew, Philip, Thomas, Bartholomew, Matthew, James, son of Alphaeus, Simon, the zealot, and Judas, brother of James. (14) These were all continuing steadfastly with one accord in prayer, with the women and Mary the mother of Jesus, and his brothers.

(15) In those days, Peter stood up in the midst of the disciples (the number was about 120) and said, (16) "Brothers, it was necessary that the Scripture be fulfilled which the Holy Spirit spoke through the mouth of David concerning Judas, who was guide to the ones taking Jesus, (17) because he was one of our number and shared this ministry."

(18) This one bought a field with the reward of unrighteousness; and there he was swollen up and ruptured in the middle and poured out all his intestines. (19) This became known to those in Jerusalem. So they called that field in their language *AKELDAMACH*, which means "Field of Blood."

(20) Peter said, "For it was written in the book of Psalms,

'Let his estate be deserted; and let no one dwell in it,'

and,

'Let another take his office.'

(21) It is therefore necessary for us to choose one of the men who have been with us all the time that the Lord went in and out among us, (22) beginning from the baptism of John until the day when Jesus was taken up from us. He must become a witness of his resurrection with us."

(23) So they brought forward two men: Joseph called Barsabbas, also known as Justus, and Matthias. (24) They prayed, "You, Lord, who

knows the hearts of all men, show us which of these men you have chosen (25) to take the ministry and apostleship, from which Judas fell to go to his own place." (26) And they cast lots and the lot fell on Matthias, and he was reckoned along with the eleven apostles.

Acts 2:1-48

(1) When the day of Pentecost was completed, the disciples were all together in one place. (2) And suddenly there was a sound like a violent wind blowing out of heaven, and it filled all the house where they were sitting; (3) and there appeared to them a distribution of tongues of fire, and one sat on each of them; (4) and they were all filled with the Holy Spirit; and they began to speak in other tongues as the spirit gave them utterance.

(5) There were residing in Jerusalem Jews who were devout men from every nation under heaven. (6) This sound caused the multitude to come together, and they were confused, because they heard them speaking in their own languages. (7) They were beside themselves and marveling (8) saying, "Are not all these speaking Galileans?" and "How can we hear in our own native language? (9) Parthians, Medes, Elamites, residents of Mesopotamia, Judea, Cappadocia, Pontus, Asia, (10) Phrygia, Pamphylia, Egypt, regions of Libya near Cyrene, visitors from Rome, (11) Jews, proselytes, Cretans and Arabians. We hear them declaring the wonderful works of God in our own languages."

(12) Being amazed and perplexed, they said to one another, "What does this mean?"

(13) Others mocking said, "They are filled with sweet new wine."

(14) Then Peter, standing with the eleven, lifted up his voice and solemnly declared to them, "Men, Jews and all Jerusalem residents, listen carefully to me as I tell you what this means. (15) For these men are not drunk as you imagine, for it is only 9:00 A.M., (16) but this is the fulfillment of that which was spoken by the prophet Joel:

(17) 'And it shall be in the last days, says God,

I will pour out my spirit on all people.

And your sons and your daughters will prophesy,

and your young men will see visions,

and your old men will dream dreams.

(18) And in those days I will pour out my spirit

on my male slaves and my female slaves,

and they will prophesy.

(19) And I will show wonders in the heaven above

and the earth below, blood and fire and vapor of smoke.

(20) The sun will be turned into darkness, and the moon into blood

before the coming of the great and glorious day of the Lord.

(21) And everyone calling upon the name of the Lord will be saved.'

(22) "Men, Israelites, hear this: Jesus, the Nazarene, a man approved by God to you by miracles, wonders and signs, which God did through him in your midst, as you know, (23) was delivered by the fixed purpose and foreknowledge of God; and you put him to death with the help of lawless men by nailing him to the cross; (24) but God raised him, loosening the pangs of death, because it was not possible for death to hold him. (25) For David said concerning him:

'I saw the Lord always before me.

Because he is on my right hand, I will not be shaken.

(26) Therefore my heart was glad and my tongue exulted,

and my flesh will dwell in hope,

(27) because you will not abandon my soul in the grave,

nor will you let your Holy One see corruption.

(28) You have made known to me the ways of life.

You will fill me with gladness with your presence.'

(29) "Men, brothers, I can speak to you with confidence concerning the patriarch David, that he died and was buried and that his tomb is with us now. (30) He was a prophet, knowing that God swore to him with an oath that one of his descendants would sit upon his throne. (31) David spoke with prophetic foresight concerning the resurrection of Christ, that his soul was not abandoned in the grave, nor did his flesh see corruption. (32) This Jesus God has raised up, and of that fact we are all witnesses. (33) Therefore having been exalted to the right hand of God, and receiving the promise of the Holy Spirit, he poured out this which you both see and hear. (34) For David did not ascend to the heavens, but he said: 'The Lord said to my Lord: Sit at my right hand (35) until I make your enemies a footstool at your feet.'

(36) "Assuredly then, let all the house of Israel know that God made this Jesus, whom you crucified, both Lord and Christ."

(37) And hearing this they were stung in the heart, and they said to Peter and the other apostles, "Men, brothers, what shall we do?"

(38) Peter said to them, "Repent and each of you should be baptized in the name of Jesus Christ for the forgiveness of your sins, and you will receive the gift of the Holy Spirit. (39) For to you is the promise, and to your children and to those far away—as many as the Lord Our God may call."

(40) With many other words Peter solemnly witnessed and exhorted them saying, "Save yourselves from this twisted generation."

(41) The ones welcoming his message, therefore, were baptized, and that day there were added about 3,000 souls; (42) and they were continuing steadfastly in the teachings of the apostles, and in the fellowship, and in the breaking of the bread, and in the prayers. (43) Everyone was reverent, and many wonders and signs were done through the apostles. (44) All the believers had all things in common. (45) They sold their real estate and possessions and distributed to each one according to his need. (46) Each day they continued steadfastly with one mind in the temple, and breaking bread

from house to house, they shared food in gladness and simplicity of heart, (47) praising God and having favor with all the people. (48) The Lord added daily to their number those who were being saved.

Acts 3:1-26

(1) Now at 3:00 P.M., the hour of prayer, as Peter and John were going up to the temple, (2) a certain man who was lame from birth was being carried. Each day they put him in front of the temple door that was called Beautiful, to ask alms from those entering into the temple. (3) The lame man, seeing Peter and John approaching the temple, asked for alms.

(4) Peter, gazing at him with John, said, "Look at us." (5) He looked at them expecting to receive something from them.

(6) Then Peter said, "I have neither silver nor gold, but what I have, this I give to you. In the name of Jesus Christ, the Nazarene, walk."

(7) Peter, seizing him by the right hand, raised him up. At once, his feet and ankle bones were made firm, (8) and leaping up, he stood and walked. And he, walking, and leaping and praising God, entered the temple with them. (9) All the people saw him walking and praising God. (10) They recognized that he was the one who had been sitting at the Beautiful Gate of the temple begging alms, and they were filled with awe and astonishment at what had happened to him. (11) As he held on to Peter and John, all the people, greatly amazed, ran together to a place called the Porch of Solomon.

(12) On seeing this, Peter replied to the people, "Men, Israelites, why do you marvel at this, as if we, by our own power or piety, made this man to walk? (13) The God of Abraham, Isaac, and Jacob, the God of our fathers, glorified his son Jesus, whom you betrayed and denied when Pilate had decided to release him. (14) You disowned the holy and just one, and you asked for the release of a murderer. (15) You killed the author of life whom God raised from the dead. To this we are witnesses. (16) By faith in the name of Jesus, this man whom you see and know was made firm in his name. Through this faith, he has perfect soundness of health, as you can see.

(17) "Now, brothers, I know that you did this in ignorance, as your rulers did. (18) But God had previously announced through his prophets concerning the suffering of the Christ and so it was fulfilled. (19) Repent, therefore, and turn to God, so your sins can be wiped away, (20) and that times of refreshing may come from the Lord, so he can send Christ Jesus who had been appointed for you. (21) Heaven is his home until the times of restitution of all things, which God has spoken through the mouth of his holy prophets in the beginning of the age. (22) Moses indeed said, "The Lord your God will raise up a prophet for you like me. Listen to him according to all things he speaks to you. (23) Everyone who does not listen to him will be utterly destroyed from the people.'

(24) "Indeed, all the prophets from Samuel on, as many as have

spoken, announced these days. (25) And you are sons of the prophets and of the covenant, which God made with our fathers, saying to Abraham, 'In your seed shall all the families of the earth be blessed.' (26) When God raised up his servant, he first sent him to you to bless you in turning you from your iniquities."

Acts 4:1-37

(1) While Peter and John were speaking to the people, the priests, the commandant of the temple, and the Sadducees came upon them, (2) being greatly troubled because they were teaching the people and proclaiming in Jesus the resurrection from the dead. (3) They arrested them in the evening and put them in jail until the next day. (4) Many of those hearing the word believed, and the number of the men came to be about five thousand.

(5) The next day the rulers and the elders and the scribes assembled in Jerusalem, (6) and Annas, the high priest, Caiaphas, John, Alexander, and all of those who belonged to the high priest's clan, met with them. (7) They stood Peter and John in the center and questioned them, "By what power or in what name did you do this?"

(8) Then Peter, filled with the Holy Spirit, said to them, "Rulers and elders of the people, (9) if we are being examined concerning a good deed done to an infirm man and how this man has been healed, (10) let it be known to all of you and to all the people of Israel that in the name of Jesus Christ, the Nazarene, whom you crucified, whom God raised from the dead, in him this man stands before you whole. (11) This is
'the stone you builders despised,
which has become the chief stone of the building.'
(12) Salvation is found in no one else. For there is no other name under heaven given to men for salvation."

(13) And beholding the boldness of Peter and John, and perceiving that they were unlettered laymen, they marveled and observed that they had been with Jesus; (14) and seeing the man, who had been healed, standing with them, they had nothing to say. (15) So having commanded them to go outside the courtroom, they discussed the problem with one another (16) saying, "What are we going to do to these men? We cannot deny that a notable miracle has been done through them, (17) but so it will not spread more to the people, let us warn them to speak no more in this name to anyone."

(18) Then calling them, they charged them not to speak at all or teach in the name of Jesus. (19) But Peter and John replied to them, "You decide if it is right in the sight of God to obey you rather than God. (20) For we cannot refrain from speaking about the things we saw and heard."

(21) After more threats, they released them, because they could not decide how to punish them, since all the people glorified God because of the

things that had happened. (22) This man who was healed was more than 40 years old.

(23) And being released, Peter and John went to their own people and reported what the chief priests and the elders had said. (24) Having heard this, they lifted their voices with one mind and said, "Master, you made the heaven and the earth and the sea and all things in them. (25) You spoke through the Holy Spirit by the mouth of your servant our father David:

'Why raged the nations
and people plotted in vain?
(26) The kings of the earth and the rulers
assembled together against the Lord
and against his Christ.'

(27) It is true that Herod and Pontius Pilate assembled with the nations and peoples of Israel in the city against your holy servant Jesus, whom you anointed. (28) They did what your hand and counsel had foreordained to happen. (29) And now, Lord, look on their threatening and give to your slaves all boldness to speak your words; (30) stretch forth your hand to heal and perform miracles and wonders through the name of your holy servant Jesus."

(31) As they were praying, the place where they were assembled was shaken; and they were all filled with the Holy Spirit, and they spoke the word of God with boldness.

(32) Now the multitude of the believers was of one heart and one soul, and no one claimed that his possessions were his own, but all things were common property. (33) With great power the apostles gave the testimony of the resurrection of the Lord Jesus, and great grace was upon all of them. (34) Neither were there any needy persons among them; for all who were owners of land and houses sold them and brought the money from the sales (35) and placed it at the feet of the apostles, and it was distributed to each according to his need.

(36) Joseph, the one called Barnabas (which means, Son of Encouragement) by the apostles, a Levite, a Cyprian by race, (37) had a field. He sold it and brought the money and placed it at the feet of the apostles.

Acts 5:1-42

(1) A man, whose name was Ananias, and his wife, Sapphira, sold some property. (2) He kept part of the money, and his wife knew about it. Bringing a part of the money, he placed it at the apostles' feet. (3) Then Peter said, "Ananias, why have you been deceived by Satan to lie to the Holy Spirit concerning the price of the land and keep part of it? (4) The land was yours, and after the sale the money was at your disposal. Why did you do this? You lied to God rather than to man!"

(5) Ananias, hearing these words and falling down, expired, and great fear came on those hearing about these things. (6) Then the young men wrapped up his body, carried him out, and buried him.

(7) After an interval of about three hours his wife, not knowing what had happened, entered. (8) Peter asked her, "Tell me, is this the payment you received for the land?"

And she said, "Yes, that is the price."

(9) Peter said to her, "Why did you agree to tempt the Spirit of the Lord? Behold, the feet of the ones who buried your husband are at the door, and they will carry you out." (10) She immediately fell at their feet and expired. The young men entering, found her dead, carried her out, and buried her beside her husband. (11) Great fear came upon all the church and the ones hearing about these things.

(12) Through the hands of the apostles many signs and wonders were performed. The believers, with one accord, met on the Porch of Solomon. (13) No one else joined them, but the people magnified them. (14) However, many more believers were added to the Lord, both men and women. (15) The people brought out the sick into the streets on pallets and mattresses so that the shadow of Peter might be cast on some as he passed by. (16) Many came from the cities surrounding Jerusalem carrying the sick and the ones being tormented by unclean spirits, and they were all healed.

(17) The high priest and the party of the Sadducees who were with him, rising up, were filled with jealousy. (18) They laid their hands on the apostles and put them in the public jail. (19) But during the night an angel of the Lord opened the doors of the jail, and leading them out said, (20) "Go stand in the temple, and speak to the people all the words of this life."

(21) As the apostles were instructed, they entered about dawn into the temple and taught.

When the high priest and those with him came and called together the council and all the senate of the sons of Israel, they sent to the jail for the apostles to be brought to them. (22) But the attendants, coming to the jail, did not find the apostles. Returning, they reported (23) saying, "We found the jail securely locked and the guards standing at the doors, but going inside we found no one." (24) As the commandant of the temple and the chief priests heard these words, they were puzzled and wondered what might have happened to them.

(25) Then someone came and reported to them, "Behold, the men you put in jail are standing in the temple and teaching the people."

(26) Then the commandant, going with his attendants, brought the apostles. They did not use force, because they feared that the people would stone them. (27) And bringing them, they stood them before the council, and the high priest questioned them, (28) saying, "We strictly charged you not to teach in this name, and behold you have filled Jerusalem with your teaching, and you intend to make us guilty of this man's blood."

(29) Peter and the other apostles answered by saying, "We must

obey God rather than men. (30) The God of our fathers raised up Jesus whom you killed, hanging him on a tree. (31) God exalted this man to his right hand as a Ruler and Savior to give repentance and forgiveness of sins to Israel. (32) And we are witnesses of these things, and so is the Holy Spirit God gave to the ones obeying him."

(33) When they heard this, they were furious and wanted to put them to death. (34) But Gamaliel, a Pharisee, a member of the council, a teacher of the law, and honored by all the people, stood up and commanded that the men be put outside for a little while. (35) Then he said to them, "Men, Israelites, consider carefully what you intend to do to these men. (36) Sometime ago Theudas stood up claiming to be somebody, and about four hundred men joined him. He was killed, and all who followed him were dispersed and came to nothing. (37) After him, Judas the Galilean stood up in the days of the census and drew away people after him. That man perished, and all who obeyed him were scattered. (38) Therefore, I say to you, keep away from these men and leave them alone. For if their purpose of activity is of human origin, it will be destroyed; (39) but if it is of God, you will not be able to destroy them. You may be found fighting against God."

Taking his advice, (40) they called the apostles back in. After beating them, they charged them not to speak in the name of Jesus, and they released them.

(41) The apostles therefore left the council rejoicing because they were deemed worthy to suffer shame for the Name. (42) Everyday in the temple and from house to house, they did not cease teaching and preaching that Jesus is the Christ.

Acts 6:1-15

(1) In those days, as the number of the disciples was increasing, there was a murmuring of the Hellenists against the Hebrews, because their widows were overlooked in the distributions of food. (2) Then the twelve, calling the multitude of the disciples together, said, "It is not good for us to neglect the word of God to serve tables. (3) So brothers, select seven men full of the Spirit and of wisdom and we will appoint them over this service; (4) but we will devote ourselves to prayer and the ministry of the word."

(5) This proposal pleased the church, so they chose Stephen, a man full of faith and of the Holy Spirit, Philip, Prochorus, Nicanor, Timon, Parmenas, and Nicholaus, a proselyte of Antioch. (6) They set these men before the apostles, and after praying, they laid their hands on them.

(7) The word of God spread; and the number of the disciples in Jerusalem grew rapidly, and many of the priests became obedient to the faith.

(8) Stephen, full of grace and power, did many great miracles and signs among the people. (9) But some of the ones who were called the

synagogue of the Freedmen—Cyrenians and Alexandrians, and some from Cilicia and Asia—were arguing with Stephen, (10) but they were not able to withstand the wisdom and the spirit with which he spoke.

(11) Then they persuaded men to say, "We heard Stephen speak blasphemous words against Moses and God."

(12) So they stirred up the people and the elders and the scribes, and rushing upon him, they seized him and dragged him to the council.

(13) They brought false witnesses who said, "This man continuously speaks against this holy place and the law, (14) for we have heard him say that Jesus the Nazarene will destroy this place and will change the customs which Moses delivered to us."

(15) And those sitting in the council, gazing at him, saw the face of him as a face of an angel.

Acts 7:1-60

(1) Then the high priest said, "Are these things true?" (2) And he said, "Men, brothers and fathers, hearken! The God of glory appeared to our father Abraham when he was in Mesopotamia before he lived in Haran. (3) God said to him, 'Leave your land and your relatives and come into the land that I will show you.'

(4) "So leaving the land of Chaldea, he dwelt in Haran. After the death of his father, he was led into this land in which you now dwell. (5) God did not give him an inheritance here—not even a foot's space—yet he promised to give it to him and to his descendants after him. At that time he had no children. (6) Thus God told Abraham that his descendants would be strangers in a foreign land and would be enslaved and ill-treated four hundred years. (7) But God said, 'I will judge the nation that enslaves them, and later they will come forth and worship me in this place.' (8) Then he gave Abraham a covenant of circumcision, and he begat Isaac and circumcised him eight days after his birth; and Isaac begat Jacob, and Jacob begat the twelve patriarchs.

(9) "The patriarchs, becoming jealous of Joseph, sold him into Egypt; and God was with him (10) and rescued him out of all his afflictions and gave him wisdom and favor before Pharaoh, king of Egypt, and Pharaoh appointed Joseph governor over Egypt and over all his household.

(11) "Then a famine came over all Egypt and Canaan, and there was great affliction so that our fathers could find no food. (12) When Jacob heard that there was grain in Egypt, he sent forth our fathers. (13) At the second visit, Joseph was made known to his brothers, and Joseph's family became know to Pharaoh. (14) Then Joseph sent for Jacob and all his seventy-five relatives. (15) So Jacob and all our fathers went to Egypt and died there. (16) Their bodies were brought back to Shechem and were put into the tomb that Abraham had bought from the sons of Emmor in Shechem.

(17) "As the time drew near for the fulfillment declared by God to Abraham, our people grew in number in Egypt, (18) until another king arose over Egypt who did not know Joseph. (19) This man, dealing craftily with our people, mistreated our fathers by destroying their babies by abusive exposure.

(20) "At this time Moses, a handsome baby, was born. He was in his father's house for three months. (21) When he was exposed, the daughter of Pharaoh took him and reared him as her son. (22) Moses was trained in all the wisdom of the Egyptians, and he became powerful in words and works.

(23) "When Moses was forty years old, he had a desire to visit the sons of Israel, his brothers, (24) and seeing one being injured, he defended him. He took vengeance by striking the offending Egyptian. (25) He thought that his brothers would understand that God, through him, would bring salvation to them, but they did not understand. (26) On the following day while two were fighting, Moses appeared to them to reconcile them in peace by saying, 'Men, you are brothers. Why do you injure one another?'

(27) "But the offending one thrust him away saying, 'Who appointed you a ruler and judge over us? (28) Do you want to kill me the way you killed the Egyptian yesterday?' (29) At this word Moses fled and became a sojourner in the land of Midian where he had two sons.

(30) "After forty years, an angel appeared to Moses in the desert on Mount Sinai in a flame of a burning thorn bush. (31) When Moses, marveling at the sight, approached to closely observe, there was a voice from the Lord: (32) 'I am the God of your fathers, the God of Abraham and of Isaac and of Jacob.' Moses trembled and did not dare to look at him.

(33) "Then the Lord said to him, 'Take off your shoes, because the place where you are standing is holy ground. (34) I saw the ill-treatment of my people; and I heard their groaning, and I have come down to rescue them. Come now, and I will send you to Egypt.'

(35) "This Moses whom they denied saying, 'Who appointed you a ruler and a judge,' was sent to be a ruler and a redeemer by the hand of the angel who appeared to him in the bush. (36) He led them forth doing wonders and signs in the land of Egypt and in the Red Sea and in the desert for forty years. (37) This is the Moses who said to the sons of Israel, 'God will raise up a prophet from your brothers like me!' (38) This is the one having been in the congregation in the desert, with the angel speaking to him in Mount Sinai, and with our fathers, who received living oracles to give to you.

(39) "Our fathers were not obedient, but thrust him away and turned their hearts to Egypt (40) saying to Aaron, 'Make us gods who will lead us; for we do not know what happened to this Moses who led us out of the land of Egypt.' (41) And they made a calf in those days and made sacrifices to the idol and made merry in the works of their hands. (42) God turned away from them and gave them over to worship the host of heaven, as it was written in the book of the prophets:
'Did you bring me victims and sacrifices

forty years in the desert, O house of Israel?
(43) But you took up the tent of Moloch
and the star of the god Rephan,
the idols you made to worship them.
So I will deport you beyond Babylon.'

(44) "Our fathers had the tent of witness in the desert, as had been commanded to Moses to make it according to the model which he had seen. (45) Our fathers with Joshua, having received it, brought it with them when they took the land from the nations whom God drove out from the face of our fathers, until the days of David, (46) who found favor with God; and he sought to provide a dwelling for the house of Jacob. (47) But Solomon built the House of God.

(48) "However, the Most High does not dwell in houses made by hands, as the prophet says,

(49) 'Heaven is my throne,
and the earth is my footstool.
What house will you build for me? says the Lord.
Or, what is the place of my rest?
(50) Did not my hands make all these things?'

(51) "You hard-necked, and uncircumcised in hearts and ears, always oppose the Holy Spirit, as your fathers also did. (52) Which of the prophets did your fathers not persecute? They even killed those who predicted the coming of the Righteous One, of whom you became betrayers and murderers, (53) you who received the law delivered by angels, but you did not keep it."

(54) When they heard these things, they were cut to their hearts, and they gnashed their teeth at him. (55) But Stephen, filled with the Holy Spirit, gazing into heaven and seeing the glory of God, and Jesus standing at the right hand of God, (56) said, "Behold, I see heaven opened and the son of man standing at the right hand of God."

(57) They closed their ears, and crying out with a great voice they, with one mind, rushed on him. (58) Then, dragging Stephen outside the city, they stoned him. The witnesses took off their garments and laid them at the feet of a young man named Saul.

(59) As they stoned Stephen, he was calling upon God, saying, "Lord Jesus receives my spirit." (60) And kneeling down he cried with a great voice, "Lord, do not hold this sin against them." Then he fell asleep.

Acts 8:1-40

(1) Saul gave approval of the killing of Stephen. On that day a great persecution of the church began in Jerusalem. The believers, except the apostles, were scattered throughout the countries of Judea and Samaria. (2) Devout men, with great lamentation, buried the body of Stephen. (3) But

Saul ravaged the church, entering each house and dragging out both men and women and putting them into prison.

(4) The dispersed disciples went everywhere preaching the word, (5) but Philip went down to the city of Samaria to preach Christ to them. (6) The crowds, with one accord, gave heed to Philip when they heard his teaching and saw the miracles which he did. (7) For unclean spirits, crying with loud voices, came out of many, and many paralytics and lame people were healed. (8) So there was much joy in that city.

(9) There was a man named Simon who had been in the city practicing sorcery and astonishing the nation of Samaria, and he claimed to be someone great. (10) The small and the great gave heed to him saying, "This man called great is the power of God." (11) They believed in him because he had astonished them for a long time by his sorceries. (12) But when they believed Philip, preaching about the kingdom of God, they were baptized, both men and women, in the name of Jesus Christ. (13) And even Simon believed, and having been baptized, attached himself to Philip. He was amazed at the signs and the wonderful miracles that were happening.

(14) When the apostles in Jerusalem heard that Samaria had received the word of God, they sent Peter and John to them. (15) As they were going, they prayed that the Samaritans might receive the Holy Spirit, (16) for the Holy Spirit had not yet fallen on any of them. They had been baptized only in the name of the Lord Jesus. (17) Then the apostles laid their hands on them, and they received the Holy Spirit. (18) When Simon saw that they received the Holy Spirit through the laying on of the hands of the apostles, he offered them money saying, (19) "Give me this power so that on whom I lay my hands he will receive the Holy Spirit."

(20) Peter replied, "Let your silver go with you to perdition, because you thought you could purchase the gift of God with money. (21) You have no part in this ministry, because your heart is not right before God. (22) Repent therefore from this wickedness and pray to the Lord for forgiveness of the thoughts of your heart. (23) For I see that you are in the gall of bitterness and in the bond of unrighteousness."

(24) Simon answering said, "Pray to the Lord for me, so that these things will not come on me."

(25) Therefore the apostles, having solemnly witnessed and spoken the word of the Lord, returned to Jerusalem, preaching the gospel to many Samaritan villages.

(26) An angel of the Lord spoke to Philip saying, "Get up and go south on the way going down from Jerusalem to Gaza, which is in the desert." (27) He got up and went. And behold there was an Ethiopian eunuch, who was in charge of all the treasury of Candace, the queen of the Ethiopians. He had worshiped in Jerusalem (28) and was returning home. He was sitting in his chariot reading the prophet Isaiah.

(29) The Spirit said to Philip, "Go and join yourself to this chariot."

(30) Then Philip ran to the chariot and heard him reading the

prophet Isaiah and he said, "Do you understand what you are reading?"

(31) The eunuch said, "How can I unless someone shows me the way," and he invited him to come up and sit with him.

(32) He was reading this passage of Scripture:
"He was led as a sheep to the slaughter,
and as a lamb before the shearers is silent,
so he did not open his mouth.
(33) In his humiliation justice was denied him.
Who can speak of his descendants?
For his life was taken from the earth."

(34) The eunuch asked Philip, "Tell me, who is the prophet talking about? Is it about him or someone else?" (35) Then Philip preached to him Jesus.

(36) As they were going down the road, they came to some water and the eunuch said, "Behold, water. What hinders me from being baptized?" (38) And he ordered the chariot to stop; and they both, Philip and the eunuch, went down into the water, and Philip baptized him. (39) When they came up out of the water, the Spirit of the Lord carried Philip away, and the eunuch did not see him again, but he went on his way rejoicing. (40) Philip was found in Azotus, and he preached the gospel as he went through all the cities until he came to Caesarea.

Acts 9:1-43

(1) Saul was still breathing out murderous threats against the disciples of the Lord; and going to the high priest, (2) he asked for letters to the synagogues in Damascus, so that if he found anyone belonging to the WAY, men or women, he might bind them and bring them to Jerusalem. (3) When he journeyed near to Damascus, suddenly a light from heaven shined around him. (4) Falling upon the ground, he heard a voice saying to him, "Saul, Saul, why do you persecute me?"

(5) Saul asked, "Who are you, Lord?"

He said, "I am Jesus whom you are persecuting. (6) Now arise and go into the city, and it will be told to you what you must do."

(7) The men journeying with him stood speechless, hearing the voice but seeing no one. (8) Saul was raised from the earth, and opening his eyes he saw no one. So they led him by the hand to Damascus. (9) He was blinded for three days and did not eat or drink.

(10) There was a certain disciple in Damascus whose name was Ananias, and the Lord said to him in a vision, "Ananias."

And he said, "Behold, here I am, Lord."

(11) Then the Lord said to him, "Get up and go to the street called Straight and ask for Saul of Tarsus in the house of Judas. For he is praying, (12) and he saw a man in a vision by the name of Ananias coming and laying

his hands on him in order that he might receive his sight."

(13) Ananias answered, "Lord, I have heard from many concerning this man and how much evil he did to your saints in Jerusalem; (14) and he is here with authority from the chief priests to bind the ones calling upon you."

(15) But the Lord said to him, "Go, for this man is my chosen vessel to bear my name before nations and their kings and before sons of Israel. (16) And I will show him how much he will have to suffer for my name."

(17) Then Ananias went and entered the house and placed his hands on him and said, "Brother Saul, The Lord Jesus, who appeared to you on your way here, sent me so that you might receive your sight and be filled with the Holy Spirit." (18) Immediately, something like scales fell from his eyes, and he received his sight. Then he arose and was baptized, (19) and taking food, he was strengthened.

Saul was with the disciples in Damascus for several days, (20) and immediately in the synagogues he proclaimed that Jesus was the Son of God. (21) Those hearing him were amazed, and they said, "Is not this he who was destroying the ones invoking this name in Jerusalem? And has he not come here to bind them and take them to the chief priests?" (22) Yet Saul grew in power, and he confounded the Jews dwelling in Damascus, proving that Jesus is the Christ.

(23) After many days, the Jews made plans to kill him, (24) but the plot was made known to Saul. The Jews carefully watched the gates both day and night so they could kill him, (25) but his disciples, taking him by night, put Saul in a basket and let him down through the wall.

(26) When Saul arrived in Jerusalem, he tried to join himself to the disciples, but they all feared him, not believing that he was a disciple. (27) But Barnabas taking hold of him brought him to the apostles, and he told them how in his journey he saw the Lord, and how the Lord spoke to him, and how Saul had spoken boldly in Damascus in the name of Jesus. (28) Then Saul stayed with the apostles in Jerusalem, going about freely and speaking boldly in the name of Jesus. (29) He spoke to and debated with the Grecian Jews, but they attempted to kill him. (30) When the brothers learned about their plot, they took Saul to Caesarea and sent him to Tarsus.

(31) So the church throughout all Judea, Galilee, and Samaria had peace. The church increased in membership, being edified and walking in the comfort of the Holy Spirit.

(32) As Peter passed through the whole area, he came down to the saints living in Lydda. (33) He found there a certain man whose name was Aeneas, a paralytic of eight years who was lying on a mattress. (34) Peter said to him, "Aeneas, Jesus Christ heals you. Arise and gird yourself." Immediately he got up. (35) All the people of Lydda and Sharon saw him and turned to the Lord.

(36) In Joppa there was a certain disciple by the name of

Tabitha.[b] She was full of good works and acts of benevolence. (37) She got sick and died. They washed her and laid her in the upper room. (38) Lydda was near Joppa and the disciples, having heard that Peter was there, sent two men to urge him to come immediately.

(39) Peter got up and went with them. When they arrived, they took Peter to the upper room where the widows stood by him weeping and showing him the dresses and robes that Dorcas had made while she was with them.

(40) Peter put them all outside; and kneeling down he prayed, and turning to the body he said, "Tabitha, arise." She opened her eyes, and seeing Peter she sat up. (41) He took her by the hand and raised her up. He called the saints and the widows and presented her to them alive. (42) This became known to all Joppa, and many believed in the Lord. (43) Peter remained many days in Joppa with a tanner whose name was Simon.

Acts 10:1-48

(1) In Caesarea there was a man named Cornelius, a centurion of the Italian Regiment. (2) He and all his family were devout and God-fearing; and he gave many alms to the people, and he prayed to God always.

(3) About 3:00 P.M. one afternoon he clearly saw an angel of God coming and saying to him, "Cornelius!"

(4) Cornelius, staring at him and becoming afraid, said, "What is it, Lord?"

The angel said, "Your prayers and alms have come up as a memorial before God. (5) Now send men to Joppa to bring back a certain man named Simon who is called Peter. (6) This man is living with a tanner named Simon who has a house by the sea."

(7) When the angel who had spoken to him went away, Cornelius called two of his slaves and a devout soldier who served him. (8) He explained to them everything and sent them to Joppa.

(9) About noon the next day, as they were journeying and coming near to the city, Peter went up on the roof to pray. (10) He became hungry and wanted to eat. While the food was being prepared, he was caught up into a trance. (11) Peter saw heaven opened and a vessel like a great sheet coming down, and it was being let down to the earth by its four corners. (12) In the sheet were all kinds of four-footed beasts and birds of the air. (13) A voice came to him, "Get up, Peter, slay and eat."

(14) But Peter said, "By no means, Lord, because I have never eaten anything profane or unclean."

(15) The voice spoke to him a second time, "What God has cleansed do not treat as profane."

---

[b] (Greek — Dorcas; English — antelope)

(16) This happened three times, and immediately the vessel was taken up into heaven.

(17) While Peter was thinking about the meaning of this vision, behold, the men sent by Cornelius, having made inquiry of the house of Simon, were at the gate; (18) and calling out, they inquired if Simon Peter was staying there.

(19) While Peter was pondering concerning the vision, the Spirit said, "Behold, three men are seeking you. (20) So get up and go downstairs, and go with them without hesitation, for I have sent them."

(21) Then Peter, going down to the men, said, "Behold, I am he whom you seek. Why have you come?"

(22) They replied, "Cornelius, a centurion, a just and God-fearing man, being honored by all the Jews, was instructed by a holy angel to send for you and bring you to his house to hear words from you." (23) Therefore Peter invited them to spend the night with them.

On the next day he got up and went with them, and some of the brothers from Joppa accompanied him. (24) The next day he entered Caesarea. Cornelius, having called together his relatives and close friends, was waiting for them. (25) When Peter entered, Cornelius worshiped him falling at his feet. (26) But Peter raised him up, saying, "Stand up, I, myself, am also a man."

(27) As he talked with him, he entered and found a large gathering of people. (28) Peter said to them, "You know how unlawful it is for Jews to associate with or come near a foreigner. But God showed me that I should not call any man profane or unclean. (29) So, being sent for, I came without asking questions; therefore, why did you send for me?"

(30) Cornelius said, "Four days ago I was praying in my house at 3:00 P.M., and behold, a man stood before me in bright clothing (31) and said, 'Cornelius, your prayer was heard and your alms remembered before God. (32) Therefore send to Joppa for a man named Simon Peter, who is staying in the house of Simon, a tanner by the sea.' (33) So I immediately sent for you, and it is good that you are here. Now, therefore, we are all here in the presence of God to hear all the things that God has commanded you to tell us."

(34) Then Peter, opening his mouth, said, "In truth I perceive that God is not a respecter of persons, (35) but in every nation the ones fearing him and working righteousness are acceptable to him. This is (36) the word which he sent to the sons of Israel proclaiming peace through Jesus Christ, who is Lord of all. (37) You know what took place throughout all Judea, beginning in Galilee after the baptism proclaimed by John— (38) how Jesus from Nazareth was anointed by God with the Holy Spirit and power, and how he went about doing good and healing all who were oppressed by the devil, because God was with him. (39) We are witnesses of all these things which he did in the country of the Jews and in Jerusalem. Yet they killed him

by hanging him on a cross. (40) This one God raised from the dead on the third day, and he was clearly seen, (41) not by all the people, but by witnesses who had been previously appointed by God — to us who ate and drank with him after he had risen from the dead. (42) He commanded us to proclaim to the people and solemnly witness that this man has been designated by God to judge the living and the dead. (43) To this man all the prophets witness that everyone believing in him receives forgiveness of sins through his name."

(44) While Peter was still speaking these words, the Holy Spirit fell on everyone hearing the message. (45) The circumcised believers who were with Peter were amazed that the gift of the Holy Spirit had been poured out even on the Gentiles. (46) For they heard them speaking in tongues and magnifying God.

Then Peter said, (47) "Surely, no one can forbid water for these who also received the Holy Spirit as we, to be baptized." (48) So he commanded them to be baptized in the name of Jesus Christ. Then they asked him to remain with them for awhile.

Acts 11:1-30

(1) The apostles and the brothers throughout Judea heard that the Gentiles had received the Gospel. (2) When Peter went up to Jerusalem, the circumcised believers disputed with him, (3) saying, "You went into the house of the uncircumcised and ate with them."

(4) Then Peter gave them an orderly account from the beginning, saying, (5) "I was in the city of Joppa praying, and in a trance I saw a vision. I saw a vessel like a linen sheet being let down by four corners out of heaven, and it came near me. (6) Gazing, I observed and saw four-footed animals, wild beasts, reptiles, and birds of the air. (7) I also heard a voice saying to me, 'Get up, Peter, slay and eat.'

(8) "I answered, 'By no means, Lord! Because nothing profane or unclean has ever entered my mouth.'

(9) "The voice, a second time, answered out of heaven, 'What God cleansed do not call profane.'

(10) "This happened three times, and then everything was pulled up again into heaven.

(11) "Then behold, immediately three men having been sent by Cornelius to me were standing at the house where I was staying. (12) And the Spirit said to me to go with them without hesitation. And these six brothers were with me, and we entered into the man's house. (13) He told us how he had seen an angel in his house standing and saying, 'Send men to Joppa for Simon Peter, (14) who will tell you, and all your household, how to be saved.'

(15) "When I began to speak, the Holy Spirit fell on them as on us in

the beginning. (16) Then I remembered the word of the Lord how he said, 'John, indeed, baptized with water, but you will be baptized in the Holy Spirit.' (17) If then God gave them the same gift as also to us when we believed in the Lord Jesus Christ, who was I to be able to restrain God?"

(18) When they heard this, they were satisfied, and they glorified God saying, "So even to the Gentiles God has granted repentance unto life."

(19) Meanwhile those who had been scattered from the persecution, which arose over Stephen, passed through Phoenicia, Cyprus, and Antioch, speaking the word only to Jews. (20) But there were some men of Cyprus and Cyrene who, coming to Antioch, spoke the word to the Greeks, preaching the Lord Jesus. (21) And the hand of the Lord was upon them, and many believed and turned to the Lord.

(22) When the report concerning them was heard in the ears of the church, they sent Barnabas to Antioch. (23) On arriving and seeing the grace of God, he rejoiced and exhorted everyone with commitment of heart to continue with the Lord, (24) because he was a good man and full of the Holy Spirit and of faith. And a great number was added to the Lord.

(25) Then Barnabas went to Tarsus to seek Saul, and finding him, he brought him to Antioch. (26) So for a whole year they met to teach a large number of people. And the disciples were first called Christians in Antioch.

(27) In these days prophets came from Jerusalem to Antioch. (28) One of them, whose name was Agabus, predicted through the Spirit that a great famine was about to come over all the inhabited earth. This happened in the time of Claudius. (29) So all the disciples, according to their ability, determined to send contributions to the brothers dwelling in Judea. (30) This they did by sending it to the elders by the hands of Barnabas and Saul.

Acts 12:1-24

(1) At that time Herod laid his hands on some of the members of the church to persecute them. (2) He killed James, the brother of John, with the sword. (3) When Herod saw that this pleased the Jews, he proceeded to arrest Peter also — these were the Days of the Unleavened Bread. (4) Seizing Peter, he put him in prison and delivered him to four squads of soldiers to guard him. Herod intended to put him on trial after the Passover. (5) Therefore Peter was kept in the prison, but the church was praying earnestly to God for him.

(6) The night before Peter was to be brought before Herod, he was sleeping between two soldiers, having been bound to him with two chains, and two guards were guarding the door. (7) And behold, an angel of the Lord came upon him and a light shined in the cell; and the angel, slapping him on the side, raised him up, saying, "Get up, Quick," and the chains fell from his hands.

(8) Then the angel said to him, "Gird yourself and put on your

shoes." So he did. Then the angel said to him, "Put on your robe and follow me." (9) Peter followed him, not knowing whether the experience was real or a vision. (10) Then going through the first and second wards, they came to the Iron Gate leading to the city, which opened for them by itself; and going through it, they went to a certain street, and immediately the angel departed from him.

(11) Then Peter said to himself, "Now I know of a certainty that the Lord sent forth his angel and has delivered me out of the hands of Herod and all the expectations of the Jews."

(12) Knowing this he went to the house of Mary, mother of John Mark, where many were gathered together praying. (13) After knocking on the door of the porch, Rhoda, a maidservant, came to listen; (14) and recognizing the voice of Peter, she did not open the door, but running in with joy, she told them that Peter was standing before the porch.

(15) They said to her, "You are crazy." But she emphatically asserted that it was true.

So they said, "It is his angel."

(16) Peter kept knocking, and having opened the door, they were amazed. (17) Peter motioned to them with his hand to be quiet, and he related to them how the Lord had led him out of the prison. He said, "Tell James and the brothers about these things." Then going out he went to another place.

(18) At daybreak, there was a great disturbance among the soldiers about what had become of Peter. (19) Herod, searching for Peter but not finding him, examined the guards and commanded that they be executed. Then Herod went from Judea to Caesarea and stayed there.

(20) Herod was fighting mad with the Tyrians and Sidonians; but they came to him, and having secured the support of Blastus, who was in charge of the king's harem, they asked for peace, because their country was dependent on the king for their food supply.

(21) On a special day Herod, clothed in royal apparel and sitting on his throne, made a speech to the people; (22) and the mob cried out, "It is the voice of a god and not of a man!" (23) Immediately, an angel of the Lord smote him because he did not give the glory to God, and being eaten by worms, he expired.

(24) Meanwhile the word of the Lord grew and increased. (25) When Barnabas and Paul had completed their mission to Jerusalem, they returned, taking with them John Mark.

Acts 13:1-52

(1) There were in the church in Antioch prophets and teachers: Barnabas, Simeon Niger, Lucius the Cyrenian, Manaen (a foster-brother of Herod the tetrarch), and Saul. (2) While worshipping the Lord and fasting,

the Holy Spirit said to them, "Set apart for me Barnabas and Saul for the work I have called them." (3) Then after fasting and praying, they laid their hands upon them and sent them away.

(4) Therefore being sent out by the Holy Spirit, Barnabas and Saul went down to Seleucia and from there sailed to Cyprus. (5) While they were in Salamis, they preached the word of God in the Jewish synagogues. They had John as their assistant.

(6) They went through the whole island and came to Paphos. There they found a certain magician named Barjesus who was a Jewish false prophet, (7) who was with the proconsul, Sergius Paulus, an intelligent man. He called for Barnabas and Saul to hear the word of God. (8) But Elymas (the name in Greek) the magician opposed them, seeking to divert the proconsul from the faith. (9) Then Saul (also called Paul), filled with the Holy Spirit, gazing at him (10) said, "You, full of all fraud and all wickedness, a son of the devil, an enemy of all righteousness, will you never cease perverting the straight ways of the Lord? (11) And now, behold, the hand of the Lord is upon you and you will be blind, not seeing the sun for a season." Immediately a mist and darkness fell upon him, and he went about seeking someone to lead him by the hand. (12) Then, the proconsul seeing what happened, believed, being astonished at the teaching of the Lord.

(13) Paul and his companions, setting sail from Paphos, came to Perga of Pamphylia, and from there John returned to Jerusalem. (14) But they, passing through Perga, arrived at Pisidian Antioch, and going into the synagogue on the Sabbath day, they sat down. (15) And after the reading of the law and the prophets, the rulers of the synagogue sent to them saying, "Brothers, if you have a word of exhortation to the people, speak."

(16) Then Paul, standing up and beckoning with his hand said, "Men, Israelites and those fearing God, listen. (17) The God of our fathers chose Israel; and he made our people great in their sojourn in Egypt, and with a mighty arm he led them out of that country (18) and endured their conduct in the desert, (19) and, having destroyed seven nations in the land of Canaan, he gave their land to them for an inheritance. (20) This took about four hundred and fifty years. After this, he gave them judges until Samuel the prophet. (21) Then they asked for a king, and God gave them Saul, son of Kish, a man of the tribe of Benjamin, who reigned for forty years. (22) And after him, he raised up David to be their king, to whom he testifies, 'I found David, the son of Jesse, a man after my heart who will do all my will.' (23) From the seed of this man, according to the promise to Israel, God raised up a Savior, Jesus. (24) John, before the coming of Jesus, had preached a baptism of repentance to all the people of Israel. (25) As John was completing his work, he said, 'Who do you think I am? I am not the Messiah, but behold, he comes after me and I am not worthy to loosen the sandals of his feet.'

(26) "Men, brothers, sons of Abraham and those fearing God, this message of salvation was sent forth to us. (27) Those dwelling in Jerusalem and their rulers did not recognize Jesus nor the voice of the prophets being

read every Sabbath; yet, they fulfilled the prophecies by condemning Jesus. (28) Though they found no cause of death in him, they asked Pilate to destroy him. (29) When they had fulfilled all the things written concerning him and taking him down from the cross, they laid him in a tomb. (30) But God raised him from the dead. (31) He appeared for many days to those who had come with him from Galilee to Jerusalem, who are now his witness to the people.

(32) "So we preach to you the good news that God promised to the fathers. (33) This promise God has fulfilled for us, their children, by raising up Jesus, as it has been written in the second Psalm,

'You are my son;

I, today, have begotten you.'

(34) "And that he raised him from the dead never to return to decay, thus he said,

'I will give you sacred and trustworthy things promised to David.'

(35) "Wherefore in another place it also says,

'You will not let your holy one return to decay.'

(36) "For David, having served God's purposes in his own generation, fell asleep and was buried with his ancestors and returned to decay. (37) But he whom God raised did not return to decay. (38) Therefore, be it known to you, brothers, that through this man is proclaimed to you the forgiveness of all your sins, from which it was not possible to be justified by the law of Moses, (39) but everyone believing in Jesus is justified. (40) Beware, therefore, so that the prophets' words will not be true to you:

(41) 'Look, you scoffers! Marvel and perish!

For a work that I am doing in your days

is something that you will not believe,

even if someone declares it to you.' "

(42) As Paul and Barnabas were leaving the synagogue, the people besought them to come the next Sabbath and to speak more about these things. (43) After the assembly was dismissed, many Jews and devout proselytes followed Paul and Barnabas, who speaking to them persuaded them to continue in the grace of God.

(44) On the following Sabbath almost all the city was assembled to hear the word of the Lord. (45) When the Jews saw the crowds, they were filled with jealousy, and they contradicted what Paul had said in abusive language.

(46) Paul and Barnabas speaking boldly, said, "It was necessary that the word of God should be spoken first to you; since you reject it you judge yourselves unworthy of eternal life; behold, we turn to the Gentiles. (47) For thus the Lord has commanded us:

'I have set you to be a light to the Gentiles,

to bring salvation to the end of the earth.' "

(48) The Gentiles, hearing this, rejoiced and glorified the word of the Lord, and as many as were ordained to eternal life believed.

(49) And the word of God was carried throughout the region. (50) But the Jews stirred up the devout women and the influential and chief men of the city. They started a persecution against Paul and Barnabas and expelled them from their borders. (51) So they, shaking the dust from their feet, went to Iconium. (52) And the disciples were filled with joy and the Holy Spirit.

Acts 14:1-28

(1) In Iconium the same thing happened to them. They went into the synagogue of the Jews and spoke in such a way that a great number of the Jews and Greeks believed, (2) but the unpersuaded Jews stirred up and embittered the minds of the Gentiles against the brothers. (3) Paul and Barnabas stayed there for a long time speaking boldly about the Lord, who was confirming the word about his grace by performing signs and wonders through their hands. (4) The people of the city were divided. Some were with the Jews, but others were with the apostles. (5) When there was a violent attempt by the Gentiles and the Jews with their leaders to insult and to stone them, (6) the apostles being aware of it, fled to the cities of Lystra and Derbe, of Lycaonia, and the surrounding territory, (7) and there they preached the good news.

(8) In Lystra there was a certain man sitting, who was weak in his feet, lame from his birth and had never walked. (9) This man heard Paul speaking. Paul, gazing at him and seeing that he had faith to be healed, (10) said with a loud voice, "Stand erect on your feet," and he jumped up and began to walk.

(11) When the crowds saw what Paul did, they raised their voices in Lycaonian, "The gods in the likeness of men have come down to us," (12) and they called Barnabas, Jupiter, and Paul, Mercury, because he was the spokesman. (13) The priest of Jupiter, at the gateway to the city, brought bulls and wreaths with the crowds to sacrifice to them.

(14) When the apostles Barnabas and Paul heard about this, they tore their garments and rushed into the crowd and cried out, (15) saying, "Men, what are you doing? We are just men like you. We are preaching to you to turn from these vanities and turn to the living God, who made the heaven and the earth and the sea and all things in them. (16) In past generations, he allowed the nations to go their own way. (17) And yet he has not left himself without evidence of his doing good: giving you rain from heaven, seasons of fruit bearing and satisfying you with food and gladness." (18) Even with these words, it was difficult to restrain the crowds from sacrificing to them.

(19) Some Jews came from Antioch and Iconium, and they persuaded the crowds to stone Paul, and they dragged him outside the city, thinking that he was dead. (20) But the disciples gathered around him, and he arose and went into the city. The next day he went with Barnabas to

Derbe.

(21) After preaching the gospel to that city and making many disciples, they returned to Lystra, Iconium and Antioch, (22) strengthening the minds of the disciples, encouraging them to continue in the faith and saying that, "We must pass through many hardships to enter into the kingdom of God." (23) And ordaining elders in each church for them and praying with fasting, they committed them to the Lord in whom they had believed.

(24) After going through Pisidia, they came to Pamphylia, (25) and speaking the word in Perga, they went down to Attalia; (26) and from there they sailed to Antioch, where they had been commended to the grace of God for the work, which they had accomplished. (27) When they arrived, they gathered together the church and reported to them the things that God did through them and that he had opened the door of faith to the Gentiles. (28) Then they remained many days with the disciples.

Acts 15:1-41

(1) Some men came down from Judea to Antioch and taught the brethren that unless one is circumcised according to the custom of Moses, he cannot be saved. (2) There was much discussion and discord with Paul and Barnabas, so they assigned Paul and Barnabas and some of the others in Antioch to go to the apostles and elders in Jerusalem concerning this problem. (3) Therefore they were sent by the church, and going through Phoenicia and Samaria, they explained to them in detail about the conversion of the Gentiles and thus caused the fellow believers to rejoice greatly. (4) When they arrived in Jerusalem, they were greeted by the church, the apostles, and the elders, and they reported to them what God had done with them.

(5) Yet some of the party of the believing Pharisees withstood them saying, "It is necessary to circumcise the Gentiles and require them to keep the Law of Moses."

(6) The apostles and the elders met to consider this problem. (7) After a long debate, Peter arose and said to them, "Men, brothers, you know from past days that God chose me among you that the Gentiles should hear through me the word of the gospel to believe. (8) God, who knows the hearts of everyone, showed his approval of the Gentiles by giving them the Holy Spirit, as also to us, (9) and there is no difference between them and us, because their hearts are also cleansed by faith. (10) Now therefore, why do you test God by putting a yoke on the neck of the disciples which neither our fathers nor we were able to bear? (11) But through the grace of our Lord Jesus, we believe to be saved in the way as they are also."

(12) The assembly was silent as they heard Barnabas and Paul relating what signs and wonders God did among the nations through them.

(13) After they listened to them, James said, (14) "Men, Brothers, hear me. Simon has declared to you how God first visited the Gentiles to take out a people for his name, (15) and this agrees with the prophets, even as it has been written:

(16) 'After this I will return
and rebuild the fallen down tent of David.
And the things having been overturned I will build again
and restore them,
(17) so the rest of men may seek the Lord,
even all the nations on whom the name of the Lord has been invoked, says the Lord who does these things'
(18) known from eternity.

(19) "Wherefore, I think that we should not burden the Gentiles turning to God, (20) but to write to them instructing them to abstain from pollution of idols, fornication, from strangled animals, and from blood. (21) For Moses from ancient generations is proclaimed in every city, being read every Sabbath in the synagogues."

(22) Then it seemed good to the apostles and the elders with all the church to send chosen men from them to Antioch with Paul and Barnabas. They chose Judas, called Barsabbas, and Silas, leading men among the brethren, (23) to deliver the following letter:

"The apostles and the elders, brothers, to the Gentile brothers in Antioch, Syria and Cilicia, send greetings. (24) Since we have heard that some from us whom we did not commission have troubled you with words unsettling your minds, (25) we are sending some men to you whom we unanimously selected, with our beloved Barnabas and Paul, (26) men who have risked their lives for the name of our Lord Jesus Christ. (27) Therefore we have sent Judas and Silas, who will announce in speech the same message as the letter. (28) For it seemed good to the Holy Spirit and to us that no burden should be put on you except these necessary things: (29) abstain from idol sacrifices, blood, from meat of strangled animals and from fornication. You will do well to keep yourselves from these things. Farewell."

(30) They therefore, being sent away, went down to Antioch, and they assembled the people and handed them the letter. (31) When they read the letter, they rejoiced at the exhortation. Judas and Silas, who were prophets, encouraged and strengthened them with many words. (33) After a time, they left Antioch to return to Jerusalem bringing peace from the church to the ones sending them. (35) But Paul and Barnabas remained in Antioch teaching and preaching, with many others, the word of the Lord.

(36) Sometime later Paul said to Barnabas, "Let us return and visit the brothers in every city where we preached the word of the Lord to see how they are doing." (37) Barnabas wanted to take with them John Mark, (38) but Paul thought that it was not right to take him with them, because he

left them at Pamphylia and did not go with them to the work. (39) There was such a sharp contention that they separated from each other, and Barnabas took Mark and sailed to Cyprus. (40) Paul, having chosen Silas, went forth, being commended by the brothers to the grace of the Lord. (41) They went through Syria and Cilicia strengthening the churches.

Acts 16:1-40

(1) Then Paul came down to Derbe and to Lystra, and, behold, there was a certain disciple there by the name of Timothy, a son of a faithful Jewish woman, but his father was a Greek. (2) He was highly esteemed by the brothers in Lystra and Iconium. (3) Paul wanted to take Timothy with them, so he circumcised him because the Jews were in those places, for they all knew that his father was a Greek. (4) As they went through the cities, they delivered the decrees that the apostles and elders had decided that they should obey. (5) Therefore the churches were strengthened, and they daily increased in numbers.

(6) They went through the region of Phrygia and Galatia, being forbidden by the Holy Spirit to speak the word in Asia; (7) and coming to the borders of Mysia, they tried to go into Bithynia, but the Spirit of Jesus would not permit them. (8) So passing by Mysia they went down to Troas. (9) In a vision, through the night, a certain Macedonian appeared to Paul who was standing and pleading with him saying, "Come over into Macedonia and help us!" (10) And when Paul saw this vision, we immediately sought to go forth into Macedonia, convinced that God had called us to evangelize them.

(11) So setting sail from Troas, we went in a straight course to Samothrace, and on the next day to Neapolis, (12) and from there to Philippi, which is the first city, a colony, in that part of Macedonia. We stayed in this city several days.

(13) On the Sabbath day we went outside the gate by a river, where we thought was a place of prayer, and sitting down, we spoke to some women who came there. (14) And there was a certain woman whose name was Lydia, a dealer in purple from the city of Thyatira. She, worshiping God, listened to us, and the Lord opened up her heart to take heed to the message of Paul. (15) When she and her household were baptized, she besought us, saying, "If you have judged me to be faithful in the Lord, come and stay in my house." And she entreated us to do so.

(16) When we went to the place of prayer, a certain maiden with a spirit of divination met us. She brought great gain to her masters by fortune-telling. (17) The maiden, following Paul and us, cried out, saying, "These men are slaves of the most high God and announce to you a way of salvation."

(18) She did this for many days. Then Paul, greatly troubled, turning to the spirit said, "I command you, in the name of Jesus Christ, come

out from her." And it came out immediately.

(19) Then her masters, seeing that the hope of their profit from her was gone, seized Paul and Silas and dragged them into the market place before the rulers; (20) and bringing them to the magistrates, they said, "These men, being Jews, are troubling our city. (21) They are teaching us customs which are not lawful for us to accept or practice, being Romans." (22) The crowd rose up against them, and the magistrates, tearing off their garments, commanded that they be flogged. (23) After whipping them with many lashes, they threw them into prison, charging the jailer to keep them securely. (24) The jailer, receiving such a charge, threw them into the inner prison securing their feet in the stocks.

(25) At midnight Paul and Silas were praying and praising God, and the prisoners were listening to them. (26) Suddenly there was a great earthquake so that the foundation of the jail was shaken, and immediately all the doors were opened and all the bonds were loosed. (27) The jailer awoke and, seeing the doors of the prison open and thinking that the prisoners had escaped, drew his sword to kill himself. (28) But Paul called out in a loud voice, saying, "Do no harm to yourself for we are all here."

(29) The jailer, asking for light, rushed in and trembling fell before Paul and Silas, (30) and leading them outside said, "What must I do that I may be saved?"

(31) They said, "Believe on the Lord Jesus, and you shall be saved and your household." (32) So they spoke to him the word of God with all his household. (33) Then the jailer, taking them in that hour of the night, washed their stripes, and he, and his entire household, was baptized immediately. (34) Bringing them to his house he fed them at his table, and he, with his entire household, rejoiced at having believed in God.

(35) When daylight came, the magistrates sent their officers saying, "Release those men."

(36) The jailer reported these words to Paul, "The magistrates have sent word that you may be released. Now, therefore, go in peace."

(37) But Paul said to them, "They beat us publicly, men who are uncondemned Romans, and they threw us into prison, and now do they expel us secretly? No, indeed, let them come and bring us out."

(38) The officers reported to the magistrates these words, and they were afraid when they heard that they were Romans. (39) They came and apologized to them and asked them to leave the city. (40) So going from the prison, they entered the house of Lydia, and when they had met with the brothers, they encouraged them and departed.

Acts 17:1-34

(1) Passing through Amphipolis and Apollonia, they came to Thessalonica, where there was a Jewish synagogue. (2) Paul, as his custom

was, lectured to them for three Sabbath days from the Scriptures, (3) opening up and explaining to them that it was necessary for the Christ to suffer and to rise from the dead; and he said "This Jesus, whom I announce to you, is the Christ." (4) Some of them were persuaded and cast in their lots with Paul and Silas, and also a multitude of worshiping Greeks, and many of the influential women joined them.

(5) The Jews, becoming jealous, gathered some of the evil loafers from the market place, and getting a mob together disturbed the city. Coming to the house of Jason, the Jews sought to bring them to the mob. (6) But, not finding them, they dragged Jason and some of the brothers to the city officials, shouting, "These men, having turned the world upside down, have arrived here, (7) and Jason has welcomed them; and they are defying the decrees of Caesar, saying that there is another king—Jesus." (8) The crowd and the city officials, hearing this, were troubled, (9) and taking bail from Jason and the others, they released them.

(10) The brothers, immediately during the night, sent Paul and Silas to Berea. When they arrived, they went into the synagogue of the Jews. (11) These men were nobler than those in Thessalonica. They received the word with all eagerness, examining the Scriptures daily to verify the truth. (12) Therefore, many of them believed, and also many of the honorable Greek women and men believed. (13) But when the Jews from Thessalonica found out that Paul was preaching the word of God in Berea, they came there also agitating and troubling the crowds. (14) Then immediately the brothers sent Paul away to go as far as the sea, but Silas and Timothy remained there. (15) The men who went with Paul brought him to Athens, and receiving instructions that Silas and Timothy should join him quickly, they departed.

(16) While Paul was waiting for Silas and Timothy, he was troubled in his spirit, seeing the city full of idols. (17) Therefore, he lectured to the Jews in the synagogue and the worshiping proselytes, and in the market place everyday to those who happened to be there. (18) Some of the Epicurean and Stoic philosophers encountered him, and some said, "What is this seed picker trying to say?"

Others said, "He seems to be talking about foreign demons." This was because he preached Jesus and the resurrection.

(19) Then, taking hold of him, they led him to the Hill of Mars, saying, "May we know what this new teaching is that you are proclaiming? (20) For some have told us about startling things, and we would like to know what this means." (21) (Now all Athenians and the strangers dwelling there spent their time doing nothing except to talk about or hear new ideas.)

(22) Then Paul, standing before them in the Hill of Mars, said, "Men, Athenians, I observe that you are extremely religious. (23) For, passing along the way, I looked at your objects of worship. I even found an altar which was inscribed: "TO AN UNKNOWN GOD." Therefore, this God whom you worship in ignorance, I proclaim to you.

(24) "The God who made the universe and all things in it is the Lord of heaven and earth and does not dwell in man-made shrines; (25) neither does he need to be ministered to by human hands, for it is he who gives to all life and breath and everything. (26) He made from one all nations of men to dwell on all the face of the earth, having fixed the seasons and boundaries of their dwellings. (27) He did this so that they may seek him and so that they might feel after him and find him, and yet God is not far from anyone of us. (28) For in him we live and move and exist, as, indeed, some of your poets have said, 'For we are his children.'

(29) "Therefore, being children of God, we ought not think of the divine nature to be like gold, or silver, or stone, or to the engraved work of the skill and meditation of man. (30) God, in times past, overlooked the ignorance of men, but now he declares to all men everywhere to repent, (31) because he has set a day in which he will judge with fairness the inhabited earth by a man whom he has designated, giving an assurance to all by raising him from the dead."

(32) Some, hearing of a resurrection of the dead, scoffed, but others said, "We will hear you again concerning this matter." (33) So Paul went out from the midst of them. (34) But some of the men, cleaving to him, believed; among them were Dionysis, the Areopagite, and a woman named Damaris, and others with them.

Acts 18:1-28

(1) After these things, Paul left Athens and went to Corinth. (2) There he met a certain Jew whose name was Aquila, a native of Pontus, and his wife Priscilla, who had recently come from Italy (because Claudius had commanded all the Jews to leave Rome). Paul went to them, (3) and because they were of the same trade, tentmakers, he remained with them and they made tents. (4) Paul lectured each Sabbath in the synagogue, persuading both Jews and Greeks.

(5) When Silas and Timothy came from Macedonia, Paul was absorbed in the word, solemnly witnessing to the Jews that Jesus was the Christ. (6) But when they resisted and blasphemed him, Paul, shaking off his garments, said to them, "Your blood is on your head. I am innocent. Now I will go to the Gentiles."

(7) From there he went into the house of a worshiper of God whose name was Titius Justus. His house was next-door to the synagogue. (8) Crispus, the synagogue ruler, and his entire household believed in the Lord; and many of the Corinthians hearing, believed, and they were baptized. (9) And in the night the Lord said to Paul through a vision, "Do not be afraid, speak and do not be silent, (10) because I am with you, and no one will mistreat you, because I have many people in this city." (11) Paul remained with them a year and six months teaching the word of God.

(12) While Gallio was proconsul of Achaia, the Jews with one mind brought Paul to the tribunal, (13) saying that Paul was persuading men to worship God contrary to the law. (14) When Paul was about to open his mouth, Gallio said to the Jews, "If it were a matter of injustice or vicious crime, O Jews, I would reason with you; (15) but since it is a dispute concerning words and names and your law, settle it yourselves. I do not intend to be a judge of these things." (16) And he sent them away from the tribunal. (17) Then they seized Sosthenes, the synagogue ruler, and struck him in front of the tribunal, but Gallio was not concerned about these things.

(18) After that, Paul stayed in Corinth for many days. Then, bidding farewell to the brothers, he sailed to Syria with Priscilla and Aquila, after having his hair cut off at Cenchreae because of a vow he had taken. (19) They came to Ephesus, where Paul left Priscilla and Aquila, and he went into the synagogue and lectured to the Jews. (20) They asked him to stay with them longer, but he declined. (21) Bidding them farewell, he said, "Again, God willing, I will return to you." Then he set sail from Ephesus. (22) Paul came to Caesarea, and after going up and greeting the church, he went down to Antioch. (23) Having spent some time there, he departed, going through the Galatian country and Phrygia, strengthening all the disciples.

(24) Appolos, a certain Jew from Alexandria, an eloquent man and mighty in the Scripture, came to Ephesus. (25) This man, being instructed in the way of the Lord and being zealous in the Spirit, spoke accurately the things concerning Jesus, knowing only the baptism of John. (26) He spoke boldly in the synagogue. Priscilla and Aquila, hearing him, took him and more perfectly explained to him the way of God.

(27) When Appolos decided to go into Achaia, the brothers encouraged him by writing to the disciples to welcome him. On arriving, he was a great source of strength to those who by grace had believed. (28) For he vehemently confuted the Jews publicly proving that Jesus was the Christ.

Acts 19:1-40

(1) When Apollos was in Corinth, Paul passed through the upper part of the province and came to Ephesus and found some disciples. (2) He said to them, "Did you receive the Holy Spirit when you believed?"

They said to him, "We have not heard about the Holy Spirit."

(3) Then Paul said, "Unto whom, therefore, were you baptized?"

And they said, "Unto the baptism of John."

(4) Then Paul said, "John baptized those repenting and saying to them that they must believe in the one coming after him, that is Jesus."

(5) So hearing this, they were baptized into the name of the Lord Jesus; (6) and as Paul laid his hands on them, the Holy Spirit came upon them, and they spoke in tongues and prophesied. (7) There were about twelve men in all.

(8) Paul, entering into the synagogue, spoke boldly for three months, reasoning persuasively about the kingdom of God. (9) But some were hardened and refused to believe, and they spoke evil of the Way before the multitude. Paul, withdrawing from them, took his disciples and lectured daily in the school of Tyrannus. (10) This continued for two years, so that all the inhabitants of Asia heard the word of the Lord, both Jews and Greeks.

(11) God did unusual, powerful miracles through the hands of Paul. (12) Handkerchiefs or aprons that had touched the body of Paul were taken to the sick, and they were healed of their diseases and the evil spirits left them.

(13) Then some of the wandering Jews, exorcists, attempted to use the name of the Lord Jesus to cast out evil spirits, saying, "I exorcise you by the name of Jesus, whom Paul proclaims." (14) And there were seven sons of Sceva, a Jewish high priest, doing this.

(15) The evil spirit, answering them, said, "I know Jesus and I have heard of Paul, but you, who are you!" (16) Then the man with the evil spirit leaped on them and so violently treated them that they, having been wounded, fled naked out of that house. (17) This became known to all the Jews and Greeks living in Ephesus, and fear fell on all of them, and the name of the Lord Jesus was magnified. (18) Many of the ones having believed came confessing and revealing what they had been doing. (19) And many of the ones practicing sorcery brought their books and burned them publicly. The estimated value of the books was five thousand pieces of silver. (20) So the power of the word of the Lord increased and was strong.

(21) After these things happened, Paul decided in his mind to go through Macedonia and Achaia and then on to Jerusalem. He said, "After I go there, I must also see Rome." (22) So he sent Timothy and Erastus, two of his assistants, to Macedonia, but he remained for a while in Asia.

(23) Now there was a great disturbance about that time concerning the Way. (24) For a man named Demetrius, a silversmith, made silver shrines of Artemis, providing a good business to the craftsmen. (25) So Demetrius assembled the workmen of the same trade and said to them, "Men, you know that from this business we make our money. (26) And you see and hear that this Paul, not only Ephesus but almost all of Asia, has persuaded and turned away a great number of people, saying that those things made by hands are not gods. (27) So, not only is our business in danger of being destroyed, but also the temple of the goddess Artemis may count for nothing, and the great majesty of her, whom all Asia and the inhabited earth worships, is about to be destroyed."

(28) When the crowd heard this, they became furious and cried out, saying, "Great is Artemis of the Ephesians." (29) And the city was filled with confusion, and they rushed, with one mind, into the theater. They seized Gaius and Aristarchus, Macedonians who were traveling companions of Paul. (30) Then Paul intended to enter the mob, but his disciples would not let him. (31) Some of the Asiarchs, friends of Paul, sent a message to him

urging him not to enter the theater.

(32) Some were crying out one thing and some another, for the assembly was confused, because most of them had no idea why they had come together. (33) Alexander, instructed by the crowd and put forward by the Jews, motioned with his hand, wishing to defend himself before the mob; (34) but knowing that he was a Jew, there was one voice from all for about two hours crying out, "Great is Artemis of the Ephesians."

(35) The city clerk, having quieted the crowd, said, "Men, Ephesians, What man is there who does not know that the city of Ephesus is the temple warden of the great Artemis and the image fallen from the sky? (36) As these things are undeniable, you ought to keep calm and do nothing rashly. (37) For you brought these men here who have not robbed temples nor blasphemed your goddess. (38) If Demetrius and the craftsmen with him have anything against anyone, the courts are held and the proconsuls are there. So let them bring charges against one another. (39) If you want to bring up anything further, it will be settled in the lawful assembly. (40) For we are in danger of being charged with insurrection concerning today, for there is no justification that we can give concerning this commotion." And saying this, he dismissed the assembly.

Acts 20:1-38

(1) After the tumult was over, Paul sent for the disciples, and after encouraging them, he left for Macedonia. (2) He went through that area speaking many words of encouragement to the disciples and went on to Greece, (3) where he stayed for three months. The Jews made a plot against him as he was about to sail for Syria, so he decided to return through Macedonia. (4) And joining him there was Sopater, son of Pyrrhus of Berea, and Aristarchus and Secundus of Thessalonica, Gaius of Derbe, Timothy, and Tychicus and Trophimus of Asia. (5) These men went on ahead and waited for us in Troas. (6) We sailed from Philippi after the Days of Unleavened Bread, and after five days we joined them in Troas and stayed there for seven days.

(7) When we came together on Saturday night to break bread, Paul lectured to them on the evening before his departure, and he continued to speak until midnight. (8) There were many lamps in the upper room where we had been assembled. (9) A certain young man, Eutychus, sitting on the window sill, being overcome by a deep sleep while Paul lectured for such a long time, fell from the third floor and was taken up dead. (10) Paul going down, fell on him and embracing him said, "Do not be alarmed, he is still alive." (11) Then going upstairs he broke bread and ate and talked with them until daylight. Then he departed. (12) Then they took the young lad home alive and were greatly comforted.

(13) Then we went ahead to the ship and set sail for Assos, intending

to take Paul on board there, for he wanted to go by land. (14) So we met him in Assos and sailed on to Mitylene. (15) We sailed from there, and on the next day we arrived off the coast of Chios; and the next day we crossed over to Samos, and the next day we came to Miletus. (16) Paul decided not to spend time in Asia so he sailed past Ephesus, for he was in a hurry to get to Jerusalem for the day of Pentecost.

(17) From Miletus, he sent a message to Ephesus to ask the elders of the church to meet him. (18) When they came to him he said, "You know how I lived the whole time I was with you, from the first day I came to Asia. (19) I served the Lord in all humility with tears and trials. You know all the things I encountered because of the plots of the Jews (20) and that I kept nothing from you that was for your own good. I taught you publicly and from house to house. (21) I solemnly warned both the Jews and Greeks to turn to God in repentance and faith in our Lord Jesus Christ.

(22) "And now, I am constrained in the Spirit to go to Jerusalem, not knowing what awaits me, (23) except that in every city the Holy Spirit solemnly witnesses to me that bonds and affliction await me. (24) I count my own life as of no value to myself, but that I may finish my course and the ministry, which I received from the Lord Jesus, to solemnly witness the grace of God.

(25) "And now behold, I know that you to whom I have gone about preaching the Kingdom of God will never see my face again. (26) Therefore, I declare to you this day that I am innocent from the blood of all men, (27) for I did not fail to declare to you the whole counsel of God. (28) Be on guard for yourselves and for all the flock in which the Holy Spirit has placed you as overseers to shepherd the church of God, which he acquired through the blood of his own Son. (29) I know that after my departure, grievous wolves will come to you, not sparing the flock. (30) And men from your own number, distorting the truth, will drag away disciples after them. (31) Therefore, be on guard, remembering that for three years, night and day, I did not cease admonishing each of you with tears.

(32) "Now I commend you to God and to the revelation of his grace, which is able to build you up and give you an inheritance among the saints. (33) I coveted no one's silver or gold or clothes. (34) You know that these hands ministered to my needs and to the needs of my companions. (35) In every way I showed you that it is necessary to work so we can help the weak, remembering the words of the Lord Jesus who said, 'It is more blessed to give than to receive.' "

(36) When Paul had finished speaking, he knelt down with them all and prayed. (37) There was much weeping as they embraced Paul and fervently kissed him. (38) They were grieved most because he said that they would never see his face again. Then they escorted him to the ship.

Acts 21:1-40

(1) When we had withdrawn from them, we set sail, taking a straight course to Cos; and the next day to Rhodes, and from there to Patara, (2) and having found a ship crossing over to Phoenicia, we set sail. (3) Seeing Cyprus on the left, we sailed into Syria and landed at Tyre, for there the ship unloaded the cargo. (4) Finding disciples there, we remained for seven days. They told Paul, through the Spirit, not to go to Jerusalem. (5) But when our time ashore was ended, we journeyed on. All the disciples, with women and children, escorted us outside the city. Kneeling on the shore and praying, (6) we gave parting greetings to one another, and embarking in the ship, the disciples returned home.

(7) We finished our voyage from Tyre and arrived in Ptolemais, and greeting the brothers we remained one day with them. (8) On the morrow, we departed and came to Caesarea, and entering into the house of Philip, the evangelist, being of the seven, we stayed with him. (9) This man had four virgin daughters who were prophetesses.

(10) After remaining there many days, Agabus, a prophet from Judea, (11) came down to us, and taking the girdle of Paul and tying his feet and hands, said, "This is what the Holy Spirit says, 'In this way the Jews in Jerusalem will bind the man whose girdle this is, and they will deliver him into the hands of the Gentiles.' "

(12) When we heard these things, we and the residents there begged Paul not to go to Jerusalem. (13) Then Paul answered, "Why are you weeping and weakening my heart? For I am not only ready to be bound in Jerusalem but also to die for the sake of the name of Jesus."

(14) When he was not persuaded, we were silent and could only say, "May the will of the Lord be done."

(15) After these days, we got ready and went up to Jerusalem. (16) Some of the disciples went with us and brought us to lodge with Mnason, one of the first disciples from Cyprus.

(17) The brothers in Jerusalem joyfully received us. (18) On the next day, Paul went in with us to James. (19) And having greeted them, Paul related in detail what God had done among the Gentiles through his ministry. (20) Hearing this, they praised God and said to him, "You see, brother, thousands of Jews have believed, and they are all zealots of the law. (21) They have been told that you teach all the Jews throughout the nations to turn away from Moses, telling them neither to circumcise their children nor to walk in our customs. (22) What shall we do? They are sure to hear that you are here. (23) Therefore we advise you to do this: We have four men who have put themselves under a vow. (24) Join these men and be purified with them and pay their expenses for the shaving of their heads. Then everyone will know the things of which they have been told about you are not true, but that you, yourself, are living in obedience to the law.

(25) Concerning the Gentile believers, we joined in writing them our decision that they should keep themselves from idol sacrifices, from blood, from strangled animals, and from fornication."

(26) Then Paul, on the next day, having been purified, went into the temple, signifying the completion of the days of purification and remained there until an offering would be made for each of them.

(27) Now when the seven days were almost completed, the Jews from Asia, seeing Paul in the temple, stirred up the entire crowd, and they laid their hands on him, (28) shouting, "Men, Israelites, help! This is the man who is teaching all men everywhere against the people and the law and this place, and he has even brought Greeks into the temple and has profaned this holy place." (29) (For they had previously seen Trophimus the Ephesian in the city with him, and they supposed that Paul had brought him into the temple.)

(30) The whole city was in turmoil, and the people rushed together; and seizing Paul, they dragged him out of the temple, and immediately the doors were shut. (31) While they were seeking to kill Paul, word came to the officer commanding the garrison that Jerusalem was in an uproar. (32) He immediately took soldiers with their centurions and rushed upon them. When the rioters saw the commander and his officers, they stopped beating Paul.

(33) Then the commander came forward and arrested Paul and commanded that he be bound with two chains, and then he demanded to know who he was and what he had done. (34) The crowd was in an uproar—some were calling out one thing and some another. So the commander, unable to get the facts, took Paul into the barracks. (35) When Paul came to the steps, the soldiers carried him because of the violence of the crowd. (36) For many of the people followed and cried out, "Put him to death!"

(37) As Paul was being brought to the barracks, he said to the commander, "May I speak with you?"

(38) And he said, "Can you speak Greek? Aren't you the Egyptian who sometime ago stirred up a rebellion and led four thousand dagger-men into the wilderness?"

(39) Paul answered, "I am a Jew from Tarsus of Cilicia, a citizen of a well-known city, and I beg of you let me speak to the people."

(40) Then Paul, being permitted to speak, stood on the steps and beckoned with his hand to the people. When there was dead silence, he addressed the people in the Hebrew language.

Acts 22:1-30

(1) "Men, brothers and fathers, hear now my defense." (2) When they heard him speaking in Hebrew, they became quiet.

Then Paul said, (3) "I am a Jew, born in Tarsus of Cilicia, and brought up in this city at the feet of Gamaliel, having been trained according to the exactness of the law of our fathers, and being zealous of God, even as all of you are today. (4) I persecuted the followers of the Way unto death, binding and delivering both men and women to prison. (5) Even as the high priest and all the council of elders can testify, I received letters to the brothers in Damascus, and I journeyed there to take those who had been bound to Jerusalem to be punished.

(6) "When I was journeying and drawing near to Damascus, about midday, suddenly out of heaven a blazing light shined around me, (7) and I fell to the ground and heard a voice saying to me, 'Saul, Saul, Why do you persecute me?'

(8) "And I answered 'Who are you, Lord?'

(9) "And he said to me, 'I am Jesus the Nazarene, whom you are persecuting.' The ones with me saw the light, but they did not hear the voice of the one speaking to me.

(10) "Then I said, 'What must I do, Lord?'

"The Lord said to me, 'Get up and go into Damascus, and there you will be told concerning the things having been arranged for you to do.' (11) And I was blinded by the glory of that light, and being led by the hand by those who were with me, I went into Damascus.

(12) "A man named Ananias, a pious man according to the law and well-spoken of by all the Jews, dwelled there. (13) He, coming and standing by me, said to me, 'Brother Saul, look up.' And in that hour I looked up and saw him.

(14) "Then he said, 'The God of our fathers has chosen you to know his will and to see the Righteous One and to hear his voice, (15) because you will be his witness of the things you have seen and heard to all men. (16) And now why do you hesitate? Arise, be baptized and wash away your sins, calling upon his name.'

(17) "When I returned to Jerusalem, I was praying in the temple, and I fell into a trance. (18) I saw the Lord speaking to me, 'Make haste and go forth out of Jerusalem, because they will not receive your witness concerning me.'

(19) " 'Lord,' I said, 'they know that I was going throughout the synagogues beating those who believed in you and putting them in prison. (20) And when the blood of Stephen, your witness, was being shed, I was standing by consenting and holding the garments of those who killed him.'

(21) "Then the Lord said to me, 'Go, because I will send you to the nations far way.' "

(22) The Jews heard him up to this point, but at these words, they lifted their voices and shouted, "Take him from the earth, for such a man is not fit to live."

(23) As they were shouting, tearing their garments, and throwing

dust into the air, (24) the commander brought Paul into the barracks and directed that he be examined by flogging so that he might fully know the cause they had against him. (25) As they stretched him forward with the thongs, Paul said to the centurion standing by, "Is it lawful for you to whip a man who is a Roman and uncondemned?"

(26) When the centurion heard this, he approached the commander and said, "What are you about to do? This man is a Roman."

(27) The commander went to Paul and asked him, "Tell me, are you a Roman?"

Paul answered the commander, "Yes."

(28) The commander said, "I paid a great sum of money to acquire this citizenship."

Then Paul said, "But I was born a citizen."

(29) Immediately, therefore, those who were about to flog him stood back. The commander also feared when he realized that he had put a Roman in chains.

(30) The next day, wishing to know why Paul was accused by the Jews, he released him and commanded the chief priest and all the council to come together, and they brought down Paul and set him before them.

Acts 23:1-35

(1) Paul, gazing at the Sanhedrin, said, "Men, brothers, I have lived in all good conscience before God to this day."

(2) Then Ananias, the high priest, gave orders to the ones standing by to strike him on the mouth. (3) Then Paul said to him, "God is about to strike you, a wall having been whitewashed, sitting to judge me according to the law, but contrary to the law commanded me to be struck!"

(4) Those standing by said, "Do you revile the high priest of God?"

(5) "Brothers, I did not perceive him to be a high priest; for it is written, 'You shall not speak evil of a ruler of your people.' "

(6) And Paul, knowing that some were Sadducees and others were Pharisees, cried out in the Sanhedrin, "Men, Brothers, I am a Pharisee, a son of a Pharisee. I am being judged concerning my hope of the resurrection of the dead." (7) As he said this, there was a division between the Pharisees and the Sadducees, and the multitude was divided. (8) For the Sadducees say that there is no resurrection, neither angels nor spirits, but Pharisees confess both.

(9) There was a vociferous yelling, and some of the scribes of the Pharisees contented vehemently saying, "We find no evil in this man. Perhaps, a spirit or an angel did speak to him." (10) The discord became so violent that the commander, fearing that Paul would be pulled apart by them, commanded the soldiers to come down and seize him from the midst of them and to bring him into the barracks.

(11) The following night the Lord said to him, "Be of good courage, for as you have solemnly witnessed the things concerning me in Jerusalem, so you must also witness in Rome."

(12) At daybreak the Jews made a conspiracy, putting themselves under an oath, saying that they would neither eat nor drink until they had killed Paul. (13) There were more than forty men involved in this plot. (14) They, going to the chief priests and elders, said, "We have bound ourselves under a solemn oath to taste nothing until we have killed Paul. (15) Now therefore, you inform the commander and the Sanhedrin to bring Paul down for more accurate information about his case, and we, as he draws near, are prepared to kill him."

(16) Paul's sister's son, hearing about the treachery, came into the barracks and told Paul.

(17) Then Paul, calling to one of the centurions, said, "Take this youth to the commander, for he has something to report to him."

(18) He therefore, taking him to the commander, said, "Paul, the prisoner, asked me to bring this young man to you. He has something to tell you."

(19) The commander, taking him by the hand and withdrawing to a private place, asked, "What do you have to report to me?"

(20) He said, "The Jews have agreed to ask you tomorrow to bring Paul to the Sanhedrin to question him more accurately about his case. (21) Therefore be not persuaded by them, for they are waiting for him in ambush. More than forty men have bound themselves under a solemn oath neither to eat nor to drink until they have killed him, and now they are waiting for you to give the word."

(22) The commander therefore dismissed the young man telling him to tell no one about the report.

(23) Then he called two of his centurions and said, "Prepare two hundred soldiers, seventy horsemen, and two hundred spearmen so they may go as far as Caesarea to leave at 9:00 P.M. tonight. (24) And prepare mounts for Paul to take him to safety to Governor Felix." (25) He sent the following letter:

(26) "Claudius Lysias, to the Most Excellent Governor Felix: Greetings.

(27) "This man, having been seized by the Jews, was about to be killed by them, and I, having learned that he was a Roman, rescued him with my soldiers; (28) and seeking to know fully the charges on which they were accusing him, I brought him to the Sanhedrin. (29) I found that they were accusing him of matters concerning their law, but there was no charge against him worthy of death or imprisonment. (30) When it was revealed to me that there was a conspiracy against him, I immediately sent him to you, and I commanded the accusers to speak against him before you."

(31) Therefore the soldiers, according to their command, took

Paul and brought him during the night to Antipatris. (32) On the next day the horsemen went with him, but the others returned to the barracks. (33) They entered into Caesarea and gave the letter to the governor and presented Paul to him. (34) After he read the letter, he asked what province he was from, and learning that he was from Cilicia, he said, (35) "I will hear you when your accusers arrive." He commanded that he be kept in Herod's palace.

Acts 24:1-27

(1) Five days later Ananias, the high priest, came with some elders and Tertullus, an orator, to present their case against Paul to the governor. (2) When Paul was summoned, Tertullus began to accuse him, saying to the governor, "Your reforms have given us great peace to this nation through your foresight, (3) and we welcome you everywhere and in everything, most excellent Felix, with all gratitude. (4) But I must not detain you, I beg of you in your kindness hear us briefly.

(5) "We have found this man to be a public pest, an inciter of insurrection among the Jews in all the world, and a ringleader of the sect of the Nazarenes. (6) He also attempted to profane the temple, but we seized him. (8) You will be able, after examining him concerning all these things, to fully understand our case against him."

(9) And all the Jews joined in affirming that all these accusations were true.

(10) Then Paul, when the governor nodded his head for him to speak, answered, "I, knowing that you have been a judge many years to this nation, cheerfully make my defense concerning these charges. (11) You can easily verify the fact that not more than twelve days ago I went to worship in Jerusalem. (12) They did not find me in the temple disputing with anyone or stirring up a crowd, neither in the synagogue nor in the city, (13) neither can they prove their accusations against me. (14) But I do confess this to you that according to the Way, which they call a sect, I do worship the God of our fathers, believing all the things concerning the law and the scriptures of the prophets, (15) having a hope toward God, as my accusers also have, that there will be a resurrection both of the just and the unjust. (16) This being so, I strive to have a blameless conscience always toward God and men.

(17) "After many years, I came to my nation bringing alms and offerings; (18) and they found me, having been purified in the temple; and I was not with a crowd nor was I causing an uproar; (19) but the Jews from Asia ought to be here to present their charges if they have anything against me. (20) Or let these men say what they found me guilty of when I stood before the Sanhedrin. (21) This one thing I did while standing before the Sanhedrin, I cried out, 'I am being judged before you today concerning the resurrection of the dead.' "

(22) Then Felix, knowing more clearly the things concerning the Way, adjourned the trial, saying, "When Lysias the commander arrives, I will decide your case." (23) Then commanding the centurion to keep Paul in custody, he gave him liberty and allowed his friends to provide for his needs.

(24) After a few days, Felix came with his wife, Drusilla, who was a Jewess, and he sent for Paul and heard him concerning his faith in Christ Jesus. (25) As he spoke concerning righteousness and self-control and the coming judgment, Felix trembled and said, "Go now, but at an opportune time, I will send for you." (26) He was also at the same time hoping to receive a bribe from Paul; therefore, he frequently sent for him and talked with him.

(27) After two years, Felix was succeeded by Porcious Festus, but Felix, wishing to gain favor with the Jews, left Paul in custody.

Acts 25:1-27

(1) Festus, three days after entering the province, went from Caesarea to Jerusalem, (2) and the chief priests and the leaders of the Jews presented their charges against Paul, and they begged Festus (3) to do them a favor of transferring Paul to Jerusalem. They planned an ambush to kill him on the way. (4) Festus answered, "Paul should be kept in Caesarea, and I will soon be there. (5) Let able men go with me, and if he is guilty of any crime let them bring charges against him."

(6) After spending eight or ten days more in Jerusalem, he went to Caesarea, and the next day, sitting on the judgment seat, he commanded that Paul be brought in. (7) When Paul came in, the Jews who came from Jerusalem stood around him. They made many serious charges against him, which they were unable to prove.

(8) Paul defended himself, "I have not sinned against the law of the Jews nor against the temple nor against Caesar."

(9) Then Festus, wishing to gain the favor of the Jews, said to Paul, "Are you willing to go to Jerusalem and there be tried on these charges before me?"

(10) Paul answered, "I appeal to the court of Caesar, where I should be tried. I have not wronged the Jews, as you very well know. (11) If, however, I am guilty of a crime worthy of death, I am ready to die, but if these charges are false, no one has the right to deliver me to the Jews. I appeal to Caesar."

(12) Then Festus, after talking with his council, said, "You have appealed to Caesar, so to Caesar you will go."

(13) After a few days King Agrippa and Bernice came to Caesarea and greeted Festus. (14) As he remained there several days, Festus told the king about the case against Paul. He said, "There is a certain man left in prison by Felix. (15) When I was in Jerusalem, the chief priests and the elders

of the Jews informed me about him and demanded judgment against him.

(16) "I told them that it was not a Roman custom to hand over any man before he had faced his accusers with the opportunity to make his defense. (17) Therefore they came with me, and on the next day I commanded that the man be brought to trial. (18) When the accusers came forward, they brought no evil charges against him as I had anticipated. (19) They only had questions concerning their own religion and about a dead man called Jesus whom Paul declared to be alive. (20) I, being perplexed about these things, asked Paul if he would go to Jerusalem to be judged about these things there. (21) But when Paul appealed for the decision of the Emperor, I ordered him to be kept until I could send him to Caesar."

(22) Agrippa said to Festus, "I would like to hear him myself."

He said, "Tomorrow you will hear him."

(23) The next day, therefore, Agrippa and Bernice entered with great pomp into the judgment hall with the commanders and chief men of the city, and at the command of Festus, Paul was brought in. (24) Festus said, "King Agrippa and all here present, you see this man whom all the multitude of the Jews petitioned me in Jerusalem and in Casesarea, clamoring for his execution. (25) But I found that he had done nothing worthy of death, and when he appealed to Caesar I decided to send him to Caesar. (26) But I have nothing to write Caesar about him. For this reason I have brought him before all of you. And especially before you, King Agrippa, that after cross-examination I may have something to write. (27) For it seems unreasonable to me to send a prisoner to Caesar without specifying charges against him."

Acts 26:1-32

(1) Then Agrippa said to Paul, "You may speak for yourself."

Then Paul stretched out his hand and made his defense. (2) "King Agrippa, I consider myself fortunate to defend myself today concerning all these things that I am accused of by the Jews, (3) because you are acquainted with all the customs and questions of the Jews; therefore, I beg of you to listen to me patiently.

(4) "The manner of my life from my youth, beginning in my country and in Jerusalem, is known by all Jews. (5) They have known me from the beginning and could testify that according to the most exact sect of our religion I lived as a Pharisee. (6) And now in the hope of the promise God made to our fathers I am being judged today, (7) to which our twelve tribes earnestly, night and day, hoped to see fulfilled. It is concerning this hope, O King, that I am accused by the Jews. (8) Why is it judged incredible with you that God should raise the dead?

(9) "Indeed, I once thought to myself that I ought to do many things contrary to the name of Jesus the Nazarene. (10) And, indeed, I did in Jerusalem. I put many saints in prison, and having authority from the chief

priests, I gave my vote to have them killed; (11) and in every synagogue I tortured them and compelled them to blaspheme, and I raged excessively against them as I persecuted them even to foreign cities.

(12) "When I was journeying to Damascus with authority and a commission from the chief priests, (13) at midday along the way I saw, O King, a light from heaven brighter than the sun shining around me and the ones journeying with me. (14) When we had all fallen down, I heard a voice saying to me in the Hebrew language, 'Saul, Saul, why do you persecute me? It is hard for you to kick against the goads.'

(15) "Then I said, 'Who are you, Lord?'

"And the Lord said to me, 'I am Jesus whom you are persecuting. (16) But now get up and stand on your feet, for I have appeared to you to appoint you to be a servant and witness of the things which you saw and which will appear to you; (17) and I will deliver you from your people and from the Gentiles, to whom I am sending you (18) to open their eyes to turn from darkness to light and from the authority of Satan to God, that they may receive forgiveness of sins and have a place among those having been sanctified by faith in me.'

(19) "Whence, O King Agrippa, I was not disobedient to the heavenly vision, (20) going first to those in Damascus, then to Jerusalem, then to the country of Judea, and then to the Gentiles, declaring that they should repent and turn to God, doing works worthy of repentance. (21) On account of these things the Jews seized me and tried to kill me. (22) God has been my helper until this day, as I stand witnessing to both small and great, saying nothing more than what the prophets and Moses said was to take place. (23) That is that Christ should suffer and that he should be first to rise from the dead and be a light both to the Jews and to the Gentiles."

(24) As Paul defended himself with these words, Festus shouted in a loud voice, "Paul, you are crazy; your excessive study is driving you insane."

(25) Paul replied, "I am not insane, most excellent Festus, but I speak words of truth and of good sense. (26) The king understands these things, before which I speak with confidence, for I am convinced that none of these things are unknown to him, for this was not done in secret. (27) King Agrippa, do you believe the prophets? I know that you do."

(28) Then Agrippa said to Paul, "In such a short time you seek to make a Christian of me!"

(29) Paul replied, "Whether it be a short time or a long time, I pray that not only you but all who hear me today would become as I am — except for these chains."

(30) The king and the governor and Bernice and the ones sitting with them arose; (31) and, having left the room, they spoke to one another, saying, "This man has done nothing worthy of death or imprisonment." (32) Agrippa said to Festus, "This man could have been released if he had not appealed to Caesar."

Acts 27:1-44

(1) When it was decided that we should sail to Italy, they delivered Paul and other prisoners to Julius, a centurion of a company of troops. (2) Embarking, we set sail in a ship from Adramyttium which was about to sail to the places on the coasts of Asia. Aristarchus, a Macedonian of Thessalonica, was with us. (3) The next day we came to Sidon. Julius treated Paul kindly, and he permitted him to visit his friends to receive help. (4) From there we sailed close to Cyprus to be protected from the adverse winds. (5) Then after sailing over the sea of Cilicia and Pamphylia, we came to Myra, a city of Lycia. (6) And there the centurion found an Alexandrian ship sailing to Italy, and he transferred us to it. (7) When we had sailed slowly for many days it was difficult for us to come near to Cnidus; as the wind would not allow us to go further, we sailed close to Crete near Salmone, (8) and with difficulty we sailed along the coast and came to a place called Fair Havens near the town of Lasea.

(9) We spent a long time there, and sailing was dangerous because it was after the Day of Pentecost; so Paul advised them, (10) saying "Men, I see that there will be injury and much loss, not only to the cargo and the ship, but also to the lives of the passengers on the voyage." (11) However, the centurion was persuaded more by the pilot and the master of the ship than by Paul. (12) The harbor was not suitable for wintering, so the majority wanted to sail from there, hoping to arrive in Phoenix and to winter there. It was a harbor of Crete, open to the south and northwest. (13) When a south wind blew gently, thinking that they could reach their destination, they raised anchor and coasted near the shore of Crete. (14) Soon afterwards, a tempestuous storm beat down upon us from the northeast, (15) and seizing the ship as it beat against the wind, we were unable to control it, so we were borne along. (16) We were able to pass near the small island called Clauda, and with difficulty we were able to secure the boat. (17) When they had put it aboard, they undergirded the ship with cables, and fearing that they might be driven into the quicksand of Syrtis, they lowered the sail and let the ship drift. (18) We were violently battered by the storm, and on the next day we threw cargo overboard; (19) and on the third day with their own hands they threw the ship's gear overboard. (20) When neither sun nor stars appeared for many days and the stormy weather continued to rage, all hope that we might be saved was taken away.

(21) Then Paul, standing in the midst of them, said, "Men, you should have listened to me and not sailed from Crete and caused this injury and loss. (22) And now I advise you to be of good cheer. There will be no loss of life, but we shall lose the ship. (23) For there stood by me in the night an angel of my God whom I serve, (24) saying 'Fear not, Paul, you must stand before Caesar, and behold God will save the lives of all the ones sailing with you.' (25) Therefore, be of good cheer, men, for I believe that God will

do that which has been spoken to me, (26) but we will be cast ashore on some island."

(27) In the fourteenth night while we were driven to and fro in the Adriatic Sea, about midnight the sailors thought that we were approaching some land. (28) They took soundings and found that the water was one hundred twenty feet deep. A little later they took sounding and found it to be ninety feet deep. (29) Then fearing that they might be wrecked on some rocky coast, they dropped four anchors from the stern and prayed for daylight. (30) And when the sailors sought to flee from the ship, lowering the boat into the sea, pretending to take the anchors from the front of the ship, (31) Paul said to the centurion and the soldiers, "Unless these men remain in the ship, you cannot be saved." (32) Then the soldiers cut the ropes of the boat and let it drift away.

(33) As day was dawning, Paul urged them all to partake of food, saying, "Today is the fourteenth day of anxiety and you have continued fasting, eating nothing. (34) Therefore, I urge you to partake of food, for this is necessary for your safety. No one will perish—even a hair of the head will not be lost."

(35) After Paul had said these things, he took bread and gave thanks to God in the presence of all, and breaking the bread he began to eat. (36) They were all of good courage, and they all ate. (37) The number of us in the ship was 276 persons. (38) When they had finished eating, they lightened the ship by throwing the wheat into the sea.

(39) When daylight came, they saw a certain bay with a sandy beach into which they decided to drive the ship upon. (40) The anchors were cut off and dropped into the sea, and they untied the ropes that held the rudders. Then they spread out the topsail to catch the breeze to reach the shore. (41) But the ship hit a reef between two deep places in the sea; and the front part was immovable on the ground, and the back part was broken by the waves.

(42) The soldiers, thinking that some of the prisoners might escape by swimming to shore, wanted to kill them. (43) But the centurion, wanting to save Paul, forbade them to do so. He commanded that those who could swim should jump first into the sea and swim to land (44) and for the rest, some on planks and others on parts of the ship, to follow. So they all reached the land safely.

Acts 28:1-31

(1) When we were safely ashore, we found that the island was called Malta. (2) The natives treated us with unusual kindness. They lit a fire because it was cold and raining, and they welcomed all of us. (3) When Paul collected a bundle of sticks and put them on the fire, a viper came out of the heat and fastened itself on his hand. (4) When the natives saw the beast hanging from his hand, they said to one another, "This man must be a

murderer saved from the sea, but justice will not allow him to live." (5) Then Paul, shaking off the beast into the fire, suffered no harm, (6) but they expected him to swell up or fall dead suddenly. However, after a long time, no harm came to him, so changing their minds, they said that he was a god.

(7) In that part of the island was an estate belonging to the chief man of the island whose name was Publius. He graciously received us, and we stayed with him three days. (8) The father of Publius became very sick and was lying down suffering from high fever and dysentery. Paul came to him praying, and putting his hands upon him, he was healed. (9) After this happened, the rest of those in the island that were sick came, and Paul healed them. (10) They honored us in many ways, and when we departed, they gave us everything we needed.

(11) After three months wintering in the island, we embarked in an Alexandrian ship with a distinguishing mark of the sons of Jupiter. (12) We went to Syracuse and remained there for three days, (13) and from there we made a circuit and arrived at Rhegium; and after one day a south wind blew, and on the second day we came to Puteoli, (14) where we found brothers who entreated us to stay with them seven days. Then we went to Rome. (15) The brothers there had heard about us, so they came to meet us as far as the Market Place of Appius and Three Taverns, and Paul seeing them and thanking God, took courage. (16) When we entered Rome, Paul was permitted to remain by himself, with a soldier guarding him.

(17) After three days he called together the chief Jews, and when they came together he said to them, "Men, Brothers, I have done nothing against our people or the customs of our fathers; yet as a prisoner, I was delivered into the hands of the Romans, (18) who examined me and were willing to release me, because they found nothing worthy of death in me. (19) But when the Jews objected, I was compelled to appeal to Caesar, not that I have anything to accuse my nation of. (20) Therefore, I have called to see and to talk to you. It is for the hope of Israel that I have this chain around me."

(21) Then they said to him, "We have received no letters concerning you from Judea, and none of the brothers have arrived here to speak evil against you; (22) but we want to know what you believe about this sect, for we know that it is denounced everywhere."

(23) They arranged to meet with Paul on a certain day. Many came to his lodging place; and he solemnly proclaimed the kingdom of God, and he was persuading them concerning Jesus from the Law of Moses and the prophets, from morning until evening. (24) Some were persuaded by his testimony, (25) but others disbelieved. They disagreed among themselves, and they departed after Paul had made his last statement, "It was true what Isaiah, the prophet, said to your fathers by the Holy Spirit:

(26) 'Go to this people and say,
"In hearing you will hear but not understand,
and in looking you will look but not see."

(27) For the heart of this people is hard,
and their ears are heavy,
and they have closed their eyes.
Lest they would see with their eyes,
and hear with their ears,
and understand with their hearts
and turn, so I could heal them.'

(28) "Know, therefore, that this salvation will be sent to the Gentiles, and they will hear."

(30) Paul remained two whole years in his own hired apartment welcoming all who came to him, (31) proclaiming the kingdom of God and teaching the things concerning the Lord Jesus Christ with all boldness and without hindrance.

The Ministry of Paul

Paul was probably born about A.D. 5 (Acts 7:58 – young man;
Philemon 1:9 – old man).
35 A.D. Martyrdom of Stephen. Conversion of Paul a little later,
perhaps in that same year.
46-48 A.D. First Missionary Journey (Acts 13:2-14:28)
48/49 A.D. Writing of Galatians
51 A.D. Writing of 1 Thessalonians from Corinth
51/52 A.D. Writing of 2 Thessalonians from Corinth
55 A.D. Writing of 1 Corinthians from Ephesus
55 A.D. Writing of 2 Corinthians from Macedonia
57 A.D. Writing of Romans from Cenchrea or Corinth
57-59 A.D. Caesarean imprisonment
60/61 A.D. Writing of Ephesians, Colossians, Philippians, Philemon
from Rome
62 A.D. Release from prison
62-67 A.D. Fourth mission journey, including ministry to Crete (Tit 1:5)
64 A.D. Rome burned
63-65 A.D. Writing of 1 Timothy and Titus from Philippi
67-68 A.D. Second Roman imprisonment (2 Timothy 4:6-8)
67/68 A.D. Writing of 2 Timothy from the Mamertime dungeon
(2 Timothy 4:6-8)
67/68 A.D. Trial and execution

The four men who delivered Paul's prison letters:
1. Epaphroditus from Philippi
> KJV Philippians 4:18: "But I have all, and abound: I am full, having
> received of Epaphroditus the things which were sent from you, an
> odor of a sweet smell, a sacrifice acceptable, well-pleasing to God."
2. Tychicus from Ephesus
> KJV Ephesians 6:21: "But that ye also may know my affairs, and
> how I do, Tychicus, a beloved brother and faithful minister in the
> Lord, shall make known to you all things...."
3. Epaphras from Colosse
> KJV Colossians 4:12: "Epaphras, who is one of you, a servant of
> Christ, saluteth you, always laboring fervently for you in prayers,
> that ye may stand perfect and complete in all the will of God."
4. Onesimus runaway slave from Colosse
> Philemon (10): "I appeal to you for my child, Onesimus, whose
> father I have become in my imprisonment."

On Paul's third missionary journey he began a far-reaching ministry in Ephesus. For two years he spoke in the school of Tyrannus, and the Gospel penetrated into every center of the province of Asia.

The Temple of Diana in Ephesus was one of the 7 wonders of the ancient world — the largest Greek temple ever constructed, 418 by 238 feet. Paul spoke boldly in the synagogue for 3 months. Then he went to the school of Tyrannus and continued there for 2 years. He stayed there longer than any other place.

Introduction to Romans

Paul wrote the letter to the Roman church when he was on his third missionary journey. He was either at Corinth or Cenchrea. He had been in Greece for 3 months (Acts 20:3), and the churches had made a collection for the poor saints in Jerusalem. Most of his time was spent with the church in Corinth, but Phoebe lived in Cenchrea (about 6 miles from Corinth), and she was going to Rome. So Paul sent the letter by her. She was a διάκονον in the church in Cenchrea. The word used for her office is used 30 times in the New Testament: 20 times it is translated minister; 7 times it is translated servant; and 3 times it is translated deacon. Paul was on his way back to Jerusalem, but he had planned a trip to Spain, and he planned to stop by and visit the Christians in Rome. He could not go to Rome at this time, but this gave him an opportunity to write to them.

The purpose of the letter was to elaborate on the fundamental doctrines of Christianity and to show that the message of Christ was for all people, whether Jew or Greek. All have sinned so all need salvation, and the Gospel of Christ is the power of salvation to all who believe.

There were both Jews and Gentiles who were members of the church in Rome. He uses 74 quotations from the Old Testament, and he sought to explain the relationship between Jew and Gentile in God's plan of redemption. This letter is the most systematic of his letters. Paul writes about eternal things that are relevant to all people in all ages, such as sin, salvation, grace, faith, righteousness, justification, sanctification, redemption, death, and resurrection. It is one of the greatest theological essays that has ever been written. It continues to be an authority on theological issues.

Romans 1:1-32

(1) Paul, a slave of Christ Jesus, called to be an apostle, set apart for the gospel of God, (2) which he promised by his prophets in the holy scriptures (3) concerning his Son, who came from the seed of David according to the flesh, (4) who was declared with power to be the Son of God according to the spirit of holiness by his resurrection from the dead — Jesus Christ our Lord, (5) through whom we received grace and apostleship to bring about obedience that comes from faith among all the nations on behalf of his name, (6) including yourselves also who are called to belong to Jesus Christ; (7) to all in Rome who are loved of God and called to be saints: Grace to you and peace from God our Father and the Lord Jesus Christ.

(8) First, I thank my God through Jesus Christ for all of you, because your faith is being reported throughout the whole world. (9) For God, whom I serve in my spirit in the gospel of his Son, is my witness how constantly I make mention of you (10) always in my prayers requesting that somehow at sometime, in the will of the Lord, I shall have a good journey to come to you.

(11) For I long to see you so that I may impart to you some spiritual gift that you may be strengthened, (12) or rather, that you and I may be mutually strengthened by our common faith. (13) I want you to know, brothers, that I have many times planned to visit you—but until now I have been prevented—in order that I might obtain some fruit among you also, even as the rest of the nations. (14) I am debtor both to the Greeks and to the Barbarians, to the wise and to the foolish. (15) That is why I am eager to preach the gospel to you also who are in Rome. (16) For I am not ashamed of the gospel, for it is the power of God unto salvation to all who believe, the Jew first, then the Greek. (17) For in it the righteousness of God has been revealed from faith to faith, as it has been written, "The righteous shall live by faith."

(18) For the wrath of God has been revealed from heaven against all ungodliness and unrighteousness of men who by their wickedness suppress the truth, (19) because that which is known of God is manifest to them, for God has manifested it to them. (20) For since the creation of the world his invisible nature—his eternal power and divinity—has been clearly seen, being understood by the things that were made, so that they are without excuse. (21) For even though they knew God, they did not honor him as God or give thanks to him, but they became vain in their speculations, and their foolish hearts were darkened. (22) Claiming to be wise, they became fools, (23) and they exchanged the splendor of the immortal God for images representing mortal man and birds and beasts and snakes.

(24) Therefore God gave them over in sinful desires of their hearts to sexual impurity for the degrading of their bodies with one another. (25) They exchanged the truth of God for a lie, and they worshiped and served the creature rather than the Creator, who is blessed forever. Amen.

(26) For this reason God gave them over to shameful passions; for even their women exchanged natural intercourse for unnatural; (27) likewise the men also, giving up natural relations with women, inflamed with passionate desire for one another, men committing shameful acts of indecency with men and receiving the wages of their own perversion. (28) They did not see fit to acknowledge God, so God gave them over to a depraved mind, to do those things which are not proper. (29) They were filled with all unrighteousness, wickedness, greed, and malice; full of envy, murder, strife, deceit, malignity, whisperers, (30 scandalmongers, haters of God, insolent, arrogant, boasters, inventors of evil, disobedient to parents, (31) without understanding, untrustworthy, without natural affection, (32) and although they know the ordinance of God that those who do such things are worthy of death, yet they not only do them, but they applaud those who practice them.

Romans 2:1-29

(1) Therefore, O man, you are without excuse; you who judge another are condemning yourself, since you are guilty of the same things. (2) We know that God's judgment falls unerringly on those who do such things. (3) Do you suppose, O man, that you who judges and does such things will escape the judgment of God? (4) Or do you despise the riches of his kindness and his tolerance and long-suffering? Do you not know that the kindness of God leads to repentance? (5) But because of your hard and unrepentant heart, you are storing up retribution for yourself for the day of wrath when the righteous judgment will be revealed. (6) For he will give to each person according to his works: (7) to those who by patient endurance in welldoing seek glory and honor and immortality, eternal life; (8) but to those who are self-seeking and reject the truth and follow evil, wrath and anger. (9) There will be affliction and anguish on everyone working evil, first to the Jew, and then to the Greek, (10) but glory, honor and peace to everyone working for the good, first to the Jews, and then to the Greeks. (11) For God is no respecter of persons.

(12) All who have sinned without law will perish without law, and all who have sinned under the law will be judged by the law; (13) for it is not the hearers of the law who are just before God, but the doers of the law will be justified. (14) When gentiles who do not have the law do by nature the requirements of the law, they are a law to themselves, even though they do not have the law, (15) since they show that the requirements of the law are written on their hearts, while their consciences bear witness and their conflicting thoughts accusing, or perhaps excusing them. (16) On that day God will judge the secrets of men according to the gospel through Christ Jesus.

(17) But if you bear the name of a Jew, and rely on the law and boast in God, (18) and know his will, but appreciate the finer moral distinctions, being instructed in the law, (19) and being confident that you are a guide to the blind, a light for those in darkness, (20) an instructor for the foolish, a teacher for the young, having the embodiment of knowledge and of the truth— (21) you teach others, why don't you teach yourself? You preach, "Do not steal," but do you steal? (22) You say, "Do not commit adultery," but do you commit adultery? You detest idols, but do you rob temples? (23) You boast about having God's law, but do you bring shame on God by breaking his law? (24) For as it is written, "The name of God is blasphemed among the nations because of you."

(25) Circumcision is of value if you keep the law, but if you are a transgressor of the law, your circumcision has become uncircumcision. (26) So, if the uncircumcised man keeps the requirements of the law, will not his uncircumcision be regarded as circumcision? (27) Then those who are physically uncircumcised but keep the law will judge you who, although you

have the written code and circumcision, break the law. (28) For he is not a Jew who is one outwardly; neither is true circumcision the external mark of the flesh; (29) but he is a Jew who is one inwardly; and circumcision is of the heart, by the spirit and not by the letter; and his praise is not from men, but from God.

Romans 3:1-31

(1) Then what advantage has the Jew? Or what is the value of circumcision? (2) Much in every way. First of all, they were entrusted with the oracles of God. (3) What if some disbelieved? Will their unbelief nullify the faithfulness of God? (4) Perish the thought! Let God be true and every man a liar, as it is written,

"That you may be justified in your words,

and you will prevail when you are judged."

(5) What shall we say then if our unrighteousness shows the justice of God? Is God unjust to inflict wrath on us? (I speak in human terms) (6) Perish the thought! Otherwise, how could God judge the world? (7) But if through my falsehood God's truthfulness abounds to his glory, why am I still condemned as a sinner? (8) And why not say (as we are slanderously reported and some affirm that we say), "Let us do evil that good may come?" Their condemnation is just.

(9) What then? Are we better than they? Not at all; for we have already declared that both Jews and Greeks are under the power of sin, (10) as it is written,

"There is none righteous, no, not one,

there is no one who understands,

(11) there is no one seeking God.

(12) All have turned away, together they have become unprofitable.

There is no one to show kindness, no, not one.

(13) Their throats are open graves,

they use their tongues to deceive,

the poison of asps is under their lips.

(14) Their mouths are full of cursing and bitterness.

(15) Their feet are swift to shed blood,

(16) in their paths are ruin and misery,

(17) and the ways of peace they do not know.

(18) There is no fear of God before their eyes."

(19) Now we know that whatever the law says, it speaks to those under the law, that every mouth may be stopped and that the entire world may be held accountable to God. (20) For by the works of the law no flesh will be justified in his sight, since through the law comes the knowledge of sin.

(21) But now the righteousness of God has been manifested apart

from the law, being witnessed by the law and the prophets, (22) the righteousness of God through faith in Jesus Christ to all who believe. For there is no difference. (23) For all have sinned and fall short of the glory of God, (24) being justified freely by his grace through the redemption which is in Christ Jesus, (25) whom God displayed publicly as a propitiation by his blood, to be received by faith; for this was to demonstrate his righteousness, because in the forbearance of God he passed over the sins previously committed. (26) It was to demonstrate his righteousness at the present time, that he himself is righteous and the justifier of those who have faith in Jesus.

(27) Where then is boasting? It is excluded. Through what law? Of works? No, but through the law of faith. (28) For we reckon that a man is justified by faith apart from works of the law. (29) Or is God of the Jews only? Is he not also the God of Gentiles? Yes, of Gentiles also, (30) since there is one God who will justify the circumcision by faith and the uncircumcision through faith. (31) Do we nullify the law through faith? Perish the thought! On the contrary, we establish the law.

Romans 4:1-25

(1) What then shall we say about the experience of Abraham our forefather in the flesh? (2) For if Abraham was justified by works, he has something to boast about, but he cannot boast before God; (3) for what does the Scripture say? "Abraham believed God, and it was credited to him as righteousness." (4) Now to the one who works, his wages are not regarded as a gift, but what is earned; but to the one not working (5) but believing on the one who justifies the ungodly, his faith is credited to him as righteousness. (6) So also David pronounces a blessing upon the man who is credited as righteous apart from works:

(7) "Blessed are those whose iniquities have been forgiven,
   and whose sins have been covered.
(8) Blessed is the man whose sin the Lord will not take into account."

(9) Then is this blessing only upon the circumcision, or is it also on the uncircumcision? For we say, "The faith of Abraham was credited to him as righteousness." (10) How then did this happen? Was it after or before he was circumcised? It was not after but before he was circumcised. (11) He received the sign of circumcision, a seal of his righteousness of the faith he had before he was circumcised, so that he was to be a father of all who believe apart from circumcision that righteousness should be credited to them; (12) and he is a father of the circumcision who are not only of the circumcision but also walk in the steps of our father Abraham before he was circumcised.

(13) For the promise to Abraham and to his descendents that he should be heir to the world was not through law, but through the righteousness of faith. (14) For if those of law are heirs, faith is made void

and the promise is nullified; (15) for the law brings wrath, but where there is no law, there is no disobeying of the law. (16) The promise is of faith, that it might be according to grace and be guaranteed to all his descendents—not only to those who are of the law but also to those who are of the faith of Abraham, who is the father of us all, (17) as it is written, "I have made you a father of many nations." So the promise is good in the presence of God whom he believed—the God who gives life to the dead and calls into being that which does not exist.

(18) When hope seemed hopeless, Abraham believed that he would become a father of many nations, according to what had been spoken, "So shall your descendents be." (19) He did not weaken in faith when he considered his body to have died, being about an hundred years old, or the fact of the barrenness of Sarah's womb. (20) He did not waver in unbelief but still had faith in the promise of God, and he grew strong in his faith and gave praise to God. (21) He was fully convinced that God was able to do what he had promised. (22) Therefore his faith was "credited to him as righteousness." (23) But the words "it was credited to him" were not for his sake only, (24) but for ours also, who believe in him who raised Jesus our Lord from the dead, (25) who was put to death because of our transgressions and was raised for our justification.

Romans 5:1-21

(1) Now that we have been justified by faith, we have peace with God through our Lord Jesus Christ, (2) through whom we also have access by faith into this grace in which we stand; and we rejoice in our hope of the glory of God. (3) And not only this, but we also rejoice in our afflictions, knowing that afflictions produces perseverance; (4) and perseverance, approved character; and approved character, hope; (5) and hope does not disappoint us, because God has poured out his love into our hearts by the Holy Spirit who was given to us.

(6) For while we were yet helpless, at the appointed time, Christ died for the ungodly. (7) Hardly anyone will die for a righteous man, though perhaps for a good man someone would dare to die. (8) But God shows his love for us in that while we were sinners, Christ died for us. (9) Much more then, having been justified by his blood, we shall be saved from wrath through him. (10) For if, while we were enemies, we were reconciled to God through the death of his Son, much more, having been reconciled, we shall be saved by his life. (11) And not only this, but we rejoice in God through our Lord Jesus Christ, through whom we have now received our reconciliation.

(12) Therefore, as through one man sin entered into the world, and death through sin, so death spread to all men, because all men sinned; (13) for sin was in the world before the law was given; but sin is not imputed when there is no law. (14) Nevertheless, death reigned from Adam to

Moses, even over those whose sins were not like the transgression of Adam, who is a type of the one who was to come.

(15) But the free gift is not like the trespass. For if many died by the trespass of one man, much more did the grace of God and the gift by the grace of the one man, Jesus Christ, abound to the many. (16) The gift is different from the sin committed by the one man. On the one hand, the sentence followed one trespass and brought condemnation, but on the other hand, the gift came after many trespasses resulting in justification. (17) For if death began its reign through one man's trespass, much more shall those who receive the abundance of the grace and the gift of righteousness reign in life through the one man, Jesus Christ.

(18) So then as the trespass of one man led to condemnation, so also one act of righteousness leads to justification and life for all men. (19) For through the disobedience of one man many were made sinners, so also through the obedience of one man many will be made righteous.

(20) Law came in order to increase the trespass; but where sin increased, grace has surpassed it, (21) so that, as sin reigned in death, grace might reign through righteousness to eternal life through Jesus Christ our Lord.

Romans 6:1-23

(1) What then, shall we say? Shall we continue in sin that grace may abound? (2) Perish the thought! How can we who died to sin still live in it? (3) Do you not know that as many as were baptized into Christ Jesus were baptized into his death? (4) Therefore we were buried with him through baptism into death, in order that as Christ was raised from the dead through the glory of the Father, so we also might walk in the newness of life.

(5) For if we have been united with him in the likeness of his death, we shall also share in his resurrection. (6) We know that our old self was crucified with him so that the sinful self might be destroyed, so that we may no longer be slaves to sin. (7) For he who is dead is freed from sin. (8) Since we died with Christ, we believe that we shall also live with him, (9) knowing that Christ, having been raised from the dead, will die no more; death no longer has dominion over him. (10) For in that he died, he died to sin once, but in that he lives, he lives to God. (11) So also consider yourselves to be dead to sin but alive to God in Christ Jesus.

(12) Therefore do not let sin reign in your mortal bodies, so that you obey the desires of your natural self; (13) and do not continue to offer the members of your body to sin as weapons of unrighteousness; but offer yourselves to God as those alive from the dead, and your members as weapons of righteousness to God. (14) For sin shall not have dominion over you, since you are not under law, but under grace.

(15) What then? Shall we sin because we are not under law but

under grace? Perish the thought! (16) Do you not know that to whom you offer yourselves as obedient slaves, you become slaves to whom you obey, whether of sin to death, or of obedience to righteousness. (17) But thanks be to God, though you were slaves of sin, you became obedient from the heart to that form of teaching which you received. (18) Having been freed from sin you became slaves of righteousness. (19) I am using this human analogy because of the weakness of your flesh. For as you offered the members of your body as slaves of uncleanness and to iniquity unto iniquity, so now offer the members of your bodies to righteousness for sanctification. (20) For when you were slaves of sin, you were free in regards to righteousness. (21) Therefore, what harvest were you then reaping from the things which now make you blush? For the end of those things is death. (22) But now, having been freed from sin and enslaved to God, your harvest is sanctification, and the end eternal life. (23) For the wages of sin is death, but the gift of God is eternal life in Christ Jesus our Lord.

Romans 7:1-25

(1) Do you not know, brothers — I am speaking to those who have knowledge of law — that the law has authority over the man only as long as he lives? (2) For example, a married woman is bound by law to her husband as long as she lives, but if the husband dies, she is released from the law of marriage. (3) So then, if her husband is living and she is married to another man, she will be called an adulteress; but if the husband dies, she is free from the law, and she will not be an adulteress if she marries another man.

(4) So, my brothers, you also died to the law through the body of Christ, so that you might belong to another, to him who was raised from the dead, in order that you might bear fruit for God. (5) For when we were controlled by our sinful nature, the sinful passions, aroused by the law, worked in our bodies to bear fruit for death. (6) But now we have been released from the law, having died to that which held us captive, so we can serve in the newness of the spirit and not in the oldness of the letter.

(7) What then shall we say? Is the law sin? Perish the thought! Yet it was only through the law that I knew sin; for I would have not known about evil desire if the law had not said, "You shall not covet." (8) But sin, taking an opportunity through the commandment, produced in me every evil desire; for without law, sin is dead. (9) Once I was living without law, but when the commandment came, sin revived (10) and I died. The commandment that was supposed to bring life brought death to me. (11) For sin, taking an opportunity through the commandment, deceived me, and through it killed me. (12) So the law is holy, and the commandment is holy, righteous and good.

(13) Therefore did that which is good cause my death? Perish the thought! It was sin that killed me, and sin exposed its true character: it was a

good thing that caused my death, in order that through the commandment sin might become utterly sinful. (14) For we know that the law is spiritual, but I am carnal, sold into the captivity of sin. (15) For I do not understand my actions. For I do not do what I want to do, but what I hate I do. (16) But if what I do is against my will, I agree that the law is good. (17) So now, it is no longer I who is doing it, but sin that dwells in me. (18) For I know that nothing good dwells in my flesh; for I want to do good, but I cannot do it. (19) The good that I want to do, I do not do, but the evil that I do not want to do, that I do. (20) Now if I do what I do not want to do, it is no longer I that do it, but sin that dwells in me.

(21) So I find this law at work: when I want to do good, (22) evil is present; for I delight in the law of God in my inmost self, (23) but I see a different law warring against the law of my mind and making me a prisoner of the law of sin which is in me. (24) What a wretched man I am! Who will deliver me from the body of this death! (25) Thanks are to God through Jesus Christ our Lord. So then, on the one hand I myself with my mind serve the law of God, but with my flesh I serve the law of sin.

Romans 8:1-39

(1) So there is now no condemnation to those in Christ Jesus. (2) For the spirit of life in Christ Jesus has freed us from the law of sin and death. (3) For God has done what the law, weakened by the flesh, could not do. By sending his own son in the likeness of sinful flesh and for sin, he condemned sin in the flesh, (4) in order that the requirement of the law might be fulfilled in us, who walk not according to the flesh but according to the spirit. (5) For those who live according to the flesh set their minds on the things of the flesh, but those who live according to the spirit set their minds on the things of the spirit. (6) For to be carnally minded is death, but to be spiritually minded is life and peace; (7) because the mind set on the flesh is hostile toward God; it does not submit to the law of God, indeed it cannot; (8)and those who are in the flesh cannot please God.

(9) But you are not in the flesh but in the spirit, since the Spirit of God dwells in you. Anyone who does not have the Spirit of Christ does not belong to him. (10) And if Christ is in you, the body is dead because of sin, but the spirit is alive because of righteousness. (11) If the spirit of the one who raised Jesus from the dead dwells in you, he who raised Jesus from the dead will also give life to your mortal bodies through his Spirit dwelling in you.

(12) So then, brothers, we are debtors, not to the flesh, to live according to the flesh— (13) for if you are living according to the flesh, you will die—but if you put to death the deeds of the body, you will live. (14) For all who are led by the Spirit of God are sons of God. (15) For you did not receive a spirit of slavery leading you back into fear, but a spirit of adoption

through which we cry out, "Abba! Father!" (16) The Spirit himself bears witness with our spirit that we are children of God. (17) Since we are children, then we are heirs, heirs of God, and joint heirs with Christ; for if we share in his sufferings we will also share in his glory.

(18) I consider that the sufferings of this present time are not worthy to be compared with the coming glory which is to be revealed to us. (19) For the creation waits expectantly but patiently for the revelation of the sons of God. (20) For the creation was subjected to futility, not of its own will, but because of him who subjected it, in hope (21) that the creation itself will be set free from its slavery to corruption into the freedom of the glory of the children of God. (22) For we know that all creation groans together and travails until now; (23) and not only the creation but we ourselves, who have the first fruits of the Spirit, groan inwardly while we wait for the adoption as sons, the redemption of our bodies. (24) In hope we were saved. But hope is no hope if its object is seen; for how can anyone hope for what he sees? (25) But if we hope for what we do not see, we wait patiently for it.

(26) Likewise, the Spirit helps us in our weakness; for we do not know what to pray for, but the Spirit intercedes for us with groanings too deep for words. (27) And he who searches the hearts knows the mind of the Spirit, because he intercedes for the saints according to the will of God.

(28) We know that all things work together for good to those loving God, who are called according to his purpose. (29) For whom he foreknew, he also predestined to be conformed to the image of his Son, that his Son might be the firstborn among many brothers. (30) And whom he predestined, he also called; and whom he called, he also justified; and whom he justified, he also glorified. (31) What then shall we say to these things? If God is for us, who is against us? (32) He who did not spare his own Son, but delivered him up for us all, will he not also freely give us all things? (33) Who will bring a charge against God's elect? It is God who justifies, (34) who is to condemn? Jesus Christ is he who died, or rather who was raised up and is at the right hand of God, who indeed intercedes for us. (35) Who will separate us from the love of Christ? Shall affliction or distress or persecution or famine or nakedness or peril or sword? (36) As it is written:

"For your sake we are being put to death all day long;
we are considered as sheep to be slaughtered."

(37) Yet in all these things we are more than conquerors through him who loved us. (38) For I am convinced that neither death, nor life, nor angels, nor rulers, nor things present, nor things to come, nor powers, (39) nor height, nor depth, nor anything else in all creation, will be able to separate us from the love of God in Christ Jesus our Lord.

Romans 9:1-33

(1) I am speaking the truth in Christ, I am not lying. My conscience

bears me witness in the Holy Spirit, (2) that I have great sorrow and constant pain in my heart. (3) For I could wish myself accursed from Christ for my brothers who are my kinsmen in the flesh, (4) the Israelites, to whom belongs the adoption as sons, the glory, the covenants, the giving of the law, the temple worship, and the promises. (5) Theirs are the patriarchs, and from them according to the flesh, came the Messiah. May God, who is over all, be blessed forever! Amen.

(6) It is not as though the word of God has failed. For not all of Israel are of Israel; (7) neither are all the descendents of Abraham the children of Abraham; but "In Isaac will your descendents be called." (8) This means that it is not the children of the flesh who are the children of God, but the children of the promise are regarded as his descendents. (9) For the promise is: "At the proper time I will visit Sarah and she will have a son." (10) And not only that, for when Rebecca had conceived twin children by one man, our father Isaac, (11) and though the children were not yet born, and had done nothing good or bad, but in order that the purpose of God might continue according to his choice, (12) not because of works but because of his calling, she was told, "The older will serve the younger." (13) Even as it has been written, "Jacob I loved, but Esau I hated."

(14) What then shall we say? Is God unrighteous? Perish the thought! (15) For he says to Moses, "I will have mercy on whom I will have mercy, and I will have compassion on whom I will have compassion." (16) So therefore, it does not depend on the man who wills or the man who runs, but on God who has mercy. (17) For in the Scripture he says to Pharaoh, "For I raised you up for this very purpose, that I might show forth my power, and that my name might be proclaimed in all the world." (18) So therefore God has mercy on whom he wishes, and he hardens whom he wishes.

(19) You will say to me then, "Why does God still blame us? For who can resist his will?" (20) But who are you, O man, to talk back to God? Will the pot say to the potter, "Why did you make me like this?" (21) Or does not the potter have the authority over the clay to make one vessel for honor and the other vessel for dishonor from the same lump of clay? (22) What if God, wishing to show his wrath and to make known his power, endured with much patience the vessels of wrath prepared for destruction? (23) And he did in order that he might make known the riches of his glory toward the vessels for mercy, which he previously prepared for glory, (24) even us whom he also called, not only of the Jews but also of the Gentiles. (25) As in Hosea he says,

"I will call them 'my people' who were not my people;
and to her who was not my beloved, I will call 'my beloved';
(26) and it shall be in the place where it was said to them,
'You are not my people,' there they will be called
'sons of the living God.' "

(27) And Isaiah cries out concerning Israel,
"Though the number of the sons of Israel are as the sand of the sea,

only the remnant will be saved.
(28) For the Lord will execute his sentence on the earth,
fully and without delay."
(29) It is as Isaiah had previously said,
"If the Lord Almighty had not left us descendents,
we would have become as Sodom
and we would have resembled Gomorra."
(30) What then shall we say? That Gentiles, who were not pursuing righteousness, have attained it, a righteousness that is by faith; (31) but Israel, pursuing a law of righteousness, never attained it. (32) Why? Because they did not pursue it through faith, but as if it were through works. They stumbled over the stumbling stone, (33) as it is written,
"Look, I place in Zion a stumbling stone, a rock of offence,
and the one believing in him will not be put to shame."

Romans 10:1-21

(1) Brothers, it is my heart's desire and prayer to God that they may be saved. (2) I can testify that they have a zeal for God, but not according to knowledge. (3) For they did not know the righteousness of God, and seeking to establish a righteousness of their own, they did not submit to the righteousness of God. (4) For Christ is the end of the law for righteousness to all who believe.

(5) Moses writes that the man who practices the righteousness of the law shall live by it. (6) But the righteousness based on faith says, "Do not say in your heart, 'Who will ascend into heaven?' (that is, to bring Christ down) (7) or 'Who will descend into the abyss?' " (that is, to bring Christ up from the dead).

(8) But what does it say?

"The word is near you, in your mouth and in your heart" (that is, the word of faith that we proclaim). (9) For if you confess with your mouth that "Jesus is Lord" and believe in your heart that God raised him from the dead, you will be saved. (10) For with the heart one believes and is justified, and with the mouth one confesses and is saved. (11) For the Scripture says, "No one who believes in him will be put to shame." (12) For there is no difference between the Jew and the Greek. For the same Lord is Lord of all and gives his riches to all who call upon him. (13) For "Everyone who calls upon the name of the Lord will be saved."

(14) How then can they call upon him in whom they have not believed? And how can they believe in him whom they have not heard? And how can they hear without the message being proclaimed? (15) And how can the message be proclaimed unless the messengers are sent? As it is written, "How beautiful are the feet of those who bring glad tidings of good things." (16) But not all have obeyed the gospel. For Isaiah says, "Lord, who

has believed our message?" (17) Then faith comes by hearing, and hearing through the word of Christ. (18) But I ask: Did they not hear? Certainly they did:

> "The sound of their voices has gone out to all the earth,
> and their words to the ends of the inhabited world."

(19) Again I ask: Did Israel not understand? First Moses says,

> "I will make you jealous of those who are not a nation,
> I will make you angry by a foolish nation."

(20) And Isaiah quite boldly says,

> "I was found by those who were not seeking for me,
> I appeared to those who were not inquiring for me."

(21) But to Israel he says,

> "All the day long I stretched out my hand
> to a disobedient and rebellious people."

Romans 11:1-36

(1) I ask then, has God rejected his people. Perish the thought! For I am an Israelite, a descendent of Abraham, of the tribe of Benjamin. (2) God did not reject his people whom he foreknew. Do you not know what the Scripture says about Elijah, how he pleads with God against Israel? (3) "Lord, they have killed your prophets, torn down your altars, and I am the only one left and they are trying to kill me." (4) But what was the divine response? "I have reserved for myself seven thousand who have not bowed the knee to Baal." (5) So also, at the present time there is a remnant chosen by grace. (6) And if by grace, it is no longer of works; otherwise, grace would no longer be grace.

(7) What then? What Israel sought was not obtained, but the elect obtained it; and the rest were hardened, (8) as it is written,

> "God gave them a spirit of apathy,
> blind eyes and deaf ears,
> to this very day."

(9) And David says,

> "Let their feasts become a trap and a net,
> a stumbling block and a retribution for them.
> (10) May their eyes be darkened so they cannot see,
> and may their backs be bent forever."

(11) So I ask, did their stumbling mean that they are forever fallen? Perish the thought! But by their trespass, salvation has come to the nations, to provoke them to jealousy. (12) Now if their trespass has enriched the world, and if their failure has enriched the Gentiles, how much more will their fullness bring!

(13) Now I am speaking to you Gentiles: In as much as I am an apostle to the Gentiles, I magnify my ministry, (14) in the hope that I may

provoke my own people to envy and save some of them. (15) For if their rejection means the reconciliation of the world, would not their reconciliation be life from the dead? (16) And if the first portion of dough is consecrated, so is the whole mass of dough; and if the root is consecrated, so are the branches.

(17) But if some of the branches were broken off, and you, a wild olive shoot, were grafted in among them and have come to share the same root and sap from the olive tree, (18) do not be arrogant toward the branches; but if you are arrogant, remember that you do not support the root, but the root supports you. (19) You therefore say: "Branches were broken off so I might be grafted in." (20) Very well; they were broken off because of their unbelief, and you stand by faith. Do not be conceited, but stand in awe. (21) For if God did not spare the natural branches, neither will he spare you.

(22) Consider therefore the kindness and the sternness of God: sternness to those who fell away, but God's kindness to you, if you continue in his kindness; otherwise, you will be cut off. (23) And they also, if they do not continue in their unbelief, will be grafted in, for God is able to graft them in again. (24) For if you were cut from your wild olive and were grafted, contrary to nature, into a cultivated olive, how much more will these natural branches be grafted into their native stock!

(25) For I do not want you to be uninformed of this mystery, brothers, lest you be wise in your own eyes; a partial hardening has come upon Israel until the fullness of the Gentiles has come in; (26) so all Israel will be saved, as it is written:

"The Deliverer will come from Zion,
he will turn away ungodliness from Jacob.
(27) And this is my covenant with them
when I take away their sins."

(28) Concerning the gospel, they are enemies for your sake; but concerning election, they are loved for the sake of the patriarchs. (29) For the gifts and calling of God are without regret. (30) For as you were once disobedient to God but now you have obtained mercy because of their disobedience, (31) so now they have become disobedient in order that by your mercy they also may receive mercy. (32) For God has imprisoned all in disobedience that he may have mercy upon all.

(33) Oh, the depth of the riches, wisdom and knowledge of God! No one can explain his decisions, and no one can understand his ways!

(34) As the scripture says,
"Who has known the mind of the Lord?
Or who has been his counselor?"
(35) And
"Who has ever given to him
that he may be repaid?"
(36) For all things are from him and through him and to him. To him be glory forever! Amen.

Romans 12:1-21

(1) I appeal to you therefore, brothers, by the mercies of God, to present your bodies as a living sacrifice, holy and well-pleasing to God, which is your reasonable service; (2) and do not be conformed to this age, but be transformed by the renewing of the mind, so that you may be able to discern the will of God, which is good, well-pleasing, and perfect.

(3) For I say through the grace given to me that everyone among you should not be conceited and think too highly of himself, but to be sober-minded, as God has given a measure of faith to each of you. (4) For as in one body, we have many members, but all the members do not have the same function. (5) So we, though many, are one body in Christ. (6) We have gifts differing according to the grace given to us. If one's gift is to prophesy, he should prophesy according to his faith; (7) or service, in serving; or teaching, in teaching; (8) or he who exhorts, in his exhortation; he who shares, in simplicity; he who leads, in diligence; and he who shows mercy, in cheerfulness.

(9) Love is without hypocrisy: shrinking from the evil, cleaving to good, (10) loving warmly one another in brotherly love, preferring one another in showing honor, (11) not slothful in zeal, fervent in spirit, serving the Lord, (12) rejoicing in hope, steadfast under pressure, persevering in prayer, (13) contributing to the needs of the saints, pursuing the love of strangers.

(14) Bless those who persecute you; bless and curse not. (15) Rejoice with those who rejoice; weep with those who weep. (16) Live in harmony with one another; do not be arrogant; fellowship with the lowly. Do not be conceited. (17) Never return evil for evil; aim to do what is right in the sight of all. (18) If possible, so far as it depends upon you, live in peace with everyone. (19) Beloved, never take revenge, but make room for wrath; for it is written,

"Vengeance is mine, I will repay," says the Lord.
(20) But,

"If your enemy is hungry, feed him;
if he is thirsty, give him a drink;
for by doing this you will heap burning coals upon his head."
(21) Do not be conquered with evil, but conquer evil with good.

Romans 13:1-14

(1) Let everyone be subject to the governing authorities. For there is no authority except by the permission of God, and those that exist are ordained by God. (2) So he who resists the authority has opposed the ordinance of God; and they who have opposed will bring judgment upon themselves. (3) For the rulers are no threats to those who do good works, but

to those who do evil. Do you want to be free from the fear of authority?
Then do good and you will gain its approval; (4) for the one in authority is
God's servant to do you good, but if you do evil, be afraid, for he does not
bear the sword in vain; for he is a minister of God to execute his wrath on the
evildoer. (5) Therefore, it is necessary to be in subjection, not only because of
his wrath but also for the sake of conscience.

(6) For the same reason we pay taxes, for the authorities are
ministers of God, who give their full time to governing. (7) Pay what you
owe to all men: tax to whom tax is due; toll to whom toll is due; respect to
whom respect is due; and honor to whom honor is due.

(8) Owe no debt to anyone, except the continuing debt to love one
another, for he who loves his fellowman has fulfilled the law. (9) For the
commandments, "You shall not commit adultery, you shall not kill, you shall
not steal, you shall not covet," and if there is any other commandment, are
summed up in this rule, "You shall love your neighbor as yourself." (10)
Love does no wrong to a neighbor; therefore love is the fulfillment of the law.

(11) And do this, knowing the time, that it is time for you to wake up
from sleep; for now salvation is nearer to us than when we believed. (12) The
night is far spent, and the day is almost here. Let us therefore lay aside the
works of darkness and put on the weapons of light.   (13) Let us live
honorably as in the day, not in reveling and drunkenness, not in sexual
promiscuity and licentiousness, not in strife and jealousy; (14) but put on the
Lord Jesus, and make no provision for the lusts of the flesh.

Romans 14:1-23

(1) Accept him who is weak in faith, but not to pass judgment on his
scruples. (2) One man has faith to eat all kinds of food, but the weak man
eats only vegetables. (3) Let not the one who eats despise the one who
abstains, and let not the one who abstains criticize the one who eats, for God
has welcomed him. (4) Who are you to judge the servant of another? He
stands or falls before his own master. He will stand because his master is
able to make him stand.

(5) One man esteems one day greater than another, another man
esteems all days alike. Let each man be fully persuaded in his own mind. (6)
He who observes the day, observes it for the Lord; and the one eating, does it
for the Lord, for he gives thanks to God; and the one who abstains, does it for
the Lord, and he gives thanks to God. (7) For none of us lives to himself, and
none of us dies to himself. (8) For if we live, we live to the Lord, or if we die,
we die to the Lord. Therefore, whether we live or die, we belong to the Lord;
(9) for to this end, Christ died and lived again, that he might be Lord of both
the dead and the living. (10) And why do you criticize your brother? Or
you, how can you despise your brother? For we shall all stand before the
judgment seat of God. (11) For it is written,

"As I live," says the Lord, "every knee will bend to me,
and every tongue will confess to God."
(12) So then each one of us must give an account of himself to God.

(13) Therefore let us no longer criticize one another, but rather that we do not put a stumbling block or a snare in the way of a brother. (14) I know and I am persuaded in the Lord Jesus that nothing is unclean in itself; but it is unclean to the one who thinks it unclean. (15) For if your brother is grieved because of what you eat, you are no longer living according to love. Do not destroy with food the man for whom Christ died. (16) Therefore do not let that which is good be spoken of as evil. (17) For the reign of God is not eating and drinking, but righteousness and peace in the Holy Spirit; (18) for he who serves Christ in this way is well-pleasing to God and approved by men.

(19) So then let us pursue the ways of peace and the strengthening of one another. (20) Do not destroy the work of God for the sake of food. Everything is pure within itself, but it is evil to the man who causes a stumbling block by what he eats. (21) It is good not to eat meat or drink wine or to do anything that causes your brother to stumble.

(22) Use your faith to be your rule in the sight of God. Blessed is he who does not condemn himself by what he approves; (23) but he who doubts is guilty if he eats, because he does not act from faith; all that is not of faith is sin.

Romans 15:1-33

(1) We who are strong ought to bear the infirmities of the weak and not to please ourselves. (2) Let each of us please his neighbor, for it is good to build him up. (3) For Christ did not please himself, but as it is written, "The insults of those who insult you fell on me." (4) For the things that were written were written for our instructions, so that through patience and the encouragement of the scriptures we might have hope. (5) And may the God of patience and encouragement grant you to be of the same mind with one another in Christ Jesus, (6) so that together with one voice you may glorify the God and Father of our Lord Jesus Christ.

(7) Welcome one another, then, as Christ also welcomed us to the glory of God. (8) For I tell you Christ became a minister to the circumcision on behalf of the truth of God, to confirm the promises made to the patriarchs, (9) and for the Gentiles to glorify God on behalf of his mercy, as it is written:
"Therefore I will praise you among the Gentiles
and sing praises to your name."
(10) And again it says,
"Gentiles, rejoice with his people."
(11) And again,
"Praise the Lord all the Gentiles, and let all the peoples praise him."

(12) And again Isaiah says,
> "The one raised from the root of Jesse
> will come up to rule the nations;
> the Gentiles will hope in him."

(13) Now may the God of hope fill you with all joy and peace in believing, so that you may abound in hope by the power of the Holy Spirit.

(14) My brothers, I myself am convinced that you yourselves are full of goodness and equipped with all knowledge, being able also to admonish one another. (15) But in some points I was very bold in what I wrote to you, reminding you of the grace given to me from God (16) that I should be a minister of Christ Jesus to the Gentiles in the priestly service of the gospel of God, so that the offering of the Gentiles may be acceptable and sanctified by the Holy Spirit.

(17) Therefore I glory in Christ Jesus in my service for God; (18) For I will not dare to speak of anything except what Christ worked through me for the obedience of the Gentiles in word and deed— (19) by the power of signs and wonders, by power of the Spirit; so that from Jerusalem and as far around as Illyricum, I fully preached the gospel of Christ. (20) Thus it was my ambition to preach the gospel where Christ was unknown, so that I would not build on someone else's foundation, (21) but as it is written:
> "Those who were never told about him will see,
> and those who have never heard will understand."

(22) This is why I have so often been hindered from coming to you. (23) But now, since there is no place in these regions, and since I have wanted to visit you for many years, (24) I hope to see you as I journey through on my way to Spain and to be sent there by your support after having been refreshed by your presence for awhile. (25) But now I am going to Jerusalem to minister to the saints. (26) For Macedonia and Achaia thought it good to make some contributions for the poor saints in Jerusalem. (27) For they were pleased to do it, and they are debtors to them; for if the Gentiles have come to share in their spiritual blessings, they ought also to minister to them in material things. (28) Therefore when I have completed this task and have made sure that they have received this contribution, (29) I will pass through you on my way to Spain; and I know that I will come to you in the fullness of the blessing of Christ.

(30) I urge you, brothers, through our Lord Jesus Christ and through the love of the Spirit, to agonize with me in your prayers to God on my behalf, (31) that I may be delivered from the unbelievers in Judea and that my ministry to Jerusalem may be acceptable to the saints, (32) in order that I may come to you in joy through the will of God and be refreshed in your presence. (33) Now may the God of peace be with all of you. Amen.

Romans 16:1-27

(1) I commend to you our sister Phoebe, who is a servant of the church in Cenchrea, (2) that you receive her in the Lord in a manner worthy of the saints and that you stand by to help her in whatever need she has; for she has indeed been a helper of many, including myself.

(3) Greet Prisca and Aquila, my fellow workers in Christ Jesus, (4) who risked their lives for my sake, to whom not only I, but also all the churches of the Gentiles give thanks. (5) Greet also the church that meets in their house.

Greet my dear friend Epaenetus, who was the first convert in Asia for Christ. (6) Greet Mary who worked hard for you. (7) Greet Andronicus and Junias, my relatives and fellow prisoners, who are well-known among the apostles, and who were in Christ before me. (8) Greet Ampliatus my dear friend in the Lord. (9) Greet Urbanus, our fellow worker in Christ and my dear friend Stachys. (10) Greet Apelles, who was tested and approved in Christ. Greet those of the household of Aristobulus. (11) Greet Herodian, my relative. Greet those in the Lord who are of the household of Narcissus. (12) Greet Tryphaena and Tryphosa, workers in the Lord. Greet dear Persis, who has worked hard in the Lord. (13) Greet Rufus, the chosen of the Lord, and his mother, who has been a mother to me. (14) Greet Asyncritus, Phlegon, Hermes, Patrobas, Hermas, and the brothers with them. (15) Greet Philologus, Julia, Nereus and his sister, and Olympas, and all the saints with them. (16) Greet one another with a holy kiss. All the churches of Christ greet you.

(17) Now I urge you, brothers, watch out for those who create divisions and put stumbling blocks in your way, contrary to the teaching which you learned; turn away from them. (18) For such men do not serve Christ, but their own base desires; and through insinuating speech and flattery, they deceive the hearts of the innocent. (19) Your obedience is known to all, therefore I rejoice over you. I want you to be wise in what is good and innocent in what is evil. (20) And the God of peace will soon crush Satan under your feet. The grace of our Lord Jesus be with you.

(21) Timothy, my fellow worker, sends you greetings and also Lucius, Jason, and Sosipater, my relatives. (22) I Tertius, who is writing this letter, greet you in the Lord. (23) Gaius, my host and host of all of the church, greets you. Erastus, the city treasurer, and Quartus the brother, greet you.

(25) Now to him who is able to strengthen you according to my gospel and the proclamation of Jesus Christ, according to the revelation of the mystery that was unknown in past ages, (26) but now has been manifested, and by the prophetic writings, according to the command of the eternal God, has been made known to all the nations so that they might believe and obey — (27) To the only wise God be glory forever through Jesus Christ! Amen.

Introduction to 1 Corinthians

Paul wrote this letter about 55 A.D. toward the close of his three years of ministry in Ephesus. Corinth had a population of about 250,000 free persons and about 400,000 slaves. In many ways it was the chief city of Greece. It was a crossroads for travelers and traders. Corinth was not a university city like Athens, but it was characterized by Greek culture and placed high value on wisdom.

Corinth was a city of at least 12 temples. Aphrodite, the goddess of love, was the temple where the worshippers practiced religious prostitution. At one time 1,000 sacred prostitutes served her temple. The Greek verb "to Corinthianize" meant to practice sexual immorality. It was in this setting that the church in Corinth was established.

Paul was in Ephesus on his third missionary journey when he received the news about the problems in Corinth. Some members of the Corinthian church had come to Paul to tell him of the problems of the church. There were 4 factions in the church. There were problems about marriage and the status of women and problems of personal relationships. The letter is characterized by its practical wisdom for solving all problems in accordance with Christian principles.

Paul used 6,828 words in his first letter to the Corinthians. People are about the same in each generation, so his advice for the Corinthians is relevant advice for us. It is in this letter that we have the thirteenth chapter of Corinthians. Charles B. Williams, theologian and seminary professor, said that it was "the most beautiful poem ever written," and he tags the fifteenth chapter of the resurrection as "a brief epic packed with keenest logic, the sublimest thoughts, and sparkling rhetoric."

1 Corinthians 1:1-31

(1) Paul, called by the will of God to be an apostle of Jesus Christ, and Sosthenes, the brother, (2) to the church of God in Corinth, to those sanctified in Christ Jesus, called to be saints, with all those calling on the name of our Lord Jesus in every place – their Lord and ours.

(3) Grace to you and peace from God our Father and the Lord Jesus Christ.

(4) I always thank God for his grace, which was given to you in Christ Jesus; (5) because you were enriched in everything in him, with outward expression and inward conviction, (6) as the testimony of Christ was confirmed in you, (7) so that you were not lacking in any gift, as you wait for the manifestation of our Lord Jesus Christ, (8) who will sustain you to the end, so that you will be blameless on the day of our Lord Jesus Christ. (9) God, through whom you were called into the fellowship of his son, Jesus

Christ our Lord, is trustworthy.

(10) I call upon you, brothers, by the name of our Lord Jesus Christ, that all of you agree so there will be no divisions, but that you will be joined together in your mind and expressed opinions. (11) Chole's people have reported to me that there is strife among you, brothers. (12) This is what I mean: someone says, "I am of Paul"; another says, "I am of Apollos"; another says, "I am of Cephas"; and another says, "I am of Christ."

(13) Has Christ been divided? Was Paul crucified for you, or were you baptized in the name of Paul? (14) I am thankful that I baptized none of you except Crispus and Gaius, (15) lest anyone should say that you were baptized in my name. (16) I also baptized the household of Stephanas. I do not remember if I baptized anyone else. (17) For Christ did not call me to baptize but to evangelize, not in words of wisdom, lest the cross of Christ becomes ineffective.

(18) For the preaching of the cross is foolishness to those who are perishing, but it is the power of God to those who are being saved. (19) For it is written: "I will destroy the wisdom of the wise, I will disregard the understanding of the prudent."

(20) Where is the wise man? Where is the scribe? Where is the debater of this age? Has not God made foolish the wisdom of this age? (21) For since in the wisdom of God, the world through its wisdom did not know God, it pleased God through the foolishness of preaching to save those who believe. (22) For Jews ask for signs and Greeks seek wisdom, (23) yet we proclaim Christ crucified, to Jews a stumbling block, and to Gentiles foolishness. (24) But to those who are called, both Jews and Gentiles, Christ is the power of God and the wisdom of God. (25) For the foolishness of God is wiser than men, and the weakness of God is stronger than men.

(26) For consider your calling, brothers. Not many of you were wise according to the flesh, not many of you were powerful, and not many of you were of noble birth; (27) but God chose the foolish things of the world to shame the wise, and the weak things to shame the strong; (28) and God chose the base and despised things and the things that are nothing that he might abolish the things that are, (29) so that no one might boast in the presence of God. (30) But it is because of him that you are in Christ Jesus, who became wisdom to us from God and righteousness, sanctification, and redemption, (31) as it is written: "Let him who boasts, boast in the Lord."

1 Corinthians 2:1-16

(1) When I came to you, brothers, I did not come proclaiming the testimony of God with eloquence or philosophy. (2) For I decided not to know anything while I was with you except Jesus Christ and him crucified. (3) I was with you in weakness, fear and much trembling. (4) My speech and message were not in persuasive words of wisdom, but in the demonstration

of the spirit and power, (5) so that your faith might not be in the wisdom of men, but in the power of God.

(6) Yet we do speak wisdom to the mature, but it is not the wisdom of this age or of the leaders of this age, who are coming to nothing. (7) We speak a hidden mystery, which God in eternity planned, for our glory. (8) None of the leaders of this age understood this. For if they had, they would not have crucified the Lord of Glory; (9) but it is written,

> "No eye has seen, nor ear heard, nor the heart of man conceived
> what God has prepared for those loving him."

(10) For God has revealed this to us through the Spirit; for the Spirit searches all things, even the deep things of God. (11) For who knows the thoughts of a man except the spirit of the man in him? So also no one knows the thoughts of God except the Spirit of God. (12) We have not received the spirit of the world but the spirit from God, so that we may know the grace that has been freely given to us. (13) We also do not speak in terms of human philosophy, but in terms of the things taught by the Spirit, interpreting spiritual things in spiritual terms.

(14) The natural man does not receive the things of the Spirit of God. They are foolishness to him, and he cannot understand them, because they are spiritually discerned. (15) The spiritual man judges all things, but he is judged by no one.

(16) For who knows the mind of God? Who will instruct him? But we have the mind of Christ.

1 Corinthians 3:1-23

(1) Brothers, I could not speak to you as spiritual men but as carnal, even infants in Christ. (2) I gave you milk to drink not solid food, for you were not ready for it then, neither are you ready for it now, (3) for you are still of the flesh. For while there is jealousy and strife among you, are you not carnal and living as other men do? (4) When one says, "I am of Paul," and another says, "I am of Apollos," are you not carnal?

(5) What then is Apollos? What is Paul? They were servants through whom you believed, even as the Lord assigned to each. (6) I planted, Apollos watered, but God caused it to grow. (7) So then neither is the one planting nor the one watering anything, but God who makes it grow. (8) The one planting and the one watering are one, and each will receive his own wages in proportion to his own labor. (9) For we are fellow workers; you are a cultivated field of God, a structure of God.

(10) In accordance with the grace of God given to me as a skilled architect, I laid a foundation, and another is building upon it. Let each one be careful how he builds. (11) For no one can lay a foundation other than the one that is laid, which is Jesus Christ. (12) If anyone builds on this foundation using gold, silver, precious stones, wood, hay or straw, (13) each

man's work will become known, for the day will declare it; because it will be revealed by fire, and the fire will test the quality of the work of each one. (14) If the work which anyone builds on the foundation survives, he will receive a reward. (15) But if the work is consumed, he will suffer loss; he himself will be saved, but only as through fire.

(16) Do you not know that you are a temple of God and that the Spirit of God dwells in you? (17) If anyone defiles the temple of God, God will defile him. For God's temple is holy, and you are that temple.

(18) Let no one deceive himself. If any among you thinks himself to be wise in this age, let him become a fool so that he may become wise. (19) For the wisdom of this world is foolishness with God. For it is written:

"He catches the wise in their trickery,"
(20) and again,
"The Lord knows the vain thoughts of the wise."
(21) So let no one boast in men, for all things are yours, (22) whether Paul or Apollos or Cephas or the world or life or death, or the present or the future— all is yours, (23) and you belong to Christ, and Christ belongs to God.

1 Corinthians 4:1-21

(1) So, men should regard us as servants of Christ and stewards of the mysteries of God. (2) It is required of stewards that they are found trustworthy. (3) It is a very small thing that you or any human court judges me. I do not even judge myself. (4) Even though I am not aware of anything against myself, that does not mean that I am innocent. The Lord is the one judging me. (5) So do not be hasty in your judging, but wait until the Lord returns; for he will bring to light the hidden things in darkness, and he will reveal the secret purposes of the heart. Then each one will receive his praise from God.

(6) These things, brothers, I have applied to myself and Apollos, so that you may learn from us to live according to the Scriptures and that none of you would be puffed up thinking that he is better than another. (7) For who conferred distinction on you? And what do you have that you did not receive? If, then, it was given to you, why are you boasting?

(8) Already you are completely satisfied; already you have become rich; and you have reigned without us! O that you did reign so we might reign with you! (9) For I think that God has put us apostles at the end of the line, sentenced to death as a spectacle to the world, both to angels and to men. (10) We are fools for Christ's sake, but you are wise in Christ. We are weak, but you are strong. You are distinguished, but we are without honor. (11) Even now we are hungry and thirsty and dressed in rags, we are violently abused and homeless. (12) We work hard at manual labor. When insulted, we bless. When persecuted, we endure. (13) When slandered, we conciliate. We are considered as worthless filth, the scum of all things, even

until now.

(14) I do not write these things to shame you, but to admonish you as my beloved children. (15) For though you had ten thousand guardians in Christ, you do not have many fathers. For I became your father through the gospel of Christ Jesus. (16) Therefore, I urge you, follow my example. (17) This is why I have sent Timothy to you. He is my beloved child and faithful in the Lord, and he will remind you of my ways in Christ Jesus, as I teach everywhere in all the churches.

(18) Some of you are puffed up, thinking that I will not come to you. (19) But I will come to you soon, if the Lord wills, and I will find out not the speech of the puffed up ones, but their power. (20) For the kingdom of God is not in talk but in power. (21) Which do you prefer, that I come to you with a rod, or in love and a gentle spirit?

1 Corinthians 5:1-13

(1) It is reported everywhere that there is fornication among you, and it is of such a kind that even the pagans condemn, that a man co-habits with his father's wife. (2) You are puffed up rather than being mortified. Should you not have removed this one from your fellowship? For I, being absent in body but present in spirit, have already passed judgment on this person who has done this deed. (4) When you are assembled in the name of our Lord Jesus, and my spirit present, and with the power of our Lord Jesus, (5) deliver this person to Satan for the destruction of the flesh, so that his spirit may be saved in the day of the Lord.

(6) Your boasting is not good. Do you not know that a little leaven leavens the whole lump? (7) Purge out the old leaven so you will have a fresh batch of dough, as unleavened loaves. For Christ, our Passover lamb, has been sacrificed. (8) So let us keep the feast, not with the old leaven, the leaven of malice and evil, but with the unleavened loaves of sincerity and truth.

(9) In the letter, I wrote to you not to associate intimately with fornicators. (10) I was not speaking of the fornicators of this world, or the greedy, robbers, or idolaters, since you would have to go out of the world to avoid them. (11) But rather I wrote to you not to associate intimately with anyone who claims to be a brother if he is a fornicator or greedy, an idolater, an abusive person, a drunkard, or a robber—do not fellowship with such a person. (12) For why should I judge the outsiders? Is it not the ones on the inside that you are to judge? (13) God will judge those outside. "Remove the evil man from your fellowship."

1 Corinthians 6:1-20

(1) Do any of you, having a grievance against another, dare to take

your case before the unrighteous rather than before saints? (2) Do you not know that the saints will judge the world? And if the world is to be judged by you, are you incompetent to judge minor things? (3) Do you not know that we will judge angels? How much more the affairs of this life! (4) If then you have cases concerning the affairs of this life, why do you seek those least esteemed by the church to try your cases? (5) I say this to shame you. Can it be that there is no one among you who can judge a dispute between believers? (6) But brother goes to court against brother, and that before unbelievers.

(7) To have lawsuits among yourselves means that you have utterly failed. Why not rather suffer wrong? Why not rather be cheated? (8) Instead, you do wrong and cheat, and that to your brothers.

(9) Do you not know that the unrighteous will not inherit the kingdom of God? Do not be led astray. Neither fornicators, nor idolaters, nor adulterers, nor the effeminate, nor sodomites, (10) nor thieves, nor the greedy, nor drunkards, nor slanderers, nor the rapacious will inherit the kingdom of God. (11) And such were some of you. But you were washed, you were sanctified, you were justified in the name of Jesus Christ and by the Spirit of our God.

(12) "All things are lawful for me," but all things are not beneficial. "All things are lawful for me," but I will not be enslaved by anything. (13) "Food is for the stomach, and the stomach is for food," but God will destroy both of them. The body, however, is not for fornication, but for the Lord, and the Lord for the body. (14) And God, who raised up the Lord, will raise us up also by his power. (15) Do you not know that your bodies are members of Christ? Shall I therefore take the members of Christ and make them members of a harlot? Perish the thought! (16) Do you not know that he who joins himself to a harlot is one body with her? For it is written, "The two shall become one flesh." (17) But he who unites himself with the Lord is one spirit with him.

(18) Flee fornication. Every other sin a man commits is outside his body, but the fornicator sins against his own body. (19) Do you not know that your body is a temple of the Holy Spirit in you, which you have from God, and that you are not your own? (20) You were bought with a price. Therefore glorify God in your body.

1 Corinthians 7:1-40

(1) In reference to the things about which you write, it would be good for a man to remain single; (2) but because of fornication, I advise every man to have his own wife and every woman to have her own husband. (3) The husband should fulfill his marital duty to his wife, and the wife also to her husband. (4) The wife does not belong to herself but to her husband; likewise, the husband does not belong to himself but to his wife. (5) Do not

refuse one another except for a time by agreement, that you may have time for prayer. Then come back together again, lest Satan tempt you through lack of self-control. (6) I say this as a concession, not a command. (7) I wish that all men were as I myself am. But each man has his own gift from God, one of one kind, and one of another.

(8) To the unmarried men and the widows, it is good for you to remain single, as I am. (9) But if they cannot exercise self-control, they should marry rather than be aflame with passion. (10) To the married I charge you, not I, but the Lord, that the wife should not leave her husband; (11) but if she leaves, she should remain single or be reconciled to her husband; and the husband should not leave his wife.

(12) To the rest I say, not the Lord, that if a brother has an unbelieving wife and she consents to live with him, he should not leave her. (13) And if a wife has an unbelieving husband and he consents to live with her, she should not leave him. (14) For the unbelieving husband is sanctified by his wife, and the unbelieving wife is sanctified by her believing husband. Otherwise your children would be unclean, but now they are holy. (15) But if the unbelieving partner leaves, let it be done. The brother or sister is not obligated in this case. For God has called us to peace. (16) Wife, how do you know if you will save your husband, or husband, how do you know if you will save your wife?

(17) Only, as the Lord has assigned to each one, as God has called each, he should live. This is my rule for all the churches. (18) Was anyone circumcised when he was called? He should not be uncircumcised. Was anyone uncircumcised when he was called? He should not be circumcised. (19) Circumcision is nothing and uncircumcision is nothing, but what matters is keeping the commandments of God. (20) Each one should continue as he was when he was called. (21) Were you a slave when you were called? Do not let that trouble you, but if you can gain your freedom, do so. (22) For he who was called in the Lord as a slave is a freedman of the Lord; likewise, he who was called in the Lord as a free man is a slave of Christ. (23) You were bought with a price. Do not become slaves of men. (24) Brothers, each of you should continue with God just as he was when he was called.

(25) Now concerning the unmarried, I have no command from the Lord, but I am one who by the mercy of the Lord is trustworthy. (26) I think that in view of the present distress, it is good for a man to remain as he is. (27) Are you married? Do not seek a divorce. Are you single? Do not seek a wife. (28) But if you do marry, you do not sin; and if a virgin marries, she does not sin. But you will have many afflictions, and I am trying to spare you.

(29) I tell you, brothers, the time is short. From now on those who have wives should be as though they had none; (30) and those who weep, as though they did not weep; and those who rejoice, as those who did not rejoice; and those who buy, as those who owned nothing; (31) and those using this world, as those abusing it. For the fashion of this world is passing

away.

(32) I want you to be free from anxieties. The unmarried cares for the things of the Lord, (33) how he may please the Lord; but the married man cares about the things of this world, how he may please his wife, (34) and his interests are divided. An unmarried woman or virgin cares for the things of the Lord, that she may be holy both in body and spirit; but the married woman is concerned about the cares of the world, how she may please her husband. (35) I am saying this for your own good and not to lay a burden upon you, but to promote good order so that you will have undistracted devotion to the Lord.

(36) But if any man thinks that he is acting improperly to his virgin and she has passed her youth, and so the concern is urgent, let him do as he wishes. He commits no sin if there is a marriage. (37) But he who stands firm in his heart, who is not under compulsion but is free to carry out his will, decides to keep his virgin, he will do well. (38) So the one who marries his virgin does well, and the one refraining from marriage does better.

(39) A wife is bound to her husband as long as he lives; but if he dies, she is free to marry anyone she wishes, only in the Lord. (40) But in my opinion, she would be happier if she remained as she is. And I think that I have the Spirit of God.

1 Corinthians 8:1-13

(1) Concerning the meat sacrificed to idols, we know that we all have knowledge. Knowledge inflates, but love edifies. (2) If anyone thinks he has superior knowledge, he does not yet know as he ought to know. (3) But if anyone loves God, he is known by him.

(4) Therefore, concerning the eating of the meat sacrificed to an idol, we know that an idol has no real existence and that there is only one God. (5) Even though there are so-called gods in heaven and earth, as indeed there are many "gods" and "lords," (6) yet to us there is one God, the Father, from whom all things came and for whom we live, and one Lord, Jesus Christ, through whom are all things and through whom we live.

(7) But not everyone has this knowledge. And some by habit, even now, eat this meat as food sacrificed to an idol, and their consciences, being weak, are defiled. (8) Food will not commend us to God. We are no worse if we do not eat, and we gain no favor by eating. (9) But be careful that this freedom of yours does not become a stumbling block to the weak. (10) For if someone sees you, one who has knowledge, at a table in an idol's temple, would he, the one who has a weak conscience, not be encouraged to eat? (11) So the weak one, the brother for whom Christ died, by your knowledge is destroyed. (12) So sinning against your brothers and wounding their weak consciences, you sin against Christ. (13) Therefore, if eating meat sacrificed to an idol causes my brother to stumble, I will not eat meat again, so that I

may not cause my brother to stumble.

1 Corinthians 9:1-27

(1) Am I not free? Am I not an apostle? Have I not seen the Lord? Are you not the product of my labor in the Lord? (2) If to others I am not an apostle, yet to you I am. For you are the seal of my apostleship in the Lord.

(3) This is my defense to my critics. (4) Do we not have a right to our food and drink? (5) Do we not have the right to be accompanied by a believing wife, as the other apostles and the brothers of the Lord and Cephas? (6) Or is it only Barnabas and I who have not the right to refrain from working for a living?

(7) Who serves as a soldier at his own expense? Who plants a vineyard without eating any of its fruit? Who shepherds a flock and does not drink milk from the flock? (8) Am I speaking only according to human reason, or does not the law say the same things? (9) For it is written in the Law of Moses, "You shall not muzzle an ox treading out the grain." Is God concerned here for the oxen? (10) Or is not this written for us? Yes, it was written for us, for the plowman should plow in hope, and the harvester should share in the crop. (11) If we have sowed spiritual things, is it a great thing that we should reap material benefits? (12) If others have shared this right with you, should we not even more? Nevertheless, we did not use this right, but we endured all hardships rather than put an obstacle in the way of the gospel of Christ. (13) Do you not know that those who perform sacred services eat the food of the temple, and those who serve at the altar share in the sacrificial offerings? (14) So the Lord ordained that those proclaiming the gospel should live by the gospel.

(15) But I have not made use of any of these rights, and I am not writing this to receive anything for myself. For I would rather die than to be deprived of my ground for boasting. (16) For if I preach the gospel, I have nothing to boast about. For I am compelled to do this. Woe to me if I do not preach the gospel! (17) If I do this work because I choose to I have a reward, but if not by choice but by compulsion, I am entrusted with a stewardship. (18) What therefore is my reward? It is the preaching of the gospel without charge and not making use of my right in the gospel.

(19) Although I am not bound to anyone, I have made myself a slave to all so that I may win the more. (20) To the Jews I became a Jew, so that I might win the Jews. To those under the law I became as one under law, though I myself was not under law, so that I might win those under law. (21) To those without law I became as one without law, not being without the law of God but under the law of Christ, so that I might win those without law. (22) I became weak to the weak so that I might win the weak. I became all things to all men so that I might save some. (23) I did it all for the sake of the gospel, so that I might share in its blessings.

(24) Do you not know that in a race all the runners compete, but only one receives the prize? So run that you may receive it. (25) Every athlete exercises self-control in all things. They do it to receive a crown of leaves that withers, but we do it for an imperishable crown. (26) So I do not run as one who loses sight of the finish line. I do not beat the air as one shadowboxing. (27) I treat my body severely and make it my slave, lest after I have preached to others I myself should be disqualified.

1 Corinthians 10:1-33

(1) Brothers, I want you to remember that our fathers were all under the cloud and they all passed through the sea, (2) and all in the cloud and in the sea were baptized into Moses. (3) They all ate the same spiritual food, (4) and they all drink the same spiritual drink. For they all drank of the spiritual rock accompanying them, and the rock was Christ. (5) But God was not pleased with the majority of them. For they were struck down in the desert.

(6) These events are examples for us so that we should not desire evil things as they did. (7) Do not be idolaters as some of them were. It is written, "The people sat down to eat and to drink, and they arose to dance." (8) Do not commit fornication as some of them did and twenty-three thousand fell in one day. (9) Do not test the Lord as some of them did and were destroyed by serpents. (10) Do not grumble as some of them did and were destroyed by the destroyer.

(11) These things happened to them as examples for us, and they were written as a warning to us, upon whom the fulfillment of the ages has come. (12) So to him who thinks he stands, watch out lest he fall! (13) No temptation has come to you that is not common to all men. But God is faithful; and he will not let you be tempted beyond your strength, but he will make a way of escape so you may be able to endure it.

(14) Therefore, my beloved, flee from idolatry. (15) I speak as to wise men. Examine what I say. (16) Is not the cup of thanksgiving for which we give thanks a participation in the blood of Christ? Is not the bread which we break a participation in the body of Christ? (17) Since there is one loaf, we who are many are one body, for we partake of the one loaf.

(18) Consider what Israel, according to the flesh, did. Did not those who served at the altar partake of the food of the sacrifices? (19) What do I imply then? Is the idolatrous sacrifice anything, or is the idol a reality? (20) No, but that which they sacrifice is to demons and not to God. I do not want you to participate with demons. (21) You cannot drink the cup of the Lord and the cup of demons. You cannot partake of the table of the Lord and the table of demons. (22) Or do we provoke the Lord to jealousy? Are we stronger that he?

(23) "All things are lawful," but all things are not profitable. "All things are lawful," but all things do not edify. (24) No one should seek his

own good, but the good of others.

(25) Eat what is being sold in the market place without raising questions of conscience. (26) For, "the earth is the Lord's and the fullness of it."

(27) If an unbeliever invites you to his table and you wish to go, eat what is set before you, without raising any question of conscience. (28) But if someone says to you, "This was slain in sacrifice," do not eat it, for the sake of the man who informed you and for conscience' sake— (29) the other man's conscience, not yours. Why should my liberty be restricted by another's conscience? (30) If I partake with thankfulness, why am I slandered concerning that for which I give thanks?

(31) Therefore, whether you eat or drink or whatever you do, do all to the glory of God. (32) Give no offense to Jews or to Greeks or to the church of God, (33) just as I also please all men in all things, not seeking my own advantage but the advantage of the many, in order that they may be saved.

1 Corinthians 11:1-34

(1) Imitate me as I imitate Christ. (2) I praise you because you remember me in everything and for holding firmly to the traditions that I passed on to you.

(3) I want you to realize that Christ is the head of every man, and the man is the head of a woman, and God is the head of Christ. (4) Every man praying or prophesying with his head covered shames his head. (5) But every woman praying or prophesying without her head covered shames her head. For it is as if her head were shaven. (6) For if a woman is not veiled, let her cut off her hair. But since it is shameful for a woman to have her hair cut off or her head shaven, she should wear a veil. (7) For a man ought not veil his head, because he is the image and glory of God, but the woman is the glory of man. (8) For man is not from woman, but woman is from man. (9) For indeed man was not created for the woman, but woman was created for the man. (10) Therefore, the woman ought to have authority on her head because of the angels. (11) Nevertheless, in the Lord, neither is the woman without the man nor the man without the woman. (12) For as the woman is from the man, so also the man is born of the woman, but all things are from God. (13) Judge for yourselves. Is it proper for an unveiled woman to pray to God? (14) Does not nature itself teach you that it is a shame for a man to wear long hair, (15) but if a woman wears long hair, it is her glory? Her long hair has been given to her instead of a veil. (16) If anyone wants to argue about this, remember that neither we nor the churches of God recognize any other mode of worship.

(17) In the following injunctions I do not commend you, for when you come together it is not for the better but for the worse. (18) I hear that

when you come together in the church, there are divisions among you, and in part, I believe it. (19) For it is necessary that there are factions among you so that those who are genuine among you may be recognized. (20) Therefore when you come together, it is not to eat the supper of our Lord. (21) For each person goes ahead and eats his own supper; and one is hungry, and another is drunk. (22) Do you not have houses to eat and drink in? Or do you despise the church of God and humiliate those who have nothing? What shall I say to you? Shall I praise you? In this I do not praise you.

(23) For I received from the Lord what also I delivered to you. In the night that the Lord Jesus was betrayed, he took bread, (24) and giving thanks, he broke it and said, "This is my body in behalf of you. Do this in remembrance of me."

(25) Likewise, he took the cup after supper, saying, "This cup is the new covenant in my blood. Do this, as often as you drink it, in remembrance of me." (26) For as often as you eat this bread and drink this cup, you proclaim the death of the Lord until he comes.

(27) So, whoever eats the bread and drinks the cup of the Lord in an unworthy manner will be guilty of the body and the blood of the Lord. (28) Let a man examine himself, and then let him eat of the bread and drink of the cup. (29) For the one who eats and drinks without discerning the body eats and drinks judgment upon himself. (30) This is why many of you are sick and feeble and many have died. (31) But if we carefully examined ourselves, we should not be judged. (32) When we are judged by the Lord, we are being disciplined so we will not be condemned with the world.

(33) So, my brothers, when you come together to eat, wait for one another. (34) If anyone is hungry, let him eat at home, so that you may not come together to be judged. And the remaining matters I will settle when I come.

1 Corinthians 12:1-31

(1) Now concerning spiritual matters, brothers, I do not want you to be misinformed. (2) You know that when you were pagans, you were led around by dumb idols as impulse drove you. (3) Therefore I tell you that no one speaking by the Spirit of God says, "Jesus is accursed," and no one can say, "Jesus is Lord," except by the Holy Spirit.

(4) There are different gifts, but the same spirit. (5) There are different ministries, but the same Lord. (6) There are different works, but the same God who accomplishes all of them in everyone.

(7) To each one is given the manifestation of the Spirit for the common good. (8) For to one is given a word of wisdom through the Spirit, to another a word of knowledge according to the same Spirit, (9) to another faith by the same Spirit, to another gifts of healing by that one Spirit, (10) to another the working of miracles, to another prophecy, to another the

discerning of spirits, to another various kinds of tongues, and to another the interpretation of tongues. (11) All these things are performed by the one and the same Spirit, distributing separately to each one as he wills.

(12) For even as the body is one and has many members, all the members of the body, though many, are one body; so it is with Christ. (13) For by one Spirit we were all baptized into one body, whether Jews or Greeks, whether slaves or free, and we all were given to drink of the one Spirit.

(14) Now the body is not one member but many. (15) If the foot says, "Because I am not a hand, I am not of the body," would that mean that it ceased to be a part of the body? (16) And if the ear says, "Because I am not an eye, I am not of the body," would that mean that it ceased to be a part of the body? (17) If the whole body were an eye, where would the sense of hearing be? If the whole body were an ear, where would the sense of smell be? (18) But as it is, God has placed each member in the body as he chose. (19) And if all were one member, where would the body be? (20) But as it is, there are many members, but one body.

(21) The eye cannot say to the hand, "I have no need of you," nor again the head to the feet, "I have no need of you." (22) On the contrary, the members of the body that seem to be weaker are indispensable, (23) and the members of the body we think to be less honorable, we honor by more abundant clothing; and our unpresentable parts are treated with greater honor, (24) which our presentable parts do not require. But God has constructed the body giving greater honor to the inferior parts, (25) so that there should be no division in the body, but that all the members should care for one another. (26) If one member suffers, all the members suffer, or if one member is honored, all the members rejoice.

(27) You are the body of Christ and individually members of it. (28) God has set in the church first apostles, second prophets, third teachers, then miracle workers, gifts of healing, helpers, administrators, and different kinds of tongues. (29) Are all apostles? Are all prophets? Are all teachers? Are all miracle workers? (30) Do all have the gifts of healing? Do all speak with tongues? Do all interpret? (31) But you should desire the greater gifts. And yet I will show you the most excellent way!

1 Corinthians 13:1-13

(1) If I speak in the tongues of men and angels, but have not love, I have become sounding brass or a tinkling symbol. (2) And if I have prophecy and know all mysteries and all knowledge, and if I have all faith so as to remove mountains, but have not love, I am nothing. (3) If I dole out all my goods and deliver my body that I may boast, but have not love, nothing I am profited.

(4) Love is long-suffering, love is kind, not jealous, not boastful, not

inflated, (5) not discourteous, not selfish, not irritable, not enumerating evil, (6) not rejoicing over the wrong, rejoices with the truth. (7) (Love) covers all things, (has) faith for all things, hopes in all things, endures in all things.

(8) Love never falls in ruins; but whether prophecies, they will be abolished; or tongues, they will cease; or knowledge, it will be superseded. (9) For we know in part and we prophesy in part. (10) But when the perfect comes, the imperfect will be superseded. (11) When I was an infant, I spoke as an infant, I thought as an infant, I reckoned as an infant; when I became a man, I abolished the things of the infant. (12) For now we see through a mirror in an enigma, but then face to face. Now I know in part, but then I shall know as also I was fully known. (13) But now remains faith, hope, love, these three; but the greatest of these is love.

1 Corinthians 14:1-40

(1) Pursue love and seek the spiritual gifts, especially that you may prophesy. (2) For the one speaking in a tongue does not speak to men but to God; for no one understands him, because he utters mysteries in the spirit. (3) On the other hand, the one who prophesies speaks to men for their edification and encouragement and consolation. (4) The one who speaks in a tongue edifies himself, but the one who prophesies edifies the church. (5) I would like for all of you to speak in tongues, but I would rather that you prophesy. For, the one prophesying is greater than the one speaking in tongues, unless the speaker interprets, so that the church may be edified.

(6) Now, brothers, if I come to you speaking in tongues, what shall I profit you unless I bring to you some revelation or knowledge or prophesy or teaching? (7) If even lifeless instruments which produce a sound, such as pipe or harp, do not give distinct notes, how will it be known what is played? (8) For if the bugle gives an uncertain sound, who will prepare himself for battle? (9) So also you, unless you give a clear word by the tongue, how will it be known what is said? For you will be speaking into the air. (10) So there are, doubtless, many different languages in the world, and none is without meaning. (11) So if I do not know the meaning of the language, I will be a foreigner to the speaker and the speaker a foreigner to me. (12) So also you, since you are zealous of spiritual gifts, seek to excel in the edification of the church.

(13) Therefore let the one speaking in a tongue pray for the ability to interpret. (14) For if I pray in a tongue, my spirit prays but my mind is unfruitful. (15) So what shall I do? I will pray with the spirit, and I will pray with the mind also. I will sing with the spirit, and I will sing with the mind also. (16) Otherwise if you praise with your spirit, how can the one in the position of the uninstructed be able to say the "amen" to your giving thanks, since he does not know what you are saying? (17) For indeed you do well in giving thanks, but the other person is not edified. (18) I thank God

that I speak in tongues more than all of you. (19) But in the church I would rather speak five intelligible words to instruct others than ten thousand words in a tongue.

(20) Brothers, do not be childish, but in your ways be childlike, and in your thinking be mature. (21) It is written in the law:

"In other tongues and lips of foreigners I will speak to this people,
but even then they will not hear me,"

says the Lord.

(22) Therefore tongues are not for a sign to the believer but to the unbeliever, and prophecy is not for the unbeliever but to the believer. (23) If therefore the whole church comes together and everyone speaks in tongues, and the uninstructed or unbelievers enters, will they not say that you are crazy? (24) But if all prophesy and an unbeliever or one uninstructed enters, he is convinced by all, he is judged by all, (25) and the secrets of his heart are disclosed, so that he will fall on his face and worship God, saying, "God is truly among you."

(26) What then shall we do, brothers? When you come together, each one has a psalm, a teaching, a revelation, a tongue or an interpretation. Let all things be done for edification. (27) If anyone speaks in a tongue, let there be only two, or most three, and each in turn, and let one interpret; (28) but if there is no interpreter, let him be silent in church, and let him speak to himself and to God. (29) Let two or three prophets speak, and let the others weigh what is said; (30) but if a revelation is given to someone sitting down, let the first be silent. (31) For all of you can prophesy one by one so that all may learn and all may be encouraged. (32) The spirits of prophets are subject to prophets. (33) For God is not a God of confusion but of peace.

As in all the churches of the saints, (34) the women should be silent in church. They are not permitted to talk, but let them be in submission, as also the law says. (35) If there is anything that they want to know, let them ask their husbands at home. For it is improper for a woman to speak in church. (36) Did the word of God originate with you, or are you the only ones it has reached?

(37) If anyone thinks he is a prophet or a spiritual man, let him acknowledge that what I am writing is a command of the Lord. (38) But if anyone ignores it, let him be ignored. (39) So, my brothers, be eager to prophesy and forbid not to speak in tongues. (40) But let all things be done decently and in order.

1 Corinthians 15:1-58

(1) Now, brothers, I want to remind you of the good news that I preached to you, which also you received and in which you stand firm. (2) By this gospel you are being saved, if you hold fast the word I preached to you, unless your faith was counterfeit.

(3) For I delivered to you that which is of first importance, what I also received: that Christ died for our sins according to the Scriptures, (4) that he was buried, that he was raised on the third day according to the Scriptures, (5) that he was seen by Cephas, and then by the twelve. (6) After that, he was seen by more than five hundred at one time, of whom the majority remains today, though some have fallen asleep. (7) Next he was seen by James, then by all the apostles. (8) Last of all, he was seen by me also, as one prematurely born. (9) For I am least of all the apostles and am not worthy to be called an apostle, because I persecuted the church of God. (10) But by the grace of God I am what I am, and his grace to me was not in vain; for I worked harder than all the others, but it was not I, but the grace of God with me. (11) So, whether it was I or they, this is what we preach, and this is what you believed.

(12) So if it is proclaimed that Christ has been raised from the dead, how can some of you say that there is no resurrection of the dead? (13) Now if there is no resurrection of the dead, then Christ has not been raised. (14) And if Christ has not been raised, then our preaching is in vain, and your faith also is in vain.

(15) Moreover, we are found to be false witnesses of God, because we witnessed that God raised Christ, whom he did not raise, if the dead are not raised. (16) For if the dead are not raised, neither has Christ been raised; (17) and if Christ has not been raised, your faith is futile, and you are still in your sins. (18) Then those also who have fallen asleep have perished. (19) If we only have hope in Christ in this life, we are of all men most to be pitied.

(20) But in fact Christ has been raised from the dead and is the first fruit of those who have fallen asleep. (21) For since through a man came death, by a man also came the resurrection of the dead. (22) For as in Adam all die, so also in Christ shall all be made alive. (23) But each one in his own order: Christ the first fruits, then at his coming those who belong to him; (24) then comes the end, when he delivers the kingdom to God the Father, when he abolishes all rule, all authority, and all power. (25) For he must reign until he has put all enemies under his feet. (26) Death is the last enemy to be abolished. For he has put all things in subjection under his feet. (27) For when Scripture says he has put all things in subjection, in saying "all things," it clearly means to exclude God who subordinates them. (28) And when all things are subject to him, then the Son himself will also be made subordinate to God, who made all things subject to him, so that God may be all in all.

(29) Otherwise, what about those who are being baptized on behalf of the dead? If the dead are not raised, why then are they baptized on behalf of them? (30) Why are we also in danger every hour? (31) Yes, truly, brothers, by my pride in you, which I have in Christ Jesus our Lord, I die daily. (32) What do I profit if, from the human point of view, I fought with wild beasts in Ephesus? If the dead are not raised, "Let us eat and drink, for tomorrow we die."

(33) Do not be led astray: "Bad company corrupts good character." (34) Wake up to righteousness, and sin no more. For some have no knowledge of God. I say this to your shame.

(35) But someone will say, "How are the dead raised? With what kind of body do they come?" (36) Foolish man! What you sow does not come to life unless it dies. (37) And what you sow is not the body that it will become, but a naked grain, perhaps of wheat or some other grain. (38) But God will give it a body that he has chosen, and to each seed with its own particular body. (39) All flesh is not the same flesh, but there is one kind for men, another for animals, another for birds, and another for fish. (40) There are heavenly bodies and there are earthly bodies, but the splendor of the heavenly bodies is one, and splendor of the earthly bodies is another. (41) There is one splendor of the sun, and another splendor of the moon, and another splendor of the stars. For each star differs from another in splendor.

(42) So also is the resurrection of the dead. The body that is sown is perishable, it is raised imperishable. (43) It is sown in dishonor, it is raised in glory. It is sown in weakness, it is raised in power. (44) It is sown a physical body, it is raised a spiritual body. If there is a natural body, there is a spiritual body. (45) Thus it is written: "The first man Adam became a living soul." The last Adam became a life-giving spirit. (46) The spiritual is not first, but the physical, then afterwards the spiritual. (47) The first man was out of the dust of the earth, the second man is from heaven. (48) As was the man of dust, so are those of the dust; and such as the man of heaven, so are those who are of heaven. (49) Just as we have borne the image of the man of dust, we shall also bear the image of the heavenly man.

(50) I tell you, brothers, that flesh and blood cannot inherit the kingdom of God. Nor does the perishable inherit the imperishable. (51) Behold, I tell you a mystery. We shall not all sleep, but we shall all be changed, (52) in a moment, at the glance of an eye, at the last trumpet. For a trumpet will sound, and the dead in Christ will be raised imperishable, and we shall be changed. (53) For the perishable must put on the imperishable, and this mortality must put on immortality. (54) When the perishable puts on the imperishable and this mortal shall put on immortality, then shall be fulfilled the written word: "Death is swallowed up in victory."

(55) "O Death, where is your victory? O Death, where is your sting?" (56) Now the sting of death is sin, and the power of sin is the law. (57) But thanks be to God who gives us the victory through our Lord Jesus Christ.

(58) Therefore, my beloved brothers, be firm, immovable, always abounding in the work of the Lord, knowing that your labor in the Lord is not futile.

1 Corinthians 16:1-24

(1) Now concerning the collection for the saints, follow the

instructions I gave to the churches in Galatia. (2) On the first day of each week, let each of you put aside and save, as you have prospered, so you will not need to take a collection when I arrive. (3) When I arrive, I will give letters of introduction to those you approve to carry your gift to Jerusalem; (4) and if it is advisable for me to go also, they shall go with me.

(5) I will visit you after I pass through Macedonia, for I am traveling by way of Macedonia— (6) and I will stay with you awhile, or even spend the winter, so that you may provide me with what I need for the rest of my journey. (7) For I do not want to make a passing visit, because I hope to spend some time with you, if the Lord permits. (8) But I will stay in Ephesus until Pentecost, (9) for a great door of opportunity stands wide open for effective work, but there are many against me.

(10) Now if Timothy comes, see that you put him at ease, for he is doing the work of the Lord, just as I am. (11) So let no one neglect him. Send him on his way in peace so that he may join me, for I am waiting for him with the brothers.

(12) As for our brother Apollos, I tried to persuade him to come with the brothers, but it was not at all his will to come now. But he will come when the time is right.

(13) Be alert, stand firm in the faith, be valiant and strong. (14) Let everything be done in love.

(15) You know that Stephanas and his family were the first converts in Achaia and that they have devoted themselves to the ministry of the saints. I urge you, brothers, (16) to submit to such men and to everyone who cooperates and toils with them. (17) I rejoice at the coming of Stephanas, Fortunatus and Achaicus, because they made up for your absence. (18) For they refreshed my spirit as well as yours. Therefore recognize such men.

(19) Greetings from the churches of Asia. Aquila and Prisca, with the church that meets in their house, send you cordial greetings. (20) Greetings from all the brothers. Greet one another with a holy kiss.

(21) I, Paul, write this greeting in my own hand. (22) If anyone does not love the Lord, let him be accursed. Come, O Lord! (23) The grace of our Lord Jesus be with you. (24) My love to all of you in Christ Jesus.

Introduction to 2 Corinthians

Paul wrote the second letter to the Corinthians about 57 A.D. from Macedonia. He had left Ephesus after his great ministry of three years there. His preaching against idol worship caused so many problems that there was a riot in the city, and he left under pressure and went to Macedonia. The letter is addressed to the church in Corinth and to the province of Achaia, which was all the territory of Greece south of Macedonia.

This letter was the most personal of all his letters. He tells of his great afflictions and his deep love for the church. He said that he was crushed beyond his power to endure and that he despaired of life itself (1:8). But his testimony was that his despair caused him to rely on God, and God delivered him. Some of the members of the church were saying bad things about Paul. They were bitterly attacking his message, his authority as an apostle, and even his character. Paul had sent Titus to the church, and after his visit there, they met in Macedonia. Titus had brought a good report. The majority of the church had endorsed his message and character; however, the judaizing party continued to be a threat to the fellowship of the church.

The purpose of the letter was to express his joy over the victory of his message, to show his intense love for them, to defend his authority as an apostle, and to urge the church to complete their contribution to the famine-stricken Christians in Judea.

This letter is 4,476 words and it is packed with teachings of eternal value. In the first chapter, he tells us that God has sealed us by his Spirit, which is a guarantee of our salvation (1:22). In chapter three, he teaches that the believers are Living Letters (3:1-4). In chapter four, he tells us that we are not to look at the seen but to the unseen, because only the unseen things are eternal (4:16-18). In chapter five, he tells us that if we are in Christ, we are a new creation and the old has passed away (5:17). In chapters eight and nine his words concerning stewardship are profound. He reminds us that we are to give according to what we have, not what we do not have (8:12). It blessed the people in Achaia in Paul's day, and it continues to bless the people in our day.

2 Corinthians 1:1-24

(1) Paul, an apostle of Jesus Christ by the will of God, and brother Timothy, To the church of God in Corinth, with all the saints in all Achaia: (2) Grace to you and peace from God our Father and the Lord Jesus Christ.

(3) Praise be to the God and Father of our Lord Jesus Christ, the Father of mercies and God of all encouragement, (4) who encourages us in all our afflictions and thus enables us to encourage those who are in any affliction with the encouragement with which we ourselves received from

God. (5) For as we share abundantly in the sufferings of Christ, we through Christ are also abundantly encouraged. (6) If we are afflicted, it is for your encouragement and salvation; if we are consoled, it is for your consolation, so that you may endure patiently the same sufferings we endure. (7) Our hope for you is firm, knowing that as you share in our sufferings, you also share in our encouragement.

(8) We, brothers, do not want you to be unaware of our sufferings in Asia. The burdens were so excessive and beyond our strength that we despaired even of life itself. (9) Indeed, we felt that we had received the sentence of death, but that was to make us trust not in ourselves but the God who raises the dead; (10) who delivered us from such a perilous death, and he will deliver us again. On him we have set our hope that he will continue to deliver us, (11) while you cooperate with us by praying for us so that thanks on our behalf may be given for the blessing granted us through the prayers of so many.

(12) Now this is our rejoicing: Our conscience assures us that we have conducted ourselves in the world, and especially with you, not in fleshly wisdom but in the grace of God. (13) For we do not write to you anything that you cannot read and understand. I hope that you will understand us fully, (14) as you have known us in part, so that you can be proud of us as we are of you on the day of our Lord Jesus.

(15) It was because I was so confident of this, that I chose to come to you first, so that you might have the benefit of a double visit. (16) I wanted to visit you on my way to Macedonia and after leaving Macedonia to visit you again, and for you to send me on to Judea. (17) That was my intention. Then did that mean that I was fickle? Or did I make my plans according to the flesh so that it would rest with me to say, "Yes, yes" and "No, no"?

(18) As surely as God is trustworthy, our word to you is not "Yes" and "No." (19) For the Son of God, Christ Jesus, who was proclaimed among you — by me, Silvanus and Timothy — was not "Yes" and "No"; but in him it was always, "Yes." (20) For all the promises of God find their "Yes" in him; wherefore it is through him that the "Amen" is spoken by us to the glory of God. (21) But it is God who establishes us with you and has anointed us, (22) and he has put his seal upon us and has given us the Spirit to dwell in our hearts, as a pledge of future blessings.

(23) Now I call God to be a witness against my life that it was to spare you that I did not come to Corinth. (24) Not that we lord it over your faith, but we work with you for your joy, for it is by faith that you stand.

2 Corinthians 2:1-17

(1) So I made up my mind not to make you another painful visit. (2) For if I grieve you, then who will cheer me up except the ones I grieved? (3) I wrote as I did so that when I come I will not be made miserable by those who

should make me rejoice. I had confidence in you that my joy would be the joy of all of you. (4) For I wrote to you through many tears and with great affliction and anxiety, not to cause you grief but to let you know what great love I have for you.

(5) But if anyone has caused grief, he has not only hurt me, but in some measure— not to put it too severely—all of you. (6) This punishment for such a one by the majority is enough, (7) so now you should forgive and comfort him, so that he may not be swallowed up in excessive grief. (8) Therefore, I urge you to reaffirm your love for him. (9) For I wrote to you to see if you are obedient in all things. (10) Anyone whom you forgive, I also forgive. What I have forgiven—if there was anything to forgive—it was for your sakes in the presence of Christ, (11) so that Satan cannot take advantage of us; for we are not ignorant of his designs.

(12) When I came to Troas to preach the gospel, a door had been opened by the Lord, but I had no peace of mind, because I could not find my brother Titus; (13) so I said goodbye to them and went on to Macedonia.

(14) But thanks be to God, who always leads us captives in Christ's triumphal procession and everywhere leads us to spread the fragrance of the knowledge of him. (15) For we are the aroma of Christ to God among those who are being saved and to those who are perishing, (16) to the latter a fragrance of death to death, to the former a fragrance of life to life. Who is adequate for such a calling? (17) For we are not like so many, adulterating the word of God, but with sincerity, as sent from God, we speak in Christ in the presence of God.

2 Corinthians 3:1-18

(1) Are we beginning to commend ourselves again? Or do we need, as some do, letters of recommendation to you or from you? (2) You yourselves are our letter of recommendation, written in our hearts, known and read by all men. (3) Clearly you are a letter from Christ delivered by us, written not with ink but with the Spirit of the living God, not on tablets of stone but on tablets of hearts of flesh.

(4) Such is the confidence we have through Christ toward God. (5) We are not competent to do anything of ourselves, but our competency is from God, (6) who has qualified us to be ministers of a new covenant, not of the letter, but of the Spirit; for the letter kills, but the Spirit gives life.

(7) The law, then, engraved by letters upon stone, dispensed death, and yet it came with such splendor that the Israelites could not gaze upon the face of Moses, even though it was fading. (8) Will not the ministry of the Spirit be with greater splendor? (9) For if the ministry of condemnation was in splendor, how much more will the ministry of righteousness abound in splendor? (10) That which once had splendor does not now have splendor because of the splendor that surpasses it. (11) For if what was fading away

came in splendor, that which endures has a much greater splendor.

(12) Since we have such hope, we speak with boldness, (13) and not as Moses, who put a veil upon his face so the Israelites could not gaze upon the final fading of that splendor. (14) But their hearts were hardened. For even now the same veil remains on the reading of the old covenant, because it is only in Christ that the veil is removed. (15) But whenever Moses is read, a veil covers their understanding; (16) but whenever anyone turns to the Lord, the veil is removed. (17) Now the Lord is the Spirit, and where the Spirit of the Lord is, there is freedom. (18) All of us, reflecting the splendor of the Lord, are being transformed into his likeness, from splendor to splendor, which comes from the Spirit of the Lord.

2 Corinthians 4:1-18

(1) Therefore, since we have this ministry through God's mercy, we do not lose courage. (2) We have renounced the hidden things of shame, not walking in craftiness nor adulterating the word of God, but by declaring the truth openly we recommend ourselves to the conscience of every man in the presence of God. (3) And if indeed our gospel is hidden, it is hidden to those who are perishing, (4) in whom the god of this age has blinded the thoughts of the unbelievers to keep them from seeing the radiance of the gospel of the glory of Christ, who is the image of God. (5) For we do not proclaim ourselves, but Christ Jesus as Lord, and ourselves your slaves for Jesus' sake. (6) For God, who said, "Out of darkness light shall shine," has shone in our hearts to give us the light of the knowledge of the glory in the presence of Christ.

(7) We have this treasure in earthen vessels, to show that such transcendent power comes from God and not from us. (8) We are afflicted in every way, but not restrained; perplexed, but not in despair; (9) persecuted, but not forsaken; knocked down, but not destroyed; (10) always carrying about in the body the dying of Jesus, so that the life of Jesus may also be revealed. (11) For we are always living in the presence of death for Jesus' sake, so that the life of Jesus may be revealed in our mortal bodies. (12) So death works in us, but life in you.

(13) Since we have the same spirit of faith of that which is written, "I believed, therefore I spoke," we believe, and therefore we speak, (14) knowing that the one who raised the Lord Jesus will raise us also and will bring us with you into his presence. (15) For all things are done for your sake, so that as grace extends to more and more people, it may cause the giving of thanks to abound to the glory of God.

(16) Wherefore we do not lose courage; though our body is in decay, yet our inner self is being renewed every day. (17) For our light, momentary affliction is achieving for us, beyond all proportion, an eternal weight of glory, (18) while we do not fix our gaze upon the things which are seen, but

upon the things which are unseen; for the things which are seen are temporal, but the things which are not seen are eternal.

2 Corinthians 5:1-21

(1) For we know that if the tent which forms our earthly dwelling is destroyed, we have a building from God, a house not made with hands, eternal in the heavens. (2) For indeed in this tent we groan, greatly desiring to be clothed with our dwelling from heaven, (3) so being thus clothed we shall not be found naked. (4) For we groan indeed, being burdened while we are in this tent, because we do not want the old body stripped off; but we want to be clothed with the new body, so that the mortal will be swallowed up by life. (5) It is God who prepared us for this very purpose, and he has given us the Spirit as a down payment.

(6) Therefore we are always of good courage, knowing that while we are at home in our bodies we are exiles from the Lord; (7) for we walk by faith, not by sight. (8) Then we are of good courage and think it good rather to be absent from the body and to be at home with the Lord. (9) Wherefore we are zealous, whether we are at home or away from home, to be well-pleasing to him. (10) For we must all appear before the judgment seat of Christ, where each must receive what is due him according to his conduct in the body—whether good or worthless.

(11) Therefore, knowing the fear of the Lord, we persuade men; and what we are is known to God, and I trust that it is known also to your conscience. (12) We are not commending ourselves to you again, but we are giving you cause to be proud of us, so that you may have a reputation to those who glory in appearance rather than what is in the heart. (13) For if we are beside ourselves, it is for God; if we are of sound mind, it is for you. (14) For the love of Christ constrains us, because we are convinced one has died for all, and therefore all have died. (15) He died for all, that they should cease to live for themselves but should live for him who for their sake died and rose again on their behalf.

(16) So from now on, we regard no one according to the flesh; even though we have known Christ according to the flesh, now we do so no longer. (17) Therefore, if anyone is in Christ, he is a new creation; the old has passed away, behold, the new has come! (18) All this is from God, who through Christ has reconciled us to himself and has given us the ministry of reconciliation. (19) For it was through Christ that God was reconciling the world to himself, not counting their trespasses against them. And he has entrusted to us the message of reconciliation. (20) Therefore we are ambassadors for Christ, as God is pleading through us; we beg on behalf of Christ: Be reconciled to God. (21) He made him who knew no sin to be sin for us, so that we might become the righteousness of God in him.

2 Corinthians 6:1-18

(1) As we work together with him, then, we entreat you not to receive the grace of God to no purpose. (2) For he says,
"In an acceptable time I listened to you,
and in the day of salvation I helped you."
Behold, now is an acceptable time; behold, now is a day of salvation.
(3) We cause no one to stumble, so that our ministry will not be discredited; (4) but in everything we make it clear that we, ourselves, are servants of God: in steadfast endurance, in afflictions, in anguish, in distress, in stripes, (5) in prisons, in tumults, in hard work and without sleep and food, (6) in purity, in knowledge, in patience, in kindness, in the Holy Spirit, in genuine love, (7) in the word of truth, in the power of God; with the weapons of righteousness for the right hand and for the left hand, (8) through glory and dishonor, through ill report and good report. We are treated as imposters, but we speak the truth; (9) as unknown, yet well-known; as dying, yet we live; as punished and yet not put to death; (10) as grieved, but always rejoicing; as poor, but enriching many; as having nothing, yet possessing all things.
(11) To you, Corinthians, we speak frankly; we have kept no secrets from you. (12) You are not restricted by us, but you are restricted in your affections. (13) As a fair exchange — I speak as to my children — open wide your hearts also.
(14) Do not become unequally yoked with unbelievers. For what does righteousness and lawlessness have in common, or what fellowship does light have with darkness? (15) Or what harmony is there between Christ and Satan? Or what has a believer in common with an unbeliever? (16) What union does a Temple have with idols? For we are the living temple of God; as God has said,
"I will dwell among them and I will walk among them,
and I will be their God, and they shall be my people."
Therefore, (17) "Come out from among them and be separate,
and do not touch what is unclean;
and I will welcome you,
(18) and I will be a father to you,
and you shall be my sons and daughters,"
says the Almighty God.

2 Corinthians 7:1-16

(1) Since we have these promises, beloved, let us purify ourselves from everything that pollutes either body or spirit, and in the fear of God let us bring our consecration to completeness. (2) Make room for us in your hearts. We have wronged no one, we have injured no one, we have cheated

no one. (3) I do not want to condemn you; I have already told you that you are in our hearts to die together or to live together. (4) I speak to you in utter frankness. I have great pride in you. I am greatly encouraged, and in all of our afflictions I am overflowing with joy.

(5) For when we came into Macedonia, our flesh had no rest, and we were oppressed in every way – conflicts on the outside and anxieties within. (6) But the God who comforts the humble comforted us by the presence of Titus. (7) And not only by his presence but also by the encouragement that he received from you. He has told us of your eager affection, your mourning, and your ardent concern for me, so that I rejoiced even more. (8) I grieved because of the letter I sent you, but I do not regret it now; however, I did regret it for a time, but now I see that you were grieved only for a short time. (9) Now I rejoice, not that you were grieved, but that your grief lead to repentance; for your grieving was a godly grief so that you might not suffer loss by anything that we did. (10) For godly sorrow leads to salvation and leaves no regrets, but the worldly sorrow produces death. (11) For look at what this godly sorrow has produced in you: what diligence to vindicate yourselves, what indignation, what fear, what zeal, what avenging of wrong! In everything you have demonstrated that you are innocent in this matter. (12) So then, although I wrote to you, it was not for the sake of the one who did wrong or for the sake of the one who was wronged, but that our care for you in the sight of God might appear to you. (13) Therefore, we are encouraged.

But besides being encouraged ourselves, we rejoiced even more at the joy of Titus, because his spirit has been refreshed by all of you. (14) For though I boasted to him about you, I was not put to shame, because everything we said to you was true, so our boasting about you to Titus has proved to be true as well. (15) And his affection is more abundant for you when he recalls the obedience of you all when you received him with fear and trembling. (16) I rejoice because I have complete confidence in you!

2 Corinthians 8:1-24

(1) We want you to know, brothers, about the grace of God that has been given to the churches in Macedonia; (2) for in a very severe time of affliction, in their abundance of joy and depth of poverty, they have abounded in the richness of their liberality. (3) I testify that they gave according to their means, and even beyond their means, (4) begging us earnestly for the privilege of sharing in the offering for the saints. (5) Beyond our expectations, they first gave themselves to the Lord and then to us by the will of God. (6) So we have asked Titus, as he had initiated the offering, to also complete this gracious contribution. (7) As you abound in everything – in faith, in speech, in knowledge and in all diligence, and in your love for us – see that you abound in this grace also.

(8) I am not saying this as a command, but by telling you the zeal of others, I am putting your love to the test. (9) For you know the grace of our Lord Jesus Christ, that though he was rich, yet for your sakes he became poor, so that you through his poverty might become rich.

(10) This is my advice to you: It is best for you now to complete what you began a year ago not only to do but also the desire to do it. (11) Now finish the work, so that the eager desire to do it will be matched by completing it from what you have. (12) For if the willingness is there, the gift is acceptable according to what one has, not according to what one does not have. (13) For it is not that others should be relieved and you burdened, but that as a matter of equality, (14) your abundance at the present time should supply their need, so that their abundance one day may supply your need, that there may be equality. (15) As it is written:

"He who gathered much had no excess,
and he who gathered little had no lack."

(16) But thanks be to God, who gave this same earnest care for you in the heart of Titus; (17) because he not only accepted our appeal, but being very eager he has gone to you of his own accord. (18) And we are sending with him the brother who is famous in all the churches for his preaching of the gospel. (19) Moreover, he has been selected by the churches to travel with us in this gracious work, which is administered by us for the glory of the Lord himself and to show our eager concern. (20) We want to avoid any criticism in our administration of this generous gift; (21) for we aim to do that which is honorable, not only before the Lord but also before men.

(22) And with them we are sending our brother, whom we have often in many ways found to be zealous, and now far more zealous because of his great confidence in you. (23) As for Titus, he is my partner and fellow worker for you; as for our brothers, they are delegates of the churches, the glory of Christ. (24) Therefore, demonstrate before the churches the proof of your love and our reason for boasting about you to these men.

2 Corinthians 9:1-15

(1) Now concerning the offering for the saints, it is unnecessary for me to write to you. (2) For I know of your desire to help, to which I boast of you to the Macedonians, telling them that Achaia has been ready since last year, and your zeal has stirred up most of them. (3) But I am sending the brothers so that my boasting about you will not be proven to be in vain, so that you will be ready, as I told them you were. (4) For if some Macedonians coming with me find you unprepared, we will be humiliated — to say nothing of yourselves — for having had this trust. (5) So I thought it necessary to urge the brothers to go on before me and arrange in advance this generous gift as you promised, so that it will be ready as a generous gift and not given under pressure.

(6) Remember this: he who sows sparingly will also reap sparingly, and he who sows bountifully will also reap bountifully. (7) Each one should give what he has decided in his own mind, not in pain or under compulsion, for God loves a cheerful giver. (8) And God is able to make all grace abound to you, so that you may always have self-sufficiency in everything and that you may have an abundance for every good work. (9) As it is written,

"He scatters his gifts to the needy,
his righteousness continues forever."

(10) Now he who supplies seed for the sower and bread for food will supply and multiply your seed for sowing and will increase the harvest of your righteousness. (11) You will be enriched enough to be generous in everything, which through us will produce thanksgiving to God.

(12) For the ministry of this service is not only supplying the needs of the saints, but it also overflows in a flood of thanksgiving to God. (13) Through the proof of this ministry they will glorify God by your submission to your confession of the gospel of Christ, and by the generosity of your contribution to them and to all, (14) while they also pray for you and yearn for you because of the surpassing grace of God in you. (15) Thanks be to God for his indescribable gift!

2 Corinthians 10:1-18

(1) Now I, Paul, appeal to you, by the meekness and kindness of Christ—I who am humble when face to face with you, but bold when I am away from you. (2) I beg that you will not force me, when I come, to be bold with the confidence with which I propose to be courageous against some who accuse us of walking in the flesh. (3) For though we live in the flesh, our war is not in the flesh. (4) For the weapons of our warfare are not of the flesh but are divinely powerful for the destruction of fortresses—tearing down calculations (5) and every barrier that is raised up against the knowledge of God, and bringing into captivity every thought to the obedience of Christ, (6) being ready to avenge all disobedience, when your obedience is complete.

(7) Face the obvious facts. If anyone is persuaded that he, himself, belongs to Christ, let him consider once more for himself that as he belongs to Christ we also belong to Christ. (8) For even though I should boast more freely about our authority, which the Lord gave us for building you up and not for tearing you down, I would feel quite justified; (9) for you must not think that I am writing empty threats. (10) For they say, "His letters are impressive and forceful, but his personal presence is weak and his speech is utterly contemptible." (11) Let such a person realize that what we say by letter when we are absent, we will act accordingly when we are present.

(12) For we do not dare to rank or compare ourselves with others who recommend themselves, for they are not wise in measuring themselves and comparing themselves with themselves. (13) But we will not boast

excessively, but we will keep within the limit that God has laid down for us, to reach even as far as you. (14) For we are not overextending ourselves, as though we did not reach you, for we came as far as you with the gospel of Christ. (15) For we are not boasting beyond our proper sphere nor in the labors of other men, but we hope that as your faith increases, our area of activity will be greatly enlarged, (16) so that we may preach the gospel in regions beyond you, without boasting over work already done in another's field. (17) But, "He who boasts, let him boast in the Lord." (18) For it is not the one who commends himself that is approved, but the one whom the Lord commends.

2 Corinthians 11:1-33

(1) I wish that you would bear with me in a little foolishness; please bear with me! (2) I feel a divine jealousy about you, for I betrothed you to Christ to present you as a pure bride to her one husband. (3) But I fear that as the serpent deceived Eve by his cleverness, your thought may be corrupted and you may lose your sincere and pure devotion to Christ. (4) For if someone comes and preaches another Jesus whom we did not preach, or you receive a different spirit from the one you received, or if you receive a different gospel from the one you received, you graciously welcome it! (5) I do not think that I am inferior to those "super-apostles." (6) Even if I am unskilled in speech, I am not in knowledge; but in every way and in all things we have made this plain to you.

(7) Or did I commit a sin by humbling myself that you might be exalted because I preached the gospel of God to you without charge? (8) I robbed other churches, taking wages from them to serve you. (9) And when I was with you and in need, I was not a burden to anyone, for my need was supplied by the brothers who came from Macedonia; and in every way I kept myself from being a burden to you, and I will continue to do so. (10) As the truth of Christ is in me, this boasting of mine shall not be stopped in the regions of Achaia. (11) Why? Is it because I do not love you? God knows I do!

(12) I will continue to do what I have been doing to undermine the claim of those who desire an opportunity to claim in their boasted mission that they work on the same terms that we do. (13) For such men are false apostles, deceitful workers, masquerading as apostles of Christ. (14) It is no wonder that they do, for Satan disguises himself as an angel of light. (15) So it is not surprising if his servants also disguise themselves as servants of righteousness. Their end will be according to their works.

(16) I repeat: let no one take me for a fool, but if you do, then receive me just as you would a fool, so that I too may boast a little. (17) In this self-confident boasting I am not speaking as from the authority of the Lord, but as a fool. (18) Since many boast according to the flesh, so I will also boast.

(19) For you, being wise, gladly welcome fools! (20) For you welcome anyone who enslaves you, exploits you, takes advantage of you, exalts himself, or slaps you in the face. (21) To my shame I say we were too weak for that!

But whatever anyone dares to boast about—I am speaking as a fool—I also dare to boast. (22) Are they Hebrews? So am I. Are they Israelites? So am I. Are they descendents of Abraham? So am I. (23) Are they servants of Christ—I am speaking as a Madman—I have done more. I have worked harder, been in prison more frequently, beaten more severely, often in danger of death. (24) Five times I was beaten by the Jews with thirty-nine lashes. (25) Three times I was beaten with rods, once I was stoned, three times I was shipwrecked, (26) a day and a night I was adrift in the sea; (I was) on frequent journeys, in danger from rivers, danger from robbers, danger from my own people, danger from Gentiles, danger in the city, danger in the wilderness, danger at sea, and danger from false brothers; (27) (I was) in labor and hardship, in sleepless nights, in hunger and thirst, often without food, cold and ill-clad. (28) And apart from external things was the daily pressure of the care of all the churches. (29) Who is weak without my being weak? Who is led into sin without my being fired with indignation?

(30) If I must boast, I will boast of the things that pertain to my weakness. (31) The God and Father of our Lord Jesus, who is to be praised forever, knows that I am not lying. (32) At Damascus, the governor under King Aretas guarded the city of the Damascenes to seize me, (33) but I was let down through the wall in a basket and escaped his hands.

2 Corinthians 12:1-21

(1) I must boast! It is unprofitable, but I will go on to visions and revelations of the Lord. (2) I know a man in Christ who fourteen years ago (whether in or outside the body I do not know—God knows) was caught up to the third heaven. (3) And I know that this man (whether in the body or apart from the body I do not know—God knows) (4) was caught up into paradise, and he heard sacred secrets which man may not repeat. (5) On behalf of this man I will boast, but on behalf of myself I will not boast, except as regards my weaknesses. (6) For if I desire to boast, I shall not be a fool, for I speak the truth. But I refrain, so that no one will credit me with more than he sees in me or hears from me.

(7) So to keep me from being too exalted because of the extraordinary revelations, there was given to me a thorn in the flesh, a messenger of Satan, to harass me. (8) Three times I begged the Lord to take it away from me. (9) But the Lord said to me, "My grace is sufficient for you, for my power is perfected in weakness." Most gladly, therefore, I will boast in my weakness, that the power of Christ may rest upon me. (10) Therefore, I

take pleasure in weaknesses, in insults, hardships, persecutions, and difficulties, for Christ's sake; for when I am weak, then I am strong.

(11) I have become a fool! For you yourselves compelled me to do it, for I ought to have been commended by you. For I was in no respect inferior to the super-apostles even though I am nothing. (12) The marks of an apostle—signs, wonders, and miracles—were performed among you with steadfast endurance. (13) In what way were you inferior to the other churches, except that I myself was not a burden to you? Forgive me for this wrong!

(14) Now I am ready to visit you for the third time, and I will not be a burden to you, for I do not seek your possessions but you. For the children ought not lay up treasures for their parents, but the parents for the children. (15) But I will most gladly spend and be spent for the sake of your souls. Am I to be loved less because I love you so intensely? (16) But even so, I did not burden you—but you say I was crafty and unscrupulous and took you by trickery. (17) Did I defraud you through any of the men I sent to you? (18) I urged Titus to go, and I sent our brother with him. Did Titus defraud you? Did we not walk in the same spirit and in the same steps?

(19) Have you been thinking all this time that we are defending ourselves to you? It is before God in Christ that we speak, and in all things, my dear people, it is our aim to build you up. (20) I fear that perhaps when I come I will find you different than what I wish you to be, and that you will find me to be different than what you wish me to be; perhaps there will be strife, jealousy, ill-feeling, rivalries, slander, gossiping, arrogance, and disorderly behavior. (21) I fear that when I come again to you my God may humiliate me before you, and I may mourn over many of those who have sinned in the past and have not repented of their impurity, sexual vice, and sensuality which they formerly practiced.

2 Corinthians 13:1-13

(1) This will be my third visit to you. Two or three witnesses must confirm any charge. (2) To those who have sinned in the past, and to everyone else, I repeat the warning I gave them in person on my second visit, and I give it now in my absence. When I come this time, I will show no leniency, (3) since you want proof of the Christ who speaks through me, and who is not weak toward you, but is powerful in you. (4) For indeed he was crucified in weakness, but he lives by the power of God. Likewise, we are weak in him, but in dealing with you we shall live with him by the power of God.

(5) You must test yourselves to see if you are in the faith; examine yourselves! Or do you not realize that Christ is in you, unless you are counterfeits? (6) I hope that you will find out that we are not counterfeits. (7) Now we pray to God that you do no evil—not that we ourselves may

appear to be approved, but that you may do what is good, even though we might appear to be counterfeits. (8) For we can do nothing against the truth, but only for the sake of the truth. (9) For we rejoice when we are weak and you are strong. We pray for your perfection. (10) For this reason I am writing these things while absent, so that when I am present I will not have to be severe in my use of the authority, which the Lord gave me for building you up and not for tearing you down.

(11) Finally, brothers, rejoice, be made complete, admonish yourselves, agree with one another, be at peace, and the God of love and peace will be with you. (12) Greet one another with a holy kiss. (13) All the saints greet you. The grace of the Lord Jesus Christ and the love of God and the fellowship of the Holy Spirit be with you all.

Introduction to Galatians

Paul's first missionary journey was to the southern area of the Roman province of Galatia (Antioch, Iconium, Lystra and Derbe). Churches were founded in each of the cities. Later, some of the members of the churches were influenced by the Judaizers. They were Jewish Christians who believed that the ceremonial practices of the OT were still binding on the NT church. They insisted that Gentile converts to Christianity be circumcised and abide by OT rites. The Zealot Jews objected to fraternizing with Gentiles. So Paul wrote this letter to them to correct this devastating turn of events.

The Judaizers had argued that Paul was not an authentic apostle and that he was just trying to appeal to the Gentiles by removing from the gospel some of the legal requirements. Paul responded by clearly establishing his authority and substantiating the gospel he preached. They had been saved by grace and nothing else and it is by grace through faith that we live out this new life in the freedom of the Spirit. And he emphatically told them if an angel from heaven should preach any other gospel, let him be eternally condemned (1:8).

In chapter 5, Paul drew a picture of the life of the flesh and the life of the spirit. He vividly portrays the "Works of the Flesh" (19-21) and "The Fruit of the Spirit" (22-23). Paul emphasized that salvation is only by grace and sanctification is only by grace and it is the only road to glorification.

Galatians has been referred to as "Luther's book," because Luther relied on this book in his writings against the theology of his day. And the book in our day is needed to keep us on the right track. Galatians was the first letter written by Paul to the churches. Of the 2,230 words used there were 524 different words used.

Galatians 1:1-24

(1) Paul an apostle—sent not from men or by man, but through Jesus Christ and God the Father, who raised him from the dead— (2) and all the brothers with me to the churches of Galatia: (3) Grace and peace to you from God our Father and the Lord Jesus Christ, (4) the one who gave himself for our sins to rescue us from this present evil age, according to the will of God our Father, (5) to whom is the glory unto the eternal ages. Amen.

(6) I am astonished that you have so quickly turned from the one who called you by the grace of Christ to another gospel, (7) which is no gospel. Those who are agitating you are trying to pervert the gospel of Christ. (8) If we, or an angel from heaven, should preach a different gospel than we preached to you, let him be accursed. (9) I will repeat what I just said: If anyone preaches to you a different gospel than we preached to you,

let him be accursed.

(10) For now do I court the favor of men or God? Am I trying to please men? If I were still pleasing men, I would not be a slave of Christ.

(11) I assure you, brothers, that the gospel I preached is not according to man, (12) for I did not receive it from man nor was I taught by man, but it came through a revelation of Jesus Christ.

(13) You have heard of my life-style in Judaism and how I excessively persecuted the church of God and ravaged it, (14) and how I advanced beyond most of my contemporaries of my race, being extremely zealous of our national traditions. (15) But when he, who had sanctified me before I was born and called me through his grace, (16) was pleased to reveal his son in me in order that I might proclaim him to the nations, I did not communicate with flesh and blood, (17) neither did I go up to Jerusalem to the apostles who were before me, but I went away into Arabia and later returned to Damascus.

(18) Then after three years, I went to Jerusalem to visit Peter and I stayed with him fifteen days. (19) I did not see the other apostles, except James the brother of the Lord. (20) (As I stand in the presence of God what I write to you is true.) (21) Later, I went to the regions of Syria and Cilicia. (22) I was unknown to the churches of Judea. (23) They only heard that, "the one who had persecuted us is now preaching the gospel that he had tried to destroy." (24) And they praised God because of me.

Galatians 2:1-21

(1) Fourteen years later, I went up to Jerusalem with Barnabas and I took Titus with me. (2) I went by revelation and I set before the authorities secretly my method of evangelism, to make sure my course of action was sound. (3) But Titus, a Greek, who was with me, was not compelled to be circumcised. (4) False brothers had slipped in to spy out our freedom which we have in Christ, to enslave us; (5) but we did not yield in subjection to them at all, so that the truth of the gospel might continue with you.

(6) As to the ones who were recognized as leaders, however (and their importance did not impress me because God shows no partiality), they had nothing to add to my message; (7) but they recognized that I had been entrusted with the gospel to the uncircumcised as Peter had been to the circumcised. (8) He who worked in Peter as an apostle to the circumcised worked in me to the Gentiles, (9) and, knowing that grace was given to me, James, Cephas and John, who were recognized as pillars, gave me and Barnabas the right hand of fellowship so that we might go to the Gentiles, but they to the circumcision. (10) Only, they would have us remember the poor, and that was the very thing that I was eager to do.

(11) When Cephas came to Antioch, I withstood him to his face, because he was in the wrong. (12) Before some men came from James, Peter

ate with the Gentiles; but when they came, he separated himself from them because he was afraid of the circumcision party. (13) The other Jews went with him in this hypocrisy, and this hypocrisy even led Barnabas astray. (14) But when I saw that they did not walk straight in the truth of the gospel, I said to Cephas in the presence of everyone, "If you, being a Jew, live like a Gentile, how can you compel the Gentiles to live like Jews?"

(15) By birth we are Jews and we are not Gentile sinners, (16) yet we know that a man is not justified by works of the law but through faith in Christ Jesus. We also believed in Christ Jesus in order that we might be justified by faith in Christ and not by works of the law, because no one will be justified by works of the law.

(17) Then, if we seeking to be justified in Christ are found to be sinners, is Christ a minister of sin? By no means! (18) For if I build again that which I destroyed, I prove that I am a transgressor. (19) For I died through the law that I might live for God. I have been crucified with Christ. (20) I no longer live but Christ lives in me, and now the life I live in the flesh I live by faith in the Son of God who loved me and gave himself for me. (21) I do not reject the grace of God. For if we are justified by the law, then Christ died in vain.

Galatians 3:1-29

(1) O foolish Galatians! Who has cast a spell upon you? Your eyes beheld the crucified Jesus Christ! (2) Only one thing I want to learn from you. Did you receive the spirit by the works of the law or by hearing and believing? (3) Are you so foolish to think that you can begin in the spirit and be perfected in the flesh? (4) Did you experience so many things for nothing? Perhaps it really was for nothing! (5) Is it because you observe the law or because you believed what you heard that God lavishes the spirit and works miracles among you? (6) So it was with Abraham. He believed God and it was credited to him as righteousness. (7) Therefore, we see that those who live by faith are the real descendants of Abraham. (8) The Scriptures foresaw that God would justify the Gentiles by faith. He told Abraham the good news, saying, "In you all the nations will be blessed." (9) So those who live by faith are blessed with Abraham, the man of faith.

(10) Those who are seeking to be justified by the works of the law are under a curse, because it is written, "Accursed is everyone who does not do all of the things written in the book of the law." (11) It is obvious that no one is justified by the law, because "the just shall live by faith." (12) But the law does not rest on faith, for it says, "The one who does them shall live by them." (13) Christ redeemed us from the curse of the law by becoming a curse for us, because it is written, "Accursed is everyone hanging on a tree" — (14) that in Jesus Christ the blessing promised to Abraham might come to the Gentiles, so that we might receive the promise of the spirit

through faith.

(15) Brothers, this is a human analogy: A man's will that has been ratified cannot be changed or set aside. (16) Now the promises were made to Abraham and to his descendants. It does not say, "and to descendants," referring to many, but, referring to one, "and to your seed," which is Christ.

(17) This is my point: A covenant, having been ratified by God, cannot be annulled by the law that came four hundred and thirty years later, so as to abolish the promise. (18) For if the inheritance is by law, it is no longer by a promise; but God gave it to Abraham by a promise.

(19) What, therefore, is the purpose of the law? It was added because of transgressions, having been ordained through angels by the hand of a mediator until the arrival of the descendent to whom the promise referred. (20) Now the mediator is not for one; but God is one.

(21) Is the law then contrary to the promises of God? Certainly not! For if a law could have been given that could impart life, then justification would have been indeed by the law. (22) But the scriptures declare that all are in bondage to sin, in order that the promise might be given to believers by faith in Jesus Christ. (23) Before faith came, we were guarded and confined under law until faith should be revealed. (24) So the law was put in charge to lead us to Christ that we might be justified by faith. (25) But now that faith has come, we are no longer under a tutor. (26) For we are all children of God through faith in Christ Jesus. (27) For as many of you who have been baptized into Christ have put on Christ. (28) There cannot be Jew or Greek, slave or freeman, male or female, for you are all one in Christ Jesus. (29) If you belong to Christ, then you are the descendants of Abraham, heirs according to the promise.

Galatians 4:1-31

(1) I tell you that the heir, as long as he is a child, is no different from the slave, even thought he is the owner of all the estate, (2) for he is under guardians and trustees until the date previously appointed by the father. (3) So it is with us. When we were children, we were enslaved by the elemental things of the world. (4) When the appointed time came, God sent forth his son, born of a woman, born under the law, (5) in order that he might redeem those under the law so that we might receive adoption as sons. (6) Now that you are sons, God has sent forth the Spirit of his Son into our hearts, crying, "Abba!" ("Father"). (7) So you are no longer a slave, but a son, then an heir, made so by God.

(8) When you did not know God, you were enslaved by false gods. (9) But now that you have come to know God — or rather, being known by God — how can you return to the weak helpless false gods? Do you want to serve them again? (10) You observe days, months, seasons and years. (11) I fear that I have wasted my time with you!

(12) Brothers, I beg you to become as I am, because I have become as you are. (13) You know that it was because of a physical problem that I first preached the gospel to you, (14) and you did not reject or despise me because of my poor health but you received me as a messenger of God, as Christ Jesus. (15) What has happened to your blessed good will? For I bear witness that if possible you would have gouged out your eyes and would have given them to me. (16) Have I become your enemy because I tell you the truth?

(17) Those men are zealous for your favor, but for no good purpose. They want to cut you off from me (18) so you will be zealous of them. It is always good to be zealous of a good thing, and not just when I am present with you. (19) My children, with whom I suffer birth pains until Christ is formed in you, (20) I would like to be with you and change my tone, because I am at a loss as to what I should do.

(21) Tell me, you who want to be under the law, do you not hear what the law says? (22) It is written that Abraham had two sons, one by a slave woman and the other by a free woman. (23) The one of the slave women was born according to the flesh, and the one of the free women was born according to the promise. (24) All this is an allegory: the two women represent two covenants. One is from Mount Sinai, bearing children for slavery, which is Hagar. (25) Now Hagar represents Mount Sinai in Arabia and corresponds to Jerusalem, for she serves as a slave with her children. (26) But the Jerusalem above is free, who is our mother. (27) For it is written:

"Rejoice, barren one, you who bears no children,

break forth and shout, you who are not travailing,

for the deserted woman had more children

than the one having the husband."

(28) Now you, brothers, are children of promise according to Isaac. (29) But just as it was then, the one born of the flesh persecuted the one born of the spirit; so it is now. (30) But what does the scripture say? "Cast out the slave woman and her son, for the son of the slave woman shall not share the inheritance of the free woman." (31) Therefore, brothers, we are not children of the slave woman, but of the free woman.

Galatians 5:1-26

(1) Christ has freed us. So stand firm in that freedom and do not get entangled again in a yoke of slavery. (2) I, Paul, say to you that if you receive circumcision, Christ will profit you nothing. (3) I testify again to every man who receives circumcision that he is obligated to obey all the law. (4) You who are trying to be justified by the law have been cut off from Christ; you have rejected the way of grace. (5) For we in the Spirit, through faith, wait expectantly for the hope of righteousness. (6) For in Christ Jesus neither circumcision nor uncircumcision has any validity. It is only faith expressing itself through love.

(7) You were running well. Who persuaded you to turn from the truth? (8) This persuasion is not from the one who called you. (9) A little leaven leavens the whole batch of dough. (10) I trust in the Lord that you will take no other view; but the one troubling you will be judged, whoever he is. (11) As for me, brothers, if I am still preaching circumcision, why am I being persecuted? In that case the cross would cease to be a stumbling block. (12) I wish those who are disturbing you would go the whole way and castrate themselves.

(13) For you, brothers, were called for freedom. Only, do not use your freedom to indulge in the flesh; but, serve one another in love. (14) For the whole law has been summed up in one commandment, "You shall love your neighbor as yourself." (15) But if you bite and devour one another, you will see that you will be destroyed by one another.

(16) So I say, walk in the spirit and you will not gratify the lust of the flesh. (17) For the flesh lusts against the spirit and the spirit against the flesh; these are contrary to each other, to prevent you from doing what you desire. (18) But if you are led by the spirit you are not under the law.

(19) The works of the flesh are obvious: fornication, uncleanness, sensuality, (20) idolatry, abuse of drugs, hostility, strife, jealousy, fits of rage, self-seeking ambition, dissension, factions, (21) envy, drunkenness, carousing, and the like. (22) I warn you, as I warned you before, those who do such things will not inherit the kingdom of God. (23) But the fruit of the spirit is love, joy, peace, long-suffering, kindness, goodness, faithfulness, meekness, and self-control. There is no law against such things. (24) And those who belong to Christ have crucified the flesh with its passions and lusts. (25) Since we live in the spirit let us walk also in the spirit. (26) Let us not become boastful, challenging one another, envying one another.

Galatians 6:1-18

(1) Brothers, if a man is caught in some sin, you who are spiritual should restore him in a spirit of meekness, watching your step lest you also become tempted. (2) Share the burdens of one another and so fulfill the law of Christ. (3) For if anyone thinks he is someone important when he is not, he deceives himself. (4) Let each man see that his own work is worthy, then he will not need to compare it with another. (5) For each man has his own pack to carry.

(6) Let the student who receives instruction in the word share all good things with his instructor.

(7) Do not be led astray, God is not mocked. For whatever a man sows he will also reap, (8) because the one who sows for his flesh will reap corruption, but the one who sows for the Spirit will reap of the Spirit eternal life. (9) Let us not be slack in doing good for at the proper time we will reap the harvest if we do not give up. (10) So then, while we have the

opportunity, let us do good to everyone, especially to those of the household of faith.

(11) See the large letters that I am writing to you with my own hand! (12) Those who are trying to force you to be circumcised are only seeking human approval so they will not be persecuted for the cross of Jesus Christ. (13) For those having received circumcision do not keep the law, but they want you to be circumcised so that they can boast about your flesh. (14) But for me, may I never glory except in the cross of the Lord Jesus Christ through whom the world has been crucified to me and I to the world. (15) For neither circumcision nor uncircumcision means anything, but the only thinking that counts is a new creation. (16) Peace and mercy on all who live by this rule, to the true Israel of God.

(17) Henceforth, let no one trouble me, for I bear the brands of Jesus in my body.

(18) Brothers, the grace of our Lord Jesus Christ be with your spirit. Amen.

Introduction to Ephesians

Paul wrote the Ephesian letter from Rome c. 60 A.D. The letter was probably meant to be a circular letter to the churches in that area. This letter is not as personal as most of his letters and he did not address any particular error or heresy. Paul made Ephesus his headquarters for about 3 years.

Ephesus was located on the most direct sea and land route to the eastern provinces of the Roman Empire. No city in Asia was more famous or more populous. It ranked with Rome, Corinth, Antioch and Alexandria as the important centers of the empire. In Ephesus was the temple of Artemis (Diana), one of the seven wonders of the ancient world. It was here that Paul spoke to large crowds of people (Acts 19:27). Paul's message was that "gods made with hands are not gods." When the people there questioned the power of the idols, the silversmiths came together and caused a riot. It caused so much confusion that Paul was forced to leave Ephesus. He went from there to Macedonia.

The purpose of the letter was to show that salvation was only in Christ and that believers can sit with Christ in heavenly places. In the second chapter he emphasizes that "by grace we are saved through faith" (Ephesians 2:8). He encourages the believers to be in one accord and to work with love for one another. He gives instructions for husbands and wives (5:21-23), and he concludes by reminding us that we must put on the whole armor of God so that we can stand against the devil (6:10-20).

Paul used 2,410 words in his letter with 128 new words. It represents his best literary efforts in thought and in treatment of the subject matter of eternal value.

Ephesians 1:1-23

(1) Paul, an apostle of Christ Jesus by the will of God, to the saints in Ephesus who are faithful in Christ Jesus:

(2) Grace to you and peace from God our Father and the Lord Jesus Christ.

(3) Praise be to the God and Father of our Lord Jesus Christ, who has blessed us with every spiritual blessing in the heavenlies in Christ, (4) who chose us before the foundation of the world, so that we would be holy and unblemished before him. In love (5) he foreordained us to be adopted as sons through Jesus Christ, in accordance with his good pleasure, (6) to the praise of the splendor of his grace, which he abundantly demonstrated to us in the Beloved. (7) In him we have redemption through his blood, the forgiveness of our transgressions, according to the riches of his grace, (8) which he made to abound to us in all wisdom and intelligence, (9) making known to us the mystery of his will, according to his good pleasure which he purposed in him, (10) to be accomplished in the fullness of time so that all

things in heaven and the things on earth might be brought under the headship of Christ.

(11) In him we were given our share of the inheritance, having been predestined according to his purpose, and operating in all things with the counsel of his will, (12) so that we, who had hoped in Christ, might be for the praise of his glory. (13) In him you also, hearing the word of truth, the gospel of your salvation, believed and you were sealed with the promised Holy Spirit, (14) who is the guarantee of our inheritance, until our redemption is complete to the praise of his glory.

(15) Therefore I also, hearing about your faith and the love you have for all the saints, (16) do not cease to give thanks on behalf of you, making mention of you in my prayers, (17) so that the God of our Lord Jesus Christ, the Father of glory, may give you a spirit of wisdom and a revelation of a full knowledge of him, (18) that you may receive the inner illumination of mind, so that you may know the hope to which he has called you, the riches of the glory of his inheritance in the saints, (19) and the transcendent greatness of the power which he is able to exercise with us who believe in him. (20) That power he exercised in Christ, raising him from the dead and seating him at the right hand of God in the heavenlies, (21) far above all rule and power and lordship and every name that is named, not only in this age but the age to come; (22) and he has put all things under his feet, and made him, thus exalted, to be head of the church, (23) which is his body, the fullness of him who fills the universe in all its parts.

Ephesians 2:1-22

(1) You were dead in your transgressions and sins, (2) when you followed the evil ways of this present age, according to the ruler of the authority of the air, which is now operating in the sons of disobedience, (3) among whom we also conducted ourselves then in the lusts of the flesh and the mind, and were by nature children of wrath, as the rest. (4) But God, who is rich in mercy, because of the great love by which he loved us, (5) and when we were dead in trespasses, made us alive in Christ Jesus—by grace you are saved— (6) and raised us up and seated us in the heavenlies with Christ Jesus, (7) in order that in the coming ages he might show the exceeding riches of his grace in kindness toward us in Christ Jesus. (8) For you have been saved by grace through faith; and this is not from you, it is the gift of God— (9) not of works, lest anyone should boast. (10) For we are his work of art, created in Christ Jesus for good works, which God had previously prepared, that we should walk in them.

(11) Therefore, when you were Gentiles in the flesh, you were called the uncircumcised by the circumcised in the flesh by hands, (12) and you were at that time without Christ, having been alienated from the commonwealth of Israel and strangers of the covenants of promise, having

no hope and godless in the world. (13) But in Christ Jesus you who were far away have come near by the blood of Christ. (14) For he himself is our peace, the one who made us both one, and has broken down the dividing wall of hostility; and by his sacrifice (15) he nullified the law with its regulations, that he might create in himself one new man in place of the two, so making peace, (16) and might reconcile both in one body to God through the cross, by it killing the hostility. (17) And he came and preached peace to those who were far away and peace to those who were near; (18) for through him we both have access in one Spirit to the Father.

(19) So then, you are no longer strangers and sojourners, but you are fellow citizens with the saints and members of the family of God, (20) having been built on the foundation of the apostles, Christ Jesus himself being the cornerstone, (21) in whom the whole building is joined together and grows into a holy temple in the Lord, (22) in whom you also are being built together into a spiritual dwelling place of God.

Ephesians 3:1-21

(1) For this reason I, Paul, am the prisoner of Christ Jesus for the sake of you Gentiles. (2) Surely you have heard of the stewardship of the grace of God given to me for your benefit, (3) how the mystery was made known to me by revelation, as I have written briefly before. (4) And when you read it, you can understand my insight into this mystery of Christ, (5) which was not made known to the men of other generations but now has been revealed to the holy apostles and prophets by the Spirit. (6) This revelation is that the Gentiles are heirs of the same inheritance and members of the same body and partakers of the same promise in Christ Jesus through the gospel. (7) I was made a servant of the gospel by the gift of the grace of God, which he gave to me through the working of his power. (8) To me, the least of all the saints, was given this grace, to preach to the Gentiles the unfathomable riches of Christ, (9) and to enlighten all people about the mysterious design which was hidden in God who created all things; (10) that through the church the manifold wisdom of God might be made known to the rulers and the authorities in the heavenlies. (11) This was the eternal purpose that he accomplished in Christ Jesus our Lord, (12) in whom we have boldness to go into God's presence in confidence through faith in him. (13) So I ask you not to be discouraged because of my afflictions for your sake, for they bring you honor.

(14) For this reason I bend my knees before the Father (15) from whom every family in heaven and on earth is named, (16) that he may give you the riches of his glory to become strong in the inner man through his Spirit, (17) so that Christ may dwell in your hearts through faith; and that you, being rooted and grounded in love, (18) may be fully able to comprehend with all the saints the breadth and length and height and depth

of it, (19) and to know the surpassing love of Christ that you may be filled with all the fullness of God.

(20) Now to him who by the power at work within us is able to do infinitely more than we can ask or imagine, (21) to him be glory in the church and in Christ Jesus to all generations, for ever and ever! Amen.

Ephesians 4:1-32

(1) So I, the prisoner for the Lord's sake, exhort you to live lives worthy of the call you have received, (2) with all humility and meekness with patience lovingly bearing with one another, (3) being eager to keep the unity of the Spirit, (4) as you were also called in one hope of your calling. (5) There is one Lord, one faith, one baptism, (6) one God and Father of us all, over all, through all and in all. (7) But grace was given to each of us according to the measure of the gift of Christ. (8) So the Scripture says,

"When he ascended on high he led prisoners into captivity,
and he gave gifts to men."

(9) What does "he ascended" mean, except that he also descended into the lower parts of the earth? (10) He who descended was also the one who ascended far above all the heavens in order that he might fill all things. (11) He gave some to be apostles, some to be prophets, some to be evangelists, some to be shepherds and teachers, (12) to prepare the saints for the work of ministry, to the building up of the body of Christ, (13) until we all arrive in the unity of faith and the full knowledge of the Son of God, to the complete measure of the fullness of Christ, (14) so that we will no longer be infants, being blown and carried around by every teaching by the sleight of men, by craftiness in deceitful scheming; (15) but speaking truth in love, we may grow into him in every way, who is Christ the head, (16) from whom all the body is being fitted and held together by that which every joint supplies, according to the proper working of each part, making the growth of the body for the building up of itself in love.

(17) So this I affirm and testify in the Lord, that you must no longer live as the Gentiles do, in the vanity of their minds, (18) their intellect being darkened and alienated from the life of God, through their ignorance on account of the hardness of their hearts. (19) They, who have no sense of shame, have given themselves to licentiousness, which leads to excessive practice of all sorts of immorality. (20) This is not what you learned in Christ. (21) For indeed you have heard about him and you were taught the truth as it is in Jesus, (22) that you take off, as to the former way of living, the old man, corrupted by the lusts of deceits, (23) being made new in spirit and mind, (24) and put on the new man, created according to God in true righteousness and holiness.

(25) So each one must stop lying and speak the truth with his neighbor, because we are members of one another. (26) Be angry but do not

sin; do not let the sun set on your anger, (27) and do not give the devil a foothold. (28) The thief must steal no more, but rather he should work, performing with his own hands what is good, so that he may be able to share with those who are in need.

(29) Do not let foul language come from your mouth, but only what is good for the occasion, so that it may bring a blessing to those who hear. (30) And do not grieve the Holy Spirit of God, by whom we were sealed for the day of redemption. (31) You must remove from you all bitterness, anger, wrath, shouting, and cursing with all malice. (32) And be kind to one another, tenderhearted, forgiving one another as God in Christ forgave you.

Ephesians 5:1-33

(1) Therefore be imitators of God, as his dearly loved children, (2) and walk in love, as Christ also loved us and gave himself up for us, a sweet smelling sacrifice to God.

(3) But sexual vice and all indecency or greed should not even be mentioned among you who are children of God, for this is not proper among saints; (4) neither should there be obscene speech nor foolish talk nor suggestive jesting, which is not proper, but rather giving of thanks. (5) For this you know, that no one who is sexually impure, immoral or greedy (which is idolatry) has any inheritance in the kingdom of Christ and God. (6) Let no one deceive you with vain arguments, for it is because of these very things that the wrath of God is coming. (7) Therefore do not associate with them.

(8) For you were once in darkness, but now you are in the light of the Lord; walk as children of the light (9) (for the fruit of the light is in all goodness, righteousness, and truth) (10) and seek to find out what is well-pleasing to the Lord. (11) Have no fellowship with the unfruitful works of darkness, but rather expose them. (12) For it is shameful to speak of the secret things they do; (13) but all things become visible when they are exposed to light, (14) for it is light that clearly reveals everything. Therefore it is said:
"Wake up! Sleeper,
and arise from the dead,
and Christ will shine upon you."
(15) So be careful how you walk, not as unwise but as wise, (16) redeeming the time, because the days are evil. (17) Therefore do not be foolish, but understand what the will of the Lord is. (18) And stop getting drunk with wine, which leads to debauchery; but be filled with the spirit. (19) Speak to one another in psalms, hymns, and spiritual songs, singing and making melody in your hearts to the Lord, (20) and in the name of our Lord Jesus Christ always give thanks for everything, to God the Father.

(21) Submit to one another because of your reverence for Christ.

(22) Likewise wives to their own husbands as to the Lord, (23) because the husband is the head of the wife as Christ is the head of the church, his body, of which he is the Savior. (24) As the church is subject to Christ, so also the wives must submit to their husbands in everything.

(25) Husbands love your wives as Christ loved the church and gave himself up for her, (26) that he might sanctify her by cleansing her by the washing with water through his word, (27) that he might present the church to himself in splendor, without spot or wrinkle or any such thing, but that she might be holy without blemish. (28) So husbands ought to love their wives as their own bodies. He who loves his wife loves himself. (29) For no man ever hates his flesh, but nourishes and cherishes it, as also Christ the church, (30) because we are members of his body. (31) For this reason shall a man leave his father and his mother and he shall cleave to his wife, and the two shall be one flesh. (32) This is a great mystery, and I understand it to mean Christ and the church. (33) However, for you individually, let each man love his wife as himself, and let each wife respect her husband.

Ephesians 6:1-24

(1) Children, obey your parents in the Lord, for this is right. (2) Honor your father and your mother, which is the first commandment with a promise, (3) in order that it may be well with you and that you may dwell long on the earth. (4) And fathers, do not provoke your children to wrath, but nurture them in the discipline and the instruction of the Lord.

(5) Slaves, obey your masters according to the flesh with fear and trembling, in singleness of heart, as to Christ; (6) not by eye-service, as men-pleasers, but as slaves of Christ, doing the will of God from the heart, (7) with goodwill serving as slaves, as to the Lord, and not to men, (8) knowing that whatever good anyone does, he will be rewarded by the Lord, whether slave or free.

(9) And masters, you do the same toward them. Stop threatening them, knowing that you and they have the same Lord in heaven, and he is no respecter of persons.

(10) Finally, be strong in the Lord and in the strength of his might. (11) Put on the complete armor of God so that you may stand against the craftiness of the devil; (12) because our struggle is not against flesh and blood, but against the rulers, against the authorities, against the world powers of this darkness, against the spiritual wickedness in the heavenlies. (13) Therefore take up the complete armor of God, so that you may be able to resist in the day of evil and having done all, to stand firm. (14) Therefore stand, with the belt of truth around your waist, and the breastplate of righteousness in place, (15) and your feet shod with the preparation of the gospel of peace; (16) in addition to all this, take the shield of faith so that you will be able to extinguish the fiery arrows of the evil one. (17) Take the

helmet of salvation and the sword of the Spirit, which is the word of God. (18) With all prayer and petitions, pray constantly in the Spirit, and with this in mind, be on the alert with all perseverance and petition for all the saints, (19) and pray for me, that the words may be given to me so I may speak with boldness to make known the mystery of the gospel, (20) for which I am an ambassador in chains, so that I may speak with authority as I should speak.

(21) Tychicus, the dear brother and faithful servant of the Lord, will tell you everything about me, and the work that I am doing. (22) I am sending him to you for this very purpose, so that you may know how we are, and that he may encourage you.

(23) Peace to the brothers, and love with faith, from God the Father and the Lord Jesus Christ. (24) Grace to all who love our Lord Jesus Christ with an undying love.

Introduction to Philippians

Paul wrote the letter to the Philippians about 61 A.D. when he was a prisoner in Rome. This was his first imprisonment. The church at Philippi was established about 50 A.D., when Paul, with Luke, came to the city on Paul's second missionary journey. Paul had a vision while he was at Troas. In that vision he saw a man, standing and begging him, "Come over to Macedonia and help us." That is where Luke joins the missionaries. Some have thought that Luke was the man in the vision. Luke stayed in Philippi when Paul left to go to Achaia.

Philippi was a Roman colony, a city of great importance in Macedonia located on the main road from the eastern provinces to Rome. Philippi was name after Philip, the father of Alexander the Great. The city enjoyed rights legally equivalent to those in Italy. The fact that Philippi was a Roman colony may explain why there were not enough Jews to have a synagogue and why Paul does not quote from the Old Testament.

Paul wrote this letter to thank them for the gift that they sent to him by Epaphroditus. The church also had helped him on other occasions. Epaphroditus had told Paul about the problems with the Judaizers and Anti-nomians. So he wrote to warn them against false teachers, and to show how his suffering had contributed to his own personal growth and the advancement of the kingdom of God. He had learned the secret of facing dire circumstances and in it to be content and rejoice in it all (4:11-13). It is indeed a personal love letter with optimism that bubbles over. This letter of 1,629 words cheered up the disciples in Philippi that day and it continues to bless those who read it today.

Philippians 1:1-30

(1) Paul and Timothy, slaves of Jesus Christ, to all the saints in Christ Jesus who are in Philippi, with the overseers and deacons, (2) grace to you and peace from God our Father and our Lord Jesus Christ.

(3) I thank my God every time I remember you, (4) and always when I pray for all of you, I do it with joy, (5) because of your partnership with me in the gospel from the first day until now. (6) For this I am sure, that he who began a good work in you will continue it until it is completed in the day of Christ Jesus.

(7) It is right for me to think of all of you in this way because you are in my heart, whether in prison or out defending and vindicating the gospel, for you are all partakers of grace with me. (8) For, God is my witness that I long for you in the compassion of Jesus Christ. (9) And this I pray that your love will abound more and more, in full knowledge and perfect discernment, (10) so that you may be able to know what is best so that you may be pure

and blameless in the day of Christ, (11) filled with the fruit of righteousness which comes through Jesus Christ, to the glory and praise of God. (12) Now I want you to know, brothers, that what has happened to me has actually served to promote the gospel, (13) so that the whole palace guard, and all the others, know that I am in chains for Christ, (14) and so most of the brothers have been encouraged by my chains, and have been exceedingly fearless and bold to speak the word of God. (15) Some indeed preach Christ because of envy and strife, but others because of good will. (16) The latter out of love, knowing that I am put here for the defense of the gospel, (17) but the former proclaim Christ because of rivalry, not sincerely, but thinking to afflict me in my chains.

(18) So what? Nevertheless, in every way, whether in pretense or in sincerity, Christ is proclaimed and in this I rejoice, and I will continue to rejoice. (19) For I know that your prayers and the provision of the Spirit of Jesus Christ will result in my deliverance, (20) and this will fulfill my eager expectation and hope that I will never disgrace myself, so that now, as always, Christ will be magnified in my body. (21) For to me to live is Christ and to die is gain. (22) But if I live in the flesh, that will be fruitful labor, and I do not know which to choose. (23) I am in a dilemma. I desire to depart and be with Christ, for this is far better. (24) But to remain in the flesh is more needful for you. (25) And this I know that I will remain and continue with you to add to your progress and joy in the faith, (26) so that when I come to you again your joy in Christ may overflow because of me.

(27) Only let your life-style be worthy of the gospel, so whether I come to see you or being absent, I may hear that you stand in unity, with one mind, working together in the faith of the Gospel; (28) and do not fear your opponents, which is to them a proof of their destruction, but to you salvation that is from God. (29) For the privilege of serving Christ has been given to you, not only to believe but also to suffer for his sake, (30) since you are having the same conflict which you once saw I had, and now hear that I still have.

Philippians 2:1-30

(1) Since you therefore have encouragement in Christ, the incentive of love, the fellowship of the Spirit, and the affectionate tenderness, (2) complete my joy by being united in your thoughts, (3) being divested of any rivalry or vainglory, but in humility esteeming one another greater than self; (4) and do not look for just your own interests, but also for the interests of others.

(5) You should have the same attitude that Christ Jesus had:
(6) Though he was in the form of God,
He did not think that equality with God
was something to be grasped.

(7) Rather, he emptied himself and took the form of a slave,
being born in the likeness of men.
(8) He humbled himself being obedient to death,
even the death of a cross.
(9) Wherefore God highly exalted him
and gave him the name that is above every name.
(10) So that at the name of Jesus every knee should bow,
in heaven and on earth and under the earth,
(11) and every tongue shall acknowledge that Jesus Christ is Lord,
to the glory of God the Father.

(12) So then, my dear friends, as you have always obeyed me when I was with you, but now much more in my absence, continue to work out your salvation with fear and trembling. (13) For it is God who is working in you both to will and to do what pleases him.

(14) Do everything without grumbling or arguing, (15) so that you may be blameless and innocent, children of God without blemish in the midst of a crooked and depraved generation, in which you shine as luminaries in the universe, (16) holding fast the word of Life, so that in the day of Christ I may rejoice because I did not run in vain or labor in vain.

(17) But even if I am poured out on the sacrifice and service of your faith, I am glad, and I rejoice with all of you, (18) and in that same way you must be glad and rejoice with me.

(19) If it is the Lord's will I hope to send Timothy to you soon, so that I may also be refreshed in knowing about your concerns. (20) For no one is like him, who is genuinely concerned about you. (21) Everyone else is concerned about their own things, not the things of Christ Jesus. (22) But you know about his character, because as a son with his father, he has served with me in the gospel. (23) Therefore I hope to send him immediately, as soon as I see how things are going with me. (24) And I trust in the Lord that I myself may come to you soon.

(25) But I think that it is now necessary to send back to you Epaphroditus, my brother, fellow worker and fellow soldier, and your apostle, and a minister to my needs. (26) He has been anxious to see all of you, and he was distressed because you heard that he was ill. (27) And indeed he was ill and almost died. But God had mercy on him, and not only him but also on me, to keep me from having sorrow upon sorrow. (28) More eagerly therefore I am to send him, so that you may rejoice to see him again and I may be less anxious. (29) Therefore receive him in the Lord with all joy, and honor men like him, (30) because for the work of Christ he almost died, risking his life, so that he might give me the help that you could not give.

Philippians 3:1-21

(1) Finally, my brothers, rejoice in the Lord. To write the same

things to you is not troublesome for me, and it is for your stability.

(2) Look out for the dogs, look out for the evil workers, look out for those mutilators of the flesh. (3) For we, who are worshipping by the Spirit of God and glorying in Christ Jesus, are not trusting in the flesh— (4) though I myself might have reason for confidence in the flesh. If anyone thinks that he has reason to put confidence in the flesh, I have more! (5) I was circumcised on the eighth day, from the race of Israel, from the tribe of Benjamin, a Hebrew of Hebrews; according to the law, a Pharisee; (6) according to zeal, a persecutor of the church; according to the law, blameless.

(7) But those things that were gain to me I have counted them as a loss for the sake of Christ. (8) Yes, I also count all things a loss in view of the surpassing knowledge of Christ Jesus my Lord, on account of whom I have suffered loss of all things; and I consider them to be refuse in order that I might gain Christ (9) and to be found in him, not having my righteousness of the law, but through faith in Christ, the righteousness of God based on faith, (10) to know him and the power of his resurrection and the fellowship of his suffering, being conformed to his death, (11) in order that I may attain to the resurrection from the dead.

(12) It is not that I have already attained to this, or that I have become perfect, but I press on that I may take hold of it, because Christ Jesus has laid hold of me. (13) Brothers, I do not yet consider myself to have taken hold of it, but this one thing I do: Forgetting the things that are behind, I am stretching forward to what lies ahead. (14) My eyes are on the goal and I am pressing on for the high calling of God in Christ Jesus.

(15) Let us therefore, as many as are mature, think like this; but if some of you think differently, God will make it clear to you. (16) Only let us hold true to what we have already attained and continue in the same course.

(17) Brothers, join in with others in following my example, and take note of those who walk according to the pattern you have in us. (18) For, as I have said before and now I say it weeping, many live as enemies of the cross of Christ. (19) Their end is destruction, their god is their stomach, and their glory is their shame, and their thoughts are on earthly things. (20) But our citizenship is in heaven, and we eagerly await a Savior from there, the Lord Jesus Christ, (21) who, by the power that enables him to bring everything under his control, will transform our lowly bodies so they will be like his glorious body.

Philippians 4:1-23

(1) Therefore, my brothers, loved and longed for, my joy and crown, by the help of the Lord, keep on standing firm, my dear friends.

(2) Euodia and Syntyche, I plead with you, be reconciled in the Lord. (3) Yes, and I ask you, my loyal partner, help these women, who have labored together with me and Clement and the other fellow workers whose

names are in the book of life. (4) Rejoice in the Lord always. I will say it again: Rejoice! (5) Let your patient steadfastness be evident to everyone. The Lord is near. (6) Do not worry about anything, but in everything, by prayer and petition with thanksgiving, let your requests be known to God. (7) And the peace of God that transcends all our dreams will guard your hearts and your thoughts in Christ Jesus.

(8) Finally, brothers, whatever is true, whatever is noble, whatever is pure, whatever is lovely, whatever is praiseworthy, yes, on moral excellence and praise—let your thoughts dwell. (9) Practice the things you learned, and received, and heard, and saw in me, and the God of peace will be with you.

(10) I rejoiced greatly in the Lord that your concern for me has been renewed, but indeed you have been concerned for me but you had no opportunity to show it. (11) I do not say this because I am in need, for I have learned to be self-sufficient regardless of the circumstances. (12) I know what it is to be humbled and I know how it is to abound. I have learned the secret of how to respond in every situation—to be filled or to be hungry, to have plenty or to be in need. (13) I can do all things through him who strengthens me.

(14) Nevertheless, it was kind of you to share with me in my hardships. (15) You Philippians yourselves know that when you first heard the gospel and when I departed from Macedonia that you were the only church that shared in the matter of giving and receiving. (16) Indeed, when I was in Thessalonica you supplied my needs more than once. (17) It is not that I seek a gift, but I seek for the increase of the balance to your account. (18) I have received everything in abundance. I am fully supplied, having received from Epaphroditus the gifts you sent, the sweet smell of an acceptable sacrifice, which is well-pleasing to God. (19) And my God will supply your every need according to his riches in glory in Christ Jesus. (20) Now to God our Father be glory forever and ever.

(21) Greetings to every saint in Christ Jesus. The brothers with me send their greetings. (22) All the saints greet you, especially those of the household of Caesar.

(23) The grace of the Lord Jesus Christ be with your spirit.

Introduction to Colossians

Paul wrote Colossians during his first imprisonment in Rome, where he spent two years under house arrest (Acts 28:16-31). During Paul's ministry in Ephesus, Epaphras had been converted and he took the gospel to Colosse (1:7-8). The church there had not been established by Paul, who had never been there (4:1). Epaphras was a member of the church in Colosse and the false teachers who were leading the church astray disturbed him. Epaphras went to Rome and visited Paul in prison and told him about the condition of the church in Colosse.

At one time Colosse had been a leading city in Asia Minor (Turkey today). It was located on the Lycus River and was a great east-west trade route leading from Ephesus to the Euphrates River. By the first century A. D. Colosse was surpassed by the neighboring towns of Laodicea and Hierapolis.

The purpose of the letter was to express his personal interest in them and to combat the heresy of the false teachers. It seems like the problem was an extreme form of Judaism and the early stage of Gnosticism. Paul affirms that it is Christ, not angels or external rules, that is sufficient for salvation and for the fullness of life.

This small letter of only 1,582 words is packed with thoughts of edification for the church in that day and also for us today. In chapter one, he talks about maturity in Christ (1:28). In chapter two, he emphasizes the purpose of baptism (2:12). In chapter three, he tells us what our life-style should be (3:8-10). In chapter four, he admonishes the recipients to be steadfast in prayer and to live with hearts of gratitude, always seeking the will of the Lord (4:1-6).

Colossians 1:1-29

(1) Paul, an apostle of Christ Jesus by the will of God, and Timothy the brother, (2) to the saints and faithful brothers in Christ in Colosse: Grace and peace to you from God our Father.

(3) We always give thanks to God, the Father of our Lord Jesus Christ, praying for you. (4) We heard of your faith in Christ Jesus and the love you have for all the saints, (5) because of the hope of what is laid up for you in heaven, of which you previously heard in the word of the truth of the gospel. (6) For it has reached you, as it has in all the world and is bearing fruit and increasing, even as it has in you since the day you heard and fully understood the grace of God in truth. (7) You learned it from Epaphras, our beloved fellow slave, who is a faithful servant of Christ, (8) and who informed us of your love in the spirit.

(9)Therefore, ever since we heard this, we have not ceased to pray for you and asking that you may be filled with the full knowledge of him in all wisdom and spiritual understanding, (10) so that you may walk worthily of the Lord, to please him in every good work, bearing fruit and growing in the full knowledge of God, (11) being strengthened with all power, according to his glorious might, that you may have all endurance and long-suffering with joy, (12) giving thanks to the Father, who made you adequate to have a part with the saints in the light. (13) He delivered us out of the dominion of the darkness and transferred us into the kingdom of his dear son, (14) in whom we have redemption, the forgiveness of sins. (15) He is an image of the invisible God, the firstborn of creation; (16) because in him, all things were created, in heaven and all things in the earth, the visible and the invisible, whether thrones, or lordships, or rulers, or authorities; all things were created through him and for him. (17) He is before all things and in him all things hold together, (18) and he is the head of the body, the church. He is the beginning, the firstborn from the dead, so that he may be in first place in all things, (19) because he was pleased to have all his fullness dwell in him (20) and through him to reconcile all things to himself (making peace through the shedding of blood offered on the cross)—whether on the earth or in heaven.

(21) And you were alienated and hostile in disposition as implied by your evil works, (22) but now he has reconciled you in the body of his flesh through his death, to present you holy and blameless and innocent before him, (23) assuming that you continue in your faith, having been grounded and steadfast and have not shifted from the hope of the gospel which you heard, which has been proclaimed to all creation, of which I, Paul, became a servant.

(24) Now I rejoice in my sufferings for your sake, and in my flesh I do my share of what is lacking in the sufferings of Christ for the sake of his body, the church, (25) of which I became a servant according to the stewardship of God, given to me for you, to fulfill the word of God, (26) the mystery which was hidden for a long time and through many generations, but now has been manifested to his saints, (27) to whom God wished to make known the riches of the glory of this mystery among the nations, who is Christ in you, the hope of glory. (28) We announce warning every man and teaching every man in all wisdom, in order that we may present every man mature in Christ. (29) I also labor, struggling according to his power which is effectively working in me.

Colossians 2:1-23

(1) For I want you to know how great a struggle I have for you and those in Laodicea and to those who have not known me personally, (2) so that their hearts may be encouraged, being joined together in love, so that they may have the full wealth of assurance which true understanding brings, so that they may have the full knowledge of the mystery of God, which is

Christ himself, (3) in whom are hidden all the treasures of wisdom and knowledge. (4) I say this in order that no one will deceive you with persuasive speech. (5) For though I am absent in body, yet I am with you in spirit, rejoicing to see your good discipline and the firmness of your faith in Christ.

(6) As therefore you received the Lord Jesus Christ, live in union with him, (7) having been rooted and built up in him and established in the faith as you were taught, and overflowing in gratitude.

(8) See to it that no one takes you captive through philosophy and empty deceit, according to the tradition of men, according to the elementary principles of the world and not according to Christ; (9) because in him dwells all the fullness of deity in bodily form, (10) and you are complete in him, who is the head over all rule and authority. (11) In him you were also circumcised with a circumcision made without hands, by putting off the sinful nature by the circumcision of Christ, (12) having been buried with him in baptism and raised up with him through faith in the power of God, who raised him from the dead; (13) and you, when you were dead in your trespasses, in your sinful nature, he made you alive together with him, having forgiven all your trespasses, (14) having cancelled the bond which the law demanded by nailing it to the cross, (15) disarming the rulers and the authorities and exposing them openly, and triumphing over them by the cross.

(16) Therefore let no one judge you in matters of eating and drinking, or in matters of annual or monthly feasts or Sabbaths. (17) These were the shadow of what was coming, but the reality is Christ. (18) Let no one disqualify you in false humility and worship of angels, claiming to be superior because of special visions, inflated without cause by sinful nature, (19) and not holding to the Head, from which all the body, being nourished and held together by the joints and ligaments, grows with a growth that God produces.

(20) Since you died with Christ to the basic principles of the world, why do you live as though you still were subject to its decrees: (21) "Do not touch! Do not taste! Do not handle!" (22) (Which refer to all the things which perish as they are used), according to the injunctions and teachings of men. (23) These rules have an appearance of wisdom in self-imposed worship and false humility and their harsh treatment of the body, but they have no value in restraining fleshly indulgence.

Colossians 3:1-25

(1) Since therefore you have been raised with Christ, seek the things that are above, where Christ is sitting at the right hand of God. (2) Set your affections on heavenly things, not the things upon the earth. (3) You died with Christ, and your life is hidden with Christ in God. (4) Whenever Christ appears, then you also will appear with him in glory.

(5) Therefore put to death your earthly nature, which is, illicit sex, filthiness, passion, lust, and greed, which is idolatry, (6) because it is on account of these things that the wrath of God is coming on the sons of disobedience. (7) Such was your behavior when you used to live that way. (8) But now you must also put away all these things: wrath, anger, malice, slander, and abusive language from your lips. (9) Do not lie to one another, having put off the old man with his actions (10) and having put on the new man, who is growing in the full knowledge of the likeness of his Creator, (11) where there is no distinction between Greek and Jew, circumcised and uncircumcised, barbarian, Sythian, slave and freeman; but everyone is the same in Christ.

(12) Clothe yourselves therefore, as chosen of God, holy and loved, with compassion, kindness, humility, meekness, and long-suffering, (13) bearing with one another and forgiving whatever complaint one may have against another. As the Lord forgave you, you must also forgive. (14) And above all put on love, which is the bond of perfection. (15) Let the peace of Christ rule in your hearts, to which indeed you were called in one body; and be thankful. (16) Let the word of Christ dwell in you richly. Teach and instruct one another with all wisdom. Sing psalms, hymns, and spiritual songs with gratitude in your hearts to God. (17) Whatever you do in word or deed, do everything in the name of the Lord Jesus, giving thanks to God the Father through him.

(18) Wives, be submissive to your husbands, as is proper in the Lord. (19) Husbands love your wives and do not be bitter toward them. (20) Children, obey your parents in all respects, for this pleases the Lord. (21) Fathers, do not provoke your children, lest they become discouraged. (22) Slaves, obey in everything those who are your earthly lords, not with eyeservice as men pleasers, but with singleness of heart, fearing the Lord. (23) Whatever you do, work diligently, as serving the Lord and not men, (24) knowing that you will receive the inheritance of your reward. You are serving the Lord Christ. (25) For the wrongdoer will be punished for his wrongdoing; there is no favoritism.

Colossians 4:1-18

(1) Masters, be fair and square with your slaves, knowing that you also have a Master in heaven.

(2) Continue in prayer and be alert and thankful as you pray. (3) Remember to pray for us also, that God may open to us a door for the word, for us to declare the mystery of Christ, for which I am in chains, (4) that I may speak, as I should, and make the message clear. (5) Walk in wisdom before the outsiders, redeeming the time. (6) Your speech should always be gracious, seasoned with salt, so that you will always have an answer for everyone.

(7) Tychicus will tell you everything about me.   He is a dear brother and a faithful servant and fellow slave in the Lord.   (8) I have sent him to you for this very purpose, so that you may know about me and be encouraged in your hearts, (9) and with him Onesimus, the faithful and dear brother, who is one of you. They will tell you about everything here.

(10) Aristarchus, my fellow prisoner, sends you greetings, and so does Mark, the cousin of Barnabas (You have already received instructions to receive him if he comes your way), (11) and Jesus, who is called Justus sends his greetings. These are the only men of the circumcision who are fellow workers with me in the kingdom of God. They have been a comfort to me. (12) Epaphras, one of you, sends his greetings. He is a slave of Jesus Christ who is always struggling for you, praying that you may stand firm, with a mature faith and with full assurance, in obedience to the will of God. (13) For I can personally testify that he has deep concern for you and those in Laodicea and in Hierapolis. (14) Luke, the beloved physician, and Demas send greetings.   (15) Give my greetings to the dear brothers in Laodicea and to Nympha and to the church in her house.   (16) When you have read this epistle see that it is read in the church of the Laodiceans, and see that you also read the letter from Laodicea. (17) Say to Archippus, "See that you fulfill the ministry that you received from the Lord."

(18) I, Paul, write this greeting with my hand.   Remember my chains.   Grace be with you.

Introduction to 1 Thessalonians

The church at Thessalonica was established on Paul's second missionary journey. Thessalonica was an important seaport city at the head of the Thermic Gulf. It was the largest city of Macedonia, with 200,000 people, and it was the capital city of its province. Some did not like Paul's preaching, so they formed a mob and started a riot in the city. It got so bad that Paul and Silas fled under the cover of darkness and went to Berea. Later, Paul fled from Berea and went to Athens and later to Corinth. Silas and Timothy stayed in Berea for awhile, but later they joined Paul in Corinth.

Timothy met Paul when he was in Athens, and Paul sent him back to Thessalonica to check on the church. So when he met Paul in Corinth he gave him the report. He had brought back good news about their faith and love (3:6). So Paul begins his letter by praising them for their deep conviction and sincere commitment in spite of severe suffering. Many of the members had just come out of paganism and were in the midst of persecution. Paul's purpose in writing this letter was to encourage the new converts in their trials (3:3-5), instruct them in godly living (4:1-8), instruct them to work (4:11-12), and to assure them of the future blessings of the Christians who die before Christ returns (4:13,15). The two Thessalonian letters are called the eschatological letters, because they emphasize the return of Christ. Each of the 5 chapters in this letter ends with a reference to the second coming of Christ.

Paul wrote this letter from Corinth in about 51 A.D. while he was on his second missionary journey. This letter of 1,841 words is as relevant today as it was in the first century.

1 Thessalonians 1:1-10

(1) Paul, Silas and Timothy, to the church of the Thessalonians in God the Father and the Lord Jesus Christ: Grace and peace to you.

(2) We always give thanks to God for all of you, mentioning you in our prayers, constantly (3) remembering before God our Father your energizing faith, your toiling love, and your enduring hope in our Lord Jesus Christ.

(4) We know, brothers, that God loved you and has chosen you, (5) because our gospel came to you not only in word, but also in power and in the Holy Spirit with full assurance. You know what our lives were for your sake. (6) You became imitators of us and of the Lord, receiving the word amid severe affliction, with joy inspired by the Holy Spirit. (7) So you became a pattern to all the believers in Macedonia and Achaia. (8) For from you sounded forth the word of the Lord not only in Macedonia and Achaia, but your faith in God has gone everywhere, so we have no need to speak

about it. (9) For they themselves report how you welcomed us, and how you turned to God from idols to serve the living and true God, (10) and to wait for his Son, from heaven, whom he raised from the dead—Jesus, who delivers us from the coming wrath.

1 Thessalonians 2:1-20

(1) You know, brothers, that our coming to you was not in vain, (2) but even though we had already suffered and had been shamefully treated at Phillipi, as you remember, we were bold in our God to speak to you the gospel in spite of much contention. (3) For our appeal to you was not from a delusion or from impure motives, nor from any form of trickery; (4) but as we have been approved by God and entrusted with the gospel, so we speak, not to please men but God, who tests our hearts. (5) For you know we never used words of flattery or a pretext for greed—God is witness! (6) We never sought glory from men, whether you or from others, (7) though we could have insisted on our authority as apostles of Christ, but we were infants among you. We were as a nurse who cherishes her children. (8) We had a strong affection for you so we were pleased to share with you not only the gospel of God but also our own lives, because you had become so dear to us. (9) For, brothers, you remember our labor and toil. We worked night and day so we would not be a burden on anyone of you while we preached to you the gospel of God.

(10) You are witnesses, and God also, how holy and righteous and blameless we lived before you who believe. (11) You likewise know how, as a father with his own children, we encouraged and comforted each one of you (12) and charged you to walk worthy of God, who calls you into his own kingdom and glory.

(13) We are also thanking God always because, when you received the word of God which you heard from us, you received it not as a word from men, but what it really is, the word of God, which operates in you who believe. (14) For you, brothers, became imitators of the churches of God in Judea in Christ Jesus, because you suffered the same things from your own people as they did from the Jews, (15) who killed the Lord Jesus and the prophets and drove us out. They displease God and are hostile to all men, (16) hindering us from speaking to the nations so that they might be saved. All this time they are heaping up their sins to the limit, but the wrath of God has come upon them at last.

(17) Brothers, when we were torn away from you for a short time (in person, not in spirit), in our intense longing we were more fervently eager to see you face to face. (18) So we tried to come to you—I, Paul, several times—but Satan blocked our way. (19) For what is our hope or joy or crown of boasting before our Lord Jesus at his coming? Is it not you? (20) You are our glory and our joy.

1 Thessalonians 3:1-13

(1) So when we could bear it no longer, we thought it best to be left alone in Athens (2) and to send Timothy, our brother and fellow worker of God in the gospel of Christ, (3) to strengthen and encourage you in your faith so that no one would be drawn away by these afflictions. You yourselves know that this is what we were called to do. (4) For even when we were with you, we told you that you were about to suffer affliction, and this, as you know, has happened. (5) For this reason, when I could bear it no longer, I sent to know about your faith, for fear that the tempter had tempted you and our labor would be wasted.

(6) Now Timothy has arrived from you and has brought us good news of your faith and your love, and that you always have good memories of us, and that you are longing to see us as we are to see you. (7) Therefore we were comforted, brothers, over all our distress and affliction, through your faith, (8) because now we live once more since you are standing fast in the Lord. (9) For what thanks can we return to God for all the joy we have which we feel because of you before our God! (10) We are earnestly praying for you night and day so we can see you in person, and to complete what is lacking in your faith.

(11) Now may our God and Father himself, and our Lord Jesus Christ, direct our way to you. (12) May the Lord make you to increase and overflow in love to one another and to everyone else, as we love you, (13) to establish your hearts blameless in holiness before God our Father and in the presence of our Lord Jesus with all his saints.

1 Thessalonians 4:1-18

(1) Furthermore then, brothers, we request and implore you in the Lord Jesus that as you learned from us how to walk and please God, as indeed you are doing, abound still more. (2) For you are aware of the instructions we gave you through the Lord Jesus. (3) For the will of God is your sanctification: that you abstain from sexual vice; (4) that each one of you may know how to control his body in holiness and honor, (5) not in lustful desires as the nations who do not know God; (6) and that no man defraud his brother in this matter, because the Lord is the avenger of all these sins, as we have previously forewarned you. (7) For God did not call us to uncleanness but to holiness. (8) Therefore those who reject this, rejects not man, but God, who gives you his Holy Spirit.

(9) It is not necessary for me to write to you concerning brotherly love, for you yourselves are taught by God to love one another. (10) For indeed you do have love for all the brothers in all Macedonia, and yet we exhort you to abound still more, (11) to be zealous, to be peaceful, and to

mind your business, and to work with your own hands as we charged you, (12) so you may walk worthy before the outsider and that you be self-supporting.

(13) We want you to know, brothers, concerning those who are sleeping, that you are not to grieve as those who have no hope. (14) We believe that Jesus died and rose again, even so those who are sleeping in Jesus, God will bring with him. (15) For this we say to you by the word from the Lord, that we the living, who survive until the Lord comes, will by no means precede those who are asleep. (16) The Lord himself will descend from heaven with a shout, at the voice of the archangel and the sound of the trumpet of God, and the dead in Christ will rise first; (17) and then we the living, who survive, will be caught up together in the clouds to meet the Lord in the air; and so we will be with the Lord forever. (18) Therefore comfort one another with these words.

1 Thessalonians 5:1-28

(1) Concerning the times and seasons, brothers, there is no need for anything to be written to you, (2) for you know perfectly well that the Lord will come as a thief in the night. (3) When they say, "Peace and safety," then suddenly destruction will come upon them as travail upon a woman with child, and there will be no way of escape. (4) But you, brothers, are not in darkness, for that day to overtake you as a thief. (5) For all of you are sons of light and sons of the day. We are not of the night or of darkness. (6) Therefore let us not sleep as others do, but let us watch and be sober. (7) For those sleeping, sleep at night, and those getting drunk, get drunk at night; (8) but we are of the day, so let us be sober, putting on the breastplate of faith and love and a helmet of the hope of salvation. (9) For God did not appoint us to wrath, but to obtain salvation through our Lord Jesus Christ, (10) who died for us so that whether we watch or sleep we will live with him. (11) Therefore, encourage one another and edify one another, as indeed you are doing.

(12) We implore you, brothers, respect those who are leading and admonishing you in the Lord. (13) Consider them highly esteemed in the Lord because of their work. Be at peace among yourselves. (14) We exhort you, brothers, to admonish the idle, console the fainthearted, help the weak, be long-suffering with everyone. (15) See that no one returns evil for evil, but always follow the good in regard to one another and in regard to everyone. (16) Rejoice always, (17) pray without ceasing, (18) give thanks in everything, for this is the will of God in Christ Jesus for you. (19) Do not quench the spirit; (20) do not despise prophecies. (21) Prove all things. Hold fast the good. (22) Abstain from every kind of evil. (23) And may the God of peace himself completely sanctify you, and may your spirit, soul and body be completely kept blameless at the coming of our Lord Jesus Christ.

(24) Trustworthy is he who calls you, therefore he will do it. (25) Brothers, pray for us. (26) Greet all the brothers with a holy kiss. (27) I adjure you by the Lord to have this letter read to all the brothers. (28) The grace of the Lord Jesus Christ be with you.

Introduction to 2 Thessalonians

Paul wrote both of the Thessalonian letters while he was at Corinth. The second letter was written about 6 months after the first letter. Paul had sent Silas and Timothy to Thessalonica to deliver the first letter, and they had returned with a report from the church. Some of the report was disturbing news. Some of the members of the church thought that the Lord's coming was imminent, and that encouraged them to become idle while they were waiting for the Lord's return.

So this letter was written to correct a misunderstanding about the Lord's return and to encourage them to be steadfast and to work for a living. There were certain things that must happen before the Lord's return. They must continue in their daily employment. There is no virtue in being idle.

When Paul was living with them he worked with his hands to build tents, and he made the rule that if a person did not work he did not eat. The word comes to him that there are some who are idle, and they go about as busybodies. Paul sternly admonished them to work in quietness and work for the bread that they eat. Then he told them if anyone will not obey these instructions, do not associate with him. Do not treat him as an enemy, but warn him as a brother.

This letter was the third letter of Paul's messages to the churches. It was written about 52 A.D. It is a small letter of only 1,055 words. Paul had eternal teaching for temporal problems. We have the same problems today, so his teachings are relevant to us as well as it was to them.

2 Thessalonians 1:1-12

(1) Paul, Silas and Timothy to the church of the Thessalonians in God our Father and the Lord Jesus Christ: (2) Grace to you and peace from God the Father and our Lord Jesus Christ.

(3) We ought to always thank God for you, brothers, for this is right, because your faith is growing abundantly and your love for one another is increasing, (4) so that we ourselves are boasting in the churches of God about your steadfastness and faith in all your persecutions and afflictions that you are enduring.

(5) This is an evidence of the righteous judgment of God, so that you may be made worthy of his kingdom for which you are suffering. (6) God is right in afflicting those who afflict you (7) and to grant rest to you who are suffering and also to us when the Lord Jesus is revealed from heaven with his mighty angels (8) in a flame of fire, inflicting vengeance upon those who do not know God and to those who do not obey the gospel of our Lord Jesus. (9) Their punishment will be eternal ruin and banishment from the presence of the Lord and from the majesty of his power (10) when he comes to be glorified in his saints and to be loved by those who have believed; and you,

who believed our testimony, will be included in that number on that day.

(11) For this reason we always pray for you that you may be worthy of his call and may fulfill every good resolve and work of faith in power, (12) so that the name of our Lord Jesus may be glorified in you, and you in him, according to the grace of our God and the Lord Jesus Christ.

2 Thessalonians 2:1-17

(1) Concerning the coming of our Lord Jesus Christ and our gathering together to meet him, we beg you, brothers, (2) not to be shaken in mind or disturbed either by a revelation, a word, or a letter alleged to have come from us, saying that the day of the Lord is here. (3) Let no one deceive you in any way, for that day will not come until the apostasy and the man of lawlessness, the son of perdition, is revealed. (4) He will set himself against and exalt himself above every so-called God or object of worship, and he seats himself in the temple of God and proclaims that he, himself, is God.

(5) Do you not remember that I told you about these things when I was with you? (6) And you know what is restraining him, but he will be revealed in his time. (7) For the mystery of lawlessness is already at work; only he who restrains will do so until he is taken out of the way. (8) Then the lawless one will be revealed, and the Lord will overthrow him by the breath of his mouth and will bring him to an end by the brilliance of his presence. (9) The presence of the lawless one is according to the working of Satan with all power and signs and false miracles (10) and with all wicked deceit to those who are perishing, because they refused the love of truth so they could be saved. (11) Therefore God will send a deluding influence so that they may believe a lie (12) and be condemned. They have not believed the truth but they have lived in the pleasures of unrighteousness.

(13) But we are bound to give thanks always for you, brothers who have been loved by the Lord, because God chose you as his first fruits for salvation by sanctification of the spirit and belief in the truth, (14) to which he called you through our gospel that you may gain the glory of our Lord Jesus Christ. (15) So then, brothers, stand and keep the teachings you were taught either by speech or through our letter.

(16) Now the Lord Jesus Christ and God our Father, who loved us and has given us eternal comfort and good hope by grace, (17) comfort and strengthen you in every good deed and word.

2 Thessalonians 3:1-18

(1) Finally, brothers, pray for us that the word of the Lord may spread rapidly and triumph as it has with you, (2) and that we may be delivered from perverse and evil men, for not all men have faith. (3) But the Lord, who is faithful, will establish and guard you from evil. (4) We are

persuaded in the Lord that you are doing and will continue to do what we command. (5) May the Lord direct your hearts into the love of God and the steadfastness of Christ.

(6) We command you, brothers, in the name of our Lord Jesus Christ to keep away from every brother who is idle and does not live according to the teachings which you received from us. (7) You know that you ought to follow our example, because we were not idle when we were with you; (8) and we did not eat anyone's bread without paying for it, but we worked hard by night and by day so we would not be a burden to anyone. (9) It was not that we did not have that right, but we gave you an example to imitate. (10) Even when we were with you, we gave you this rule: If anyone will not work, neither let him eat. (11) For we hear that some are loafing, doing no work but meddling. (12) To such people we command and exhort in the Lord Jesus Christ that they should work in quietness and eat their own bread. (13) And you brothers, do not lose heart in doing good.

(14) If anyone refuses to obey the instructions of this letter, mark that man and do not mix with him, so he will see his irresponsibility and be put to shame; (15) but do not regard him as an enemy, but admonish him as a brother.

(16) Now may the Lord of peace, himself, continually give you peace in every way. The Lord be with you all!

(17) I, Paul, write this greeting with my hand as a signature in every letter I write. (18) May the grace of our Lord Jesus Christ be with you all.

Introduction to 1 Timothy

Timothy was from Lystra. On Paul's first missionary journey, he healed a crippled man who had been a cripple from birth in Lystra. The people were so impressed with Paul and Barnabas that they wanted to worship them as gods. Some of Paul's enemies came and spoke against them and turned the city against them. They stoned Paul and thought they had killed him, so they dragged him outside the city. On the second missionary journey, Paul went back to Lystra. At that time Timothy was one of the disciples. Paul took him with them for the rest of the journey and from that time he became a companion to Paul in his ministry. Timothy's mother was a Jew, and his father was a Greek. Paul had Timothy circumcised so he would not be offensive to the Jews.

There is reason to believe that Paul made a fourth missionary journey after he was released from his first imprisonment in Rome. Paul had declared his plans to go to Spain, and there is a record in the early church literature that Paul did take the gospel as far as Spain. So Paul was probably released from prison in 62 A.D. and went to Spain (62-64). Then he went to Crete, Miletus and Ephesus. Timothy was with him, and he left Timothy in Ephesus and went to Philippi.

The three letters (1 & 2 Timothy & Titus) are referred to as "The Pastoral Letters," and they were written after his release from his first imprisonment. So Paul is on his fourth missionary journey when he writes to Timothy while he is caring for the church in Ephesus. The purpose of the letter written to Timothy is to give him instructions in the care of the church in Ephesus. He was to refute the false teachers, give proper supervision to the church, and to appoint qualified leaders for the church. This letter gives us guidelines for the supervision of the churches as well as it did for them.

1 Timothy 1:1-20

(1) Paul, an apostle of Christ Jesus by a commission of God our Savior and of Christ Jesus our hope, (2) to Timothy my true son in the faith: Grace, mercy and peace from God our Father and Christ Jesus our Lord.

(3) As I urged you when I went to Macedonia, remain in Ephesus so that you may give strict orders that certain people are not to teach a different doctrine, (4) nor to be concerned about myths and endless genealogies, which promote speculation rather than the stewardship of God, which is by faith. (5) But the purpose of our charge is love, from a pure heart, a good conscience and a genuine faith; (6) but some have missed the point and have turned aside to idle chatter. (7) They desire to be teachers of the law, but they do not understand the words they use, nor the opinions that they dogmatically affirm.

(8) We know that the law is good if it is used right. (9) We understand that the law was not made for the just, but for the transgressor and rebellious, for the ungodly and sinners, for the unholy and profane, for parricides and matricides, for murderers, (10) fornicators, homosexuals, kidnappers, liars, perjurers, and for whatever else is contrary to wholesome teaching, (11) according to the glorious gospel of the blessed God, of which I have been entrusted.

(12) I thank Jesus Christ our Lord, who empowered me and, thinking me trustworthy, called me to his service, (13) though I had been a blasphemer, a persecutor, and a sadist. Nevertheless I obtained mercy, because I did it in ignorance and unbelief. (14) The superabundance of the divine grace of our Lord has come upon me, accompanied by faith and love, which are in Christ Jesus.

(15) Faithful is the saying and worthy of universal acceptance that "Christ came into the world to save sinners" — of whom I am the greatest. (16) But for this reason I was shown mercy, that in me, the greatest of sinners, Jesus Christ might show forth his perfect patience for an example to those who would believe in him for eternal life. (17) Now to the King of the ages, incorruptible, invisible, the only God, be honor and glory forever and ever. Amen.

(18) Timothy, my son, this charge I commit to you in accordance with the prophecies previously made concerning you, that by them you may fight the good fight, (19) having faith and a good conscience. Some have rejected conscience and made shipwreck of their faith; (20) among them are Hymenaeus and Alexander, whom I have delivered to Satan that they may be taught not to blaspheme.

1 Timothy 2:1-15

(1) First of all, I urge you to make petitions, prayers, intercessions, and thanksgivings for all men, (2) for kings and those in prominent places, so that we may live peaceful and quiet lives with all reverence and dignity. (3) This is good and acceptable before God our Savior, (4) whose will is that all should be saved with a full knowledge of the truth. (5) For there is one God and one mediator between God and men, the man Christ Jesus, (6) who gave himself as a ransom for all, with the testimony at the proper time. (7) For this I was appointed as a herald and an apostle (I am speaking the truth, I am not lying) and a teacher of nations in faith and truth.

(8) Therefore I wish that all men would pray everywhere lifting up holy hands unstained by anger and dissension.

(9) I also wish that women would clothe themselves in proper apparel with modesty and self-control, not with elaborate hair styles or gold or pearls or expensive clothing, (10) but with good deeds, for this is appropriate for women who profess godliness.

(11) A woman should learn in quietness and complete submission. (12) I do not permit a woman to teach or exercise authority over a man, but she is to be silent. (13) For Adam was first created, then Eve. (14) And Adam was not deceived, but the woman was deceived and became a transgressor. (15) Nevertheless she will be saved through childbearing, if she continues in faith, love, and holiness with self-control.

1 Timothy 3:1-16

(1) Faithful is the saying: If anyone desires to be a pastor he desires a good work. (2) So the pastor must be a man without reproach, the husband of one wife, clearheaded, self-controlled, dignified, lover of strangers, qualified to teach, (3) not addicted to strong drink, not pugnacious, but gentle and not contentious, and not a lover of money. (4) He must manage well his own household, having control over his children with all dignity. (5) (If a person cannot control his own household, how can he care for the church of God?) (6) He must not be a recent convert, lest he be puffed up and fall into the condemnation of the devil. (7) And he should be a good witness to the outsiders, so that he may not fall into reproach and fall into the devil's trap.

(8) Deacons likewise must be dignified, not double-tongued, not addicted to wine, not greedy of gain, (9) but holding the mystery of the faith with a clear conscience. (10) They should first be examined, then approved, and then, being irreproachable, let them serve as deacons.

(11) Wives likewise must be dignified, not slanderers, clearheaded, trustworthy in all things.

(12) The deacon must be the husband of one wife and must manage his children and household well. (13) For those who have served well acquire for themselves a good position and great boldness in Christ Jesus. (14) These things I am writing to you though I am hoping to come to you soon. (15) But if I am delayed, you may know how to live in the household of God, which is the church of the living God, the pillar and foundation of the truth. (16) And by common confession, great is the mystery of godliness:
"He was manifested in the flesh,
He was vindicated in the Spirit,
He was seen by angels,
He was proclaimed among the nations,
He was believed in by the world,
He was taken up in glory."

1 Timothy 4:1-16

(1) The Spirit clearly declares that in later times some will depart from the faith, giving attention to misleading spirits and teachings of

demons, (2) through the hypocrisy of liars, men whose consciences are cauterized, (3) who forbid marriage and insist on abstaining from foods which God created to be shared with thanksgiving by believers who know the truth. (4) For everything created by God is good, and nothing is to be rejected if it is received with gratitude; (5) for it is sanctified by the word of God and prayers.

(6) If you put these instructions before the brothers, you will be a good servant of Christ Jesus, being nourished by the words of faith and the good teachings, which you have followed. (7) Have nothing to do with profane myths and old wives' tales. But train yourself for godliness. (8) For physical exercise is of some value, but godliness is profitable for all things, since it has promise for the present life and the life to come.

(9) Faithful is the saying and worthy of full acceptance; (10) for to this end we labor and struggle, because our hope is in the living God, who is the Savior of all men, especially of believers.

(11) Continue to command and teach these things. (12) Let no one underrate you because you are young, but be an example in speech, in conduct, in love, and in faith to the believers. (13) Until I come, continue to give attention to the reading, the exhortation and the teaching. (14) Do not neglect your gift, which was given to you by the prophetic utterance and the laying on of the hands of the body of elders. (15) Attend to these things, so that all may see your progress. (16) Pay close attention to yourself and in your teaching. Persevere in them; for in doing this you will save yourself and those who hear you.

1 Timothy 5:1-25

(1) Do not severely censure an older man, but exhort as a father, younger men as brothers, (2) older women as mothers, younger women as sisters, with all purity.

(3) Care for widows who are really in need. (4) But if any widow has children or grandchildren, let them first fulfill their religious obligation to their parents; for this is pleasing to God. (5) She who is a widow indeed and has been left alone has fixed her hope in God and continues in supplications and prayers night and day; (6) but she who gives herself to pleasure is dead, even while she lives.

(7) Continue to give these instructions so that they will be above reproach. (8) If anyone provides not for his own people, especially those of his own household, he has denied the faith and is worse than an infidel. (9) Widows should be over sixty years of age to be enrolled, having been the wife of one husband, (10) having a reputation for doing good works, such as rearing children, entertaining strangers, washing the feet of the saints, relieving the afflicted and doing good works in every way.

(11) Do not enroll younger widows, because when their sensuous

impulses alienate them from Christ, they desire to marry, (12) and deserve censure for breaking their previous pledge. (13) But at the same time they go from house to house, and they are not only idle but also gossips and busybodies, talking about things that are not proper. (14) Therefore, I would council younger women to marry and to bear children, rule their households, and give the enemy no occasion for slander; (15) for already some have turned aside to follow Satan. (16) If any woman who is a believer has widows, let her assist them, so they will not be a burden to the church.

(17) Let the elders who rule well be considered worthy of double honor, especially those who labor in preaching and teaching. (18) For the scripture says, "You shall not muzzle an ox when he is treading out grain," and the workman is worthy of his pay.

(19) Do not receive an accusation against an elder except on the evidence of two or three witnesses. (20) Those who continue in sin should be rebuked in the presence of all, so the rest may stand in reverence.

(21) I solemnly charge you before Christ Jesus and the chosen angels to keep these rules without prejudice and to do nothing from partiality.

(22) Do not be hasty in laying on of hands, nor participate in the sins of others; but keep yourself pure.

(23) Stop drinking only water, but use a little wine to strengthen your stomach and relieve its frequent infirmities.

(24) The sins of some men are clearly seen, and they go before them to judgment, but for others they follow them. (25) Likewise, the good works of some are clearly seen, and even when they are not, they cannot be completely concealed.

1 Timothy 6:1-21

(1) Let all who are under the yoke of slavery esteem their masters as worthy of all honor, so the name of God and our teaching may not be slandered. (2) Those who have believing masters must not despise them because they are brothers, but rather they are to serve them better, because those who benefit are believers and are dear to them.

These are the things you should teach and preach. (3) If anyone teaches a different doctrine and does not agree with the words of our Lord Jesus Christ, and it is not according to godly teachings, (4) he is puffed up and knows nothing; but he has a diseased mind with intellectual curiosity about trifles and disputes about words, which produce envy, strife, blasphemies, evil conjectures, (5) and perpetual friction of men with corrupted minds, who have been deprived of the truth, who think that godliness is a means of gain.

(6) There is great gain in godliness with self-sufficiency. (7) For we brought nothing into the world and we cannot carry out anything. (8) If we have food and clothing we will be satisfied. (9) But those who seek to be rich

fall into temptation and snares and many foolish and injurious lusts which cause men to sink into ruin and destruction. (10) For the love of money is a root of all kinds of evils, of which some craving after wandered away from the faith and have pierced themselves with many pains.

(11) But you, O man of God, flee these things, and pursue righteousness, godliness, faith, love, endurance and meekness. (12) Fight the good fight of the faith, lay hold on eternal life, to which you were called, when you made the good confession before many witnesses. (13) Before God who gives life to all things and Christ Jesus who witnessed the good confession before Pontius Pilate, I solemnly entreat you, (14) to keep this commandment unstained and without reproach until the appearing of our Lord Jesus Christ, (15) which will be brought about in his own time by the blessed and only Sovereign, the King of kings, the Lord of lords, (16) the only one having immortality and dwells in unapproachable light, whom no man has ever seen or can see. To Him be the honor and eternal dominion. Amen.

(17) Instruct the rich in this present age to not be haughty, nor to set their hope in the uncertainty of riches, but on God who richly gives us everything to enjoy. (18) Instruct them to do good, to be rich in works, generous and ready to share. (19) In this way they will lay up treasures for themselves that forever endure in the life to come, so that they may take hold of the life that is life indeed.

(20) O Timothy, guard what has been entrusted to you. Turn away from profane and frivolous talk and contradictions (21) of pseudoscience, which some have professed and have deviated from the faith. Grace be with you.

Introduction to 2 Timothy

Paul was released from his first imprisonment in Rome about 62 A.D., and it was at that time that he wrote the letters to Timothy and Titus. Paul was imprisoned again under Emperor Nero about 66 A.D. It was at this time that he wrote the second letter to Timothy. He was in a cold dungeon and chained to a Roman soldier like a common criminal (1:16; 2:9). Paul knew that his work on earth was about over, as he was waiting to be executed (4:6-8). But he knew that he had fought the good fight, that he had finished the race, and that he had kept the faith.

In this dingy dungeon Paul was no more popular. Most of his friends had forsaken him. He writes, "everyone in the province of Asia has deserted me, including Phygelus and Hermogenes"(1:16). Demas deserted him and had gone to Thessalonica because he loved this world (4:10). Crescens, Titus, and Tychicus had gone on special mission trips. Then he says, "Only Luke is with me." He instructs Timothy to "get Mark and bring him with you." And when you come "bring my coat that I left at Troas and my scrolls" (4:13).

Paul was concerned about the welfare of the churches, because during this time Nero was persecuting the churches. Paul admonishes Timothy to guard the gospel (1:14), live by its precepts (3:14), preach it in season and out of season (4:2), and be prepared to suffer for it (1:8; 2:3). This letter was a personal letter to Timothy, but the plural "you" in the closing verse suggests that the letter was intended for public use.

Paul's ministry was ageless, and through his letters he still ministers to the people of the world. There were 32,394 words in his 13 letters. We are prone to think that he wrote more of the New Testament than anyone else, but Luke, with his Gospel and Acts, wrote 37, 897 words. They worked closely together, and adding them together they wrote 70,291 words, which is more than half of the 136,872 words in the New Testament. Paul and Luke made a wonderful team, and we will ever be indebted to them.

2 Timothy 1:1-18

(1) Paul, apostle of Christ Jesus by the will of God, according to the promise of the life which is in Christ Jesus, (2) to Timothy, my dear son: Grace, mercy and peace from God our Father and Christ Jesus our Lord.

(3) I thank God, whom I serve with a clean conscience as my forefathers did, as night and day I constantly remember you in my prayers, (4) longing to see you, having been reminded of your tears, so that I may be filled with joy. (5) I am reminded of your sincere faith, which first dwelt in your grandmother Lois, then in your mother Eunice, and I am persuaded that it dwells in you now. (6) For this reason I remind you to fan the flame

of the gift of God, which came upon you when I laid my hands upon you. (7) For God did not give us a spirit of cowardice, but a spirit of power, of love, and of self-control.

(8) Therefore do not be ashamed of the testimony of our Lord, nor of me, his prisoner, but suffer for the gospel according to the power of God. (9) He saved us and called us with a holy calling, not according to our works but according to his own purpose and grace, given to us in Christ Jesus, planned before the beginning of time, (10) but now has been manifested through the appearance of our Savior Christ Jesus, who abolished death and brought life and immortality to light through the gospel. (11) For this gospel I was appointed a herald, an apostle, and a teacher. (12) For this reason I suffer, but I am not ashamed, for I know in whom I have believed, and I am persuaded that he is able to guard my deposit until that day. (13) Continue to be an example of wholesome instructions, which you heard from me, with faith and love in Christ Jesus. (14) Guard the truth that has been entrusted to you by the aid of the Holy Spirit who dwells in us.

(15) You know that everyone in Asia has turned against me, including Phygelus and Hermogenes. (16) May the Lord grant mercy to the household of Onesiphorus, because he often cheered me up and he was not ashamed of my chains; (17) and when he came to Rome, he diligently searched for me and found me. (18) May the Lord give to him mercy in that day, and you know very well that in many ways he helped me in Ephesus.

2 Timothy 2:1-26

(1) So you, my son, be strengthened by the grace that is in Christ Jesus; (2) and the things you heard from me, before many witnesses, you must commit to trustworthy men who will be able to teach others also. (3) Endure hardships as a good soldier of Jesus Christ. (4) No one serving as a soldier is involved with civilian affairs, because he must be at the disposal of his commanding officer. (5) Also the wrestler will not receive the crown unless he wrestles according to the rules. (6) The laboring farmer should be the first to partake of the harvest. (7) Consider what I say, and the Lord will give you understanding in everything.

(8) Remember Jesus Christ, risen from the dead, descended from David, according to my gospel, (9) for the sake of which I am suffering and bound in chains as a criminal; but the Word of God is not chained. (10) Therefore I endure all things for the sake of the chosen ones, so that they also may obtain in Christ Jesus salvation with eternal glory. (11) Faithful is the saying:

"If we died with him, we shall also live with him;

(12) if we endure, we also shall reign with him;

if we deny him, he will also deny us;

(13) if we are without faith, he remains faithful,

for he cannot deny himself."

(14) Remind them of these things. Solemnly charge them before God to stop fighting with words that are useless and bring destruction to the hearers. (15) Be eager to present yourself, approved by God, a workman who is unashamed, cutting straight the word of truth. (16) Avoid profane and empty talk; for it will lead people into more ungodliness, (17) and their talk will spread like gangrene. This is the case of Hymenaeus and Philetus, (18) who missed the truth, saying that the resurrection is past already, and destroyed the faith of some. (19) However the foundation of God stands firm, having this seal, "The Lord knows his own" and "Let everyone who bears his name abstain from evil."

(20) In a large house there are not only vessels of gold and silver, but also wood and clay, and some for noble purposes and others for ignoble. (21) Therefore if anyone cleanses himself from the latter, he will be a sanctified vessel, suitable for the master, having been prepared for every good work.

(22) Flee from youthful lusts, but pursue righteousness, faith, love, and peace, with those who call on the Lord with pure hearts. (23) But avoid foolish and senseless arguments; for they produce strife. (24) A slave of the Lord must not fight, but he should be gentle toward all men, skilled in teaching, and not resentful when wronged. (25) With meekness he must instruct his opponents, for God might grant them repentance that would lead to a full knowledge of the truth, (26) so that they might escape from the trap of the devil, after being caught by him to do his will.

2 Timothy 3:1-17

(1) But know this: In the last days there will be difficult times. (2) For men will be lovers of self, lovers of money, braggarts, haughty, abusive, disobedient to parents, unthankful, unholy, (3) without natural affection, irreconcilable, slanderers, without self-control, uncivilized, haters of good, (4) treacherous, reckless, conceited, lovers of pleasure rather than lovers of God, (5) having the form of godliness but negating its power. Avoid such people. (6) For some of them worm their way into houses and take captive idle women who are overwhelmed with the weight of their sins and are led about with all sorts of evil impulses, (7) who are always learning but never able to come to a full knowledge of the truth. (8) In the same way Jannes and Jambres opposed Moses as these oppose the truth, men of perverted minds and counterfeit faith. (9) But they will not go far because, as in the case of those men, their folly will be clear to everyone.

(10) Now you have observed my teaching, my conduct, my purpose, my faith, my long-suffering, my love, my endurance, (11) my persecutions and my sufferings, which happened to me at Antioch, Iconium and Lystra. And the Lord delivered me out of all the persecutions I endured. (12) Indeed

everyone who wants to live a godly life in Christ Jesus will be persecuted. (13) But evil men and imposters will become more evil, deceiving and being deceived. (14) But you, continue in the things you have learned and have been assured of, because you know from whom you were taught, (15) and that from childhood you have known the sacred Scriptures, which are able to make you wise for salvation through faith in Christ Jesus. (16) Every Scripture is God-breathed and is profitable for teaching, for convicting, for correction and for training in righteousness, (17) that the man of God may be adequate and fully equipped for every good work.

2 Timothy 4:1-22

(1) I solemnly charge you before God and Jesus Christ, who is coming to judge the living and the dead, by his appearing and his reign, (2) preach the word, be diligent, when it is convenient and when it is inconvenient, convict, rebuke, encourage, with all patience in teaching. (3) For the time will come when they will not tolerate wholesome teaching, but because of their own lusts, surround themselves with teachers who tickle their ears; (4) and they will turn away form listening to the truth and turn aside to myths. (5) But you, be sober in all things, suffer evil, do the work of an evangelist, fulfill your ministry.

(6) For I am already being sacrificed, and the time of my departure has come. (7) I have fought the good fight, I have finished the course, I have kept the faith; (8) therefore the crown of righteousness is reserved for me, which the Lord, the righteous judge, will give me in that day and not only to me but to all who have loved his appearing. (9) Hasten to come to me soon. (10) For Demas, because of his love for the present age, has forsaken me and gone to Thessalonica; Crescens to Galatia; Titus to Dalmatia. (11) Only Luke is with me. Get Mark and bring him with you, for he is useful in helping me. (12) I sent Tychicus to Ephesus. (13) When you come bring the cloak which I left with Carpus in Troas, and the scrolls, especially the leather scrolls. (14) Alexander the coppersmith did me great harm; the Lord will repay him according to his deeds. (15) Watch out for him for he greatly opposed our message.

(16) At my first trial, no one stood by me, but everyone forsook me; may it not be held against them. (17) But the Lord stood with me and gave me power to proclaim the word that all might hear it, and I was delivered from the mouth of the lion. (18) The Lord will deliver me from every evil work and save me for his heavenly kingdom. To him be the glory forever and ever. Amen

(19) Greet Prisca and Acquila and the household of Onesiphorus. (20) Erastus remained in Corinth, but I left Trophimus sick in Miletus. (21) Hasten to come before winter. Eubulus, Pudens, Linus, Claudia, and all the brothers greet you. (22) The Lord be with your spirit. Grace be with you.

Introduction to Titus

Titus was a Gentile Christian, apparently from Antioch (Gal 2: 1-3), and he was a beloved friend and co-worker with Paul. He is not mentioned in Acts, but in Corinthians, Galatians, Timothy and Titus, his name is mentioned 13 times. When Paul left Antioch to discuss the gospel with the Jerusalem leaders, he took Titus with him (Gal 2:3-5). Titus worked with Paul in Ephesus during his third missionary journey, and from there he sent Titus to Corinth to help with the Corinthian church. When Paul was released from prison, he and Titus worked briefly in Crete (Tit 1:5). When Paul left Crete, he commissioned Titus to remain there and complete the work that needed to be done. Later, he met Paul at Nicopolis (west coast of Greece), and from there he went to Dalmatia (Yugoslavia).

Crete, south of the Aegean Sea, is the fourth largest island in the Mediterranean Sea. Life in Crete had sunk to a deplorable level. They were thought of as thieves, gluttons and slothful (1:12). Titus was left there to encourage the believers and to instruct them in their responsibilities.

Paul sent the letter with Zenas and Apollos, who were going through Crete (Tit 3:13). The purpose of the letter was to give Titus authorization and guidance in ministering to the church. He also informed Titus of his future plans for him.

Titus 1:1-16

(1) Paul, a slave of God and an apostle of Jesus Christ, for the faith of those chosen of God and for the knowledge of the truth of godliness, (2) in hope of eternal life, which God, who never lies, promised us ages ago, (3) but in his own time has made know in his word through the proclamation of the message which I have been entrusted by the command of God our Savior, (4) to Titus, my true son in our common faith: Grace, mercy, and peace from God our Father and Christ Jesus our Savior.

(5) I left you in Crete so that you might set in order what was needed and to appoint elders in each city, as I directed you. (6) An elder must be above reproach, the husband of one wife, and having children who believe, not accused of dissipation or rebellion. (7) For the pastor must be above reproach as steward of God, not self-pleasing, not quick-tempered, not addicted to wine, not pugnacious, not greedy of shameful gain, (8) but a lover of strangers, a lover of goodness, sensible, just, holy, and disciplined. (9) He must hold firmly to the trustworthy message as it is taught, so that he can encourage others with wholesome teaching and refute those who oppose him.

(10) For there are many rebellious men, idle talkers, deceivers, especially those of the circumcision. (11) They must be stopped, for they overturn whole households by teaching things they ought not teach—and

that for the sake of dishonest gain. (12) Even one of their own prophets said, "Cretans are always liars, evil beasts, lazy gluttons." (13) This witness is true. Therefore rebuke them sharply, so that they may be sound in the faith, (14) by ceasing to give heed to Jewish myths and to commandments of men, which pervert the truth. (15) To the pure, all things are pure, but both their minds and consciences are impure. (16) They profess to know God, but by their works they deny him; they are detestable, disobedient and disqualified to do anything good.

Titus 2:1-15

(1) But you, teach that which is sound doctrine. (2) Teach the older men to be sober, dignified, sensible, and sound in the faith, in love, and in perseverance. (3) Likewise, teach the older women to have a reverent disposition, not slanderers, not enslaved to wine but teachers of good things. (4) Then they may train the younger women to love their husbands and to love their children, (5) to be sensible, pure, homemakers, virtuous, and submissive to their own husbands, so that the Gospel will not be brought into disrepute.

(6) Likewise, exhort the younger men to be sensible (7) in all things, showing yourself to be a pattern of good works, and in your teaching show integrity and dignity, (8) and let your message be wholesome and unobjectionable, so that the opponent may be put to shame, having nothing bad to say about us.

(9) Teach slaves to be subject to their own masters in everything, to be well-pleasing, not argumentative, (10) not stealing from them, but showing all good faith that they may adorn, in everything they do, the teaching of God our Savior.

(11) For the grace of God has appeared for the salvation of all men, (12) instructing us to renounce ungodliness and worldly desires and to live sensibly, righteously, and godly in this present age, (13) looking for the blessed hope and appearance of the glory of our great God and Savior Jesus Christ, (14) who gave himself for us so that he might ransom us from all iniquity and purify for himself a people for his own possession, zealous for good works. (15) Teach these things and exhort and reprove with all authority. Let no one disregard you.

Titus 3:1-15

(1) Remind them to be submissive to rulers and authorities, to be obedient, to be ready for every good work; (2) do not slander anyone, be not contentious, be meek in the midst of difficult circumstances.

(3) For we were once foolish, rebellious, deceived, enslaved to our lusts and various pleasures, living in malice and envy, hateful and hating

one another. (4) But when the gentleness and loving kindness of God our Savior appeared, he saved us, (5) not because of our works of righteousness, but by his mercy; he saved us through the washing of regeneration and renewal by the Holy Spirit, (6) which he abundantly poured out upon us through Jesus Christ our Savior, (7) so that we might be justified by his grace and become heirs having the hope of eternal life.

(8) Trustworthy is this message, and I want you to affirm confidently these things, so that those who believe in God will be diligent in doing good. These things are good and profitable for everyone. (9) But avoid foolish controversies, genealogies, strife, and legal fights; for they are unprofitable and vain. (10) Admonish a divisive person once or twice; after that avoid him, (11) knowing that such a man is perverted, sinful and is self-condemned.

(12) When I send Artemas or Tychicus to you, hasten to meet me at Nicopolis; for I plan to winter there. (13) Speedily send forth Zenas the lawyer and Apollos and see that they have everything that they need. (14) Our people must do honest work to provide for the necessary needs and not to live unfruitful lives.

(15) Everyone with me sends greetings to you. Greet those who love us in the faith. Grace be with all of you.

Introduction to Philemon

The letter to Philemon is a short letter with only 335 words, but it has been a powerful influence for the sake of brotherhood. Perhaps the letters to Ephesus, Colosse, and Philemon were delivered at the same time. Tychicus was an Ephesian and he was the one who delivered the letter to Ephesus (Eph 6:21). Tychicus also delivered the letter to Colosse, and with him is Onesimus (Col 4:7). Philemon lived in Colosse and a church met in his house. Onesimus was a slave of Philemon. He stole from Philemon and fled to Rome.

Paul had never been in Colosse, but it was through the evangelism of Paul that Philemon became a brother in Christ. Colosse was only a few miles from Ephesus, so probably it was there where Paul led Philemon to Christ. Onesimus fled from Colosse and went to Rome, and it was there that Paul led Onesimus to Christ. Onesimus becomes a great helper to Paul, and he would like for him to remain with him, but he is led to send Onesimus back to his master.

Onesimus is willing to return to his master, so Paul writes a letter of recommendation for Onesimus. His name meant Useful, but he was useless in the past; but Paul writes that "he now is useful to you and to me" (1:11). Paul tells Philemon that he is no longer a slave but a beloved brother (1:16), and he admonishes him saying, "So if you consider me your partner, receive him as you would me" (1:17). Paul went ahead to say that "if he owes you anything just charge that to my account and I will pay it" (1:19). This little letter has done more to obliterate social and class distinctions than many books written on the subject.

Philemon 1:1-25

(1) Paul, a prisoner of Jesus Christ, and brother Timothy, to Philemon our dear fellow worker, (2) to sister Apphia, to our fellow soldier Archippus, and to the church that meets at your house: (3) Grace and peace to you from God our Father and the Lord Jesus Christ.

(4) I always thank my God every time I mention you in my prayers, (5) because I continue to hear about your love to all the saints and your faith in the Lord Jesus; (6) and I pray that in the sharing of your faith you may have a full understanding of every good thing we have in Christ. (7) For I have felt great joy and encouragement over your love, because the hearts of the saints have been refreshed through you, my brother. (8) Therefore, I have full freedom in Christ to order you to do your duty, (9) yet for the sake of love I prefer to appeal to you. I am Paul, an old man and now even a prisoner of Jesus Christ. (10) I appeal to you concerning my son, Onesimus, who became my son in prison. (11) Formerly, he was useless to you, but now

he is useful, both to you and to me.

(12) I am sending him — my dear friend — back to you. (13) I wanted to keep him with me that he might, on your behalf, minister to me while I am in prison for the gospel, (14) but without your consent I would not do it, so that whatever you do will be voluntarily done and not by pressure. (15) For perhaps he departed for awhile that you might have him back forever, (16) no longer as a slave, but more than a slave, a dear brother, especially to me and much more to you, both as a man and as a brother in the Lord.

(17) Therefore, since you consider me as a partner, receive him as you would me. (18) And if he has wronged you or owes you anything, charge it to me. (19) I, Paul, write with my hand. I will repay it — not to mention the fact that you owe me yourself. (20) Yes, brother, help me in the Lord. Refresh my heart in Christ. (21) Having confidence in your obedience, I write you knowing that you will do more than I request. (22) At the same time prepare a guest room for me, for I hope, through your prayers, to be visiting you.

(23) Epaphras, my fellow prisoner for Christ Jesus, sends you greetings. (24) Mark, Aristarchus, Demas, and Luke, my fellow workers, also send you greetings.

(25) The grace of the Lord Jesus be with your spirit.

Introduction to Hebrews

The writer of this letter does not identify himself, but he was well-known to the recipeints. From c. 400 A.D. to 1600 A.D. the book was commonly called "The Epistle of Paul to the Hebrews," but there was no agreement in the first few centuries about who was the author of the book. Tertullian, about 200 A.D., quotes from "an epistle to the Hebrews under the name of Barnabas." Some think that it was Apollos who wrote the book, but we really do not know who wrote it. I shall always remember what Dr. W. T. Conner, teacher of Systematic Theology at SWBTS, concerning the authorship of the book said, "I do not know who wrote the book but I know who did not write it, Paul."

The book must have been written before the destruction of Jerusalem and the temple in A.D. 70. The author still refers to the temple and the priestly activities in the present tense. The letter was addressed primarily to Jewish converts who were familiar with the Old Testament.

The theme of the book is the absolute sufficiency of Jesus Christ as revealer and mediator of the grace of God. The prophecies and promises of the Old Testament are fulfilled in the New Testament. Christ is superior to the prophets, to the angels, to Moses, to Aaron and the priests descended from him. Some have called Hebrews "the book of better things" since the expression is used 15 times in the book. There is no turning back to the old Jewish system, because the unique priesthood of Christ has superceded it. His atoning death and resurrection have opened the way to the true heavenly sanctuary of God's presence. There are 4,954 words in the book with 1,031 different words. Chapter 11 is the faith chapter of 633 words. That chapter alone has blessed millions of people, and it is still the subject of many sermons and Bible studies.

Hebrews 1:1-14

(1) In times past, God spoke to our fathers through the prophets in many ways and with many methods of disclosure, (2) but in these last days he has spoken to us through his son, whom he appointed heir of all things and through whom he created all things. (3) He is the radiance of his glory and the exact reproduction of his being, and he sustains all things by his powerful word. When he had provided purification for sins, he sat down at the right hand of the Majesty on high, (4) having become as far superior to angels as the title of his inheritance is to theirs.

(5) For to what angel did God ever say,
"You are my son; today I have begotten you"?
Or again,
"I will be a father to him. And he will be a son to me"?

(6) When he brought the firstborn into the world he said,
> "Let the angels of God worship him."

(7) With regard to the angels he said,
> "He makes his messengers winds,
> and his ministers flames of fire."

(8) But with regard to the son,
> "Your throne, O God, is forever and ever,
> the righteous scepter is the scepter of your kingdom.
> (9) You love righteousness and hate iniquity;
> therefore, God, your God, has anointed you
> with the oil of gladness more than your comrades."

(10) And,
> "You, Lord, in the beginning the earth was established by you,
> and the heavens are the works of your hands.
> (11) They will perish but you will remain;
> they will grow old like a garment,
> (12) like a cloak you will fold them up
> and like a garment they will be changed;
> but you are the same and your years will not end."

(13) But to what angel has he ever said,
> "Sit at my right until I make your enemies a footstool for your feet"?

(14) Are not all angels ministering spirits sent forth to serve for the sake of those who are to inherit salvation?

Hebrews 2:1-18

(1) Therefore, it is necessary for us to pay closer attention to the things we have heard, lest we drift away. (2) For if the word spoken by angels was valid, and every transgression and disobedience received an appropriate penalty, (3) how shall we escape if we neglect so great a salvation? It was declared first by the Lord and then confirmed by those who heard him, (4) while God continued to bear witness with them, both by signs and wonders and by various miracles and gifts of the Holy Spirit according to his will.

(5) For it is not to angels that he gave authority over the world to come, of which we are speaking. (6) But it has been solemnly declared,
> "What is man that you remember him,
> or a son of man that you should care for him?
> (7) You made him a little less than angels,
> you have crowned him with glory and honor,
> (8) and put everything under his feet."

Now in putting everything under his feet, there is nothing that is not under his control. But at the present time we do not see everything under his control. (9) But we see Jesus, who was made less than angels; because of his suffering and death, he was crowned with glory and honor, so that by the grace of God he might taste death for the sake of all men.

(10) For it was appropriate for God, for whom and through whom all things exist, in bringing many sons to glory, to make the author of their salvation perfect through suffering. (11) For both the sanctifier and the sanctified are of the same family; and that is why he is not ashamed to call them brothers, (12) saying,

"I will announce your name to my brothers,

in the midst of the assembly I will praise you."

(13) And again,

"I will put my trust in him."

And again,

"Here am I and the children God has given me."

(14) Since therefore the children share in flesh and blood, he himself likewise shared the same things, in order that through death he might destroy the one who has the power of death, that is, the devil, (15) and release all who had been held in slavery by their fear of death. (16) For assuredly it was not angels that he came to help, but he came to help the seed of Abraham; (17) therefore he had to become like his brothers in every way, in order that he might become a merciful and faithful high priest in the service of God, to make atonement for the sins of the people. (18) For since he suffered in his testing, he is able to help those who are tested.

Hebrews 3:1-19

(1) Therefore, holy brothers, sharers of a heavenly calling, consider Jesus, the apostle and high priest of our confession, (2) who was faithful to God who appointed him, just as Moses was faithful in the household of God; (3) but Jesus has been counted worthy of more glory than Moses, as the builder of the house has more honor than the house. (4) For every house is built by someone, but the builder of all things is God. (5) Moses was faithful as a servant in all the household of God, testifying to what would be spoken later, (6) but on the other hand Christ is faithful as a son, set over his household. And we are his household if we hold fast our confidence and the hope of which we boast.

(7) Therefore, as the Holy Spirit says:

"Today, if you hear his voice,

(8) do not harden your hearts as they did in the provocation,

in the day of the temptation in the desert,

(9) where your fathers tested me,

and for forty years saw my works.

(10) Therefore I was angry with that generation,

and I said, 'They always err in their hearts,

and they have not known my ways.'

(11) So I swore in my anger,
'They shall never enter my rest.' "
(12) Take care, brothers, lest there be in any of you a wicked heart of unbelief causing you to depart from the living God. (13) But encourage one another every day, as long as "Today" shall last, so that no one of you is hardened by the deceitfulness of sin. (14) For we share in Christ, if indeed we hold fast our original confidence to the end, (15) while it is said,
"Today, if you hear his voice
do not harden your hearts as in the provocation."
(16) Who were those who heard and yet provoked him? Was it not all those who were led out of Egypt by Moses? (17) And with whom was he angry for forty years? Was it not those who sinned, whose bodies fell in the desert? (18) Was it not to those who disobeyed him that he swore that they would never enter into his rest? (19) And we see that they were not able to enter because of unbelief.

Hebrews 4:1-16

(1) Therefore, since the promise of entering his rest is still valid, let us fear lest anyone of you should fail to enter it. (2) For indeed we have heard the good news as they did; but they did not profit from hearing the word, because they did not mix faith with what they heard. (3) For we who believe enter into that rest, as God has said,
"As I swore in my wrath:
'They shall not enter into my rest,' "
although his work was finished when he created the world. (4) For he has spoken about the seventh day: "And on the seventh day God rested from all his works." (5) And again he says, "They shall not enter my rest."
(6) Since therefore it remains for some to enter, and the ones who previously had received the good news failed to enter because of disobedience, (7) God once more set a day, "Today," saying through David after a long time the same as was said before,
"Today, if you hear his voice,
do not harden your hearts."
(8) For if Joshua had given them rest, God would not speak later of another day. (9) Then there remains a Sabbath rest for the people of God. (10) For whoever enters into God's rest also rests from his works as God did from his. (11) Let us therefore be diligent to enter into that rest, so that no one will fall by following their example of disobedience.
(12) For the word of God is living and energetic and sharper than any two-edged sword, piercing to the division of soul and spirit, of joints and marrow, able to discern the thoughts and intention of the heart. (13) No creature is hidden from his sight, but all things are open to the eyes of him to whom we have to give account.

(14) Since then we have a great high priest, Jesus the Son of God who has gone through the heavens, let us hold fast our confession. (15) For we do not have a high priest who is unable to suffer with our weaknesses, because he has been tempted in every way, just as we are, yet without sin. (16) So let us come boldly to the throne of grace, that we may receive his mercy and find grace to help in the time of need.

Hebrews 5:1-14

(1) For every high priest is chosen from among men and is appointed on behalf of men in things pertaining to God to offer both gifts and sacrifices for sins. (2) He is able to sympathize with the ignorant and wayward, since he is also subject to weakness. (3) And for this reason he ought to make sacrifices for sins for the people and also for himself. (4) And no one of his own accord takes this honor, but he is called by God, even as Aaron was.

(5) So also Christ did not glorify himself to become a high priest, but the one who spoke to him said,
"You are my son,
today I have become your Father."
(6) Also another Psalm says,
"You are a priest forever,
according to the rank of Melchizedek."
(7) In the days of his flesh, Jesus offered up prayers and supplications with bitter cries and tears to him who was able to save him from death, and he was heard because of his reverent submission; (8) and though he was a son, he learned obedience by the things which he suffered, (9) and being made perfect, he became the source of salvation to those who obey him (10) and was designated by God to be high priest according to the rank of Melchizedek.

(11) On this subject we have much to say, but it is hard to explain, because you have become dull in your spiritual understanding. (12) For by this time you ought to be teachers, but you need to be taught again the elementary principles of the oracles of God. You need milk, not solid food. (13) For everyone who lives on milk is unskilled in the doctrine of righteousness, for he is an infant. (14) But solid food is for the mature, for those whose mental faculties have been trained to distinguish good from evil.

Hebrews 6:1-20

(1) Therefore, leaving the elementary doctrines of Christ let us go on to maturity, not laying again a foundation of repentance from dead works and a faith toward God, (2) of ceremonial washings, laying on of hands, of the resurrection of the dead and eternal judgment. (3) And this we will do, if

God permits.

(4) For it is impossible to restore and bring them again to repentance those who have tasted the heavenly gift and become sharers of the Holy Spirit (5) and have tasted the Word of God and the mighty powers of the coming age, (6) if they should fall away, since they are crucifying again the Son of God and putting him to an open shame. (7) For the ground that absorbs the rain that often falls upon it and produces a good harvest for the farmers who till it, receives a blessing from God. (8) But if it brings forth thistles and thorns, it is worthless and is soon cursed, and finally is burned.

(9) But concerning you, dear friends, we are confident of better things – of things that point to your salvation. (10) For God is not unjust to forget your work and the love you showed in ministering to the saints, and as you still do. (11) And we desire that each of you shows the same eagerness in realizing the full assurance of the hope to the end, (12) lest you become dull; but be imitators of those who through faith and long-suffering inherited the promises.

(13) When God made a promise to Abraham, since there was no one greater by whom to swear, he swore by himself, (14) saying, "Surely, blessing I will bless you and multiplying I will multiply you." (15) So Abraham, with long-suffering, obtained the promise. (16) For men swear by the greater and the oath confirms what is said and puts an end to all disputes. (17) So when God resolved to show more abundantly to the heirs of the promise the unchangeableness of his purpose, he confirmed it with an oath, (18) so that through two unchangeable things, in which it is impossible for God to lie, we have fled to lay hold of the hope set before us. (19) We have this as an anchor for the soul both safe and firm, a hope that enters into the Holy of Holies, (20) where Jesus, the forerunner, entered on behalf of us, when he became a high priest forever according to the order of Melchizedek.

Hebrews 7:1-28

(1) For this Melchizedek, king of Salem, priest of the highest God, met Abraham returning from the slaughter of the kings and blessed him, (2) and Abraham gave him a tenth of everything. His name means "king of righteousness"; he was also king of Salem, which means "king of peace." (3) He was without father, without mother, and without genealogy; neither did he have beginning of days or end of life, but he was like the Son of God, who remains a priest forever.

(4) See the greatness of this man to whom Abraham gave a tenth of all the spoils. (5) The law provides that the sons of Levi who receive the office of priesthood should receive tithes from the people, that is, their brothers, even though they are also descendents of Abraham. (6) But Melchizedek, who has no genealogy, received tithes from Abraham and blessed him who had received the promises. (7) It is without dispute that

the inferior is blessed by the superior. (8) On the one hand men who die receive tithes, on the other hand the Scriptures testify that this man lives on. (9) We might say that Levi, who receives tithes, paid tithes through Abraham; (10) for he was still in the loins of his father when Melchizedek met him.

(11) Therefore if the Levitical priesthood had been perfect (for under it the people received the law), what further need would there have been for another priest to arise according to the order of Melchizedek instead of the one according to Aaron? (12) For when there is a change in the priestly office, there is need for a change in the law. (13) For he of whom we speak belongs to another tribe, from which no one has ever served at the altar. (14) It is perfectly clear that our Lord came from the tribe of Judah, a tribe about which Moses said nothing about priests. (15) It is still more overwhelmingly clear when another priest arises according to the likeness of Melchizedek, (16) who has become a priest, not in a law expressed in a commandment concerning physical descent, but by the power of an imperishable life. (17) For the Scripture bears witness:

"You are a priest forever, according to the order of Melchizedek."

(18) For on the one hand the former commandment was weak and unprofitable (19) (for the law made nothing perfect); on the other hand, there is a better hope through which we draw near to God.

(20) This was confirmed by taking an oath. The Levites became priests without taking an oath, but his appointment was ratified by an oath, when God said to him,

"The Lord has sworn, and he will not repent,

'you are a priest forever.' "

(22) So Jesus has become the guarantee of a better covenant.

(23) There were many priests under the old covenant, because death prevented them from continuing in office, (24) but Jesus has a permanent priesthood, for he remains forever; (25) whence he is able to save completely those who come through him to God, because he is always living to intercede for them.

(26) For it was fitting that we should have such a high priest: holy, blameless, stainless, separated from sinners, and exalted above the heavens. (27) He has no need to sacrifice daily as the other high priests, to offer up sacrifices for his own sins and then for the sins of the people; for he offered up himself once for all. (28) For the law appoints men who are weak as high priests, but the word of the oath, which came after the law, appoints a Son who is perfectly qualified to be a high priest forever.

Hebrews 8:1-13

1) Now to summarize what has been said: we have such a high priest, one who is seated at the right hand of God's majestic throne in heaven,

(2) a minister of holy things in the true tabernacle which is erected by God, not man. (3) For every high priest is appointed to offer gifts and sacrifices; therefore it is necessary for the priest to have something to offer. (4) Now if he were on the earth, he would not be the priest offering the gifts according to the law. (5) They serve as an example and a shadow of the heavenly things, as Moses was warned, as he was about to complete the tabernacle. For he was instructed, "Make all things according to that which was shown to you on the Mountain." (6) But now a more excellent ministry has been attained, by so much as he is a mediator of a better covenant, on which were enacted better promises.

(7) For if the first covenant would have been without fault there would have been no need for a second to replace it. (8) But God, finding fault with them, says,

"Days are coming, says the Lord,
when I will make a new covenant with the house of Israel
and the house of Judah.
(9) It will not be like the covenant I made with their fathers
in the day when I took their hand and lead them out of Egypt,
because they did not continue in my covenant,
so I had no concern for them, says the Lord.
(10) This is the covenant that I will make with the house of Israel
after those days, says the Lord.
I will put my laws into their minds
and write them on their hearts,
I will be their God
and they shall be my people.
(11) They shall not teach their fellow citizens or their brothers,
saying, 'Know the Lord'
because all shall know me from the least of them to the greatest.
(12) For I will be merciful toward their iniquities,
and I will not remember their sins anymore."

(13) When he speaks of the "new" covenant he has made the first one obsolete; and that which is obsolete and growing old is soon to vanish away.

Hebrews 9:1-28

(1) So then the first covenant had regulations for worship services and a material sanctuary. (2) For the outer part of the tabernacle was equipped with the lampstand, the table, and the bread set forth in two rows; this is called the Holy Place. (3) Behind the second curtain is a room called the Holy of Holies (4) with a golden altar of incense and the chest of the covenant, which was completely covered with gold, and in it was a golden pot of the manna, the rod of Aaron that budded, and the tablets of the

covenant. (5) Above it were the cherubim of gold overshadowing the mercy seat; but of these things we cannot now speak in detail.

(6) Now these things having been thus prepared, the priests are continually entering into the outer tabernacle and performing their ritual services; (7) but into the inner one only the high priest enters once each year, and not without blood which he offers for himself and for the people's sins of ignorance. (8) By this the Holy Spirit is teaching that as long as the outer tabernacle is still standing, the way into the sanctuary is not yet revealed. (9) This is symbolic of our time. Gifts and sacrifices are being offered but they are not able to purge and make perfect the conscience of the worshipper, (10) since they are only concerned with food, drinks and various ceremonial washings: external regulations in force until the time of the new order.

(11) But when Christ appeared as a high priest of the good things to come, through the greater and more perfect tabernacle (not made by hands, that is, not of this creation), (12) not through the blood of goats and of calves, but through his own blood, he entered once for all in the sanctuary, thus securing eternal redemption. (13) For if the sprinkling of the blood of goats and of bulls and of the ashes of a heifer sanctifies and cleanses the flesh of those who have been polluted, (14) how much more the blood of Christ, who through the eternal Spirit offered himself without blemish to God, will cleanse our conscience from dead works to serve the living God.

(15) Therefore he is the mediator of a new covenant; now that there has been a death to bring deliverance to those who have sinned under the first covenant, those who have been called may receive the promises of the eternal inheritance. (16) For where there is a will, the death of the one who made it must be established; (17) for the will takes effect at death, since it is not in force as long as the one who made it is alive. (18) Whence the first covenant was not dedicated without blood. (19) For when Moses had declared to the people every commandment of the law, he took the blood of calves and of goats, with water and scarlet wool and hyssop, and sprinkled it on the scroll itself and all the people, (20) saying, "This is the blood of the covenant which God commanded you." (21) And in the same way he sprinkled with blood the tabernacle and all the sacred vessels. (22) According to the law almost all things are purified with blood, and without the shedding of blood there is no forgiveness.

(23) So it was necessary for the copies of the heavenly things to be purified with these rites, but the heavenly things themselves require better sacrifices than these. (24) For Christ did not enter a sanctuary made by hands, a copy of the true one, but into heaven itself, now to appear in the presence of God on our behalf; (25) nor was it to offer himself repeatedly, as the high priest enters into the sanctuary each year with the blood of others; (26) for then he would have had to suffer repeatedly since the creation of the world. But as it now is, he has appeared once for all at the climax of history to put away sin by his sacrifice. (27) And as it is appointed for men once to die, and after that judgment, (28) so also Christ, offered up to bear the sins of

many, will appear a second time, not to bear sin, but bring salvation to those waiting for him.

Hebrews 10:1-39

(1) Since the law is only the shadow, and not the true image, of the good things coming, it was never able by the same sacrifices offered continually every year to make perfect those who draw near. (2) If those serving had once been cleansed, would they not have ceased making sacrifices because they would no longer have a consciousness of sins? (3) But in the yearly sacrifices there is a reminder of sins. (4) For it is impossible for the blood of bulls and goats to take away sins.

(5) Hence, when he came into the world, he said,
"Sacrifice and offering you did not desire,
but a body you prepared for me;
(6) in burnt offerings and sin offerings you were not pleased.
(7) Then I said, 'Lo, I have come, as it was written of me in the book,
to do your will, O God.' "
(8) As he said above, "You were never pleased with sacrifices and offerings, burnt offerings and sin offerings" — all of which are offered according to the law. (9) And then he said, "Lo, I have come to do your will." He takes away the first in order to establish the second. (10) It is by this will of God that we have been sanctified through the offering made once for all of the body of Jesus Christ.

(11) Every priest stands daily ministering and often offering sacrifices that can never take away sins. (12) On the other hand when this priest offered for all time one sacrifice for sins, he sat down at the right hand of God. (13) Henceforth he waits until his enemies are made a stool for his feet. (14) For by one offering he has perfected the ones being sanctified.

(15) And the Holy Spirit witnesses to us, for having said,
(16) "This is the covenant I will make with them after those days,"
says the Lord: "I will put my laws in their hearts,
and I will engrave them in their minds."
(17) Then he continues,
"Their sins and their iniquities I will never remember again."
(18) Now where there is forgiveness of sins there is no longer a need for an offering for sins.

(19) Therefore, brothers, with the blood of Jesus we can enter boldly into the sanctuary (20) by the new and living way, which he opened up for us, through the veil, that is, his human nature, (21) and he is a great priest over the household of God. (22) Let us draw near with a true heart in full assurance of faith, our hearts having been purified from an evil conscience and having been bathed with clean water. (23) Let us hold fast the confession of our hope without wavering, for he who promised will not fail us; (24) and

let us consider how to stimulate one another to love and good works, (25) not forsaking the assembling of ourselves, as the habit of some, but exhorting one another, and all the more as you see the final day drawing near.

(26) For when we sin willfully after receiving the full knowledge of the truth, there is no longer a sacrifice for sins, (27) but a fearful prospect of judgment and the fury of a burning wrath that will consume the enemies of God. (28) Anyone rejecting the Law of Moses dies without mercy on the evidence of two or three witnesses. (29) How much more do you think the one is worthy of a greater punishment who trampled on and profaned the blood of the covenant, by which he was sanctified, and has arrogantly insulted the Spirit of grace? (30) For we know him who said,

"Vengeance is mine, I will repay."

And again,

"The Lord will judge his people."

(31) It is a fearful thing to fall into the hands of a living God.

(32) But remember the former days when, after you were enlightened, you endured a much greater conflict with sufferings, (33) on the one hand by insults and persecutions, and on the other you stood by those who were so treated. (34) You suffered together with those who were in prison, and you joyfully accepted the seizure of your possessions, knowing that you yourselves have a better possession and one that is permanent.

(35) Therefore you must never give up your courage, which has a great reward. (36) For you need to endure and do the will of God so that you will obtain the promise. (37) For yet very soon,

"He who comes will come without delay;

(38) but my just one shall live by faith,

and if he withdraws,

my soul is not pleased with him."

(39) But we are not of those who withdraw and are destroyed, but we have faith to possess our souls.

Hebrews 11:1-40

(1) Faith is the assurance of the things hoped for, the evidence of the things not seen.

(2) For by it the elders received divine approval.

(3) By faith we understand that the world was created by the word of God, so that what is seen was made from the unseen.

(4) By faith Abel offered to God a better sacrifice than Cain, through which he was declared to be righteous, God bearing witness by accepting his gift, and though he died, yet by his faith he still speaks.

(5) By faith Enoch was translated so that he did not see death, and he was not seen because God took him. (6) For before he was translated, he was recognized as one who pleased God. Now without faith it is impossible to

please God. For whoever comes to God must believe that he exists, and that he rewards those who seek him.

(7) By faith Noah, being divinely instructed by God of things yet unseen, moving with godly fear, prepared an ark for the saving of his household, through which he condemned the world and became an heir of the righteousness that comes by faith.

(8) By faith Abraham, when he was called, obeyed by going forth to a place, which he was to receive as an inheritance, and he went out, not knowing where he was going. (9) By faith he dwelled in the land of promise as a foreigner, living in tents with Isaac and Jacob, the joint heirs of the same promise. (10) For he was looking for the city, which has foundations, whose architect and builder is God.

(11) By faith Sarah herself received power to conceive even beyond the time of conception, since she considered faithful the one who had promised. (12) Therefore, there came from one who had no prospects for an heir, as the stars in the sky in number, and as the sand of the seashore that cannot be counted.

(13) These all died in faith, not receiving the promises, but seeing them and welcoming them from a distance, and they admitted that they were strangers and pilgrims on the earth. (14) For people who talk this way make it clear that they are seeking a country of their own. (15) If they had been thinking about the place that they had left, they might have had an opportunity to return. (16) Instead, they were yearning for a better place, that is, a heavenly one. Therefore God is not ashamed to be called their God, for he has prepared for them a city.

(17) By faith Abraham, when tested, offered up Isaac; he who had received the promises was offering up his only begotten son, (18) of whom it was said, "Through Isaac shall your posterity be reckoned." (19) He considered that God was even able to raise the dead; figuratively speaking that is what he did.

(20) By faith Isaac invoked future blessings on Jacob and Esau.

(21) By faith Jacob, when he was dying, blessed each of the sons of Joseph, and bowed in prayer over the top of his staff.

(22) By faith Joseph, when he was dying, spoke of the departure of the children of Israel and gave orders concerning his bones.

(23) By faith Moses, when he was born, was hid three months by his parents, because they saw that he was a beautiful child, and they did not fear the decree of the king.

(24) By faith Moses, when he grew up, refused to be known as the son of Pharaoh's daughter, (25) choosing rather to suffer ill-treatment with the people of God than to enjoy the temporary pleasures of sin. (26) He considered the reproach of Christ of greater value than the treasurers of Egypt, for his eyes were fixed on the future reward. (27) By faith he left Egypt, not fearing the king, for he endured because of his vision of the

invisible one. (28) By faith he established the Passover and the sprinkling of the blood, so that the destroying angel might not touch the firstborn.

(29) By faith the people crossed the Red Sea as on dry land, while the Egyptians, when they attempted it, were drowned.

(30) By faith the walls of Jericho fell down after they had been encircled for seven days.

(31) By faith Rahab the prostitute, who received the spies with peace, did not perish with the disobedient.

(32) What more shall I say? I do not have time to give a detailed account of Gideon, Barak, Samson, Jephthah, of David and Samuel and the prophets. (33) Through faith they overcame kingdoms, established righteousness, received promises, stopped the mouths of lions, (34) quenched the power of fire, escaped the edge of the sword, were strengthened in their weakness, made mighty in war, and overcame foreign armies. (35) Women received their dead by resurrection, but others were beaten to death, refusing to receive deliverance, so that they might obtain a better resurrection. (36) Others had trials and were mocked and whipped, and were bound and put in prison. (37) They were stoned; they were tempted; they were sawn in two; they were killed by the sword; they went about in sheepskins, in goatskins, destitute, persecuted, and ill-treated — (38) of whom the world was not worthy — wandering over desserts and mountains and caves and holes in the ground.

(39) These all made a good witness through their faith, but they did not receive the promise, (40) since God had provided something better for us, so that without us they could not reach their goal.

Hebrews 12:1-29

(1) So then, since we have such a great cloud of witnesses surrounding us, let us lay aside every weight and the sin that entangles us; let us run with patient endurance the race that is set before us, (2) focusing our eyes on Jesus, the author and finisher of the faith, who because of the joy set before him endured the cross, despising the shame, and is now seated at the right hand of the throne of God. (3) Consider him who endured such great hostility against himself so that you may not grow weary and faint.

(4) You have not yet resisted to the shedding of blood in your struggle against sin, (5) and you have forgotten the exhortation, which addresses you as sons:

"My son, do not regard lightly the discipline of the Lord,

nor faint when he corrects you.

(6) For the Lord disciplines those he loves,

and he scourges those he receives."

(7) Endure your trials as discipline. God deals with you as sons; for what son is there whom his father does not discipline? (8) But if you are

without discipline, in which all sons share, then you are illegitimate children and not sons. (9) Furthermore we have earthly fathers who corrected us and we respect them. Shall we not much more be subject to our spiritual father and live? (10) For they disciplined us for a short time as seemed best for them, but he disciplined us for our good that we could share in his holiness. (11) For the present time, discipline does not seem to be joy but grief, but later it yields the peaceful fruit of righteousness to those who have been trained by it.

(12) Therefore straighten the weary hands and the paralyzed knees, (13) and make straight the tracks of your feet, lest the lame legs be dislocated, but rather be healed.

(14) Seek to be at peace with all men and to be holy, for without holiness no one will see the Lord. (15) See that no one comes short of the grace of God, so that no root of bitterness grows up to cause trouble and defile many; (16) see that there be no fornicator or profane person like Esau, who sold his birthright for a meal. (17) For you know that later on when he wished to inherit the blessing he was rejected, for he found no place for repentance, though he sought it with tears.

(18) For you have not come to that which can be touched and to a blazing fire, and darkness, and deep gloom, and stormy weather, (19) and the sound of a trumpet, and the sound of audible words. Those who heard begged that no other word be spoken; (20) for they could not bear the command: "Even if a beast touches the mountain it shall be stoned." (21) So fearful was the appearance that Moses said, "I am trembling with fear"; (22) but you have come to Mount Zion, even to the city of the living God, the heavenly Jerusalem, to myriads of angels, (23) to the festive gathering and church of the firstborn whose names are enrolled in heaven, and to God the judge of all man, and to the spirits of righteous men made perfect, (24) and to Jesus the mediator of a new covenant, and to the sprinkled blood which speaks more eloquently than the blood of Abel.

(25) See that you do not refuse the one who is speaking, for if they did not escape when they refused the one who warned them on earth, much less shall we escape if we turn away from him who warns us from heaven. (26) Then his voice shook the earth, but now he has promised, "Yet once again I will shake not only the earth but also the heaven." (27) Now the phrase "yet once again" declares the removal of the things being shaken as the things having been made, in order that the things not shaken will remain.

(28) Therefore let us be grateful that we have received an unshakable kingdom, through which we may offer to God an acceptable service with reverence and awe; (29) for our God is a consuming fire.

Hebrews 13:1-25

(1) Let brotherly love continue. (2) Do not neglect to love strangers;

for some, without knowing it, have entertained angels. (3) Remember the prisoners as if you were bound with them, and those who are ill-treated as yourselves, since you yourselves also are in the body.

(4) Let marriage be held in honor in every way and the marriage bed undefiled; for God will judge fornicators and adulterers. (5) Let your manner of life be free from the love of money, and be content with what you have, for God has said,

"I will never leave you, nor forsake you."
(6) So we can boldly say,

"The Lord is my helper: I will not fear.
What can man do to me?"

(7) Remember your leaders who taught you the word of God; and reflecting upon the results of their lives, imitate their faith. (8) Jesus Christ is the same yesterday and today and forever.

(9) Do not be carried away by diverse and strange teachings; for it is good that the heart be strengthened by grace, and not by foods that have not benefited those who have lived by them. (10) We have an altar from which the ones serving have no authority to eat. (11) For the blood of animals for the sacrifice for sins is brought into the sanctuary by the high priest; the bodies of these animals are burned outside the camp. (12) Therefore Jesus also suffered outside the gate that he might sanctify the people by his blood. (13) So let us go forth to him outside, bearing the shame with him; (14) for we do not have a permanent city, but we seek the everlasting one. (15) Therefore, through Jesus, let us always offer to him a sacrifice of praise, which is the speech of lips that confess his name. (16) But do not forget to do good and share with others; for such sharing is well-pleasing to God.

(17) Obey your leaders and submit to them, for they watch over your souls as men who must give an account of their trust. Make their work a joy rather than a burden, for that would be of no advantage to you.

(18) Pray for us; for we are convinced that we have a good conscience, desiring to live honorably in every way. (19) And more earnestly I beg you to pray that I may quickly be restored to you.

(20) May the God of peace, who brought again from the dead our Lord Jesus Christ, the great shepherd of the sheep, with the blood of an eternal covenant, (21) make you complete in every good thing to do his will, working in us that which is well-pleasing before him through Jesus Christ, to whom be glory forever and ever! Amen.

(22) Brothers, I beg you to endure my word of exhortation, for I have written to you briefly. (23) Our brother, Timothy, has been released. If he comes soon he will come with me to see you. (24) Greet all the leaders and the saints. Greetings to you from those who are in Italy. (25) Grace be with all of you.

Introduction to James

James, the brother of Jesus and leader of the church in Jerusalem, wrote the epistle by that name. At first James did not believe in Jesus, but later he became very prominent in the church. Jesus appeared to him after his resurrection (1Cor 15:7). Paul called him a "pillar" of the church. Paul saw James on his first and last visit to Jerusalem. James was martyred c. A.D. 62.

By the year 51 A.D. James was the honored pastor of the Jerusalem church, when he resided over the conference held there to settle the controversy over circumcision. After they had made their decision, James brought the keynote address to the conference.

This may have been the first book of the New Testament written. At this time most of the members of the church were Jews and they were suffering persecution. Some scholars have dated the book as early as 50 A.D. The Greek term synagogue is used for the meeting place of the church (2:2).

The laborers were being deprived of their wages, while their rich employers were getting rich and living in luxury. The Christian officials were prone to favor the rich and slight the poor. James warns the oppressors that judgment day is coming. This book is a very practical side of Christianity.

James 1:1-27

(1) James, a slave of God and of the Lord Jesus Christ, sends greetings to the twelve tribes of the dispersion.

(2) Count it all joy, my brothers, when you are involved in various trials, (3) for you know that the testing of your faith produces steadfastness. (4) And let steadfastness finish its work, so that you may be perfect and complete, lacking in nothing. (5) If anyone of you lacks wisdom, let him ask God, who gives to all generously and without insulting, and it will be given to him. (6) But he must ask in faith, never doubting; for the doubting person is like a wave of the sea that is driven and tossed by the wind. (7) That person should not think that he would receive anything from the Lord, (8) for he is double-minded and unsettled in all his ways.

(9) Let the brother in his humble circumstances boast in his exaltation, (10) and the rich man in his humiliation, because he is like a flower that will soon pass away. (11) For the sun rises with the scorching wind and dries up the plant, and the petals fall off and the beauty of its appearance is destroyed; so also the rich man in the pursuit of his business will fade away.

(12) Blessed is the man who remains steadfast under trial, because when he is approved he will receive the crown of life that God has promised to those who love him. (13) Let no man say when he is tempted, "I am being

tempted by God." For God cannot be tempted with evil, and he does not himself tempt anyone. (14) For each person is tempted by his own passions when he is allured and enticed by them. (15) Then lust, being conceived, gives birth to sin, and sin, when it has reached maturity, brings forth death.

(16) My dear brothers do not be led astray. (17) Every good giving and every perfect gift comes down from above from the Father of lights, with whom there is no variation, or a shadow cast by turning. (18) Of his will he brought us forth through the word of truth that we should be a kind of first fruits of his creatures.

(19) Know this my dear brothers. Every man must be quick to hear, slow to speak, and slow to anger; (20) for the wrath of man does not work the righteousness of God. (21) Therefore put away all filthiness and every vicious excess and in meekness receive the implanted word, which is able to save your souls.

(22) Be doers of the word and not only hearers of the word, deceiving yourselves. (23) For if anyone is a hearer of the word and not a doer, he is like a man looking at his natural face in a mirror; (24) for he sees himself but he goes away, and immediately he forgets what he looked like. (25) But the person who looks in the perfect law of freedom, and continues to do so, not being a hearer who forgets, becomes a doer of works. That person will be blessed in what he does.

(26) If anyone thinks he is religious but does not bridle his tongue, but deceives his own heart, his religion is worthless. (27) Religion that is pure and stainless before God is this, to visit the orphans and widows in their affliction, and to keep oneself unstained by the world.

James 2:1-26

(1) My brothers, as you have faith in the glory of our Lord Jesus Christ, never show favoritism. (2) For if two visitors enter into your assembly, one a man with a golden ring on his finger and dressed in splendid apparel, and the other a poor man in filthy clothes, (3) and if you look at the one dressed in splendid apparel and say, "Sit here in this good place," and you say to the poor man, "Stand there, or sit on the floor by my footstool," (4) you discriminate among yourselves and become judges of evil thoughts.

(5) Listen, my dear brothers. Has not God chosen the poor in the world to be rich in faith and heirs of the kingdom he has promised to those loving him? (6) But you have dishonored the poor man. Is it not the rich who oppress you and drag you into the courts? (7) Is in not they who scoff at the good name you bear?

(8) If, however, you are fulfilling the sovereign law according to the Scripture, "You shall love your neighbor as yourself," you do well. (9) But if you show favoritism, you sin and are convicted by the law as transgressors. (10) For whoever keeps the whole law, yet stumbles in one point, is guilty of

all. (11) For he who said, "Do not commit adultery," also said, "Do not murder." Now if you do not commit adultery, but you do commit murder, you have become a transgressor of the law.

(12) Speak and act as those who are going to be judged by the law of freedom. (13) In that judgment there will be no mercy for the one who has not been merciful. Mercy triumphs over judgment.

(14) My brothers, what does it profit a man if he says he has faith but he has no works? Can faith save him? (15) If a brother or a sister is naked and is lacking daily food, (16) and if any of you say to them, "Go in peace, be warmed and filled," but if you do not help them with their physical needs, what profit is it? (17) So faith by itself, without works, is dead.

(18) But someone may say, "You have faith, and I have works."

Show me your faith without works and I will show you my faith by my works. (19) Do you believe that there is one God? You do well; the demons also believe and they tremble. (20) But, O vain man, can you not see that faith without works is barren? (21) Was it not that our father Abraham was justified, not by his faith, but by offering up his son Isaac on the altar? (22) You see that faith was working with his works and by works his faith was perfected. (23) And the Scripture was fulfilled, saying, "Abraham believed God, and it was reckoned to him as righteousness," and he was called a friend of God.

(24) You see that man is justified by works and not by faith alone. (25) Likewise, was not Rahab, the prostitute, justified by works when she entertained the messengers and sent them out by a different way? (26) For as the body without the spirit is dead, so faith without works is dead.

James 3:1-18

(1) My brothers, not many of you should be teachers, because we know that we who teach will be judged with greater strictness. (2) For we all stumble in many ways. If anyone does not stumble in speech, he is a mature man; he is able to control his whole body also. (3) If we put bits into the mouths of horses to make them obey us, we can direct their whole body. (4) Consider also the ships. They are great and driven by violent winds, but they are steered by a very small rudder wherever the will of the pilot directs. (5) So also the tongue is a small member, but it boasts of great things. See how a tiny spark of fire sets a huge forest ablaze! (6) And the tongue is a fire, the world of iniquity among our members, contaminating the whole body, and sets on fire the circle of nature, and is set on fire by hell.

(7) Beasts and birds of every kind, reptiles, and sea creatures can be subdued and have been subdued. (8) But no one can subdue the tongue; it is an unruly evil and full of deadly venom. (9) We use it to praise the Lord and Father, and with it we curse men who are made in the image of God. (10) Out of the mouth comes forth blessing and cursing. My brothers, this is

not proper; it ought not be done. (11) Can a fountain gush forth with fresh water and salt water from the same source? (12) My brothers, can a fig tree produce olives? Neither can salt water yield fresh.

(13) Who is wise and understanding among you? By his good life-style let him show his good works in the meekness of wisdom. (14) But if you have bitter jealousy and selfish ambition in your heart do not boast and be false to the truth. (15) This is not the wisdom that comes down from above; it is earthly, natural and devilish. (16) For with jealousy and selfish ambition there is disorder and every worthless practice. (17) But the wisdom that comes from above is first pure, then peaceable, reasonable, willing to yield, full of mercy and good fruits, without uncertainty and without hypocrisy. (18) And the harvest of righteousness is grown from the seed of peace sown by the peacemakers.

James 4:1-17

1) What is the source of your feuds and fights among you? Is it not because of the war of your lusts in your bodies? (2) You covet, but you do not have, so you commit murder, and you are jealous but you cannot acquire, so you fight and quarrel. You do not have, because you do not ask. (3) You ask, but you do not receive, because you ask with evil motives, to indulge in sensual pleasures.

(4) You adulteresses! Do you not know that the friendship of the world is hostility toward God? So whoever chooses to be a friend of the world becomes an enemy of God. (5) Or do you think that Scripture vainly says, "The spirit which dwells in you has envious desires"; (6) but he gives greater grace. Thus Scripture says, "God resists the arrogant, but gives grace to the humble."

(7) Submit yourselves therefore to God. Resist the devil, and he will flee from you. (8) Draw near to God, and he will draw near to you. Cleanse your hands, you sinners, and purify your hearts, you double-minded. (9) Be penitent and mourn and weep. Let your laughter be turned to mourning and your joy to gloom. (10) Humble yourselves in the presence of the Lord, and he will exalt you.

(11) Brothers, do not speak evil against one another. He who speaks evil against a brother or judges his brother speaks evil against law and judges law; but if you judge law, you are not a doer of law but a judge. (12) There is one lawgiver and judge, who is able to save and to destroy. But you – who are you to judge your neighbor?

(13) Come now, you who say, "Today or tomorrow we will go to a certain city and we will be there a year and trade and make money." (14) Yet you have no knowledge of what your life will be tomorrow. For you are a vapor which appears for a little while then disappears. (15) You should say, "If it is the Lord's will, we will do this or that." (16) But now, you boast in

your arrogance. All such boasting is evil. (17) Therefore to him who knows to do good but does not do it, to him it is sin.

James 5:1-20

(1) Come now, you rich, weep and cry aloud over the hardships that are coming upon you. (2) Your riches have rotted and your clothes are moth-eaten. (3) Your gold and your silver have rusted and the poison of them testify against you, and they will eat your flesh like fire. You have stored up treasurers in the last days. (4) Behold, the wages you kept back from the workers who reaped your land are crying out against you, and the cries of the workers have reached the ears of the Lord of Hosts. (5) You have lived in luxury and sensual pleasures on the earth, and you have fattened your hearts in a day of slaughter. (6) You have condemned and murdered the righteous, without resistance.

(7) Be patient, therefore, brothers, until the Lord comes. Note how the farmer waits for the precious fruit of the earth, being patient over it until the early and the late rains. (8) You also must be patient. Stand firm in your hearts because the coming of the Lord is near. (9) Brothers, stop your murmuring against one another, lest you be judged. Look, the judge is standing at the door.

(10) Brothers, for an example, take the ill-treatment and the long-suffering of the prophets who spoke in the name of the Lord. (11) See how we count blessed those who have persevered. You have heard of the perseverance of Job and what the Lord did in the end, because the Lord is very compassionate and merciful.

(12) My brothers, never swear, neither by heaven or by the earth, or with any other oath, but let your "Yes" be yes, and your "No" be no, lest you fall under condemnation.

(13) Is there anyone among you who is sick? Let him pray. Is there anyone cheerful? Let him sing praises. (14) Is anyone weak among you? Let him call the elders of the church and let them pray over him, anointing him with oil in the name of the Lord. (15) And the prayer of faith will save the sick, and the Lord will raise him up. And if he has sinned, he will be forgiven. (16) Therefore, confess your sins to one another, and pray for one another, so that you may be healed. The petition of a righteous man is very powerful and effective.

(17) Elijah, a man just like us, prayed earnestly that it might not rain, and it did not rain for three years and six months. (18) Again he prayed, and the clouds burst forth with rain, and the land produced its crop.

(19) My brothers, if anyone of you strays from the truth and someone brings him back, (20) let him know that the one who turns a sinner from his wandering will save his soul from death and cancel a multitude of sins.

Introduction to 1 Peter

The author of 1 Peter is the apostle Peter (1:1). This letter reflects the history and the terminology of the Gospels and Acts (Peter's speeches, etc.). Some have thought that the idiomatic Greek of this letter is beyond the competence of Peter. There is a difference in the style of 1 Peter and 2 Peter. The first letter is more polished Greek than the second letter. The explanation may be in 1 Peter 5:12. Peter says that he has written this letter "through Silas." That could mean "with the help of" or "by means of." So it could mean that Silas was Peter's secretary for this occasion. It was common for a secretary in those days to compose documents in good Greek for those who were not capable of doing so. There is no indication that Silas was with Peter when he wrote his second letter.

Peter tells us that he is writing from Babylon. There are various interpretations of the meaning of Babylon. In Revelation 17:9-10 it is obvious that the Babylon in that passage is Rome. That seems to be the most likely interpretation here, because Peter was in Rome in the 60's. The writing of the letter could not be dated before 60 A.D., because he is familiar with Paul's prison letters. It cannot be dated later than 67/68, because Peter was martyred in Rome during Nero's reign. And there is an elapse of some time between the first and second letters.

Peter wrote this letter to the Jewish Christians in Pontus, Galatia, Asia, Cappadocia, and Bithynia who were suffering bitter persecution. The main purpose of the letter was to encourage them in their trials (5:12).

1 Peter 1:1-25

(1) Peter, an apostle of Jesus Christ, to the chosen exiles who are sojourners scattered over Pontus, Galatia, Cappodacia, Asia, and Bithynia, (2) the people chosen according to the foreknowledge of God the Father and sanctified by the spirit, to obey Jesus Christ and sprinkled by his blood: May grace and peace be multiplied to you.

(3) Praise be to the God and Father of our Lord Jesus Christ, who according to his great mercy he has regenerated us and given us a living hope through the resurrection of Jesus Christ from the dead, (4) to an inheritance that is incorruptible, undefiled and unfading, and is kept in heaven for you (5) by the power of God and guarded through faith to a salvation ready to be revealed in the last day. (6) In this you rejoice, even though you suffer now through various trials, (7) so that your genuineness is proven by your faith, which is much more precious than gold, which though perishable is tested by fire, and may result in your praise and glory and honor at the revelation of Jesus Christ. (8) Without having seen him you love him, and without seeing him you have been glorified with an unspeakable exalted joy, (9) which is the outcome of your faith, the salvation of your

souls.

(10) The prophets, who prophesied about the spiritual blessings for you, sought out and inquired about this salvation. (11) They inquired about the nature and the times, which were made clear within by the Spirit of Christ, foretelling the sufferings of Christ and the subsequent glory. (12) It was revealed to them that they were not serving themselves but you, in the things which were announced through those who preached the good news to you by the Holy Spirit sent from heaven, things which the angels desire to look into.

(13) Therefore gird up your minds, be sober, and fix your hope completely in the grace that is coming to you at the revelation of Jesus Christ. (14) As obedient children, do not fashion yourselves by the passions of your former ignorance, (15) but according to the Holy One who called you so that you will be holy in all your conduct. (16) For it is written, "You shall be holy, for I am holy."

(17) For if you call upon the Father, who judges by deeds rather than by partiality, be reverent in your sojourning of your time on earth, (18) knowing that you were redeemed from the vain conduct of your fathers, not with perishable things like silver and gold, (19) but with the precious blood of Christ, as a lamb without blemish or spot. (20) This was God's plan from the foundation of the world but was made manifest in these last days for your sake. (21) Through him you believe in God, who raised him from the dead and gave him glory, so that your faith and hope are in God.

(22) By obedience to the truth, you have purified your souls for a sincere love for the brothers. Love one another earnestly from the heart. (23) You have been regenerated, not by corruptible but by incorruptible seed, through the living and abiding word of God. (24) Because,

"All flesh is like grass,
and all its glory like a flower of grass.
The grass withers,
and the flower falls off;
(25) but the word of God remains forever."
And this is the good news preached to you.

1 Peter 2:1-25

(1) So, putting away all malice and all deceit and hypocrisy and envy and all slander, (2) crave, as new born babes, the pure milk of the word, so that by it you may grow in salvation, (3) since you have tasted of the kindness of the Lord.

(4) Come to him, a living stone, rejected by man, but chosen and precious in the sight of God, (5) and like living stones you are being built into a spiritual house to be a holy priesthood, to offer up spiritual sacrifices acceptable through Jesus Christ. (6) For it is written,

"Look, I am laying a stone in Zion, a chosen precious corner stone,
and he who believes in him will not be put to shame."
(7) Therefore to you who believe, he is precious, but to those who do not believe,
"A stone rejected by the builders
has become the head of the corner,"
(8) and
"A stumbling stone and a falling rock."
For they stumble because they disobey the word, and to this they were destined to do.

(9) But you are a chosen race, a royal priesthood, a holy nation, a people for God's possession, so that you may declare the manifestation of the power of him who called you out of darkness into his marvelous light. (10) Once you were no people, but now you are the people of God; once you had not received his mercy, but now you have received his mercy.

(11) Dear friends, I beg you, as sojourners and aliens, to abstain from carnal lusts, which war against the soul. (12) Live honorable lives among the pagans, so if they slander you as evildoers, they may see your good works and glorify God in a day of visitation.

(13) Submit yourselves to every authority of man for the sake of the Lord, whether to a king as supreme, (14) or to governors, as sent by him to punish the evildoers and to praise those who do right. (15) For it is the will of God to silence the ignorance of foolish men. (16) Live as free men, but do not use your freedom as a cloak for evil, but live as slaves of God. (17) Honor everyone, love the brotherhood, fear God, and honor the king.

(18) Servants be submissive to your masters with utmost respect, not only to the good and gentle, but also to the unreasonable. (19) For to suffer injustice and endure hardships with the awareness of God is a work of grace. (20) For what credit do you have if you are whipped for doing wrong and endure it? (21) For to this you have been called, because Christ also suffered for you, leaving an example for you to follow in his steps. (22) He committed no sin, and no guile was found in his mouth. (23) When he was reviled, he did not revile in return; when he suffered he did not threaten, but he trusted himself to him who judges righteously. (24) He himself bore our sins in his body on the tree, that we might die to sin and live to righteousness. By his stripes we are healed. (25) For you were as wandering sheep, but now you have returned to the Shepherd and Overseer of your souls.

1 Peter 3:1-22

(1) Wives, in the same way be submissive to your husbands, so that if any of them are disobedient to the word, they may be won over without a word by the conduct of their wives, (2) by observing the purity and

reverence of your lives. (3) Let not your beauty come from the outward adornment, such as braided hair, the wearing of gold jewelry and fine clothing, (4) but by the hidden person of the heart, an incorruptible meek and quiet spirit, which is of great value before God. (5) For this is the way the holy women who hoped in God adorned themselves and were submissive to their husbands, (6) as Sarah obeyed Abraham and called him lord; and you, who do good and letting no anxieties disturb you, are now her children.

(7) Husbands likewise, live together with understanding, and treat your wives with respect and honor them as the weaker sex, as joint heirs of the grace of life, so that your prayers may not be hindered.

(8) Finally, all of you, be of one mind, sympathetic, loving as brothers, compassionate, humble, (9) never returning evil for evil or reviling for reviling, but on the contrary, blessing instead, because for this you were called that you might inherit a blessing. (10) For,

"Whoever loves life and would see good days

let him keep his tongue from evil

and his lips from speaking guile,

(11) let him turn away from evil and do good,

let him seek peace and pursue it.

(12) For the eyes of the Lord are on the righteous

and his ears are open to their petitions.

But the face of the Lord is against those who do evil."

(13) Who is going to harm you if you are zealous to do good? (14) But it you should suffer because of righteousness, you are blessed. But do not be afraid of their threats, and do not be troubled; (15) but in your hearts be consecrated to Christ as Lord, and always be ready to make a defense to everyone who asks you concerning the hope that is in you, (16) but with meekness and reverence, and with a good conscience, so that those who slander you may be put to shame because of your good behavior in Christ. (17) For it is better, if it is God's will, to suffer doing good than doing evil. (18) For Christ also died for sins once for all, the innocent for the guilty, so that he might bring us to God, being put to death in the flesh, but made alive in the spirit; (19) in which he also preached to the spirits in prison, (20) who disobeyed God when Noah was preparing the ark, but God had been patient with them. Only a few, which were eight, were saved through water. (21) As a figure of speech, you are saved through baptism, not the putting away of the filth of the flesh, but the answer of a good conscience before God, through the resurrection of Jesus Christ, (22) who, having gone to heaven, is at the right hand of God, with angels, authorities and powers subject to him.

1 Peter 4:1-19

(1) Therefore, since Christ suffered in the flesh, you also should arm yourself with the same mindset, because whoever has suffered in the flesh

has ceased from sin, (2) so as to live the rest of his life no longer in the lusts of the flesh but in the will of God. (3) For you have spent enough time doing what the pagans like to do, living lives of sensuality, lust, drunkenness, carousals, drinking parties and abominable idolatries. (4) They are surprised that you do not run with them into this excess of dissipation, and they slander you; (5) but they will give an account to him who is ready to judge the living and the dead. (6) For this is why the good news was preached to the dead, that though they are judged according to men in the flesh, they may live according to God in the spirit.

(7) The end of all things is near. Therefore be of sound mind and a clear head for prayers; (8) and above all things have a love for one another, because love covers a multitude of sins; (9) practice hospitality without complaining; (10) use your gift to minister to one another as good stewards of the manifold grace of God. (11) Whoever speaks, let him speak as the oracles of God; whoever ministers, let him do it with the strength given to him by God, so that in all things God may be glorified through Jesus Christ, to whom is the glory and the might unto the ages of the ages. Amen.

(12) Dear friends, do not be surprised at the fiery trial coming upon you to test you, as though something strange was happening to you. (13) But rejoice as you share the sufferings of Christ, so that when his glory is revealed you may rejoice exceedingly. (14) If you are insulted for the name of Christ, you are blessed, because the glorious Spirit of God rests upon you. (15) But let not any of you suffer as a murderer, or a thief, or an evildoer, or an agitator; (16) but as a Christian let him not be ashamed, but glorify God by that name. (17) For the time has come for judgment to begin with the household of God; and if it begins with us, what will be the end of those who disobey the gospel of God? (18) And,

"If it is difficult for the righteous to be saved,
where will the ungodly and sinner appear?"

(19) Therefore let those who suffer according to the will of God continue in doing good and entrust their lives to their faithful Creator.

1 Peter 5:1-14

(1) Therefore I exhort the elders, as a co-elder and witness of the sufferings of Christ, and a partaker of the glory that is about to be revealed, (2) shepherd the flock of God among you, not by constraint, but willingly, according to God; not for personal gain, but eagerly; (3) and do not lord it over those allotted to your charge, but be an example to your flock. (4) And when the Chief Shepherd appears, you will receive the unfading crown of glory.

(5) You younger men must also submit to older men; and all of you, clothe yourselves with humility toward one another, because "God resists the arrogant, but gives grace to the humble."

(6) Be humble therefore under the mighty hand of God, so that he may exalt you in due time, (7) casting all your anxiety on him, for he cares for you.

(8) Be sober and stay awake. Your adversary, the devil, is like a roaring lion walking about and looking for someone to devour. (9) Stand up against him, being firm in the faith, knowing that you are suffering the same kind of suffering as your brothers throughout the world. (10) And the God of all grace, who called you to his eternal glory in Christ, after you have suffered a little while, will himself restore, establish and strengthen you.

(11) To him be the power to the eternal ages. Amen.

(12) I have written to you through Silas, whom I regard as a faithful brother, exhorting and declaring this to be the true grace of God; stand fast in it.

(13) She who is in Babylon, chosen together with you, and Mark, my son, sends you greetings. (14) Greet one another with a kiss of love. Peace be to all of you who are in Christ.

Introduction to 2 Peter

The author of this letter is Simon Peter, and he identifies himself as a slave and apostle of Jesus Christ. He uses the first person singular pronoun to make the letter a very personal one (1:12-15). He refers to his experience at the transfiguration of Jesus (1:16-18), and he claims that this is his second letter (3:1). He refers to Paul as "our beloved brother Paul." He seemed to be familiar with Paul's prison letters. He says that there are some things in them that are hard to understand, which the ignorant and unstable twist to their own destruction (3:15,16).

This letter was written near the end of Peter's life (1:12-15). It is interesting to note that Paul's second letter to Timothy was near the end of his life (2 Ti. 4:6). Peter and Paul were both executed by Nero. Peter was crucified, but Paul was a Roman, so they could not crucify him. But both died about the same time in the reign of Nero.

Greedy, false teachers threatened the health of the church. Peter warns them against the evil effects of these immoral teachers. He compares them to the dog, which turns to his own vomit, and the sow that wallows in the mud. Peter tells us that he has written both letters "as reminders to stimulate you to wholesome thinking" (3:1). The letters are still relevant for us today, because we still need to be stimulated for wholesome thinking.

2 Peter 1:1-21

(1) Simon Peter, slave and apostle of Jesus Christ, to those who through the righteousness of our God and Savior Jesus Christ share a faith as precious as ours. (2) May grace and peace be multiplied to you through the knowledge of God and Jesus our Lord.

(3) His divine power has given us all things pertaining to life and godliness through the knowledge of the one who called us into his glory and excellence, (4) through which he has given us very great and precious promises, so that we can become sharers of his divine nature, escaping from the corruption of the world caused by evil desires.

(5) For this very reason, make every effort to add to your faith moral excellence; and to moral excellence, knowledge; (6) and to knowledge, self-control; and to self-control, fortitude; and to fortitude, godliness; (7) and to godliness, brotherly affection; and to brotherly affection, love. (8) For if these qualities are in you and are abounding, they will keep you from being useless or unfruitful in the full knowledge of our Lord Jesus Christ. (9) For whoever lacks these qualities is blind or near-sighted, being forgetful of the cleansing of his past sins. (10) Therefore, brothers, be more diligent to confirm your calling and election, for it you do these things you will never fail. (11) Then you will be triumphantly admitted into the eternal kingdom

of our Lord and savior Jesus Christ.

(12) So I will always remind you concerning these things even though you are grounded in the truth that you have. (13) And I think that it is right that I continue to arouse you as long as I remain in the tent of this body, (14) knowing that I will soon be putting off this earthly tabernacle, as indeed our Lord Jesus Christ informed me. (15) But I will seek to make it possible for you to always remember these things after I have departed.

(16) For we did not follow cleverly devised fables when we made known to you the power and presence of our Lord Jesus Christ, but we have seen with our eyes the majesty of that one. (17) For when he received honor and glory from God the Father, the voice came to him by the majestic splendor, "This is my beloved son with whom I am well-pleased." (18) We ourselves heard this voice out of heaven when we were with him on the holy mountain. (19) And this more firmly establishes the message of the prophets, to which you will do well to take heed as a lamp shining in a murky place, until the day dawns and the morning star rises in your hearts. (20) First of all you must know that no prophecy of scripture is a personal interpretation, (21) because no prophecy ever came by the will of man, but men spoke from God by the Holy Spirit.

2 Peter 2:1-22

(1) But there were also false prophets among the people, as there will also be false teachers among you, who will secretly bring in heresies of destruction, even denying the Master who bought them, bringing upon themselves swift destruction. (2) Many will follow the licentiousness of them, and because of them the way of the truth will be blasphemed. (3) And in their greed they will exploit you with their counterfeit arguments; their punishment for a long time has not been idle, and perdition is not asleep.

(4) For if God did not spare sinning angels, but consigning them to gloomy dungeons to be kept until judgment; (5) and if he did not spare the ancient world (except Noah, preacher of righteousness, whom he watched over with seven others), but brought a flood on a world of ungodly men; (6) and if he covered with ashes the cities of Sodom and Gomorra and condemned them, making them an example of what is going to happen to the ungodly; (7) and if he rescued Lot, who was distressed by the lascivious lives of the wicked (8) (for that righteous man, living among them day after day, was tormented in his righteous soul by seeing and hearing about their wicked deeds)— (9) The Lord knows how to deliver the godly out of trials, but he keeps the unjust under chastisement until the Day of Judgment.

(10) Most of all he will punish those who follow the corrupt desires of the sinful nature and despise authority. Arrogant and bold, they are not afraid to insult celestial beings, (11) yet even angels being greater in strength and power do not bring slanderous accusations against them in the presence

of the Lord.

(12) These men are like wild beasts without reason, born to be captured and destroyed, sneer at what they do no understand, and in their corruption they will perish, (13) suffering the reward of their wickedness. They count it a pleasure to revel in the daytime. (14) With eyes full of adultery they cannot cease form sinning. They entice weak souls. They have hearts trained in greed, accursed children! (15) They erred, forsaking a straight way, and following the way of Balaam, the son Beor, who loved the wages of unrighteousness; (16) but he was rebuked for his own transgression; a dumb donkey spoke with the voice of a man and restrained the prophet's madness.

(17) These men are springs without water and mists driven by a storm. The gloom of darkness has been reserved for them. (18) For speaking big words of vanity, and by appealing to the lustful desires of the sinful nature, they entice those who barely escape from those who live in error. (19) While they promise them freedom, they themselves are slaves of corruption; for a man is a slave to whatever has mastered him. (20) For if, after they have escaped the defilement of the world by a full knowledge of Jesus Christ, they are again entangled and defeated, the last state has become worse than the first. (21) For it would have been better for them not to have known the way of righteousness than after knowing it to turn back from the holy commandment. (22) For to them the proverbs are true, "The dog returns to his own vomit," and, "The sow is washed to wallow in the mud."

2 Peter 3:1-18

(1) This is the second letter I have written to you, and both of them as reminders to arouse you to wholesome thinking, (2) bringing to remembrance the words spoken by the holy prophets and your apostles of the commandments of our Lord and Savior.

(3) First of all, you must know that in the last days there will be mockers who will scoff, following the desires of the flesh, (4) and saying, "Where is the promise of his coming? For ever since our fathers fell asleep, everything remains as it was from the beginning of creation." (5) They take their view and ignore the fact that by the word of God the heavens existed and earth was formed out of water and by water, (6) through which the ancient world was flooded by water and destroyed. (7) The present heavens and earth by the same words are stored up for fire, being kept for the Day of Judgment and the destruction of ungodly men.

8) But, dear friends, remember that one day with the Lord is as a thousand years, and a thousand years is as one day. (9) The Lord is not slow concerning his promise as some understand slowness; but he is long-suffering toward you, and it is not his will for anyone to perish, but for all to come to repentance.

(10) But the Lord will come as a thief, and the heavens will pass away with a rushing sound, and the elements will be dissolved by fire. (11) Since all these things are to be dissolved, what sort of people should you be? You should live holy and godly lives, (12) waiting patiently and working eagerly for the coming of the day of God; that day the heavens will be set on fire and dissolved and the elements will melt with fire! (13) But we wait, according to his promise, for new heavens and a new earth in which righteousness dwells.

(14) Therefore, dear friends, since you look for these things, be diligent to be found by him to be spotless and unblemished and at peace; (15) and consider that the long-suffering of our Lord means salvation, as also Paul, our dear friend, wrote to you according to the wisdom given to him, (16) speaking of these things as he does in all his letters. There are some things in his letters difficult to understand, which the ignorant and unstable twist to their own destruction as they do the rest of the scriptures. (17) Therefore, dear friends, since you have been forewarned, be on guard lest you are lead astray by lawless men and lose your own stability. (18) But grow in grace and knowledge of our Lord and Savior Jesus Christ. To him be the glory both now and unto the eternal day.

Introduction to 1 John

John, the son of Zebedee, is the author of this letter. He is the Apostle John who wrote the Gospel of John, the other two letters of John, and the Revelation. He was a first cousin of Jesus, being a son of Salome, a sister of Mary. He was a fisherman when Jesus called him to follow him, and he became one of Jesus' inner circle, together with James and Peter. He was "the disciple whom Jesus loved" (John 13:23).

It is difficult to be certain about the date of the letter, but there are certain factors that we can consider. The early form of Gnosticism reflected in the denunciations of the letter and the advanced age of John suggest the end of the first century. The letter was addressed to believers, but it did not indicate who they were or where they lived. This suggests that it was a circular letter sent to many places. Early Christian writers indicate that John lived in Ephesus during most of his later years (c. 70 A.D.– 100 A.D.).

John wrote this letter with two basic purposes in mind: to expose false teachers, and to give believers the assurance of salvation. The false teachers taught that matter was evil. Since the body was evil, it was to be treated harshly. This also led to licentiousness. Since matter – and not the breaking of God's law (1 John 3:4) – was considered evil, the breaking of his law was of no consequence. John struck at this heresy by showing them that the new life of salvation brings forth a new life-style of righteousness. John showed that the eternal Son of God was actually made a man in the person of Jesus and that a believer can have the assurance of eternal salvation. Real faith and divine love are expressed in our love for others, and we no longer live in sin, because we have been born of God and the seed of righteousness controls our daily walk (3:9,10).

1 John 1:1-10

(1) What was from the beginning, what we have heard, what we have seen with our eyes, what we saw and touched with our hands, concerning the word of life – (2) and the life was revealed, and we have seen and bear witness and proclaim to you the life eternal, which was with the Father and was revealed to us. (3) What we have seen and have heard, we proclaim to you so that you may have fellowship with us. Indeed our fellowship is with the Father and his son, Jesus Christ. (4) These things we write to you so that our joy may be complete.

(5) This is the message we heard from him and we proclaim it to you, that God is light and in him there is no darkness. (6) If we say we have fellowship with him and walk in darkness, we lie and do not practice the truth. (7) But if we walk in the light as he is in the light, we have fellowship with each other and the blood of Jesus Christ cleanses us from all sin. (8) If we say that we have no sin, we deceive ourselves and the truth is not in us.

(9) If we confess our sins, he is faithful and righteous to forgive us of our sins and cleanse us from all iniquity. (10) If we say that we have not sinned, we make him a liar and his word is not in us.

1 John 2:1-29

(1) My dear children, I am writing these things to you so that you may not sin. But if anyone does sin we have an advocate with the father – Jesus Christ, the righteous; (2) and he is the atonement for our sins, and not only for our sins but also for the sins of the whole world. (3) And by this we know that we have known him if we keep his commandments. (4) The person who says, "I know him," but does not keep his commandments, is a liar and the truth is not in him. (5) But whoever keeps his word, truly the love of God has been perfected in him. By this we know that we are in him: (6) the person who says that he abides in him ought to walk as that one walked.

(7) Beloved, I am not writing a new commandment to you but an old commandment you have had from the beginning; the old commandment is the word which you have heard. (8) Yet a new commandment I am writing to you, which is true in him and in you, that the darkness is passing and the true light is now shining. (9) The person who says he is in the light but hates his brother is still in the darkness. (10) The person who loves his brother abides in the light, and there is no cause for sin in him. (11) But the person who hates his brother is walking in darkness, and he does not know where he is going, because the darkness has blinded his eyes.

(12) My dear children, I am writing to you because your sins have been forgiven through his name. (13) Fathers, I am writing to you because you know him who is from the beginning. Young men, I am writing to you because you have overcome the evil one.

(14) Children, I wrote to you because you know the father. Fathers, I wrote to you because you have know him who is from the beginning. Young men, I wrote to you because you are strong and the word of God abides in you and you have conquered the evil one.

(15) Do not love the world or the things in the world. If anyone loves the world, the love of the father is not in him. (16) For all that is in the world – the lust of the flesh, the lust of the eyes and the vainglory of life – does not come from the father but from the world. (17) And the world and all its allurements are passing away, but the one doing the will of God abides forever.

(18) Children, it is the last hour, and as you have heard that the antichrist is coming, now many antichrists have appeared; so we know that this is the last hour. (19) They went out from us, but they were not of us; for if they had been of us they would have remained with us, but their going out from us made it clear that they were not of us. (20) But you have an

anointing from the Holy One, so that all of you know the truth. (21) I did not write to you because you did not know the truth, but because you know it and because no lie comes from the truth. (22) Who is the liar? It is the one who denies that Jesus is the Christ. The one denying the Father and the Son is the antichrist. (23) No one who denies the Son has the Father. The one confessing the Son has the Father. (24) Keep what you heard from the beginning. If you keep what you heard from the beginning, both the Son and the Father will remain in you. (25) And the promise he gave us is the promise of eternal life.

(26) I wrote to you about those who would deceive you. (27) The anointing you received from him abides in you, and you have no need that anyone should teach you, because his anointing teaches you about all things, and it is true and is not a lie; just as it has taught you, abide in him.

(28) And now, dear children, abide in him, so that when he appears you will have boldness and not be ashamed in his presence. (29) If you know that he is righteous, you know that everyone walking in righteousness has been born of him.

1 John 3:1-24

(1) See what great love the Father has given us so that we should be called the children of God, and so we are. Therefore the world does not know us, because it did not know him. (2) Beloved, now we are children of God, but it does not yet appear what we shall be. We know that when he appears, we shall be like him, because we shall see him as he is. (3) Everyone who has this hope purifies himself, as he is pure.

(4) Everyone continuing in sin is transgressing the law: sin is transgressing the law. (5) You know that he came to take away sins, and in him there is no sin. (6) No one abiding in him continues to sin. No one who continues in sin has seen or knows him.

(7) Dear children, let no one lead you astray. He who practices righteousness is righteous, as he is righteous. (8) The one who continues in sin is of the devil, because the devil has sinned from the beginning. The reason the Son of God appeared was to destroy the works of the devil. (9) No one who is born of God will continue to sin, because his nature abides in him, and he cannot continue in sin because he has been born of God. (10) By this it is clear who are the children of God and who are the children of the devil; anyone who does not practice righteousness is not of God, nor he who does not love his brother.

(11) For the message which you heard from the beginning is this: that we should love one another. (12) We should not be like Cain, who was of the evil one and murdered his brother. And why did he murder him? It was because his works were evil and his brother's were righteous. (13) Do not be surprised, brothers, if the world hates you. (14) We know that we

have passed from death to life because we love our brothers. He who does not love remains in death. (15) Everyone who hates his brother is a murderer, and we know that no murderer has eternal life abiding in him.

(16) By this we know what love is: that Christ laid down his life for us, and we ought to lay down our lives for our brothers. (17) If anyone has material possessions and sees his brother in need but has no compassion for him, how does the love of God abide in him? (18) Dear children, let us not love in theory or in speech but in practice and in sincerity.

(19) By this we shall know that we are of the truth, and our hearts are at rest in his presence (20) when our hearts condemn us, for God is greater than our hearts and he knows all things. (21) Beloved, if our hearts do not condemn us, we have confidence with God, (22) and whatever we ask we receive from him, because we keep his commandments and do the things that are pleasing in his sight. (23) And this is his commandment: to believe in his Son Jesus Christ and love one another as he commanded us. (24) All who keep his commandments abide in him and he in them. And by this we know that he abides in us, by the spirit which he has given us.

1 John 4:1-21

(1) Beloved, do not believe every spirit, but test the spirits to see if they are from God, because many false prophets have gone out into the world. (2) This is how you may recognize the Spirit of God: every spirit which acknowledges that Jesus Christ has come in the flesh is of God, (3) and every spirit that does not acknowledge Jesus is not of God. This is of the spirit of the antichrist, which you have heard is coming, and now is already in the world. (4) You are from God, dear children, and you have overcome them, because greater is He who is in you than he who is in the world. (5) They are of the world; therefore they speak the language of that world and the world listens to them. (6) We are of God; he who knows God listens to us; he who is not of God does not listen to us. From this we know the spirit of truth and the spirit of deception.

(7) Beloved, love one another, because love is of God, and everyone who loves is born of God and knows God. (8) The one who does not love does not know God, for God is love. (9) In this the love of God has been manifested in us, that God sent his only begotten Son into the world so that we might live through him. (10) In this is love, not that we loved God, but that he loved us and sent his Son for the atonement of our sins. (11) Beloved, since God so loved us, we also ought to love one another. (12) No one has ever seen God. If we love one another, God abides in us and his love is perfected in us.

(13) By this we know that we abide in him and he in us, because of the spirit he has given us. (14) And we have seen and witness that the Father sent the Son to be the Savior of the world. (15) Whoever confesses that Jesus

is the Son of God, God abides in him, and he in God. (16) Thus we have come to know and believe the love, which God has for us.

God is love. The one abiding in love abides in God and God abides in him. (17) By this, love is perfected with us that we will have confidence in the Day of Judgment, because as he is so also are we in this world. (18) There is no fear in love, but perfect love casts out fear, because fear involves punishment, and the one who has fear has not been perfected in love. (19) You love, because he first loved you. (20) If anyone says, "I love God," but hates his brother, he is a liar. For the one who does not love his brother, whom he has seen, cannot love God, whom he has not seen. (21) This is the commandment we have from him: he who loves God must also love his brother.

1 John 5:1-21

(1) Everyone who believes that Jesus is the Christ has been born of God, and everyone who loves the parent loves the child. (2) We can be sure that we love the children of God when we love God and obey his commandments. (3) For to love God is to keep his commandments, and his commandments are not burdensome, (4) for everyone born of God overcomes the world. The victory that overcomes the world is our faith. (5) Who, then, is the one who overcomes the world? It is the one who believes that Jesus is the Son of God.

(6) This is the one who came through water and blood, Jesus Christ, not by water only, but by the water and the blood. It is the Spirit who testifies, because the Spirit is truth. (7) There are three that testify, (8) the Spirit, the water, and the blood; and these three are in one accord. (9) We receive the testimony of men, but the testimony of God is greater; for this is the testimony of God concerning his son. (10) The one who believes in the Son of God has the testimony in himself. The one who does not believe has made God a liar, because he has not believed in the testimony of God concerning his Son. (11) This is the testimony: God gave us eternal life, and this life is in his Son. (12) Whoever has the Son has life, and whoever does not have the Son does not have life.

(13) I have written these things to you, who believe in the name of the Son of God, so that you may know that you have eternal life. (14) This is the confidence that we have in him: if we ask according to his will he listens to us. (15) And we know that if he listens to us in whatever we ask, we know that we have received the answer to our requests.

(16) If anyone sees his brother committing a sin, which is not a deadly sin, he shall ask, and God shall give him life to any whose sins are not deadly. There is a deadly sin; and I do not say that you should pray about that. (17) All iniquity is sin, but not all sin is deadly.

(18) We know that everyone born of God does not live in sin, but the

Son of God keeps him, and the evil one does not touch him. (19) We know that we are of God, and the whole world lies in the power of the evil one. (20) We know also that the Son of God has come and has given us understanding that we might know who is true, and we are in him who is true even in his Son Jesus Christ. This is the true God and eternal life.

(21) Dear children, watch out for false gods!

Introduction to 2 John

The author is John the Apostle. There are several similarities to 1 John and the Gospel, which indicates that the same person wrote all three books. Note the following comparisons of Scriptures:

Gospel	1 John	2 John	
new commandment	John 13:34-35	1 John 2:7	2 John 5
the love of God	John 14:23	1 John 5:3	2 John 6
confess Jesus	1 John 4:2-3	2 John 7	
your joy may be full	John 15:11; 16:24	1 John 1:4	2 John 12

There are differences of opinion about who the chosen lady is. Some think that it is some Christian woman in the province of Asia. And the children are her children. Others think that the chosen lady is a figurative designation of a local church and that her children are members of that local church.

During the first two centuries there were traveling evangelists that took the gospel from place to place. Usually members of the church would take these missionaries into their homes and give them lodging and provisions for their journey. Gnostic teachers also relied on this practice. This letter was written to urge discernment in supporting traveling teachers; otherwise, they might unintentionally contribute to the promotion to heresy rather than truth.

2 John 1:1-13

(1) The elder to the elect Lady and her children, whom I love in the truth and not I alone but all who know the truth, (2) because of the truth which lives in us and will remain with us forever:

(3) Grace, mercy and peace from God the Father and from Jesus Christ the Son of the Father will be with us in truth and love.

(4) I was greatly delighted to find some of your children walking in the truth, as we were commanded by the Father. (5) And now, Lady, I make this entreaty not as a new commandment but one which we have had from the beginning—that we love one another. (6) And this is love: that we walk in obedience to his commandments, just as you have heard from the beginning, that you walk in love.

(7) Many deceivers, who do not acknowledge that Jesus Christ has come in the flesh, have gone out into the world. Such a one is the deceiver and the antichrist. (8) Be careful yourselves that you do not lose what you worked for, but that you may have a full reward. (9) Everyone who runs ahead and does not abide in the teaching of Christ does not have God. The

one who abides in the teaching has both the Father and the Son. (10) If anyone comes to you and does not have this teaching, do not receive him into your house or welcome him; (11) for the one who welcomes him shares in his evil works.

(12) Though I have many things to write to you, I would rather not use paper and ink, but I am hoping to speak to you face to face, so that our joy may be complete.

(13) The children of your elect sister greet you.

Introduction to 3 John

The author is John the Apostle. The John who wrote the Gospel and Revelation wrote all three epistles. And perhaps they were all written late in the first century. Diotrephes, a dictatorial leader of the church, rejected evangelists that were sent out by John. He even excommunicated members who showed hospitality to John's messengers.

Gaius was a Christian in one of the churches in the province of Asia. Gaius was a common Roman name. Diotrephes must have been a man of considerable influence to be able to exclude people from the church fellowship.

The main purpose of this letter is to secure hospitality and support for the missionaries sent out by John. Diotrephes, the ambitious leader of the church rejects the elder's authority and refuses to receive the missionaries and tries to force others to do likewise. John, to gain his purpose despite Diotrephes' opposition, writes Gaius. He urges him to continue supporting the evangelists. John also recommends Demetrius to Gaius. He also mentions that he plans to visit them and at that time he will talk to Diotrephes. This gives us some insight into the problem of authority and influence in the church at the end of the first century.

3 John 1:1-15

(1) The elder to the beloved Gaius whom I truly love.

(2) Beloved, I pray that you may prosper in all things and that you will be in good health, even as your soul prospers. (3) For I was thrilled with joy when the brothers came and testified of your fidelity to the truth as you continue walking in the truth. (4) I have no greater joy than to hear that my children are walking in the truth.

(5) Beloved, you are being faithful to care for the brothers even though they are strangers. (6) They have told the church of your love; and you will do well to send them on their way in a manner worthy of God. (7) For they went out for the sake of the Name, taking nothing from the Gentiles. (8) Therefore we ought to support such men so that we can be partners in the truth.

(9) I wrote to the church, but Diotrephes, who loves to be first, does not acknowledge our authority. (10) Therefore, if I come, I will call attention to what he is doing, bringing unjustified charges against us with evil words. And not satisfied with that, he himself refuses to receive our brothers, and he interferes with those who would do so, and expels them from the church!

(11) Beloved, do not imitate what is evil, but what is good. The one doing good is of God; the one doing evil has not seen God. (12) Demetrius is well-spoken of by everyone, even from the truth itself; we also give our

witness, and you know that our witness is true.

(13) I had many things to write to you, but I do not wish to write to you with ink and pen. (14) But I hope to see you soon and we will talk face to face. (15) Peace to you. The friends greet you. Greet the friends by name.

Introduction to Jude

The author identifies himself as Jude (1:1). It is the form of the Hebrew name, "Judah," and the Greek, "Judas." It was a common name among the Jews. Jude says he is the brother of James. Usually a person would describe himself as the son of his father but he identifies himself as the brother of James. Perhaps that was because of the prominence of James in the church of Jerusalem.

There are similarities between 2 Peter and Jude (cf. 2 Pe 2:4-9 with Jude 1:4-18). One may have borrowed from the other or they may have both had a common source.

The recipients of the letter are Jews or Gentiles, or both. There is no reference to the location. Jude had planned to write to them about salvation, but certain immoral men had infiltrated the church and were perverting the grace of God. It seems that these false teachers were trying to convince the believers that being saved by grace gave them license to sin. So Jude thought it imperative that they know the truth about God's saving grace. We still need to be on guard against such insidious teachings.

Jude 1-25

(1) Jude, a slave of Jesus Christ and brother of James, To those who have been called, who are loved by God the Father and are kept by Jesus Christ: (2) May mercy, peace and love be multiplied to you.

(3) Dear friends, while I was making all haste to write to you about our common faith, I was constrained to write and exhort you to contend for the faith once delivered to the saints. (4) For some men, whose doom was written down long ago, have secretly slipped in. They are ungodly men who pervert the grace of our God and make it a license for immorality and disown our only Master and Lord, Jesus Christ.

(5) Though you already know, I want to remind you that the Lord rescued his people from the land of Egypt, but afterward destroyed those who did not believe. (6) And the angels who did not keep their own dominion but left their proper habitation have been kept in everlasting chains in darkness until the great day of judgment, (7) just as Sodom and Gomorra and the surrounding cities, who in like manner committed fornication and indulged in unnatural lust, serve as an exhibit of perpetual punishment of everlasting fire.

(8) Likewise these dreamers defile the flesh, despise authority, and revile celestial beings. (9) But even the archangel Michael, when he was contending with the devil about the body of Moses, did not dare to condemn him in insulting words, but said, "The Lord rebuke you." (10) But these men revile the things they do not understand, and they are corrupted by the

natural instincts, like brute animals, by things that they do understand. (11) Woe to them! They have gone the way of Cain; they have abandoned themselves to Balaam's error for pay, and they have perished in the rebellion of Korah.

(12) They are hidden reefs in your love feasts, eating with you without reverence, caring only for themselves, rainless clouds carried away by winds, autumn trees without fruit and uprooted — twice dead. (13) They are fierce waves of the sea, casting up the foam of their own shame, wandering stars for which the gloom of darkness has been reserved forever.

(14) Enoch, the seventh from Adam, prophesied about these men, saying, "Look! The Lord comes with myriads of his saints (15) to execute judgment upon all, and to convict all the ungodly concerning their works of ungodliness and all the harsh things the ungodly sinners have spoken against him." (16) These men are grumblers and faultfinders, following the desires of their lusts; their lips speak arrogant things, and they flatter others for personal gain. (17) But you, dear friends, remember the words spoken by the apostles of our Lord Jesus Christ, (18) because they told you, "In the last days there will be mockers who will follow the desires of their own lusts." (19) These worldly men, who do not have the Spirit, are the ones who cause division.

(20) But you, dear friends, build up yourselves in your most holy faith and pray in the Holy Spirit. (21) Keep yourselves in the love of God, waiting for the mercy of our Lord Jesus Christ for eternal life. (22) Have mercy on those who are wavering; (23) snatch them out of the fire; have mercy on others with fear, hating even the clothes defiled by the flesh.

(24) Now to him who is able to keep you without stumbling and to set before you his glory unblemished with exultation, (25) to the only God, our Savior through Jesus Christ our Lord, be glory, majesty, power and authority before all ages, now and forever. Amen.

Introduction to Revelation

John the Apostle is the author of Revelation. He identifies himself 4 times (1:1,4,9; 22:8). He was a Jew, well-versed in Scripture, a leader in the church who was well known to the churches of Asia Minor, and a devout Christian fully convinced that the Christian faith would soon triumph over the demonic forces of evil. It was a severe time of persecution in the latter part of the reign of Domitian. The Roman authorities were beginning to enforce the cult of emperor worship. They demanded that people proclaim that Caesar was Lord, but the Christians proclaimed that Christ was Lord. That put the Christians in bitter hostility with the authorities.

John writes the book to the Christians in the province of Asia. They were being persecuted because they would not worship the statue of the Roman emperor, which was erected in the leading cities. They refused to do so because they were loyal to Jesus. John was loyal to Jesus, so he was sent to the Island of Patmos for punishment. John was in the Spirit on the Lord's Day when he received these divine visions. He was instructed to record them and send them to the seven churches in Asia Minor. The message was that Christianity would triumph over all evil. God's people are sealed and protected against any spiritual harm. When Christ returns, the wicked will be destroyed, and God's people will enter into glory and be forever blessed.

Different methods of interpreting the book:

Preterists understand the book in its first-century setting.

Historicists believe it describes from Patmos to the end of history.

Futurists understand the book telling about the end time.

Idealists view it as symbolic pictures of good over evil.

Whatever view you may have, you are blessed if you read it (1:3). The central message of the book is that Jesus is Lord, and if we serve him, we will be blessed in this life and the life to come.

Revelation 1:1-20

(1) A Revelation given by Jesus Christ, which God gave to show his slaves what was soon to happen; and he made it known by sending his angel to his slave John, (2) who testifies to the word of God and the witness of Jesus Christ to all things that he saw. (3) Blessed is the one who reads aloud the words of this prophecy, and blessed are those who hear and keep that which is written in it, for the time is near.

(4) John to the seven churches in Asia:

Grace and peace from the one who is, and who was, and who is coming, and from the seven spirits which are before his throne, (5) and from Jesus Christ, the faithful witness, the firstborn from the dead, and the ruler of the kings of the earth. To the one who delivered us from our sins by his blood— (6) and he has made us a kingdom of priests for his God and Father—to him be glory and power forever and ever.   Amen.

(7) Look! He comes on the clouds, and every eye shall see him, even those who pierced him, and all the tribes of the earth mourn because of him. So may it be.   Amen.

(8) "I am the Alpha and the Omega," says the Lord, "the God, who is, and who was, and who is coming, the Almighty."

(9) I, John, your brother and partaker with you in the affliction and the kingdom and the perseverance in Jesus, was on the island called Patmos because of the word of God and the testimony of Jesus. (10) I was in the Spirit on the Lord's day, and I heard a voice behind me like a trumpet, (11) saying, "What you see write in a book and send it to the seven churches, to Ephesus, and to Smyrna, and to Pergamum, and to Thyatira, and to Sardis, and to Philadelphia, and to Laodicea."

(12) Then I turned to see the voice that was speaking to me. And when I turned I saw seven golden lampstands, (13) and in the middle of the lampstands one like a son of man, clothed in a robe reaching to his feet and with a golden girdle around his breast. (14) His head and his hair were white as white wool, as white as snow, and his eyes were like a flame of fire; (15) his feet were like burnished bronze, refined as in a furnace, and the voice of him was as the sound of many waters; (16) in his right hand were seven stars, and out of his mouth came a sharp two-edged sword; and his face was like the sun shining at midday.

(17) And when I saw him, I fell at his feet as though dead. And he laid his right hand upon me, saying, "Do not be afraid, I am the first and the last, (18) and I am the living one, I was dead but now I am alive for evermore, and I have the keys of death and of Hades. (19) Write therefore what you have seen, the things that are about to take place. (20) The mystery of the seven stars which you saw in my right hand, and the seven golden lampstands, is this: The seven stars are the messengers of the seven churches, and the seven lampstands are the seven churches.

Revelation 2:1-29

(1) "To the messenger of the church in Ephesus write:

"The one holding the seven churches in his right hand and walking in the midst of the seven golden lampstands says, (2) I know your works, your labor and patient endurance, and that you cannot tolerate evil men, and you did test those who were calling themselves apostles, but are not, and you found them to be impostors. (3) And I know your patient endurance and that you have suffered for my name and that you have not grown weary.

(4) "But I have this against you, that you have left your first love. (5) Think how far you have fallen. Repent and do as you once did. Unless you repent I will come and remove your lampstand from its place. (6) But you do

hate the works of the Nicolaitans, and so do I.

(7) "The one who has an ear, let him hear what the Spirit says to the churches. To him who conquers I will give the right to eat of the tree of life in the paradise of God.

(8) "To the messenger of the church in Smyrna write:

"The one who is first and last, who was dead but has come to life, says, (9) I know your affliction and your poverty (but you are rich). Those who are slandering you call themselves Jews but they are not, but they are a synagogue of Satan. (10) Do not fear what you are about to suffer. See, the devil is about to cast some of you into prison so that you may be tried, and you will be afflicted for ten days. Be faithful until death, and I will give you the crown of life.

(11) "The one who has an ear, let him hear what the Spirit says to the churches. He who overcomes shall not be hurt by the second death.

(12) "To the messenger of the church in Pergamum write:

"The one who has the sharp two-edged sword says, (13) I know you live in the place where Satan has his throne, and you hold fast my name; and you have not renounced your faith in me, even in the days of Antipas, my faithful witness, who was put to death among you, where Satan dwells.

(14) "But I have a few things against you, because you have some there who hold to the teaching of Balaam, who taught Balak to cast a stumbling-block before the sons of Israel, to eat things sacrificed to idols and to commit fornication. (15) And you also have some who, in the same way, hold the teachings of the Nicolaitans. (16) Therefore repent; otherwise, I will come to you quickly and fight with them with the sword of my mouth.

(17) "The one who has an ear, let him hear what the Spirit says to the churches. To him who overcomes, I will give the hidden manna, and I will give him a white stone, and on the white stone is written a new name, which no man knows, only the one receiving it.

(18) "To the messenger of the church in Thyatira write:

"The words of the Son of God, whose eyes are like a flame of fire and whose feet like burnished bronze: (19) I know your works, love, faith, and service, and your perseverance, and that your works now are greater than at first.

(20) "But I have this against you that you tolerate the woman Jezebel, who calls herself a prophetess; and her teaching is leading my slaves astray, so that they commit fornication and eat food sacrificed to idols. (21) I gave her time to repent, but she did not want to repent of her immorality. (22) So I will cast her into a sickbed, and the ones committing fornication with her I will put into terrible suffering, unless they repent of her works; (23) and her children I will put to death; and all the churches will know that I am the one who searches minds and hearts, and I will reward each of you according to your works. (24) But I say to the rest of you in Thyatira, who do not adhere to this teaching, who do not know what they call the deep secrets of Satan, I will put no other burden on you; (25) Nevertheless hold fast to

what you have until I come.

(26) "And to the one who overcomes and continues in doing my will to the end, I will give him authority over the nations, just as I also receive authority from my father; (27) and he will shepherd them with an iron staff, and shatter them like clay vessels, just as I also received authority from my Father. (28) And I will give him the morning star. (29) The one who has an ear, let him hear what the Spirit says to the churches.

Revelation 3:1-22

(1) "To the messenger of the church in Sardis write:

"The one having the seven spirits of God and the seven stars says, Wake up! Secure the things left that are about to die, (2) for your works have not measured up to godly standards. (3) Remember how you accepted what you heard; obey it and repent. If you will not wake up, I will come as a thief, and you will not know the hour that I will come upon you.

(4) "But there are a few people in Sardis who have not soiled their clothes, and they will walk with me in white, for they are worthy. (5) So whoever overcomes will be clothed in white clothes, and his name will never be blotted out of the book of life, and I will confess his name before my Father and before his angels. (6) The one who has an ear, let him hear what the Spirit says to the churches.

(7) "To the messenger of the church in Philadelphia write:

"The true and Holy one, who has the key of David, who opens and no one shuts, and who shuts and no one opens says, (8) I know your works. Behold, I have set before you an open door that no one can shut. Even though you have little power, you have kept my word and have not denied my name. (9) Behold, I will make some of those of the synagogue of Satan, who claim to be Jews but are lying frauds, to come and worship before your feet, and they will learn that I have loved you. (10) Because you have kept my plea to stand fast, I also will deliver you from the hour of trial that is about to come upon all the earth, to test those living upon the earth.

(11) "I am coming quickly; hold fast to what you have, so that no one will take your crown. (12) To the one who conquers I will make him a pillar in the temple of my God, and he will never leave it; and I will write upon him the name of my God and the name of the city of my God, the new Jerusalem, which is coming out of heaven from my God, and my own new name. (13) The one who has an ear, let him hear what the Spirit says to the churches.

(14) "To the messenger of the church in Laodicea write:

"The Amen, the faithful and true witness, the prime source of the creation of God says, (15) I know your works, that you are neither cold nor hot. I wish you were either cold or hot. (16) So, because you are lukewarm, and neither cold nor hot, I am about to vomit you out of my mouth. (17) For you say, 'I am rich; I have become wealthy and I have everything I need,' and you do not know that you are wretched, miserable, poor, blind and naked. (18) I counsel you to buy from me refined gold, so you may be rich; and white clothes to wear, so you will not show the shame of your nakedness; and eye salve to anoint your eyes, so you can see.

(19) "As many as I love I rebuke and discipline; be hot therefore and repent. (20) Behold, I stand at the door and knock; if anyone hears my voice and opens the door, I will enter and we will dine together.

(21) "To the one who overcomes, I will sit with him on my throne, as I also overcame and sat with my Father on his throne. (22) To the one who has an ear, let him hear what the Spirit says to the churches."

Revelation 4:1-11

(1) After this I looked, and behold a door standing open in heaven, and the voice that I had first heard speaking to me like a trumpet said, "Come up here, and I will show you what must happen after this." And immediately I was in the Spirit. (2) And behold, there was a throne in heaven and on the throne sat one (3) whose appearance was like jasper and carnelian, and a rainbow around the throne, bright as emerald. (4) Around the throne were twenty-four thrones, and twenty-four elders were sitting upon the thrones, clothed in white clothes, and on their heads were golden crowns. (5) Out of the throne came forth lightening and voices and thunder; and seven lamps were burning before the throne, which are the seven spirits of God. (6) And before the throne was a sea like glassy crystal.

In a circle around the throne were four living creatures, full of eyes in front and behind. (7) The first living creature was like a lion, the second living creature was like a calf, the third living creature had the face of a man, and the fourth living creature was like an eagle in flight. (8) The four living creatures, each with six wings and full of eyes, around and within, never ceased, day or night, saying:

"Holy, holy, holy is the Lord God, the Almighty,
who was, and is, and is to come."

(9) Whenever the living creatures give glory and honor and thanks to the one sitting on the throne, who lives for ever and ever, (10) the twenty-four elders fall down before the one sitting on the throne, and they worship him who lives for ever and ever, and they cast their crowns before the throne, saying,

(11) "Worthy you are, our Lord and God,
to receive glory and honor and power,
for you created all things;
you willed that they exist so you created them."

Revelation 5:1-14

(1) I saw in the right hand of the one who sat on the throne a scroll written on both sides and sealed with seven seals, (2) and a mighty angel was proclaiming in a loud voice saying, "Who is worthy to break the seals and unroll the scroll?" (3) And no one in heaven or on the earth or under the earth was worthy to unroll the scroll and read it, (4) and I wept bitterly because no one was worthy to unroll the scroll and read it. (5) Then one of the elders said to me, "Do not weep; behold the lion of the tribe of Judah has conquered so that he can break the seven seals and unroll the scroll."

(6) And I saw between the throne and the four living creatures and in the midst of the elders a lamb standing having been slain and having seven horns and seven eyes, which are the seven spirits of God sent out into all the earth; (7) and he went and took the scroll from the one who sat on the throne. (8) And when he had taken the scroll the four living creatures and twenty-four elders fell down before the lamb, each with a harp and golden bowls full of incense which are the prayers of the saints, (9) and they sang a new song, saying, "You are worthy to break the seals and unroll the scroll for you were slain and by your blood you purchased men for God from every tribe and people and nation (10) and you made them to be a kingdom of priests, and they will reign upon the earth."

(11) I looked and I heard the voice of many angels, and the living creatures and the elders were around the throne; and the number of them was myriads of myriads and thousands of thousands. (12) They were saying in a loud voice,

"Worthy is the lamb who was slain
to receive power and wealth and wisdom and strength
and honor and glory and praise!"

(13) And I heard every creature in heaven and on the earth and under the earth in the sea, and all things therein, saying,

"To him who sits on the throne and to the Lamb
be blessing and honor and dominion forever and ever."

(14) Then the four living creatures said, "Amen!" and the elders fell down and worshipped.

Revelation 6:1-17

(1) I watched the Lamb open one of the seven seals, and I heard one of the living creatures saying with a sound of thunder, "Come!" (2) And behold I saw a white horse, and the one sitting on it had a bow, and a crown was given to him, and he went forth victorious and to conquer yet again.

(3) When he opened the second seal, I heard the second living creature say, "Come!" (4) And another horse, a fiery red one, went forth, and to its rider was given the power to take peace from the earth, so that men

should slay one another, and a great sword was given to him.

(5) When the third seal was opened, I heard the third living creature say, "Come!" And behold, I saw a black horse, and its rider had a balance in his hand. (6) I heard a voice in the midst of the four living creatures, saying, "A quart of wheat for a denarius, and three pecks of barley for a denarius, and do no harm to the oil and the wine."

(7) When he opened the fourth seal, I heard the fourth living creature say, "Come!" (8) And behold, I saw a pale green horse, and the name of the rider was Death, and Hades followed him. They were given authority over a fourth part of the earth to kill with the sword, and with famine and with pestilence, and by the wild beasts of the earth.

(9) When he opened the fifth seal, I saw under the altar the souls of the ones who had been slain for the word of God and for the testimony they bore. (10) They cried out with a great voice, "How long, Sovereign Lord, holy and true, until you vindicate us and avenge our blood on those who dwell upon the earth?" (11) Each of them was given a white robe; and they were told to wait a little longer, until the complete number of their fellow slaves and brothers were killed as they had been.

(12) When he opened the sixth seal, I saw that a great earthquake had occurred; and the sun became black as sackcloth made of black goat hair, the full moon became like blood, (13) and the stars of heaven fell to the earth, as unripe figs shaken loose by a strong wind; (14) and the sky vanished like a scroll being rolled up, and every mountain and island were moved from their places.

(15) The kings of the earth, the great men, the military commanders, the rich and the strong—everybody, whether slaves or free—hid themselves in the caves and the rocks of the mountains, (16) calling to the mountains and the rocks, "Fall on us and hide us from the one sitting on the throne and from the wrath of the Lamb, (17) for the great day of their wrath has come, and who can stand?"

Revelation 7:1-17

(1) After this I saw four angels standing on the four corners of the earth, holding back the four winds of the earth to prevent any wind from blowing on land or sea or on any tree. (2) Then I saw another angel coming up from the rising of the sun, having the seal of the living God, and he cried out in a loud voice to the four angels who had been given power to harm the land and the sea, (3) "Do not harm the earth nor the sea nor the trees until we have sealed the slaves of our God on their foreheads." (4) And I heard the number of those who had received the seal. From all the tribes of the sons of Israel there were one hundred forty-four thousand sealed:

(5) twelve thousand from the tribe of Judah,
twelve thousand from the tribe of Reuben,

twelve thousand from the tribe of Gad,
(6) twelve thousand from the tribe of Asher,
twelve thousand from the tribe of Naphtali,
twelve thousand from the tribe of Manasseh,
(7) twelve thousand from the tribe of Simeon,
twelve thousand from the tribe of Levi,
twelve thousand from the tribe of Issachar,
(8) twelve thousand from the tribe of Zebulun,
twelve thousand from the tribe of Joseph,
and twelve thousand from the tribe of Benjamin.

(9) After this I saw a huge crowd that no one could count, from every nation, tribe, people and language, standing before the throne and in front of the Lamb, dressed in white robes with palm branches in their hands. (10) They cried out in a loud voice, "Salvation to our God who sits upon the throne and to the Lamb."

(11) All the angels were standing around the throne and the elders and the four living creatures. They fell down before the throne upon their faces and worshipped God, (12) saying, "Amen! Praise and glory and wisdom and thanksgiving and honor to our God forever and ever. Amen!"

(13) One of the elders asked me, "Who are these dressed in white robes, and where did they come from?"

(14) And I said to him, "My Lord, you know."

Then he told me, "These are the ones who have survived the great persecution; they have washed their robes in the blood of the Lamb. (15) Therefore they are before the throne of God, and they serve him day and night in his temple, and the one sitting upon the throne will shelter them with his presence. (16) They will never again be hungry or thirsty, and the sun and the scorching heat will not beat down on them, (17) because the Lamb who is in the midst of the throne will shepherd them, and he will lead them to fountains of water; and God will wipe away every tear from their eyes."

Revelation 8:1-13

(1) When the Lamb opened the seventh seal, there was silence in heaven for about half an hour. (2) Then I saw seven angels who stood before God, and seven trumpets were given to them.

(3) Another angel with a golden censer came and stood on the altar; and much incense was given to him to add to all the prayers of the saints on the golden altar that stood before the throne. (4) And the smoke of the incense, with the prayers of the saints, ascended out of the hand of the angel before God. (5) Then the angel took the censer and filled it with fire from the altar and threw it to the earth, and there followed peals of thunder with its rumblings, flashes of lightening, and an earthquake.

(6) Then the seven angels with the seven trumpets prepared to blow them.

(7) The first one blew his trumpet, and there was hail and fire mixed with blood, and it was thrown to the earth; and a third of the earth was burned up, and a third of the trees were burned up, and all the green grass was burned up.

(8) Then the second angel blew his trumpet, and something that looked like a huge mountain burning with fire was thrown into the sea, and a third of the sea was turned into blood. (9) A third of the living creatures in the sea died, and a third of the ships were destroyed.

(10) Then the third angel blew his trumpet, and a great star, blazing like a torch, fell from heaven, and it fell on a third of the rivers and on the fountains of water. (11) The name of the star is Wormwood. A third of the waters became wormwood, and the waters caused many of the men to die because they had turned bitter.

(12) Then the fourth angel blew his trumpet, and a third of the sun was struck, and a third of the moon, and a third of the stars, so that one third of them were darkened; and there was no light for one third of the day and for one third of the night.

(13) Then I looked, and I saw an eagle flying high in the sky and crying in a loud voice, "Woe, woe, woe it will be for the inhabitants of the earth, because the remaining three angels are about to blow their trumpets."

Revelation 9:1-21

(1) Then the fifth angel blew his trumpet, and I saw a star that had fallen from heaven to the earth; and the key of the shaft of the abyss was given to him. (2) And he opened the shaft of the abyss and smoke went up out of the shaft like the smoke of a huge furnace, and the sun and the air were darkened by the smoke from the shaft. (3) Then over the earth locusts came forth out of the smoke, and they were given power like that of the scorpions of the earth. (4) They were told not to harm the grass of the earth or any plant or any tree, but only the men who did not have the seal of God on their foreheads. (5) They were allowed to torment them for five months, but not to kill them. The torment is like the torment of a scorpion when it stings a man. (6) And in those days men will seek death, but they will not find it; they will long to die, but death keeps fleeing from them.

(7) The locusts looked like horses prepared for battle. On their heads were what looked like crowns of gold, and their faces were like faces of men; (8) and their hair was like the hair of women, and their teeth looked like lions' teeth; (9) and they had breastplates like breastplates of iron, and the sound of their wings was like many chariots and horses rushing into battle. (10) Their tails had stingers like scorpions, and in their tails was enough venom to harm men for five months. (11) Their king over them was

the angel of the abyss. His name in Hebrew is Abaddon, in Greek it is Apollyon.

(12) The first woe is past; behold, there are yet two more woes to come.

(13) Then the sixth angel blew his trumpet, and I heard a voice from the four horns of the golden altar before God, (14) saying to the sixth angel who had the trumpet, "Release the four angels who are tied up at the great river Euphrates!" (15) So the four angels, who had been prepared for the hour, the day, the month, and the year, were released to kill a third of mankind. (16) The number of the troops of the cavalry, whose count I heard, was two hundred million.

(17) This is how I saw the horses and their riders in my vision: The riders wore breastplates the color of fire and of sapphire and sulphur; and heads of the horses looked like the heads of lions, and out of their mouths came fire and smoke and sulphur. (18) By these three plagues, the fire, the smoke, and the sulphur that came out of their mouths, a third of mankind was killed. (19) For the power of the horses was in their mouths and in their tails; for their tails were like snakes with heads ready to strike.

(20) The rest of mankind, who were not killed by these plagues, did not repent of the works of their hands, so they might not worship demons and idols of gold and silver and stone and wood, which cannot see or hear or walk; (21) and they did not repent of their murders, their sorceries, their sexual immorality or their thefts.

Revelation 10:1-11

(1) Then I saw another mighty angel coming down out of heaven, clothed with a cloud, and a rainbow over his head; his face was like the sun, his legs were as pillars of fire, (2) and in his hand was a little scroll that had been unrolled. He placed his right foot on the sea and his left foot on the land, (3) and he cried out with a loud shout, like the roar of a lion. And when he shouted, the seven thunders spoke. (4) And when the seven thunders spoke, I was about to write; but I heard a voice from heaven saying, "Keep the secret of the seven thunders and do not write it down."

(5) Then the angel I had seen standing on the sea and on the land lifted his right hand to heaven, (6) and swore by the one who lives forever and ever, who created the heaven and the things in it, the earth and the things in it, and the sea and the things in it, and said, "There will be no more delay; (7) but when the seventh angel blows his trumpet, the mystery of God, as he proclaimed to his slaves the prophets, will be fulfilled."

(8) Then the voice I had heard from heaven spoke to me again, saying, "Go, take the unrolled scroll in the hand of the angel standing on the sea and on the land."

(9) So I approached the angel, asking him to give me the little scroll.

And he said to me, "Take and eat all of it; and it will be sour in your
stomach, but it will be as sweet as honey in your mouth." (10) I took the little
scroll from the hand of the angel and ate all of it. It was as sweet as honey in
• my mouth; but when I swallowed it, my stomach turned sour.

(11) Then I was told, "You must again prophesy about many
peoples, nations, tongues and kings."

Revelation 11:1-19

(1) Then a stick that looked like a measuring rod was given to me,
and I was told, "Rise and measure the temple of God and the altar and those
worshipping there, (2) but do not measure the outside court of the temple;
leave it out, because it has been given to the nations, and they will trample on
the Holy City for forty-two months. (3) And I will commission my two
witnesses to prophesy for those one thousand two hundred and sixty days,
dressed in sackcloth."

(4) The two witnesses are the two olive trees and the two
lampstands that stand before the Lord of the earth. (5) If anyone tries to
harm them, fire comes out of the mouths of these witnesses and devours
their enemies; so if anyone desires to harm them they will be killed. (6)
These witnesses have power to shut the sky so that it will not rain during the
days of their prophesying; and they have power over the waters to turn them
into blood, and to strike the earth with every kind of plague as often as they
please.

(7) Then, when they have completed their testimony, the beast will
come up out of the abyss and will make war with them, and he will
overcome them and kill them. (8) And their corpse will lie in the street of the
great city, which is allegorically called Sodom and Egypt, where their Lord
was crucified. (9) Peoples from all nations, tribes, tongues, and races will
look at their corpse for three and a half days and will not allow them to be
buried. (10) Those dwelling on the earth will rejoice over them, and they will
celebrate and send gifts to one another, because these two prophets had
tormented those dwelling on the earth.

(11) After three and a half days a spirit of life from God entered into
them, and they stood on their feet, and great fear came upon those who saw
them. (12) And they heard a loud voice from heaven saying to them, "Come
up here!" And they went up to heaven in a cloud as their enemies looked on.
(13) At that hour there was a great earthquake, and a tenth of the city fell.
Seven thousand men were killed in the earthquake, and the rest were
terrified and they gave glory to the God of heaven.

(14) The second woe is past. The third woe is coming quickly!

(15) Then the seventh angel blew his trumpet, and there were voices
in heaven shouting:

"The kingdom of the world has become the kingdom of our Lord

and his Anointed One, and he shall reign for ever and ever!"
(16) Then the twenty-four elders, seated on their thrones before God, fell on
their faces and worshipped God, (17) saying:
> "We thank you, O Lord God, the Almighty,
> who is, and who was,
> because you have taken your great power
> and have begun to reign.
> (18) The nations raged,
> but now your wrath has come,
> and it is time to judge the dead
> and to reward your slaves the prophets,
> the saints, those reverencing your name,
> to the small and to the great,
> and to destroy those destroying the earth."

(19) Then the Temple of God in heaven was opened, and within the
temple was seen the ark of the covenant, and there came flashes of
lightening, and sounds, and peals of thunder, and an earthquake, and a
violent hailstorm.

Revelation 12:1-18

(1) A great sign appeared in heaven, a woman clothed in the sun,
and the moon underneath her feet, and on her head was a crown of twelve
stars. (2) She was pregnant, and she cried out in anguish of pain as she
labored to give birth. (3) And another sign appeared in heaven. It was a
huge red dragon with seven heads and ten horns, and on his heads were
seven diadems. (4) His tail swept a third of the stars of heaven and cast them
down to the earth. And the dragon stood before the woman to devour her
child as soon as it was born. (5) The woman gave birth to a son, who is to
shepherd all nations with a scepter of iron; but the child was caught up to
God and to his throne. (6) The woman fled into the desert, to a place that
God had prepared for her, where she will be taken care of for one thousand
two hundred and sixty days.

(7) Then war broke out in heaven; Michael and his angels fought
against the dragon. The dragon and his angels fought, (8) but they did not
prevail, and they had no place left in heaven. (9) So the huge dragon, the old
snake known as the Devil, or Satan, the deceiver of the whole world, was
thrown to the earth with his angels.

(10) Then I heard a loud voice in heaven say:
> "Now has come salvation and power,
> the reign of God and the authority of his Anointed One.
> For the accuser of our brothers,
> who accused them before God both day and night,
> has been thrown out.

(11) They overcame him by the blood of the lamb
and by the word of their testimony;
for they did not cling to life in the face of death.
(12) Rejoice then, O heaven and you who live there!
But woe to you, O earth and sea,
for the devil has come down to you!
He is filled with rage because he knows that his time is short."
(13) When the dragon saw that he had been thrown to the earth, he pursued the woman who had given birth to the son. (14) But the woman was given the two wings of the great eagle, so that she could fly from the snake to the desert to a place prepared for her, where she could be nourished for a time and times and half a time. (15) The snake spewed out of his mouth a river of water after the woman to carry her away in the flood. (16) The earth helped the woman by opening its mouth and swallowing the river that had been spewed out by the dragon. (17) The dragon was enraged with the woman and went away to make war with the rest of her descendents, those keeping the commandments of God and having the testimony of Jesus. (18) And he stood on the sand of the sea.

Revelation 13:1-18

(1) I saw a beast, coming up out of the sea, with ten horns and seven heads, and on the horns were seven diadems, and on its heads were blasphemous names. (2) The beast I saw was like a leopard, and the feet like a bear, and the mouth as a lion. And the dragon gave to it his power and his throne, and great authority. (3) One of its heads appeared to have been mortally wounded, but the mortal wound was healed. And the whole world was amazed and followed after the beast. (4) Men worshipped the dragon because he had given his authority to the beast, and they worshipped the beast, saying, "Who is like the beast, and who can make war against it?"
(5) The beast was given a mouth boasting of great things and words of blasphemies. Authority was given the beast for forty-two months. (6) And he uttered blasphemies against God, reviling his name and his dwelling place and those living in heaven. (7) The beast was given power to make war with the saints and to overcome them. He was given authority over every tribe and people and tongue and nation. (8) All those dwelling on the earth will worship him, except those whose names have been written before the foundation of the world in the book of the Lamb who was slain.
(9) If anyone has an ear, let him listen. (10) If anyone is destined for captivity, to captivity he goes! If anyone slays by the sword, by the sword he will be slain! Here is the perseverance and the faith of the saints.
And I saw another beast coming up out of the earth, and it had two horns like a lamb, but it spoke like a dragon. (12) He exercised the full authority of the first beast on his behalf, and he made the earth and all those

dwelling in it to worship the first beast, whose mortal wound was healed. (13) He performed great miracles, even making fire come down from heaven to the earth in the sight of men. (14) He deceived the earth dwellers by the miracles he performed in behalf of the first beast, telling the earth dwellers to erect an image of the first beast, which was wounded by the sword and yet has lived. (15) He was given power to impart breath to the image of the beast, and to kill those who would not worship the beast. (16) He caused all men, the small and the great, the rich and the poor, the free and the slaves, to have a mark on their right hands and on their foreheads, (17) and no one could buy or sell unless they had the mark—the name of the beast or the number of him. (18) Here is wisdom. Let the one who has wisdom count the number of the beast; for it is the number of a man. And the number is six hundred and sixty-six.

Revelation 14:1-20

(1) I looked, and I saw the Lamb standing on Mount Zion, and with him one hundred forty-four thousand who had his name and the name of his Father written on their foreheads. (2) And I heard a sound from heaven like the sound of roaring water and the sound like loud thunder, and the sound had the melody of musicians playing on their harps. (3) They sang a new song before the throne and before the four living creatures and the elders; and no one could learn the song except the one hundred and forty-four thousand who had been purchased from the earth. (4) These are men who had not defiled themselves with women; for they are virgins. They follow the Lamb wherever he goes. These men have been purchased from men as the first fruits for God and the Lamb; (5) and no lie was found in their mouths, for they are blameless.

(6) Then I saw another angel flying in midheaven, having an eternal gospel to preach to those who dwell on earth, to every nation and tribe and tongue and people, (7) and he said with a loud voice, "Fear God and give glory to him, because his hour of judgment has come; and worship him who made the heaven and the earth and the sea and the fountains of water."

(8) A second angel followed, saying, "Fallen! Fallen, is Babylon the great! She made all the nations drink the wine of the passion of her fornication."

(9) A third angel followed saying in a loud voice, "If anyone worships the beast and its image and receives the mark on his forehead or on his hand, (10) he also shall drink of the wine of the anger of God which has been mixed undiluted in the cup of his wrath; and he will be tormented by fire and sulphur before the holy angels and before the Lamb. (11) The smoke of their torment goes up forever and ever; and there is no rest, day or night, for those worshipping the beast and its image, and those who receive the mark of its name." (12) Here is a call for the perseverance of the saints, the ones keeping the commandments of God and are faithful to Jesus.

(13) Then I heard a voice from heaven saying, "Write: Blessed are the dead who die in the Lord henceforth."

"Yes," says the Spirit, "they will rest from their toils, and their works will follow them."

(14) Then I looked, and behold, a white cloud and sitting on the cloud was one like a son of man, having a golden crown on his head and in his hand a sharp sickle.

(15) And another angel went forth from the temple, crying in a loud voice to the one sitting on the cloud, "Thrust in your sickle and reap, because the harvest of the earth is ripe." (16) And the one sitting on the cloud thrust in his sickle over the earth, and the earth was reaped.

(17) Then another angel went forth from the temple in heaven and he also had a sharp sickle. (18) And another angel, who had power over the fire, went forth from the altar and spoke in a loud voice to the one having the sharp sickle, saying, "Thrust in your sharp sickle and gather the clusters of the vine of the earth, because its grapes are ripe." (19) And the angel thrust his sickle into the earth and gathered the grapevine of the earth and cast it into the winepress of the anger of the great God. (20) And the winepress was trodden outside the city, and blood flowed from the winepress as high as a horse's bridle, for one thousand six hundred stadia.

Revelation 15:1-8

(1) I saw another sign in heaven, great and amazing. There were seven angels with seven plagues, which are the last ones, for with them the wrath of God is ended.

(2) Then I saw what looked like a glassy sea mixed with fire, and those who had overcome the beast and its image and the number of its name were standing on the glassy sea with harps of God. (3) They sang the song of Moses, the slave of God, and the song of the Lamb, saying,

"Great and marvelous are your works,
Lord God Almighty!
Righteous and true are your ways,
O King of the nations!
(4) Who will not reverence and glorify your name, O Lord?
For you alone are holy.
For all the nations will come and worship before you.
For your righteous acts have been revealed."

(5) After this I looked and the temple of the tabernacle of the testimony was opened in heaven, (6) and the seven angels, having the seven plagues, came out of the temple. They were clothed in clean, bright linen and they were girded around the breast with golden girdles. (7) And one of the four living creatures gave to the seven angels seven golden bowls full of the anger of the God who lives forever and ever. (8) And the temple was

filled with the smoke of the glory of God and of his power, and no one could enter into the temple until the completion of the seven plagues of the seven angels.

Revelation 16:1-21

(1) I heard a loud voice from the temple saying to the seven angels, "Go and pour out the seven bowls of the wrath of God on the earth."

(2) The first went and poured out his bowl on the earth; and loathsome and malignant sores broke out upon men with the mark of the beast and who worshipped its image.

(3) The second poured out his bowl on the sea; and it became like the blood of a dead man and all the living creatures in the sea died.

(4) The third poured out his bowl upon the rivers and the springs of water; and they became blood. (5) Then I heard the angel of the waters cry out:

"You are righteous, Holy One, who is and who was,

because you brought these judgments.

6) To those who have shed the blood of saints and prophets

you have given them blood to drink; they deserve it."

(7) Then I heard the altar cry out:

"Yes, Lord God Almighty, true and righteous are your judgments!"

(8) The fourth poured out his bowl on the sun; and he was commissioned to burn men with fire. (9) Men were burned with great heat, and they blasphemed the name of God, who had authority over these plagues, but they did not repent nor give glory to him.

(10) The fifth poured out his bowl on the throne of the beast; and darkness covered the kingdom; and men gnawed their tongues because of their pain, (11) and they blasphemed the God of heaven because of their pain and their sores, but they did not repent of their works.

(12) The sixth poured out his bowl on the great river Euphrates, and it was dried up to prepare the way for the kings of the east. (13) I saw three unclean spirits like frogs leap from the mouth of the dragon and from the mouth of the beast and from the mouth of the false prophet. (14) They are demoniac spirits performing miracles, which go out to the whole world to gather them together for the war of the great day of the Almighty God.

(15) "Look, I am coming as a thief! Blessed is the one who stays awake and keeps his clothes on so he will not walk naked and be seen in his shame."

(16) So they gathered the kings together in the place called in Hebrew Harmagedon.

(17) The seventh poured out his bowl on the air; and a loud voice came out of the temple from the throne, saying, "It is done!" (18) Then there were flashes of lightening, rumblings and peals of thunder, and there was a

great earthquake, such as had not been in the history of man, so great was the earthquake. (19) The great city was split into three parts, and the cities of the nations fell. And God remembered the great Babylon to give her the cup of the fury of his wrath. (20) And every island fled, and mountains disappeared. (21) Great hailstones, the size of a talent, fell out of heaven on men; and they blasphemed God for the plague of hail, because the plague of the hail was extremely severe.

Revelation 17:1-18

(1) One of the seven angels with the seven bowls came and spoke to me, saying, "I will show you the judgment of the great harlot, sitting on many waters, (2) with whom the kings of the earth committed fornication; and with the wine of her fornication, the earth dwellers have become drunk." (3) And he carried me away in the Spirit into a wilderness; and I saw a woman sitting on a scarlet beast, covered with blasphemous titles, having seven heads and ten horns. (4) The woman was clothed in purple and scarlet and adorned with gold and precious stones and pearls, having in her hand a golden cup full of her obscene and filthy things of her immorality, (5) and upon her forehead was a name of symbolical meaning: "BABYLON THE GREAT, THE MOTHER OF HARLOTS AND OF THE ABOMINATIONS OF THE EARTH." (6) I saw the woman drunk from the blood of the saints and the blood of the martyrs of Jesus.

When I saw her, I was greatly amazed. (7) And the angel said to me, "Why are you amazed? I will tell you the mystery of the woman and the beast with the seven heads and the ten horns carrying her.

(8) "The beast, which you saw, was, and is not, and is about to come up out of the abyss and go to destruction. The earth dwellers will be amazed — all whose names have not been written in the book of life from the foundation of the world — when they see the beast; for he was, and is not, and will come.

(9) "Here is the mind of wisdom. The seven heads are seven mountains, where the woman is seated, and they are seven kings. (10) Five have fallen, one is, and another is yet to come; and when he comes he must remain a little while. (11) And the beast, which was, and is not, even he is the eighth, and he is like the seventh, and goes to destruction.

(12) "And the ten horns, which you saw, are ten kings, who have not yet received a kingdom, but they will receive authority from the beast for one hour. (13) They are of one mind and they receive power and authority from the beast. (14) They will make war with the Lamb, and the Lamb will overcome them, for he is Lord of lords and King of kings, and those with him are called and chosen and faithful."

(15) He said to me, "The waters which you saw, where the harlot sits, are peoples and crowds and are nations and tongues. (16) And the ten

horns which you saw, they and the beast will hate the harlot; and they will make her desolate and naked, and they will eat her flesh, and will consume her with fire; (17) for God put it into the hearts of them to do his will, by agreeing to give their kingdom to the beast, until the words of God shall be fulfilled. (18) The woman you saw is the great city which has dominion over the kings of the world."

Revelation 18:1-24

(1) After this I saw another angel coming down from heaven, having great authority, and the earth was illuminated by his splendor. (2) He cried out with a loud voice, saying: "Fallen! Fallen is Babylon the great! She has become a dwelling place for demons and a prison for every unclean spirit and every unclean bird and a prison for every unclean beast and every detestable creature; (3) for all nations have drunk of the wine of the wrath of her fornication, and the kings of the earth have committed fornication with her, and the merchants of the earth have become rich from the wealth of her sensuality."

(4) Then I heard another voice from heaven saying, "Come out of her, my people, lest you share in her sins, and lest you receive her plagues; (5) because her sins are piled up to heaven, and God has remembered her evil deeds. (6) Pay her back as she has paid others, and give her double according to her works; in the cup that she mixed make a double portion for her; (7) and by the things she glorified herself and lived in sensuality, give her torment and sorrow. Because in her heart she says, 'I sit as a queen and not a widow and I will not see sorrow.' (8) Therefore her plagues will come in one day, pestilence and sorrow and famine, and she shall be destroyed by fire; because the Lord God, who judges her, is strong.

(9) "The kings of the earth who committed fornication with her and lived in sensuality will weep when they see the smoke of her burning. (10) They will stand a long way off because of the fear of the punishment inflicted upon her, saying,

'Woe, woe to that great city! For judgment has come in one hour!'

(11) "The merchants of the earth weep and mourn over her, because no one buys their cargo anymore— (12) cargo of gold, silver, precious stones and pearls; fine linen, purple, silk and scarlet cloth; all kinds of fragrant wood, all kinds of goods in ivory and all kinds of expensive wooden furniture; bronze, iron and marble; (13) cinnamon, spices, incense, perfume, frankincense; wine, olive oil, fine meal and wheat; cattle, sheep, horses, chariots; bodies and souls of men.

(14) "The fruit that you longed for has gone from you, and all your luxury and splendor has perished, never to be found again.

(15) "The merchants who became wealthy from business with her will stand far from her because of the fear of the punishment inflicted on her,

and weeping and mourning, (16) they cry out,
> 'Woe, woe, the great city,
> clothed with fine linen and purple and scarlet,
> adorned with gold, precious stones and pearls;
> (17) because in one hour this great wealth has been destroyed!'

"All shipmasters, seafaring men, sailors and all whose trade is on the sea, stood afar off and (18) seeing the smoke of her burning cried out,
> 'What city is like the great city?'

(19) They threw dust on their heads and weeping and mourning they cried out, saying,
> 'Woe, woe, the great city,
> in which all which had ships at sea became rich by her wealth,
> for in one hour she has been destroyed.
> (20) Rejoice over her,
> heaven and the saints and the apostles and the prophets,
> for God has taken vengeance on her for you.' "

(21) A strong angel lifted a great millstone and threw it into the sea, saying, "Thus will Babylon the great be thrown with violence, and will never be found again. (22) The sound of harpists, musicians, flute players and trumpeters will never be heard in you any longer; and no craftsman of any craft will ever be heard in you any longer; and the sound of the mill will never be heard in you any longer; (23) and the light of a lamp will never shine in you any longer; and the voice of the bridegroom and the bride will not be heard in you any longer; for your merchants were the great ones in the earth; because by your sorcery all nations were deceived; (24) and in her was found the blood of prophets and saints and all who have been slain on the earth."

Revelation 19:1-21

(1) After this I heard something like the roar of a great multitude in heaven, shouting, "Hallelujah! Salvation and glory and power belong to our God; (2) for his judgments are true and righteous; because he has judged the notorious harlot who defiled the earth with her fornication, and he brought vengeance upon her because she slaughtered his slaves!"

(3) Then a second time they shouted, "Hallelujah! And the smoke from her goes up forever and ever."

(4) Then the twenty-four elders and the four living creatures fell down and worshipped God who sits on the throne, saying, "Amen! Hallelujah!"

(5) A voice coming from the throne cried out, "Praise our God, all his slaves who reverence him, both small and great!"

(6) Then I heard the sound of a great multitude, like the sound of a roaring waterfall and loud claps of thunder, saying,

"Hallelujah! The Lord, our God, the Almighty, is king!
(7) Let us rejoice and be glad, and we will give him the glory;
for the time has come for the marriage of the Lamb,
and his bride has prepared herself.
(8) She was given a gown of fine linen, shining and clean."
(For the fine linen is the righteous deeds of the saints.)

(9) Then he said to me, "Write: 'Blessed are those who have been invited to the marriage of the Lamb.' " And he said to me, "These are true words of God."

(10) And I fell before his feet to worship him, but he said to me, "No, not that! I am a fellow slave with you and your brothers who have the testimony of Jesus. Worship God." For the testimony of Jesus is the spirit of prophecy.

(11) Then I saw heaven standing open and behold, a white horse! Its rider was called Faithful and True, and in righteousness he judges and fights his battles. (12) His eyes are a flame of fire, and on his head are many diadems; and he has a name inscribed that no one knows except himself; (13) and he is clothed with a garment dripped in blood, and his name is called The Word of God. (14) The armies in heaven, dressed in fine linen, white and clean, on white horses, followed him. (15) Out of his mouth went a sharp sword to smite the nations, and he will shepherd them with a staff of iron; and he treads the winepress of the wine of the wrath of the Almighty God. (16) A title was written on his cloak that covered his thigh: "KING OF KINGS AND LORD OF LORDS."

(17) Then I saw an angel standing in the sun, and he cried out in a loud voice saying to all the birds flying in midheaven: "Come, assemble for the great supper of God, (18) so that you may eat the flesh of kings, generals, mighty men, and horses and their riders, the flesh of all men, the free and the slave, the small and the great."

(19) I saw the beast and the kings of the earth and their armies assembled to make war with the one sitting on the horse with his army. (20) And the beast was seized, and with it was the false prophet who performed miracles in its presence, by which he deceived those who had the mark of the beast and worshipped its image. These two were cast alive into the lake of fire burning with sulphur. (21) The rest were killed by the sword proceeding out of the mouth of the one sitting on the horse, and all the birds were gorged with their flesh.

Revelation 20:1-15

(1) I saw an angel descending from heaven with the key of the abyss and with a huge chain in his hand. (2) He seized the dragon, the ancient serpent, who is the Devil, or Satan, and bound him for a thousand years; (3) and he threw him into the abyss, and closed and sealed the lid over him, to

keep him from deceiving the nations until the completion of the thousand years. After this, he must be released for a short time.

(4) Then I saw thrones, and those who were seated on them were given authority to judge. Then I saw the souls of those who had been beheaded because of their witness for Jesus and for their witness of the word of God, who refused to worship the beast or his image, and who had not received the mark upon their foreheads or their hands. They came to life and reigned with Christ for a thousand years. (5) The rest of the dead did not come to life until the completion of the thousand years. This is the first resurrection. (6) Blessed and holy are those who have part in the first resurrection! The second death has no power over these, but they will be priests of God and of Christ and they will reign with him the thousand years.

(7) When the thousand years are completed, Satan will be released from his prison, (8) and he will go forth to deceive the nations in the four corners of the earth, Gog and Magog, to gather them for battle; the number is like the sand of the seashore. (9) And they invaded the whole land and surrounded the camp of the saints of the beloved city; and fire came down from heaven and destroyed them. (10) The Devil, their seducer, was cast into the lake of fire and sulfur, where the beast and the false prophet are also; they will be tormented day and night forever and ever.

(11) Then I saw a great white throne and him who sat on it, from whose presence earth and sky fled away, until they could no longer be seen. (12) And I saw the dead, the great and the small, standing before the throne, and books were opened; and another book, the book of life, was opened; and the dead were judged by the things written in the books in accordance with their works. (13) The sea gave up its dead, and Death and Hades gave up their dead; and they were judged according to their works. (14) Then Death and Hades were thrown into the lake of fire. This, the lake of fire, is the second death. Anyone whose name was not found recorded in the book of life was thrown into the lake of fire.

Revelation 21:1-27

(1) Then I saw a new heaven and a new earth, for the first heaven and the first earth had passed away, and there was no longer the sea. (2) I saw the holy city, the New Jerusalem, descending out of heaven from God, beautiful as a bride prepared to meet her husband. (3) I heard a loud voice from the throne, saying, "Look! The tabernacle of God is with men, and he will dwell with them, and they will be his people and he, himself, will be with them. (4) He will wipe away every tear from their eyes, and death will be no more; neither shall there be sorrow nor crying nor pain anymore, for the former things have passed away."

(5) The one who sat on the throne said, "Look! I am making all things new!" And he said, "Write, because these words are trustworthy and

true." (6) Then he said to me, "It is done. I am the Alpha and the Omega, the beginning and the end. To the thirsty I will give to him water from the fountain of life without cost. (7) He that overcomes shall have this heritage, and I will be his God and he will be my son. (8) But as for the coward, the faithless, the depraved, the murderers, the fornicators, the sorcerers, the idolaters and all liars, their place will be in the lake of fire and sulfur, which is the second death."

(9) One of the seven angels, having the seven bowls filled with the seven last plagues, spoke with me, saying, "Come, I will show you the bride, the wife of the Lamb." (10) He carried me away in the spirit to the top of a very high mountain, and he showed me Jerusalem, the holy city, descending out of heaven from God, (11) and shining with the glory of God. The brilliance of it was like a very precious stone, as a crystal-clear jasper stone; (12) it had a huge, high wall with twelve gates, and at the gates were twelve angels; and on the gates were written the names of the twelve tribes of Israel; (13) on the east three gates, on the north three gates, on the south three gates, and on the west three gates. (14) The wall of the city had twelve foundations, and on them were the names of the twelve apostles of the Lamb.

(15) The one who was speaking with me had a golden measuring rod to measure the city and its gates and its wall. (16) The city is square with the length the same as the width. The city, measured by the golden rod, was twelve thousand stadia; the length and the width and the height are equal. (17) He measured its wall and it was one hundred forty-four cubits, by human measurements, which the angel was using. (18) The wall was made of jasper, and the city was pure gold, like clear glass. (19) The foundations of the wall of the city were adorned with every precious stone; the first foundation was jasper, the second sapphire, the third chalcedony, the fourth emerald, (20) the fifth sardonyx, the sixth carnelian, the seventh chrysolite, the eighth beryl, the ninth topaz, the tenth chrysoprase, the eleventh turquoise, and the twelfth amethyst. (21) The twelve gates were twelve pearls; each gate was of one pearl. And the streets of the city were pure gold like transparent glass.

(22) I did not see a temple in it, for its temple was the Lord God Almighty and the Lamb. (23) The city has no need for the sun or the moon to shine upon it, for the glory of God illuminated it and its lamp is the Lamb. (24) The nations shall walk by its light, and the kings of the earth shall bring their glory into it. (25) The gates of it will never be closed by day, for there will be no night. (26) The nations will bring their glory and honor into it. (27) And nothing unclean will enter it, nor anyone whose life is shameful or false, but only those whose names have been recorded in the Lamb's book of life.

Revelation 22:1-21

(1) Then he showed me a river of living water, clear as crystal, flowing out of the throne of God and the Lamb. (2) In the midst of it and of the river was a tree of life bearing twelve kinds of fruit, yielding a different kind each month, and the leaves were for the healing of the nations. (3) Nothing under God's curse will be there. The throne of God and the Lamb will be in it and his slaves will serve him; (4) and they will see his face, and his name will be on their foreheads. (5) There will be no night, so they will not need the light of lamp or sun, because the Lord God will shine on them, and they will reign forever and ever.

(6) Then he said to me, "These words are trustworthy and true, and the Lord, the God of the spirits of the prophets, sent his angel to show his slaves what must soon take place."

(7) "Listen," says Jesus, "I am coming soon! Blessed are those who obey the words of the prophesy of this book."

(8) It is I, John, who heard and saw these things. When I had heard and seen them, I fell down to worship at the feet of the angel who had been showing these things to me. (9) And he said to me, "Do not do that. I am a fellow slave with you, of the prophets and of those who keep the words of this book. Worship God!"

(10) Then he said to me, "Do not seal the words of the prophecy of this book, for the appointed time is near. (11) Let the wicked continue in his wickedness, the depraved in their depravity, the righteous in their righteousness, and the holy in their holiness."

(12) "Listen! I am coming soon! My reward is with me, to give to each one according to his works. (13) I am the Alpha and the Omega, the first and the last, the beginning and the end.

(14) "Blessed are those who have washed their robes, so they will have the authority over the tree of life and they may enter by the gates of the city. (15) Outside are the dogs, the sorcerers, the fornicators, the murderers, the idolaters and all who loves and practices falsehood.

(16) "I, Jesus, sent my angel to witness to you about these things for the churches. I am the Root and the Offspring of David, the bright morning star."

(17) The Spirit and the bride say, "Come."

Let those who hear say, "Come." Let the thirsty come; let the one who wishes come and take the water of life without cost.

(18) I witness to everyone hearing the words of the prophecy of this book: If anyone adds to them, God will add to him the plagues record in this book; (19) and if anyone takes away from the words of the prophecy of this book, God will take from him his part in the tree of life and the holy city, which are recorded in this book.

(20) He who testifies to these things says, "Yes, I am coming soon!"

Amen! Come, Lord Jesus!

(21) The grace of the Lord Jesus be with you all.